Site Engineering for
LANDSCAPE ARCHITECTS

FIFTH EDITION

Steven Strom

Kurt Nathan

Jake Woland

WILEY

John Wiley & Sons, Inc.

To the memory of Steve Strom,
a mentor and friend

To Corrie Rosen, without whom this edition
would not have been completed

Copyright © 2009 by John Wiley & Sons, Inc. All rights reserved

Published by John Wiley & Sons, Inc., Hoboken, New Jersey
Published simultaneously in Canada

For general information about our other products and services, please contact our Customer Care Department within the United States at (800) 762-2974, outside the United States at (317) 572-3993 or fax (317) 572-4002.

Wiley also publishes its books in a variety of electronic formats. Some content that appears in print may not be available in electronic books. For more information about Wiley products, visit our web site at www.wiley.com.

Library of Congress Cataloging-in-Publication Data:
Strom, Steven.
    Site engineering for landscape architects / Steven Strom, Kurt Nathan, Jake Woland. —5th ed.
      p.   cm.
    Includes bibliographical references and index.
    ISBN 978-0-470-13814-4 (cloth/website)
     1. Building sites. 2. Landscape architecture. 3. Landscape construction. I. Nathan, Kurt.
II. Woland, Jake. III. Title.
TH375.S77   2009
624—dc22
                                                           2008019008

Printed in the United States of America

10 9 8 7 6 5 4 3 2 1

Contents

Preface   vii

Acknowledgments   ix

1 Site Engineering IS Design   1

Why Is an Understanding of This
    Material Important?   1
The Design Language of Site
    Engineering   1
Summary   21

2 Grading Constraints   23

Environmental Constraints   23
Functional Constraints   27
Summary of Critical Constraints   36

3 Contours and Form   37

Definition   37
Constructing a Section   41
Characteristics of Contour Lines   42
Contour Signatures and Landform   44
Case Studies   58

4 Interpolation and Slope   71

Topographic Data   71
Interpolation   72
Calculating Slope   76
Slopes Expressed as Ratios and
    Degrees   78
Slope Analysis   79

5 Grading of Simple Design Elements   85

Grading of Linear Elements   85
Grading by Proportion   96
Visualizing Topography from Contour
    Lines   98
Grading of Planar Areas   98
Swales to Divert Runoff   106
Area Grading Process   107

6 Grading Process   109

Introduction   109
Applying the Grading Process   111
Grading Plan Graphics   117

7 Soils in Construction   123

Role of Soil in Site Planning   123
Implications of Soils for Site
    Construction   123
Geotechnical Exploration and Soil
    Investigation   125
Soil Characteristics   127
Soil Classification   128
Engineering Properties of Soils   130
Structural Soils   131
Lightweight Soils   132
Geotextiles   132
Construction Sequence for Grading   133
Placing and Compacting Soils   136
Earthwork Specifications   137

8 Earthwork   139

Definitions   139
Grading Operations   140
Computation of Cut-and-Fill Volumes   141

9 Storm Water Management   157

Storm Runoff   157
Hydrologic Cycle   158
Nature of the Problem   159
Management Philosophy   160
Storm Water Management Strategies   161
Principles and Techniques   163
Case Studies   183
Summary   194

10 Soil Erosion and Sediment Control 195

Introduction   195
Regulatory Requirements   195

Soil Erosion Factors   196
Erosion and Sedimentation
    Processes   197
Erosion and Sediment Control
    Principles   197
Development of an Erosion and
    Sediment Control Plan   199
Runoff Considerations   199
Construction Sequencing   200
Erosion Control Measures   200
Sediment Control Measures   205
Case Studies   206
Summary   209

11 Determining Rates and Volumes of Storm Runoff: The Rational and Modified Rational Methods   211

Introduction   211
Rational Method   212
Modified Rational Method   223
Volumes of Runoff, Storage, and
    Release   228
Required Storage for Detention or
    Retention Ponds by the Modified
    Rational Method   229
Summary   233

12 Natural Resources Conservation Service Methods of Estimating Runoff Rates, Volumes, and Required Detention Storage   235

Introduction   235
Rainfall   237
Procedures of TR55   237
Volume for Detention Storage   250
Summary   253

13 **Designing and Sizing Storm Water Management Systems** **255**

Management Systems   255
Design and Layout of Drainage
     Systems   261
Applications   263
Subsurface Drainage   284
Summary   289

14 **Site Layout and Dimensioning** **291**

Hierarchy of Dimensioning   292
Dimensioning Guidelines   293
Horizontal Layout Methods   295
Layout Plans   301

15 **Horizontal Road Alignment** **303**

Types of Horizontal Curves   303
Circular Curve Elements   305
Circular Curve Formulas   306
Degree of Curve   308
Stationing   310
Horizontal Sight Distance   313
Construction Drawing Graphics   314

Horizontal Alignment Procedures   314
Superelevation   316
Case Study   318

16 **Vertical Road Alignment** **323**

Vertical Curve Formula   324
Equal Tangent Curves   325
Calculating the Locations of High and
     Low Points   326
Unequal Tangent Curves   330
Construction Drawing Graphics   333
Vertical Sight Distances   335
Road Alignment Procedure   335

Appendix I: Table of Metric Equivalents **341**

Appendix II: Metric Drawing Scales **342**

Glossary **343**

Bibliography **349**

Index **353**

Preface

The shaping of the earth's surface is one of the primary functions of site planners and landscape architects. This shaping must not only display a sound understanding of aesthetic and design principles, but also ecological sensitivity and technical competency. The last point, the technical ability to transform design ideas into physical reality, is the focus of this book. It should also be understood that the authors believe that technical ability should be used in conjunction with and intimately connected to principles of design.

Specifically, the book emphasizes principles and techniques of basic site engineering for grading, drainage, earthwork, and road alignment. The authors strongly believe that, in most cases, it is difficult to separate the design procedure from the construction and implementation process and that technical competency ultimately will lead to a better finished product. In this regard, the authors also feel that collaborative efforts among the landscape architecture, engineering, and ecological professions will result in the most appropriate solutions to design and environmental problems.

Although appropriate as a reference for practitioners, the book has been developed primarily as a teaching text. Based on the authors' experience, the material, numerous examples, and problems have been organized to provide students with a progressive understanding of the subject matter. First, landform and the language of its design are discussed descriptively. This is followed by an investigation into environmental and functional constraints that can guide site engineering decisions. In Chapter 3, the concept of contour lines is introduced and a baseline of common contour signatures is delineated. Chapter 4 expands on these concepts with explanations of interpolation and slope formulas and examples of their applications. Grading of linear elements and planar areas is outlined in Chapter 5, while a procedure for developing grading solutions involving these different parts working in conjunction is the focus of Chapter 6. The integrated relationship between site design and site engineering is also emphasized in these chapters. Soils and earthwork including soil properties, soil classification, grading terminology, construction sequencing, and the computation of earthwork volumes are presented in Chapters 7 and 8. Storm water management, soil erosion, and the design and sizing of management systems are discussed in Chapters 9, 10, 11, 12, and 13, with particular emphasis on the Rational, Modified Rational, and TR55 Natural Resources Conservation Service methodologies. Chapter 14 includes methods for site dimensioning and layout. Procedures for designing horizontal and vertical road alignments are presented in Chapters 15 and 16. In an effort to give real-life context to the information being learned, case studies have been introduced throughout the book, typically at the end of the chapters most closely associated with their information. In summary, the authors believe that the book provides a strong foundation in the essential aspects of site engineering and an approach to site development that is environmentally sensitive and intellectually stimulating.

THE USE OF THE METRIC SYSTEM

The Metric Conversion Act of 1975, as amended by the Omnibus Trade and Competitiveness Act of 1988, establishes the modern metric system, referred to as the International System of Units (or SI from Système International d'Unitès), as the preferred system of measurement in the United States. In 1991, Executive Order 12770, Metric Usage in Federal Government Programs, mandated that each federal agency develop a Metric Transition Plan. Many federal agencies now require construction projects to be designed and constructed using the metric system.

The approach in this book is to provide a discussion of metric units, applications, sample problems, and exercises. A table of equivalents is provided in Appendix I, and a comparison of drawing scales and a method of metric notation are provided in Appendix II. We have specifically avoided the use of dual notation for the example problems, since we feel it is cumbersome and interferes with the learning process. However, dual notation is used where dimensional standards or recommendations appear in the book.

All formulas based on plane or solid geometry, such as those pertaining to interpolation, slope determination, areas, and volumes, are applicable to the metric system as long as consistent dimensional values are used. Empirical equations, such as some of those used, for example, in storm water management, must be modified for use with the metric system.

COMPUTERS AND SITE ENGINEERING

Most computational and drafting tasks associated with site engineering have become completely automated. In addition, great strides have been made in terms of three-dimensional visualization, enhancing the ability of designers and clients to envision proposed designs.

There is much computer software available today to accomplish many of the site engineering computations presented in this book, including interpolation, slope, cut-and-fill volumes, hydrology, and hydraulics for the determination of storm water runoff rates and the sizing of drainageways, pipes, culverts, and storage reservoirs, and horizontal and vertical road alignment.

A computer, however, is only a tool that is dependent on reasonable input based on the judgment of a well-prepared and knowledgeable person. Computers should be used for computations and design only if the methodology used is fully understood and the output can be evaluated for reasonableness. The designer is still responsible for potential failures and cannot blame negligence on a computer program.

Acknowledgments

As this is the first edition without direct input, coordination, and support from Steve Strom and Kurt Nathan, Jake Woland would like to thank Beth Strom and Kurt Nathan for allowing him to continue refining Steve and Kurt's significant work.

We would like to thank the following people who have contributed to the most recent edition: the staff of Mathews Nielsen Landscape Architects, and particularly Michael Cluer and Jennifer Cooper, for photographs and discussions that informed the green roof and lightweight soil portions of the book; Mark Garff and the Watershed Company for contributing stream restoration photography for Chapter 1; and Karen Janosky for her help in developing the High Point Neighborhood Redevelopment case study.

We would also like to acknowledge the people who contributed to the previous editions. Their efforts are still an integral part of this work. Denise Andrews at Seattle Public Utilities for the S.E.A. Streets case study, Stuart Appel of Wells Appel for providing the Pennswood Village case study, Berson Ackerman & Associates (Henry Albert, Bernard Berson, Andrew Birtok, Frederick Kish, Thomas Miller, and Richard O'Connor) for computer-generated solutions for several of the example problems, Peter del Tredici of the Arnold Arboretum and Glen Valentine from Reed Hilderbrand for the Leventritt Garden case study, Carol Franklin and John Nystedt at Andropogon Associates for the Loantaka Brook Preserve case study, Elizabeth Grady Strom for illustrations, Jason Harkins for illustrations, Lorna Jordan for providing the Waterworks Gardens case study, and Paul Szmaida for the computer-generated slope analysis and digital terrain model in Chapter 4. Case study information was supplied by Andropogon Associates (Morris Arboretum), Günther Grzimek (Olympic Park), Richard Haag (Gasworks Park), and Nancy Leahy (Earthworks Park). Kathleen John-Alder produced the plan drawings for Earthworks Park, Gasworks Park, and Olympic Park. Robert Moore supplied the photograph for Figure 13.8b.

Many sources have contributed to the authors' interest and growth in the fields of site development, engineering, and construction. The classic book by Parker and MacGuire and the work of David Young and Donald Leslie deserve special mention among them. Publications of the USDA-Natural Resources Conservation Service, formerly SCS, particularly in the areas of storm water management and swale design, have been invaluable.

Leland Anderson and Lee Holt of the Natural Resources Conservation Service reviewed several portions of the manuscript for the first edition. David Lamm, contributing author for this edition, also reviewed the entire text of the first edition and the storm water chapters of the second edition. Vincent Abbatiello and Guy Metler performed the photographic processing for the first edition. Their assistance is gratefully acknowledged.

Finally, the authors would like to express their thanks to the faculty of the Department of Landscape Architecture, Cook College, Rutgers—The State University of New Jersey for their continued support and to all who have made helpful suggestions for improving the book over its several iterations, particularly Marvin Adleman, Stephen Ervin, and John Roberts.

CHAPTER 1

Site Engineering IS Design

WHY IS AN UNDERSTANDING OF THIS MATERIAL IMPORTANT?

Simply put, grading is design.

With regard to the relationship between grading and design, three points must be emphasized: First, grading and site design are two highly related and dependent processes. To achieve an appropriate as well as successful final product, both must be integrated in a holistic manner at the outset of the project. Second, before manipulating contours on a grading plan, it is important to have a clear understanding of the form of the desired final product. Without this knowledge, the manipulation of contours is aimless and futile. To reinforce this point, any appropriate three-dimensional form can be expressed by contours on a grading plan. However, without a preconception of what that form should be, it can never be attained. Finally,

a change in grade must be purposeful, whether for functional or aesthetic reasons, and not arbitrary. The intent to change a grade 2 in. is no less important than the intent to change a grade 20 ft.

THE DESIGN LANGUAGE OF SITE ENGINEERING

It is extremely important to realize that grading is one of the primary design tools available to the landscape architect. Every site design project requires some change in grade. How these grade changes are integrated into the overall design concept will influence the success of the project functionally, visually, and experientially. The necessity for grade changes creates opportunities for site engineering to play a role in the aesthetic, perceptual, spatial, and environmental considerations of a design.

(a)

(b)

(c)

(d)

Figure 1.1. (a) Geomorphic: A stream restoration carved in a floodplain to look as if it was created by natural processes (photo: The Watershed Company). (b) Architectonic: Terraces defining the central lawn of the Leventritt Garden at the Arnold Arboretum. (c) Sculptural: The playful mounds of vegetation interact with the curvilinear benches in a dance to provide seating in the sun in the Jacob Javits Federal Courthouse Plaza *(Photo: Michael Cluer)*. (d) Naturalistic: In this large urban park, the land was manipulated to create a meadow within a valley-like space.

Aesthetics

The visual form of grading may be broadly categorized into three types. The selection of a particular type is appropriate within a given landscape or design context, but it is possible to combine types within the same project. The four categories are geomorphic, architectonic, sculptural, and naturalistic (Figure 1.1). It is worth mentioning that many designed landscapes feature a blending of the different aesthetic categories discussed below.

Geomorphic

The proposed grading blends ecologically and visually with the character of the existing natural landscape. It reflects the geologic forces and natural patterns that shape the landscape by repeating similar landforms and physiographic structure. Generally, the intent of this category is to minimize the amount of regrading necessary in order to preserve the existing landscape character, though in some cases it is used to restore character and ecological function that have been lost.

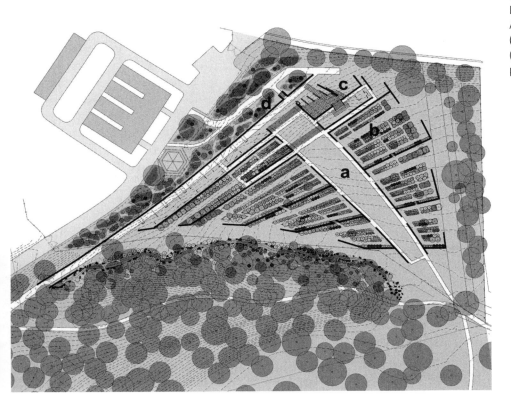

Figure 1.2. Plan of the Leventritt Garden at the Arnold Arboretum. (a) Central lawn panel. (b) Terraces. (c) Garden pavilion. (d) Great wall.

A more detailed discussion of the range of environmental factors this aesthetic type is employed to work with can be found later in this chapter.

Architectonic

The proposed grading creates uniform slopes and forms, which usually are crisply defined geometric shapes. The lines along which planes intersect are clearly articulated rather than softened by rounded edges. This type of grading is appropriate where the overall impact is human-dominated or where a strong contrast is desired between built and natural landscapes.

Leventritt Garden at the Arnold Arboretum[1]

This language can be used to reinforce the geometry of an associated building or provide a legible organization system, as in the Leventritt Garden, Boston, Massachusetts, at the Arnold Arboretum. The design for the garden draws upon the long, rich tradition of terracing the landscape to create usable and dramatic spaces, whether for agriculture, habitation, or gardens. The area selected for

---

[1]Landscape Architect: Reed Hilderbrand
Architect: Mary Thompson
Engineers: Green Associates

Figure 1.3. Walls delineate the fan-like arrangement of terraces.

Figure 1.4. Great wall and steel trellises for vine collection.

Figure 1.5. View of the central lawn, terraces, and garden pavilion.

the garden was a somewhat triangular open space with an east-facing slope that rose a bit more steeply along its western edge. The designers reworked this form to create a more constant grade change.

The constant slope established an opportunity to develop a series of terraces that are arranged in a fan-like manner, described by the designers as an "organic parterre" (Figure 1.3). The terraces provide order and organization to the collection, while the terrace walls frame the displays. A central lawn (Figure 1.1b) establishes an axis that divides the terraces into manageably sized spaces and creates the main approach to the garden. Stairs at the uphill end of the lawn, together with the great wall and pavilion, form a structured terminus to the space and a focal point for the garden (Figures 1.4 and 1.5).

This garden is a good example of a strong concept translated into a cohesive composition. The structure and beautiful craftsmanship of the fieldstone walls recall the New England agricultural landscape and provide a timeless framework to display the plant collection. Of particular note is the approach to providing accessibility, which is so well integrated into the design that it could easily be overlooked.

Sculptural

This category is really a bridge between the architectonic and naturalistic categories. There is a range of forms that fall between the sharp, crisp planar architectonic forms and the fluid curves of the natural forms. On a continuum of landscape forms between these two categories, Earthworks Park, a landscape with more abstract forms and fewer hard lines, would be considered sculptural and yet still closely related to the architectonic category. At the other end of that spectrum is Waterworks Gardens, with fluid forms that directly reference nature but would not have been formed by nature. A brief discussion of these two landscapes follows.

Earthworks Park[2]

Earthworks Park in Kent, Washington, demonstrates how grading can be used to solve a pragmatic storm runoff and erosion problem while creating

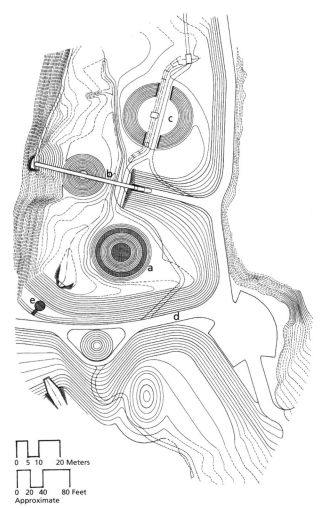

Figure 1.6. Site plan of Earthworks Park. (a) Circular pond. (b) Bridge structure. (c) Ring-shaped mound. (d) Embankment. (e) Spillway structure.

---

[2]Designer: Herbert Bayer
Engineers: URS Engineers

sculptural landforms and a park area for passive recreation. The design and reclamation of the Mill Creek Canyon site were undertaken to alleviate erosion and flooding problems as part of a public art project entitled "Earthworks: Land Reclamation as Sculpture," sponsored by the King County Arts Commission and King County Department of Public Works during the 1970s.

The park is located at the lower end of a 1,500-ac drainage basin. Approximately 460 ft^3/s of storm runoff would flow through the site during a 100-year storm. The goal of the storm water management project was to reduce the discharge so that it would not exceed 100 ft^3/s for a 100-year storm. To meet this goal, a large detention basin was created by constructing an earth dam across the steeply walled valley formed by Mill Creek. The resulting detention basin has a water storage capacity of 652,000 ft^3 (approximately 15 ac-ft).[2]

A series of abstract circular forms consisting of ring-shaped and cone-shaped mounds were created in the area of the park on the upstream side of the dam. The sculptural landforms establish the overall spatial and visual character of the park (Figure 1.6). These landforms reflect an earlier earth sculpture work by Bayer, entitled "The Grass Mound," in Aspen, Colorado. The role of the park as a storm water management facility is visually reinforced by a number of design elements. A circular pond containing an inner grass ring (Figure 1.7) retains water most of the year, thus providing a sense of the storm water detention function of the larger park landscape. A small stream passes under the bridge, shown in Figure 1.8, during dry periods; however, the capacity to accommodate much greater volumes of water is readily apparent to the park user by the scale of the bridge structure. A ring-shaped mound provides a more enclosed space within the larger landscape. Retaining walls are used to define the entry into this smaller space (Figure 1.9). The three primary sculptural elements

Figure 1.7. Circular pond with inner grass ring.

Figure 1.8. Bridge structure.

Figure 1.10. Access stair at valley wall.

Figure 1.9. Ring-shaped mound with retaining walls.

Figure 1.11. Overlook platform at access stair.

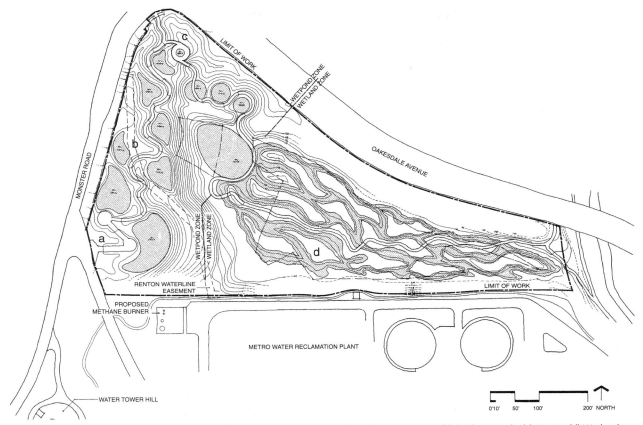

Figure 1.12. Site plan of Waterworks Gardens. (a) Main entry, where water flows beneath grates. (b) Settling ponds. (c) Grotto. (d) Wetlands. *(Plan: Lorna Jordan)*

(ring, bridge, and circular pond) are physically and visually linked by the stream running through the park.

A set of access stairs at one of the valley walls is an interesting detail. Rather than switchback or scissor-type stairs, which would appear to reduce the height of the valley wall, the stairs ascend directly up the slope (Figure 1.10). This technique accentuates the steepness of the landform. A small platform provides a resting and vantage point approximately halfway up the stairs. The placement of the platform next to the stairs is important to note, since it does not interrupt the steep character created by the line of the stair structure (Figure 1.11).

Waterworks Gardens[3]

Waterworks Gardens is 8 ac (3.2 ha) of land located on the northern edge of the Renton, Washington, wastewater treatment facility. Initially, the design of the treatment facility called for the storm water

---

[3] Artist and Lead Designer: Lorna Jordan
Landscape Architects: Jones + Jones Architects and Landscape Architects
Consulting Engineer: Brown & Caldwell Engineering
Wetland Science and Geotechnical Engineering: Shannon & Wilson
Irrigation Design: Dragonfly Irrigation.

runoff to be treated along with the sewage, which would have been a clear case of treatment overkill. It also would have set a precedent for the plant that was undesirable because it did not already treat storm water from other sources. The municipality decided that the storm water should drain into Springbrook Creek to the north of the site treated instead of into the Green River, where drainage for the 50 ac (20.2 ha) of roads and other impervious surfaces was already directed. To do this, a vault and pump had to be installed to redirect the runoff. This provided the opportunity to create what eventually became Waterworks Gardens.

The initial design proposed three featureless square detention ponds to be sandwiched between two already environmentally degraded wetlands. After successful advocacy by Lorna Jordan, the design team's artist, an alternative design was developed, led by the artist, that incorporated a natural storm water treatment system and enhanced wetlands accessible to the public through a series of paths (Figure 1.12). Realization of this design required the merger of the art and storm water budgets as well as additional funding to enhance the wetlands.

The gardens start at the top of the hill and cascade down slope to the wetlands below. The storm water being pumped from the south end of the treatment plant flows under metal grates on its way to the first of 11 settlement ponds (Figure 1.13). From the top of the hill, views extend across the site to the treatment plant and Springbrook Creek. The pedestrian path proceeds downhill, weaving between seven leaf-shaped pools edged with native vegetation that are connected through a series of standpipes. The top two pools are graded to allow vehicular access to the pool bottom to periodically remove sediment buildup. The series of seven pools leads into a shotcrete, a grotto with a tumbled stone mosaic. This grotto appears as a dissected seed pod emerging from

Figure 1.13. View of the metal grates where the water starts its journey toward the first settlement pond, visible just beyond the railing in the distance. *(Photo: Lorna Jordan)*

Figure 1.14. View across the wetlands with the treatment plant in the background on the right. *(Photo: Lorna Jordan)*

an earthen mound, damp and seeping with water. From this room, the path meanders between three circular pools to arrive at the final egg-shaped pool on the edge of the wetlands that comprise the rest of the composition. This final pool is also graded for vehicular access. The pools range between 4 and 7 ft (1.2–2.1 m) deep, with a total volume of 102,081 ft³ (2,889 m³), with 16,215 ft³ (459 m³) being designed as sediment storage. The treatment process is completed in the wetlands shown in Figure 1.14, where the water winds its way through islands, some with human access and others

strictly for animal habitat, to its connection with Springbrook Creek.

Created through collaboration between an artist, landscape architects, and engineers, this wonderful set of garden rooms is a dramatic alternative to the original landscape proposal that would have surrounded the site with a fence of trees and treated water in three square pools. Not only is the infrastructure revealed, but a place of wonder is created where humans can trace the purification and habitat functions of storm water or simply walk and enjoy the new and vibrant plant and animal life that surrounds them.

Naturalistic

Central Park[4]

This last category is perhaps the most common type of grading, particularly in suburban and rural settings, but has also been used to great effect in the urban work of Frederick Law Olmsted, as in Central Park in New York City. It is a stylized approach in which abstract (or organic) landforms are used to represent or imitate the natural landscape. The design is so successful that the landscape is believed to be a product of natural forces. The way the landforms respond to the remaining bedrock leads many to the conclusion that the landforms are natural (Figure 1.15). That misconception may also result from the great range of environmental experiences that are possible within the park's boundaries and the attention paid to the design of thresholds into the park, truly separating the experience of the park from the city beyond (Figure 1.16). There are wild-feeling places (Figure 1.17) nearby adjacent to land rolling manicured

[4] Landscape Architect: Frederick Law Olmsted
Architect: Calvert Vaux

Figure 1.15. Landform is sculpted to look as if it is draped off of bedrock outcrops. *(Photo: Michael Cluer)*

Figure 1.16. Boating in a constructed lake with the city in the distance over the treeline. *(Photo: Michael Cluer)*

Figure 1.17. Rough-hewn rock corridors feel like undiscovered country in the midst of the city. *(Photo: Michael Cluer)*

Figure 1.18. Expansive rolling lawns juxtapose with the skyline. *(Photo: Michael Cluer)*

Figure 1.19. Bridges and tunnels are found throughout the park, often separating pedestrians from automobile or other traffic, but in this case separating two pedestrian pathways. *(Photo: Michael Cluer)*

lawns (Figure 1.18). These experiences are deftly sewn together with a multilayered circulation system (Figure 1.19).

Perception

Slope

The perception of slope is influenced by the texture of the surface material and the relationship to surrounding grades. The coarser the texture, the less noticeable the slope. For example, the slope of smooth pavement, such as troweled concrete, is more noticeable than coarse pavement, such as cobblestone. Generally, slopes of 2% or greater on pavements can easily be perceived. However, horizontal reference lines, such as brick coursing or the top of a wall, increase the awareness of slope even in unpaved situations (Figure 1.20).

The relationship of one slope to another will also influence the perception of steepness. For example, when one travels along a walk with an 8% slope, which then changes to a 4% slope, the 4% slope will visually appear to be less than half the original slope.

Topography, landform, and changes in grade break the landscape into comprehensible units, which establish a sense of scale and sequence. The manner in which these grade changes occur affects the spatial and visual perception and image of a place.

Elevation Change

Being at a higher elevation relative to the surrounding landscape is potentially dramatic for a variety of

Figure 1.20. The clean square edges of the planter walls exaggerate an already steep slope running adjacent to them.

reasons. First, a rise in grade may provide a feeling of expansiveness by extending views and the overall field of vision. Also, being at a higher elevation may provide a sense of superiority, which may contribute to a feeling of control or dominance of a place. In addition, an upward change in elevation can provide an opportunity to contrast or exaggerate the steepness or flatness of the surrounding landscape. The abruptness of an elevation change will affect how space is perceived. The more gradual the ascent, the more subtle the experience. The steeper the grade, the greater the sense of enclosure at the lower elevations, while the opportunity for drama and excitement is increased at the higher elevations.

Convex and Concave Slopes

Generally, a plane is visually less pleasing than a convex or concave landform, although this depends on scale and contrast (Figure 1.21). In comparing the two rounded forms, the concave one appears more graceful from the downhill side, since it exhibits an uplifting quality. From the downhill side both forms foreshorten the view, with the foreshortening being much more abrupt with the convex slope. From the uphill side of a convex slope the sense of height is accentuated. Also, the sense of distance appears compressed, since the middle ground is foreshortened. The following quote from Arthur Raistrick's *The Pennine Dales* (1968), illustrates the influence landform can have on experience:

> The most impressive approach to a view of one of the dales is to come upon it from the high moors—what the dalesfolk call, so expressively, from off the "tops". One has spent the day, perhaps, up in this world of

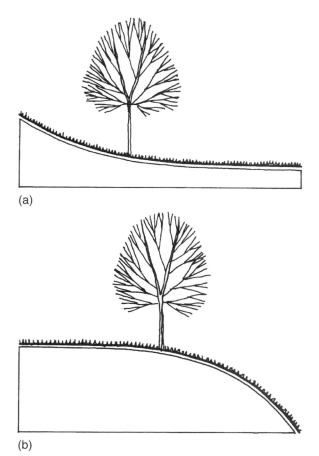

(a)

(b)

Figure 1.21. Rounded slopes. (a) Concave. (b) Convex.

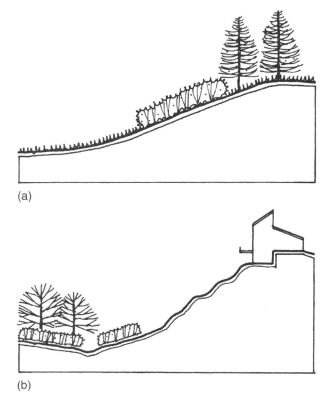

(a)

(b)

Figure 1.22. Enhancing topography with design elements.
(a) Planting. (b) Architecture.

heather, with grouse or curlew providing a commentary to one's movement, and with wide views of moorland cut by faint runnels and gullies, many of which are, in fact, the gaps of the dale lip seen in foreshortened perspective. The high ground begins to decline and one may come to the edge of the heather and peat and enter a world of benty grass and occasional stream heads. Then comes the moment when one looks "over the edge"—the convexity of the hill has reached the point where one can look back up the gentler slope of moorland, or forward down what often appears to be an almost precipitous slope into the valley. (p.29)

Enhancement

By analyzing the existing topography and landscape character, proposed landforms, grade changes, and design elements may be constructed or placed to emphasize, negate, or have little impact on the visual structure of the landscape. The basic considerations when proposing design alternatives are whether they will enhance, complement, contrast with, or conflict with that particular landscape context. In Figure 1.22a, the steepness of the slope is exaggerated by planting taller vegetation at the top of the slope. The prominence of the house in the landscape of Figure 1.22b is heightened by the lack of surrounding vegetation that would give the structure scale. The plantings in the valley also provide a picturesque view from the house.

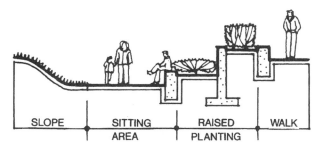

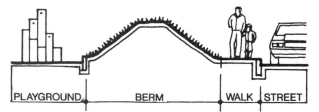

Figure 1.25. In this section, a berm is used to separate a playground from a street.

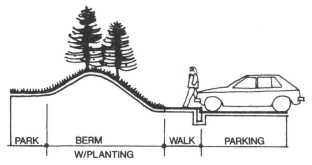

Figure 1.23. Level changes for privacy. Raised planting separates and visually screens the sunken sitting area from the sidewalk. The slope is used to add to the spatial enclosure of the sitting area.

Figure 1.24. Visual screen. Topography, particularly in conjunction with planting, can be used to screen or block undesired views. In the illustration, a planted berm is used to screen the view of a parking lot from a park area.

Spatial Considerations

Proposed grade changes may perform a variety of spatial functions. The appropriateness of the application of these functions is determined by a careful analysis of the potentials of the site and the demands of the design program. Several grading design applications are discussed and illustrated in this section.

Enclosure

Enclosure may be used to perform several tasks, including containment, protection, privacy, and

screening. Seclusion, intimacy, and privacy may be achieved through the use of containment, as in the section of the sitting area illustrated in Figure 1.23. Screening is a form of visual containment, since it terminates sight lines and eliminates undesirable views (Figure 1.24).

Enclosure, possibly in the form of a berm, as illustrated in Figure 1.25, also may be used to provide safety and protection, such as restraining children from running into the street from a playground or serving as a backstop for various types of athletic activities. However, this type of application should be used with caution for two reasons. First, it may inadvertently promote careless recreational uses. Second, the enclosure reduces visibility into the area, creating a potentially unsafe condition. It should be noted that properly designed and placed landforms can be an excellent outlet for creative play.

Berms are vegetated or paved embankments, somewhat dike-like in appearance, commonly used by landscape architects for enclosure and separation purposes. However, the use of these devices must be carefully evaluated, since in many cases the scale and proportion of berms have been insignificant or inappropriate with regard to the surrounding context.

Separation

A very basic application of grading is the separation of activities to reduce potential conflicts, such as

Figure 1.26. The low wall at the edge of some portions of Central Park in New York City provides both enclosure and separation while allowing the park and the city beyond to benefit from views in and out. *(Photo: Michael Cluer)*

separating auto traffic from pedestrians and bicyclists, bicyclists from pedestrians, and sitting areas from walkways. In the design of New York's Central Park, Olmsted and Vaux showed great vision in using grade changes and overpasses to separate the traffic on the transverse roads from the park. Grade changes in the park were also often designed for the dual purposes of separation and enclosure, as shown in Figure 1.26. Even a change in grade of only a few inches may sufficiently define the territory in which an activity may occur (Figure 1.27). Separation may be accomplished by a variety of techniques, two of which are illustrated in Figure 1.28.

Channeling

Landform may be used to direct, funnel, or channel auto and pedestrian circulation. It may also be used to direct and control viewing angles and vistas as well as wind and cold air drainage. An amphitheater is a special use of landform to both focus attention and enclose space (Figure 1.29).

It must be realized that, in all the applications listed above, the functions of landform and grade changes are reinforced and strengthened by the use of plantings and structural elements, such as walls and fences.

Environmental

Storm Water Management

The acts of grading and controlling and managing storm water runoff are inextricably linked. Almost all site development projects result in the remolding and sculpting of the earth's surface as well as changes in surface character. The complexity of this topic, as well as its prevalence across all scales

Figure 1.27. A small grade change is enough, when supported by planting, to make this space feel very separate from the Great Lawn in Central Park. *(Photo: Michael Cluer)*

(a)

(b)

Figure 1.28. Separation of activities. (a) Along a riverfront promenade a grade change, which incorporates seating, is used to separate the pedestrian walk from the bicycle and service lane. (b) An underpass is used to separate pedestrian and vehicular circulation in Central Park.

of design, merits detailed discussion, which will be undertaken in Chapter 9.

Wildlife Habitat Enhancement

Landforming can play a large role in wildlife habitat enhancement. One of the best examples of this is the listing of the Pacific salmon on the endangered species list and the resultant effort to improve their habitat in the Pacific Northwest.

In many parts of the United States, waterways have been channelized because the conventional wisdom at the time dictated that moving water

(a)

(b)

Figure 1.29. Amphitheaters. There are many good examples of places where topography has been used effectively to create a theater setting, two of which are presented here. (a) A Roman amphitheater built in Caesarea, Israel, about 25 B.C.E. The theater has been reconstructed and is in use today. (b) An amphitheater constructed at the site of the 1972 Olympics in Munich. Note how the edge of the theater has been blended into the surrounding earth form.

(a)

(b)

Figure 1.30. Beebe Springs Creek Restoration, Chelan, Washington. (a) The channelized stream. (b) Oblique view of the project, showing the channelized stream still flowing in the upper right corner and the new channel still under construction below and to the left. *(Photos: The Watershed Company)*

(c)

(d)

Figure 1.30. (cont'd)
Beebe Springs Creek
Restoration, Chelan,
Washington. (c) Heavy
machinery was used to
carve the new channel
into the floodplain. (d)
The resulting stream has
a great deal of complexity
and offers a much more
habitable environment
to salmon making
the journey upstream.
*(Photos: The Watershed
Company)*

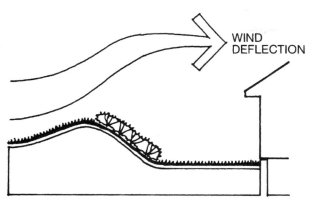

WIND
DEFLECTION

Figure 1.31. Microclimate modification. Topography can be used to channel or deflect winds, capture solar radiation, and create cold or warm pockets.

away faster was the goal of storm water management. This has caused great stress to river-dwelling wildlife populations. It is among many stresses that caused the Pacific salmon to be put on the endangered species list. As a result, a great deal of effort has gone into understanding how best to improve conditions for their health and survival. One way to improve conditions for the salmon directly involves the use of landform to re-create meandering stream conditions where streams have

been channelized to mimic the original dynamic natural environment. The images in Figure 1.30 (see the Color Plates) chronicle the stream's transformation from a fast-flowing straight channel to a meandering and complex stream.

Landform may also be involved in habitat enhancement by providing cues to help guide animals toward underpasses or bridges over highways designed especially for them.

Microclimate Modification

The use of enclosure mentioned earlier in the chapter can provide protection from climatic elements (Figure 1.31). Properly placed landforms can control drifting snow and significantly reduce the impact of wind on structures and even over large areas such as playfields and parking lots.

SUMMARY

Landforms and site engineering are at the heart of high-quality design of all types. Mastering the concepts laid out in the chapters ahead will build a foundation for the capacity to create high-quality designs that are responsive to the benefits and constraints of site engineering.

CHAPTER 2

Grading Constraints

Grading is more than a mechanical process dictated by a predetermined set of criteria. Designing an appropriate grading scheme is a decision-making process based on a variety of constraints and opportunities.

The grading process must be viewed as a response to program concerns, design intent, and contextual conditions. The last consist primarily of the existing physical conditions and the regulations that govern the development of a site. These establish the framework within which the program and design concept may be formulated. In turn, all three elements (program, site, and intent) create constraints that guide the decision-making process.

Although difficult to classify neatly, constraints may be placed in two broad categories: environmental and functional. Environmental constraints are those that deal with the natural conditions of the site. Functional constraints relate to the requirements of the activities that must be accommodated and other restrictions, including laws and regulations such as building and zoning codes. The following discussion examines each of the categories in more detail.

ENVIRONMENTAL CONSTRAINTS

Topography

The most obvious constraint is the existing topography. The existing landform should be analyzed carefully in order to guide the design of the proposed development. High and low points should be located, percentages of slope inventoried, and the extent of relatively level and steep areas determined. Coordinating the proposed grading with the existing conditions, in most cases, reduces development costs and can result in a more desirable final product.

Drainage

It is difficult to separate the act of grading from the act of accommodating and controlling storm water runoff, since one directly affects the other. This section briefly discusses storm drainage as a grading constraint. A more complete discussion of storm runoff and drainage systems is presented in Chapters 9 through 12.

A good rule of thumb to follow in order to reduce impacts and potential problems is to conform as closely as possible to the established natural, as well as constructed, drainage pattern within the proposed development. Before conforming, however, it is important to evaluate the existing system to determine whether it is functioning correctly, both ecologically and hydraulically, and whether it has the capacity to absorb any anticipated changes. Hydrologic problems that result from changes in the character of the environment have been well documented. Increased use of impervious surfaces such as pavements and roofs, channelization of streams, and floodplain encroachment, particularly in urban and suburban areas, have lowered water tables; increased the fluctuation of water levels in streams, ponds, and wetlands; and increased potential flood hazards. The impacts of these problems are also obvious. Flooding is a threat to safety, health, and personal well-being, while lowering the water table directly affects the water supply. Fluctuation of water levels will have an impact on plant and animal habitats, since such conditions require a high degree of tolerance to ensure survival. Acknowledging and understanding these problems will lead to more sensitive handling of storm water runoff.

Vegetation

Disturbing the earth around existing vegetation generally has a detrimental effect on the health of plants. The impacts are often not readily apparent.

There have been instances where architects and landscape architects have developed areas quite close to specimen trees. The photographs taken immediately after completion of the project provided an excellent and sensitive impression, but the reality of the design became apparent 2 or 3 years later, when the dead trees were removed. Although not necessarily assuring survival, protection of existing plant material is best accomplished by avoiding grade changes within the drip line of the plants. Cutting soil within the drip line removes surface roots, while filling within the same area reduces the amount of air available to the root system. The consequence of any changes will depend on the plant species and soil conditions. If a change in grade within the drip line of a tree is absolutely necessary, it is recommended to work with a licensed arborist to determine the best course of action for attempting to preserve the tree.

Protective systems, as illustrated in Figure 2.1, may be used where it is necessary to change the elevation around existing vegetation, particularly trees. However, these systems increase the cost of a project and still do not guarantee plant survival. A better approach is to develop a grading system that minimizes these types of disturbances.

Existing vegetation may also be affected by changes in drainage patterns. Directing storm runoff to areas that are normally dry, draining areas that are usually wet, or lowering the water table alters the environmental conditions to which plants have adapted. These alterations may cause severe physiological stress and result in a change in the plant community that inhabits the area.

Soils

In any building process, it is important to understand the nature of the construction material used. In the case of grading, the construction material is soil. For landscape architects, some knowledge of its engineering, as well as its edaphological

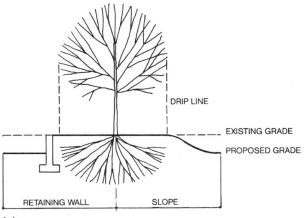

DRIP LINE

EXISTING GRADE

PROPOSED GRADE

RETAINING WALL   SLOPE

(a)

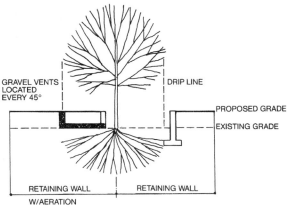

GRAVEL VENTS
LOCATED
EVERY 45°

DRIP LINE

PROPOSED GRADE

EXISTING GRADE

RETAINING WALL   RETAINING WALL
W/AERATION

(b)

(c)

(d)

(e)

Figure 2.1. Grade changes at existing trees. (a) For cut conditions, either a slope or a retaining wall can be used beyond the drip line to attain the desired grades. (b) In fill situations, a retaining wall can be placed beyond the drip line or within the drip line if proper aeration measures, such as gravel vents, are provided. (c) A wood retaining wall used to protect a tree in a fill condition. (d) A concrete retaining wall used to protect a tree in a cut condition. (e) For a tree to survive either a cut or fill condition, great care must be taken to protect the tree during construction. The tree is surrounded by fencing during construction, and large signs have been posted on the fencing noting the fines that will occur if the tree is harmed.

and pedological properties, is necessary, since soil is used as both building material and growing medium. Properties such as bearing capacity, angle of repose, shear strength, permeability, erodibility, frost action potential, pH level, and organic content establish the capabilities and limitations of a soil. As part of the preliminary planning process for any major project, an investigation of the soil and geologic conditions must be conducted and an engineering report prepared by qualified professionals. Such a report can help determine the feasibility of a project; impact the layout of the site design; and form the basis for structural design decisions.

As emphasized throughout this book, a team approach to planning and design should yield better project outcomes in relation to environmental, social, and economic needs. Site planners and landscape architects need to know when it is necessary and appropriate to engage specialized expertise. Soil and foundation engineers and soil scientists are excellent examples of such specialists.

As stated previously, landscape architects are interested in soil both as a growing medium and as a construction material. In most cases, optimization of the performance of soils for these disparate functions requires specifications and criteria that are, for the most part, diametrically opposed. In order to support vegetation, soils must have adequate pore space for air and water. In soils used as construction materials that must support structures like footings and pavements, organic content must be eliminated and pore space minimized. The development and use of structural soils, which will be discussed in more detail in Chapter 7, is an effort to minimize these opposing functions in certain design situations.

During the reconnaissance and exploration phase, it is essential to identify critical conditions that may drastically affect cost or feasibility, or be related to the potential failure of a project. Soils that pose particular difficulties and should be avoided or removed are loose silts, soft clays, fine water-bearing sands, and soils with high organic content such as peat. Other critical conditions are a high water table or rock close to the surface.

Evidence of earth movement can normally be observed directly. Earth movement includes landslides, subsidence, and creep. Such conditions are a safety threat and must be thoroughly investigated. Knowledge of the underlying geology and past history of the site will increase awareness of the potential for these conditions. Examples of such features include subsurface mining activities and the presence of water-soluble limestone deposits. Landfills and unconsolidated fills provide highly unstable conditions. Such circumstances may not be obvious without subsurface investigation and an understanding of the history of the site.

Site planning and design decisions should acknowledge any limitations posed in terms of environmental, engineering, and/or economic constraints or consequences. In critical situations such as those previously discussed, development programs may have to be significantly changed or an alternative site selected.

Erodibility

All soils are susceptible to erosion. This is especially true during the construction process, since stabilizing surface material such as vegetation is removed and soils become unconsolidated due to excavating and scraping. One of the most effective strategies for minimizing erosion is to minimize the area to be disturbed by new construction.

Erosion not only results in the loss of soil but also causes problems by depositing the soil in undesirable places such as lakes, ponds, and catch basins. Many communities now require the submission of a soil erosion and sedimentation control plan prior to the start of construction. The plan is called a TESC plan, where TESC stands for Temporary Erosion and Sedimentation Control. This plan indicates the temporary control measures to be taken during construction and often includes the permanent measures that will remain once construction has been completed. An extremely important step is to strip and stockpile the existing topsoil layer properly in order to prevent unnecessary loss of this important resource. After regrading has been completed, the topsoil can be replaced on the site. Erosion and sediment control are discussed further in Chapter 10.

Topographic factors influencing erosion are the degree and length of slopes. The erosion potential increases as either or both of these factors increase. Knowing the erosion tendency of a soil, therefore, will influence the proposed grading design by limiting the length and degree of slope.

Organic and Nutrient Content and pH Level

Tests to determine the nutrient and organic content and pH are performed to assess the ability of a soil to support plant growth, since slope stabilization is often achieved through vegetative means. If the chemical condition of the soil prevents vegetation from becoming established, erosion will occur. By knowing the pH, the nutrient level, and the amount of organic matter, corrective steps can easily be taken to improve the growing environment.

FUNCTIONAL CONSTRAINTS

Functional constraints have been broadly interpreted to include not only the limitations resulting from the uses that must be accommodated, but also factors such as maintenance, economics, and existing restrictive conditions.

Restrictive Conditions

The first set of functional constraints is determined by legal controls and physical limitations. Property lines establish legal boundaries beyond which a property owner does not have the right to modify or change existing conditions. Therefore, grades along property lines cannot be altered and thus become a controlling factor. In urban situations where land is

Figure 2.2. Retaining walls are used to support a series of raised public terraces at Seattle's City Hall.

expensive and sites are relatively small, costly grade change devices may be necessary along property lines to maximize the usability and development potential of a site (Figure 2.2).

In addition to the prohibition of physical change, it is usually illegal to increase the rate of flow of storm water runoff from one property to adjacent properties (Figure 2.3). To be in compliance, the rate of runoff after completion of construction must not exceed the rate prior to construction. Pre- and post-construction runoff rates will be discussed in Chapter 9.

Most design projects come under the jurisdiction of a political authority, whether it be at the municipal, state, or federal level, and usually must comply with a variety of building and zoning code regulations. In order to obtain permits, approvals, and certificates of occupancy, it is necessary to meet the criteria and standards set by these regulatory authorities. Items that typically may be regulated include maximum allowable cross slope for public sidewalks, maximum height of street curbs, acceptable riser/tread ratios for stairs, maximum number of stair risers without an intermediate landing, maximum slope for handicapped ramps, slope protection, drainage channel stabilization, retention

Figure 2.3. A ridge has been formed in the sidewalk to separate runoff between the road right of way and the park property.

ponds, and vegetative cover. Before starting a project, the designer should become familiar with all applicable regulations.

Existing as well as proposed structures establish controls that affect grading design. Door entrances and finished floor elevations must be met, window openings may limit the height of grades, and structural conditions may limit the amount of soil that can be retained or backfilled against a building. The ability to waterproof or not waterproof a particular structure may determine whether soil can be placed against it. The response to these various conditions will influence the form of the grading design.

Utility systems, particularly those that flow by gravity or gravity-induced pressure, such as storm drainage, domestic water supply, and sanitary sewers, establish additional criteria that may control the grading process. If a proposed storm drainage system is connected to an existing system, then obviously the elevation of the existing system cannot be higher than that of the proposed system at the point of connection; if it is, pumping stations will be required. To prevent this from occurring, it

is wise to work back from the known elevation at the outlet when establishing grades along the new drainage system. Also, the capacity of the existing system, including pipes and swales, must be evaluated to determine if additional storm runoff can be accommodated. Domestic water and sanitary sewer connections also may require pumping if the required flow cannot be achieved naturally by gravitational pressure.

Activities and Uses

The two most prevalent structures that must be accommodated by grading are buildings and circulation systems. Typically, these create the most difficult problems and the most limiting constraints that must be dealt with in the grading process. In a holistic sense, the placement of buildings in the landscape and the resultant pedestrian and vehicular access patterns should work in concert with each other as well as with the natural and cultural context in which they are placed. This has not always been the case.

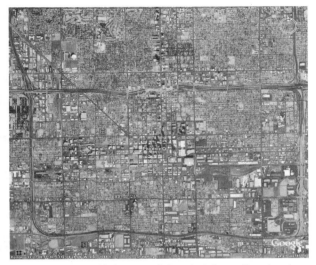

Figure 2.4. The gridded streets of Phoenix, Arizona. Note that the highway was even forced to make a right angle in the lower left corner of the image. *(Image: Google Earth™ Mapping Service and Europa Technologies, Ltd)*

At the same time, the growth of urban and suburban trail systems along historic rail corridors, rails-to-trails projects, is the result of the decline of one transit system whose design criteria fit well with its adapted reuse as a pedestrian circulation system. The rail system was developed throughout the United States and around the world at low slopes. These low slopes are ideal for pedestrian use. In this case, the historic development of one circulation system has made possible the present use.

Quite often the decision to locate a building is based on one criterion, such as zoning setbacks, initial cost, or the view from the site, without a complete understanding of how this placement will affect the construction of roads, parking areas, and walks. The criterion may be achieved, but at the expense of increased construction costs, high visual and/or natural impacts, user inconvenience, and increased long-term maintenance costs.

The reverse condition is also common. The grid street patterns of many North American cities were plotted with little regard for existing natural and topographic features (Figure 2.4). The consequences have been the loss of landscape character and uniqueness and the development of a rather homogenized environment. There are exceptions, San Francisco perhaps being the most noteworthy. San Francisco serves not only as an example of lack of coordination between development and environment, but also as an excellent example of contradiction and happenstance. If the city had been laid out according to current environmental principles, it might have been denied the charm, drama, and attraction it displays today. The lesson to be learned here is that all principles, even those described in this book, must be viewed as guidelines. A successful designer applies these principles with flexibility and knows when it is appropriate to bend or break the rules.

Fitting buildings into the landscape is related to the type of structural foundation, the method of construction, and ultimately the form of architecture employed. There are three general types of structural foundations: slab, continuous wall, and pole (Figure 2.5). A *slab foundation* forms a horizontal plane with a relatively thin profile, which results in the least amount of grading flexibility. Depending on the length of the building, slopes up to 3% may typically be achieved along the building face. A *continuous wall foundation* forms a line that provides for a moderate degree of flexibility. Depending on the height of the foundation wall, grade changes of a story or more may be achieved. *Pole*, or *pier, construction* provides the greatest amount of grading flexibility and potentially the least amount of grading impact, since there is minimal ground disturbance. This technique uses poles or piers as the primary method of transferring the structural load to the ground. The poles form points rather than lines where they meet the ground and the building is placed above the landscape, thus allowing drainage to continue

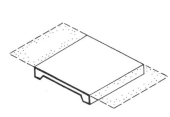

(a)

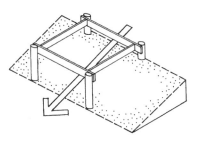

(b)   (c)

Figure 2.5. Foundation systems.
(a) Slab. (b) Continuous wall.
(c) Pole. (d) Example of a continuous wall foundation system used to overcome a large grade change on the site and provide underground parking.

(d)

uninterrupted. This normally reduces the amount of grading required to redirect storm runoff around structures.

The method of connection between the foundation and the wall system and the material composition of the wall may also create grading constraints. As illustrated in Figure 2.6a, soil should not be placed directly against wood frame construction. To reduce moisture problems, 8 in. (200 mm) is recommended as a minimum distance between the wood frame and the exterior grade. It should be noted that pressure-treated or preservative-treated lumber may come in contact with soil, but usually this material is used for conditions and purposes other than wood frame construction detailing. Concrete and masonry, when properly waterproofed, will allow somewhat more flexibility in varying the exterior grade. This is particularly true when the foundation and wall are an integral system, as indicated in Figure 2.6c.

At the risk of considerable oversimplification, architectural design may be categorized as either

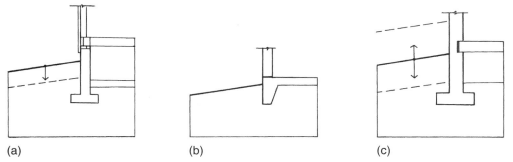

(a)   (b)   (c)

Figure 2.6. Exterior wall details. (a) Standard wood frame construction places wood floor joists on top of a concrete foundation, and the exterior siding material extends below the joist/foundation connection. The grade at the foundation should be at least 8 in. below the siding material. If a continuous wall foundation is used, there is obviously some flexibility downward with the grades. (b) Walls are normally constructed directly on slab foundations. Since it is very difficult to waterproof this connection, this condition offers the least amount of flexibility. (c) Where the exterior wall forms a continuous plane uninterrupted by floor connections, greater grading flexibility, both up and down, can be achieved.

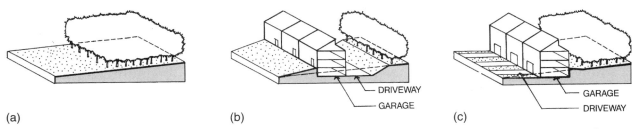

(a)   (b)   (c)

Figure 2.7. Relationship of building to topography. (a) Wooded, sloping site prior to construction. (b) Site as constructed, creating a valley across the slope. (c) An alternative site design that reduces the amount of excavation and preserves more of the wooded area.

flat-site buildings or sloping-site buildings with respect to grading. Flat-site buildings are characterized by the fact that there is relatively little change in grade from one side of the building to the opposite side. Sloping-site buildings, on the other hand, attempt to accommodate any existing changes in topography by stepping or terracing the structure with the slope. Each building type is appropriate when used in the proper context.

An example of an actual case where building-site relationships have different results, depending on functional or aesthetic priorities, is illustrated in Figure 2.7. In this situation, a three-story townhouse complex with garages on the first level was placed on a sloping parcel of land. Entrances to the garages were placed at the rear of the units, which went against the slope and required additional excavation. This decision may have been based on aesthetic concerns, placing the garage doors behind the units out of view from the street and creating the traditional image of a large lawn in front of the units. An alternative solution would have been to place the garage doors at the front of the units. As a result of this placement, less excavation would have been necessary, more of the existing vegetation could have been preserved, and a private area could have been provided at the back of each unit at the second-floor level, thus allowing the building to step with the site. This example demonstrates that grading and design are an integral process and that the decision-making process may result in trade-offs or compromises. Although both solutions

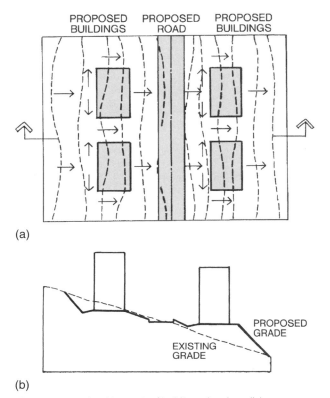

(a)

(b)

Figure 2.8. Road and long axis of buildings placed parallel to contours. (a) Plan indicating the proposed drainage pattern. (b) Section indicating the typical terrace conditions for this configuration.

may be correct from a site engineering perspective, the appropriateness of the design is determined by its cultural and environmental context.

Often the framework for building placement and development is established by street patterns. There are three basic ways in which street layout is related to topography. The first is to locate the street parallel to the contours. As indicated in Figure 2.8, buildings placed with their long axis parallel to the road create obstacles, or dams, for the natural drainage pattern, since there is little pitch in the longitudinal direction. To compensate for this obstruction, the proposed grading must direct the storm water runoff around the buildings. The section that

normally results from this arrangement is a terraced condition formed by cutting on the uphill side and filling on the downhill side. The advantage of this layout is that it normally results in easy access between circulation system and building.

The second way is to locate the street perpendicular to the contours (Figure 2.9). Since the most common practice is to place the long axis of the building parallel to the street, the task of directing storm water around the structure is made somewhat easier by this configuration. However, three potential problems arise from this arrangement. The first is that the gradient of the road may be excessive, since the steepest slope occurs perpendicular to the contours. The second is the awkward relationship that may result at access points from the street, since paths or drives placed perpendicular to the direction of the road must be cross-sloped. Finally, costly grade changes may be required between buildings, as illustrated in Figure 2.9b. Part of this problem may be alleviated by stepping the architecture, as shown in Figure 2.9c.

The third option for street layout is to place the street diagonally across the contours (Figure 2.10). This arrangement usually results in a more efficient storm drainage design, a better relationship between access and structure, and less steep gradients than those of the perpendicular arrangement. It should also result in the least amount of disturbance to the landscape, since this option should minimize the amount of regrading required.

More than likely, most development situations will be a composite of the three layout options. The actual criteria applied to the grading of any pedestrian or vehicular circulation system depend on many factors. For both systems, such factors as type, volume, and speed of traffic; climatic conditions; and existing topography must be addressed.

Specific activities and land uses also establish limits and constraints on the grading process.

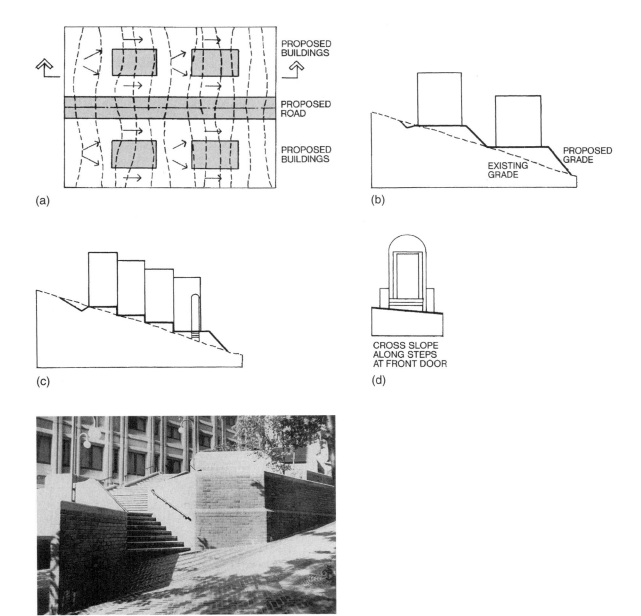

(a)

PROPOSED
BUILDINGS

PROPOSED
ROAD

PROPOSED
BUILDINGS

(b)

EXISTING
GRADE

PROPOSED
GRADE

(c)

(d)

CROSS SLOPE
ALONG STEPS
AT FRONT DOOR

(e)

Figure 2.9. Road and long axis of buildings placed perpendicular to contours. (a) Plan indicating the proposed drainage pattern. (b) Section indicating stepped terraces. (c) Section indicating stepped buildings. (d) Elevation illustrating the cross-slope condition at entrances. (e) Height varies along the first riser, where the stair meets the steep cross-slope.

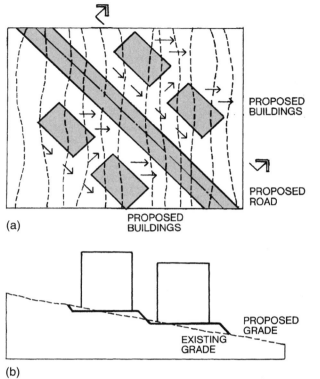

(a)

(b)

Figure 2.10. Road and long axis of buildings placed diagonally to contours. (a) Plan indicating proposed drainage pattern. (b) Section illustrating a reduced amount of required grade change as compared with Figures 2.8 and 2.9.

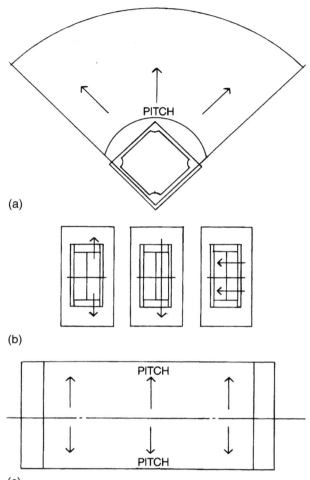

(a)

(b)

(c)

Figure 2.11. Grading for sports facilities. (a) Baseball and softball fields are normally pitched toward the outfield. (b) Court sports such as tennis and basketball may be pitched from the center to both ends, from one end to the other, or from one side to the other. They may also be diagonally cross-sloped. (c) Playfields like football and soccer fields are crowned at the center and pitched to both sides.

Athletic facilities, including playfields and game courts, are excellent examples. Facilities such as football and soccer fields, baseball and softball diamonds, and tennis courts have specific guidelines for layout, orientation, and grading (Figure 2.11). The preciseness of these guidelines is determined by the anticipated level of play (e.g., international vs. intramural competition or professional baseball vs. Little League) and the governing athletic association. Guidelines and standards extend beyond the world of sports. Highway departments, zoning ordinances, and city, state, and federal agencies have a variety of regulations and standards that must be adhered to in the design and grading process. Table 2.1 lists a number of site conditions and the suggested range of acceptable slopes for each. These guidelines are based on experience and represent common uses under average

Table 2.1 Grading Standards and Critical Gradients

Type of Use	Extreme Range (%)	Desirable Range (%)
Public Streets	0.5–0	1–8
Private Roads	0.5–20	1–12
Service Drives	0.5–15[a]	1–10[a]
Parking Areas	0.5–8	1–5
Parking Ramps	up to 20	up to 15
Collector Walks	0.5–12	1–8
Entrance Walks	0.5–8	1–4
Pedestrian Ramps	up to 12	up to 8
Stairs	25–50	33–50
Game Courts	0.5–2	0.5–1.5
Playfields	1–5[b]	2–3[b]
Paved Gutters	0.25–100	1–50
Grassed Swales	0.5–15	2–10
Terrace and Sitting Areas	0.5–3	1–2
Grassed Banks	up to 50[c]	up to 33[d]
Planted Banks	up to 100[c]	up to 50[c]

[a] Preferred gradient at loading/unloading areas is 1% to 3%.
[b] Playfields, such as a football field, may be level in the longitudinal direction if they have a 2% to 3% cross-slope.
[c] Dependent on soil type.
[d] Maximum slope recommended for power mower. AV 25% slope is preferred.

General Comments
1. Minimum slopes should be increased based on drainage capabilities of surfacing materials.
2. Maximum slopes should be decreased based on local climatic conditions, such as ice and snow, and maintenance equipment limitations.
3. All standards should be checked against local building codes, public work and highway departments, and other governing agencies.

conditions. They should be applied with flexibility, particularly in unique or atypical situations.

Economics and Maintenance

Economic constraints relate to both initial construction costs and long-term maintenance and operational costs. As an approach to grading design, an optimum solution is one that balances the amount of cut and fill on site. This means that soil does not have to be imported to or exported from the site. If this cannot be achieved, usually the less costly option is to have an excess of cut material. This will be discussed in more detail in Chapter 7.

The types of equipment and labor required during the construction process directly affect cost. Historically, earthmoving was accomplished primarily by extensive human effort with the aid of animals and rudimentary machinery. The gardens at Versailles and New York's Central Park are excellent examples of landscape designs that required large-scale earthmoving and grading, executed to a great extent by hand labor. In the twentieth century, labor-intensive grading became costly as wages increased and human energy was replaced by powerful, efficient earthmoving equipment. The development of this equipment increased the feasibility of large-scale earthmoving projects, since construction time was reduced and the ratio of the amount of work achievable per dollar spent was greatly increased. However, even with the current trend of increased equipment operation costs due to higher energy prices, earthmoving remains one of the most cost-effective construction processes. Generally, grading designs that utilize standard construction equipment and a minimum of hand labor in their implementation will be the least costly. Factors influencing the method of construction include the configuration of the site and of the proposed landforms, available maneuvering and staging space, and the preciseness of the grading required.

Grading designs that require elaborate storm drainage systems will be more expensive than designs that conform to natural drainage patterns. In urban areas it may be difficult to avoid such conditions. In these instances, both the grading and storm drainage designs must be evaluated for unnecessary intricacy. Simplification, but not at the expense of the overall design concept, will result in the most cost-effective system.

Once a project is completed, it must be maintained. Obviously, each design requires a different level of maintenance. Developing an understanding of a client's expertise, staffing and budget capabilities, and attitudes toward maintenance at the beginning of a project will influence design decisions. Providing a client with a design that cannot be maintained due to impracticality or budget constraints will, in the long run, destroy the project and one's credibility as a design professional. However, there must be a balance between maintenance demands and other aesthetic and functional design criteria.

One of the primary maintenance concerns in grading design is the extent and steepness of sloped areas. Where turf must be mowed, steep slopes will require hand mowers rather than tractor or gang mowers. Improperly maintained steep slopes may also result in soil erosion. This is not only unsightly, but the transported sediment may clog storm drainage structures. This, in turn, creates a safety problem and an additional maintenance concern.

In northern climates, steep slopes along circulation routes may increase the amount of snow removal required and may result in an excessive use of salt or sand to reduce slippery conditions. Also, in these climates, where stairs are used extensively and intricate or constricted sidewalk patterns occur, the amount of snow removal done by hand is increased. This slows the clearing process and increases snow removal budgets.

SUMMARY OF CRITICAL CONSTRAINTS

Various constraints and factors influencing grading design decisions have been presented briefly in this chapter. At this point, a few are worth repeating because of their importance.

1. Consult the applicable local codes to determine how they constrain the site design. This should occur very early in the analysis phase of a project to identify any constraints that may require a change in the design program.

2. To avoid moisture and structural problems, storm water must be drained away from buildings. This is referred to as *positive drainage*.

3. Grade changes should be avoided within the drip line of existing trees in order to protect the health of the plants.

4. Legally, grades cannot be changed beyond the property lines of the site.

5. The rate of storm runoff leaving the site after construction has been completed should not exceed the preconstruction rate.

6. New construction should disturb the smallest area possible to minimize erosion.

7. The proposed grading and landform design should respond to the function and purpose of the activities and uses to be accommodated.

CHAPTER 3

Contours and Form

DEFINITION

A clear understanding of what a contour represents is fundamental to the grading design process. Technically defined, a *contour* is an imaginary line that connects all points of equal elevation above or below a fixed reference plane or datum. This datum may be mean sea level or a locally established benchmark. A *contour line* is the graphic representation of a contour on a plan or map. In this book, however, the terms *contour* and *contour line* will be used synonymously.

A difficulty with understanding contours arises from the fact that they are imaginary and therefore cannot be easily visualized in the landscape. Abstractly, water in any vessel, a bottle or a bathtub, for instance, defines a line of equal elevation when undisturbed (Figure 3.1). The best example of a naturally occurring contour is the shoreline of a pond or lake (Figure 3.2; see the Color Plates). These examples also illustrate the concept of

closed contours. A closed contour is one that reconnects with itself. All contours eventually close on themselves, although this may not occur within the boundaries of a particular map or plan.

Figure 3.1. Water in this sink defines a line of equal elevation.

37

(a)

Figure 3.2. Two examples of lines of equal elevation in the landscape. (a) The edge of this detention pond defines a line of equal elevation. (b) The edges of these terraced rice patties also define lines of equal elevation. *(Photo: Corrie Rosen)*

(b)

A single closed contour may describe a horizontal plane or a level surface, again illustrated by a pond or lake. However, more than one contour is required to describe a three-dimensional surface. Rows of seating in an athletic stadium or amphitheater (Figure 3.3) provide an excellent way to visualize a series of contours that define a bowl-shaped form. It is important to emphasize here that contour drawings are two-dimensional representations of three-dimensional forms. A basic skill that landscape architects and

(a)   (b)

Figure 3.3. Visualizing contour lines. (a) The stepped levels formed by stadium benches demonstrate the concept of contour lines. (b) Small terraces created for spectators at the site of the 1972 Olympic kayak run provide an excellent example of contour lines as they appear on the ground.

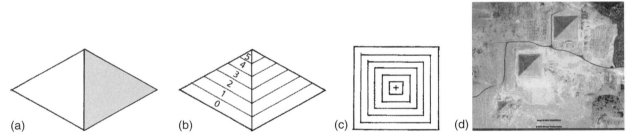

(a)   (b)   (c)   (d)

Figure 3.4. Relationship of contour lines to three-dimensional form. (a) Isometric drawing of a pyramidal form. (b) Contour lines illustrated on the isometric drawing. (c) Contour plan of a pyramid (concentric squares). (d) The courses of stone that the pyramids at Giza are constructed from mark the pyramids with lines that act like contours, defining lines of equal elevation, as seen in this Google Earth™ image. *(Image: Google Earth™ mapping service, Digital Globe and Europa Technologies, Ltd)*

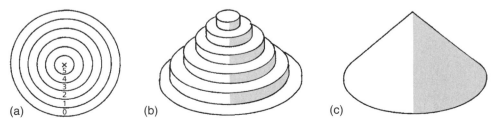

(a)   (b)   (c)

Figure 3.5. Alteration of form by changing contour lines. (a) Square contour lines of a pyramid altered to concentric circular contour lines. (b) Horizontal planes of circular contours stacked in a layer-cake-like manner. (c) Isometric of the resultant conical form.

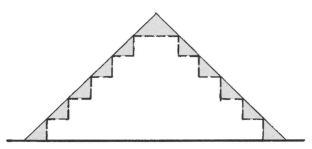

Figure 3.6. Surface smoothing between adjacent contour lines.

Figure 3.7. A monumental run of stairs showing step-like character, created by contours where a smooth transition has not been taken into consideration.

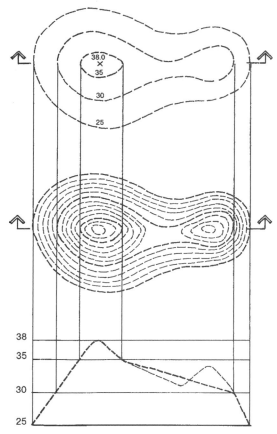

Figure 3.8. Contour interval and accuracy of form.

site designers must develop is the ability to analyze, interpret, and visualize landforms from contour maps and plans, commonly referred to as *topographic maps*. Designers must not only understand existing contours and landforms, they must also understand the implications of changes, both aesthetically and ecologically, that result from *altering* contours. The illustrations in Figures 3.4 and 3.5 demonstrate how contours define form and how a form may be altered by changing contours. The contour plan of the pyramid results in a series of concentric squares. By changing the squares to circles, the form is redefined from a pyramid to a cone. Figure 3.5 illustrates this transformation, starting with the contour plan.

Another aspect of contours and form is illustrated by Figures 3.5(b and c) and 3.6. A *gradual* rather than an abrupt change is assumed to occur between adjacent contours. In Figure 3.6, a section (see the definition in the following section) has been taken through the center of the cone. (Note that a section taken through the center of the pyramid results in the same two-dimensional form.) The step-like form that results from stacking the successive planes is indicated by the dashed line, and the smoothing effect that results from assuming a gradual transition is indicated by the shaded triangles. It is this smoothing effect that gives the cone and pyramid their true form. Again, stadium seating or a long run of monumental stairs provides a good example of the step-like character created by adjacent contours where a smooth transition has not been taken into consideration (Figure 3.7).

These examples are oversimplified in their approach, since they deal with basic geometric forms and straightforward alterations. However, the landscape consists of numerous geometric shapes occurring in complex combinations. The ability to dissect landforms into their various component shapes and to understand the relationship of the shapes to each other will make the task of analyzing, interpreting, and visualizing the landscape easier.

The difference in elevation between adjacent contour lines, as illustrated by the steps in Figure 3.6, is defined as the *contour interval*. In order to interpret a topographic map properly, the scale, direction of slope, and contour interval must be known. The most common intervals in U.S. Customary units are

1, 2, 5, 10, and multiples of 10 ft. In metric units, common intervals are 0.20, 0.50, and 1.00 m. Selection of a contour interval is based on the roughness of the terrain and the purpose for which the topographic plan is to be used. It is obvious that as the map scale decreases (for example, changing from 1 in. = 20 ft to 1 in. = 100 ft or from 1:250 to 1:1,000 for the same area) or the contour interval increases, the amount of detail, and therefore the degree of accuracy, decreases (Figure 3.8).

CONSTRUCTING A SECTION

Topography and landform can be analyzed by constructing a section. A *section* is a drawing made on a plane, which vertically cuts through the earth and/or an object like a building. The ground line delineates the interface between earth and space and illustrates the relief of the topography. To draw a section, follow the procedure outlined in Figure 3.9.

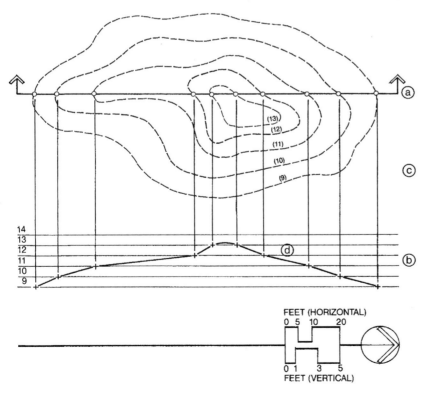

Figure 3.9. Drawing a section. (a) Indicate the cutting plane. (b) Draw parallel lines according to the contour interval and proposed vertical scale. (c) Project perpendicular lines from the intersection of the contour line with the cutting plane to the corresponding parallel line. (d) Connect the points to complete the section and delineate the ground line.

In Figure 3.9 the highest elevation of the landform occurs between the 13-ft and 14-ft elevations. Therefore, a peak, or high point, must occur between the two intersections along the 13-ft elevation line. A similar condition, and how it may be misinterpreted due to degree of accuracy, is illustrated in Figure 3.8.

Digital technology has made the creation of sections from contour plans a simple and efficient process. Modeling programs such as Google SketchUp™ include features that allow for quick visualization of landform in three dimensions.

CHARACTERISTICS OF CONTOUR LINES

The points listed below summarize the essential characteristics of contour lines. Since many of the concepts and principles discussed in subsequent chapters relate to these characteristics, a thorough understanding must be achieved before proceeding.

1. By definition, all points on the same contour line are at the same elevation (Figure 3.10).

2. Every contour line is a continuous line, which forms a closed figure, either within or beyond the limits of the map or drawing (Figure 3.11).

3. Two or more contour lines are required to indicate three-dimensional form and direction of slope (Figure 3.12).

4. The steepest slope is perpendicular to the contour lines. This is a result of having the greatest vertical change in the shortest horizontal distance (Figure 3.12).

5. Consistent with the preceding point, water flows perpendicular to contour lines (Figure 3.12).

6. For the same scale and contour interval, the steepness of slope increases as the map distance between contour lines decreases.

7. Equally spaced contour lines indicate a constant, or uniform, slope (Figure 3.13; see the Color Plates).

8. Contour lines never cross except where there is an overhanging cliff, natural bridge, or other similar phenomenon (Figure 3.14).

Figure 3.10. The edges of the stairs on this roof deck are at the same elevation as joints on the adjacent ramp and therefore are on the same contour line.

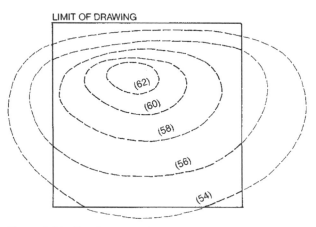

LIMIT OF DRAWING

(62)
(60)
(58)
(56)
(54)

Figure 3.11. Closed contours. Contours are continuous lines creating closed figures. However, closure may not always occur within the limits of a drawing or map.

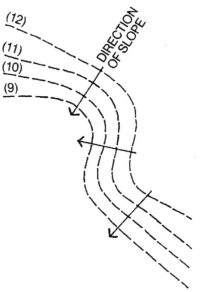

(12)
(11)
(10)
(9)

DIRECTION OF SLOPE

Figure 3.12. Direction of slope. The steepest slope is perpendicular to the contour lines. Consequently, surface water flows perpendicular to contour lines.

Figure 3.13. The dots in this image show where contour lines would hit the horizon along this sloping lawn. Their even spacing denotes a uniform slope, as traced by the arrow above.

Figure 3.14. Drawing contour lines for the intersection of the highway and the overhanging park would require crossing contour lines.

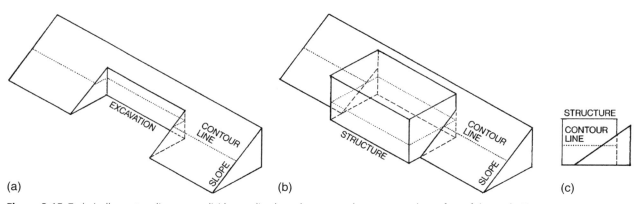

Figure 3.15. Technically, contour lines never divide or split where they are used to represent the surface of the earth. However, at structures, contour lines may also be drawn across the face of the constructed object, thus providing a split appearance. (a) The contour line follows along the face of an excavation made in a slope. (b) The contour line follows along the face of the excavation as well as along the face of the structure placed in the excavated area. (c) End section illustrating the relationship between the slope and the structure.

9. In the natural landscape, contour lines never divide or split. However, this is not necessarily true at the interface between the natural and built landscape as illustrated in Figure 3.15.

CONTOUR SIGNATURES AND LANDFORM

It becomes apparent in analyzing a landform that certain geomorphic features are described by distinct contour configurations. These configurations may be referred to as *contour signatures*. Typical contour signatures are identified on the contour maps (portions of United States Geological Survey quadrangles) in Figures 3.16 and 3.17.

Ridge and Valley

A *ridge* is simply a raised, elongated landform. At the narrow end of the form the contours point in the downhill direction. Typically, the contours along the sides of the ridge will be relatively parallel, and there will be a high point or several high points along the ridge. (See Figure 3.18 in the Color Plates.)

A *valley* is an elongated depression that forms the space between two ridges. Essentially, valleys and ridges are interconnected, since the ridge side slopes create the valley walls. A valley is represented by contours that point uphill. (See Figure 3.19 in the Color Plates.)

The contour pattern is similar for both the ridge and the valley; therefore, it is important to note the direction of slope. In each case, the contours reverse direction to create a U or V shape. The V shape is more likely to be associated with a valley, since the point at which the contour changes direction is the low point. Water collects along the intersection of the sloping sides and flows downhill, forming a natural drainage channel at the bottom.

Summit and Depression

A *summit* is a landform, such as a knoll, hill, or mountain, that contains the highest point relative to the surrounding terrain. The contours form concentric, closed figures with the *highest* contour at the center. Since the land slopes away in all directions, summits tend to drain well. (See Figure 3.20 in the Color Plates.)

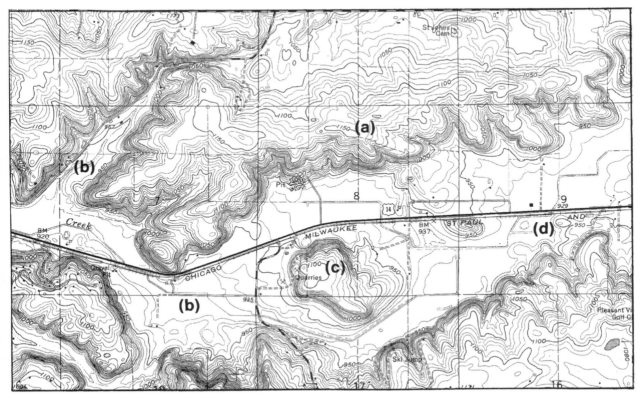

Figure 3.16. Contour signatures. (a) Ridge. (b) Valley. (c) Summit. (d) Depression.

A *depression* is a landform that contains the lowest point relative to the surrounding terrain. Again, the contours form concentric, closed figures, but now the *lowest* contour is at the center. To avoid confusion between summits and depressions, it is important to know the direction of elevation change. Graphically, the lowest contour is often distinguished by the use of hachures. Since depressions collect water, they typically form lakes, ponds, and wetlands. (See Figure 3.21 in the Color Plates.)

Concave and Convex Slopes

A distinctive characteristic of *concave* slopes is that the contour lines are spaced at *increasing* distances in the downhill direction. This means that the slope is steeper at the higher elevations and becomes progressively more flat at the lower elevations.

A *convex* slope is the reverse of a concave slope. In other words, the contour lines are spaced at *decreasing* distances in the downhill direction. The slope is flatter at the higher elevations and becomes progressively steeper at the lower elevations. (See Figure 3.22 in the Color Plates.)

Uniform Slope

Along a uniform slope, contour lines are spaced at *equal* distances. Thus, the change in elevation occurs at a constant rate (see Figure 3.13). Uniform slopes are more typical in constructed than in natural environments.

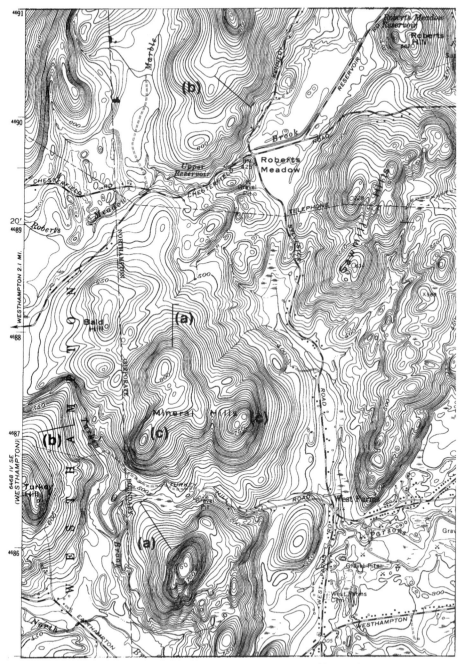

Figure 3.17. Contour signatures. (a) Concave slope. (b) Convex slope. (c) Summit.

Figure 3.18. A small-scale urban ridge. Contours are delineated with black dashed lines, while white arrows show the direction of water flow.

Figure 3.19. A small-scale urban valley. Contours are delineated with black dashed lines, while white arrows show the direction of water flow.

Figure 3.20. The Great Mound at Gasworks Park in Seattle, Washington, is a summit with complex curvilinear topography. For plan view contour drawings, see the site plan in Figure 3.41.

Figure 3.21. Steps act as contours tracing this depression in an urban plaza.

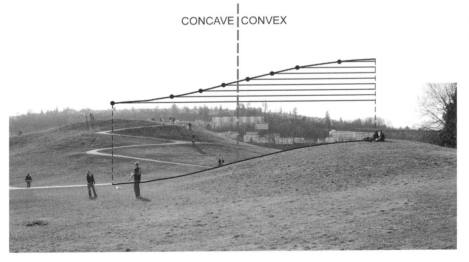

Figure 3.22. The profile of this hill in Gasworks Park contains both concave and convex slopes.

CONCAVE | CONVEX

Grade Change Devices

Breaking from the comparison of natural and human-made forms in the landscape, the following elements are specifically designed or human-made forms. The function that binds them as a group is one of the basic responsibilities of a landscape architect: accommodating changes in elevation in outdoor environments. There are many devices that can accomplish these changes, including stairs, ramps, perrons, walls, slopes, and terraces. Concern for the experiential, functional, and visual manner in which these grade transitions are executed should result in good landscape design.

Figure 3.23. Stairs as a grand public gathering space.

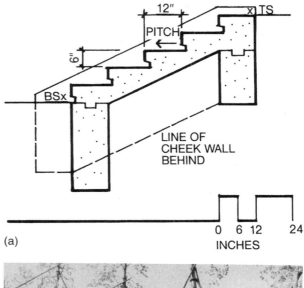

(a)

Stairs

Use of stairs is the most common technique to accommodate pedestrian circulation where an abrupt change in grade is necessary or desired. The width of a stair depends on the design intent but should be a minimum of 3 ft (900 mm). A desirable minimum width to allow two people to pass comfortably is 4 ft (1200 mm).

The proportion of riser height to tread width is critical to the ease and comfort of the user. A standard rule of thumb that has evolved for *exterior* stairs is that two risers plus one tread should equal 24 to 26 in. (600–660 mm). Common ratios in the U.S. Customary system are a 6-in. riser with a 12-in. tread and a 5-in. riser with a 15-in. tread, while a 150-mm riser with a 300-mm tread is common in the metric system. Preferably, there should be a minimum of 3 risers and a maximum of 10 to 12 risers for a set of stairs. The minimum number is suggested to make the stair more visible to prevent tripping. Where the number of risers exceeds 12, an intermediate landing is recommended to reduce the apparent scale of the stair and provide a comfortable resting point. Again, both of these guidelines must be applied with flexibility. Handrails are normally required on stairs with five

(b)

Figure 3.24. Stairs. (a) Typical stair section. (b) Stair spiraling up a steep slope. Both the stair and the path are pitched to a gutter on the uphill side, which also intercepts the runoff from the slope.

or more risers, although this must be checked against local building code requirements. Stair treads should pitch 1.0% in the downhill direction to ensure proper drainage. Low curbs, referred to as *cheek walls,* are commonly used along the edges of stairs for safety and maintenance purposes (Figure 3.24).

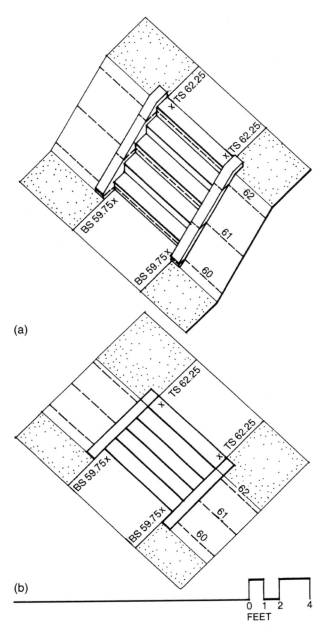

(a)

(b)

0 1 2 4
FEET

Figure 3.25. Grading at stairs. (a) Plan oblique illustrates how contour lines follow along the face of the stair risers. (b) On construction drawings the contour lines are drawn only to the edge of the stairs or cheek walls. Spot elevations are given at the top and bottom of the stairs and *not* for each step.

The configuration of contour lines where they cross stairs is illustrated in Figure 3.25. However, contour lines are drawn only to the outside edge of the cheek walls on grading plans, and the grades at the top and bottom of the stair are indicated by spot elevations. It is not necessary to indicate the spot elevation for each step, since this information is provided by dimensions on construction detail drawings.

Ramps

Ramps (Figure 3.26) are simply inclined sidewalks or driveways, usually at a uniform slope. Typical slope ratios range from 20:1 (horizontal:vertical) to 12:1 for pedestrian use and can be as great as 7:1 where handicapped access is not a constraint. Again, 4 ft (1,200 mm) is a recommended minimum width to allow people to pass. Handrails, particularly for handicapped access, are normally required on ramps of 20:1 and greater slopes. Where ramps exceed 30 ft in length, an intermediate landing is usually required. Based upon current Americans with Disabilities Act (ADA) guidelines, the maximum rise for ramps ranging in slope between 12:1 and 16:1 must not exceed 30 in. (760 mm), and an intermediate landing must be provided at least every 30 ft (9.0 m). For slopes ranging between 16:1 and 20:1, the maximum rise cannot exceed 30 in. (760 mm), and a landing must be provided every 40 ft (12.0 m). Ramps may be graded to slope perpendicular to the direction of travel or preferably cross-pitched for drainage purposes. The cross pitch must not exceed 50:1. Contours are drawn across ramps on grading plans, and spot elevations are used to indicate the grades at the top and bottom of a ramp (Figure 3.27).

Curb ramps, sometimes referred to as *drop curbs*, *curb-cut ramps*, or *sidewalk approaches*, are used to provide accessibility at street crosswalks, parking lots, and building entrances. ADA guidelines and state and local standards should be consulted for slope, width, and landing requirements.

(a)

(b)

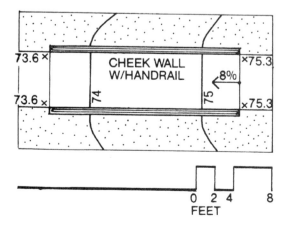

(c)

(d)

Figure 3.26. Ramps. (a) A sensitive retrofit to provide accessibility to an existing historic building. (b) Ramp integrated into sitting steps. Although this ramp was constructed prior to the establishment of ADA standards, it demonstrates the potential for highly creative solutions for accessibility. (c) A curb ramp where the curb has been partially dropped and the gutter partially raised to achieve a sloped transition. (d) In this example, the street has been ramped up to meet the elevation at the top of the curb at the crosswalk rather than installing a curb ramp. This solution may be appropriate for low-speed roads with low traffic volumes.

Figure 3.27. Grading at ramps. Spot elevations are indicated at the top and bottom of a ramp, and contour lines are drawn across the ramp. An arrow, normally pointing downhill, is shown with the slope of the ramp. It should be noted that the slope on ramps to be used by the handicapped cannot be more than 12:1 or approximately 8%.

73.6 ×   ×75.3

CHEEK WALL
W/HANDRAIL   ↗8%

73.6 ×   74   75   ×75.3

0 2 4   8
FEET

Stairs and ramps may be used in combination. The arrangement may be sets of stairs alternating with ramps, as illustrated in Figure 3.28a, or lengthened and ramped treads, as in Figure 3.28b. Many examples of the latter arrangement can be found, most of which are uncomfortable to use. Not only are the height of the risers and the distance between risers important in this situation, but so is the percentage of slope between risers, since in the uphill direction the slope shortens a person's stride and lengthens it in the downhill direction.

Accessibility and Universal Design

Grade change devices (curbs, stairs, ramps, and walls) are common elements in the landscape. The selection and use of these devices are normally related to function, aesthetics, perceptual experience, spatial enclosure, or a combination of these objectives. However, each time one of these elements is used, a potential obstacle to accessibility is created. (See Figure 3.29 in the Color Plates.)

To avoid exclusionary design, the principles of *universal design* must be integrated into the design's problem-solving process. The basic tenet of universal design is to be inclusionary by striving to provide equal choices and opportunities for people with a wide range of abilities. It is obvious that all people (including children, the elderly, and people with permanent or temporary disabilities) have different needs in terms of access and interaction with their environment.

Historically, the design of the built environment has been oriented to the able-bodied, "average" person. This approach resulted in the user's having to adapt to the environment rather than the environment adapting to the user. Issues such as accessibility, if addressed, were treated as an afterthought, often segregating or isolating the user.

Universal design should become the norm rather than the exception. Creatively integrating

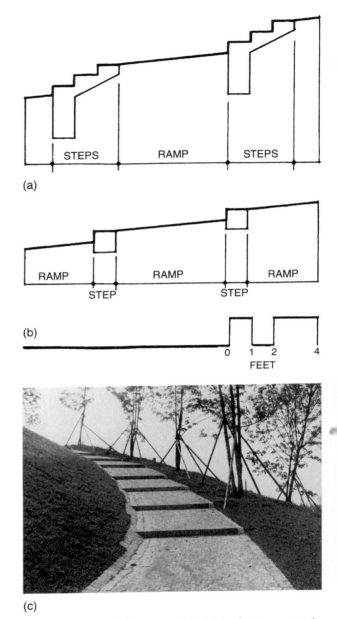

(a)

(b)

(c)

Figure 3.28. Combination ramp stairs. (a) Sets of stairs connected by a short ramp. (b) Alternating arrangement of ramp and step. (c) Photograph illustrates the condition in part b. Again, the walk has been pitched toward the uphill side.

(a)

Figure 3.29. Accessible approaches. (a) This ADA accessible ramp was created as a sculptural entrance feature to a park that all users could enjoy. (b) This ADA accessible ramp provides those using it with a unique experience of the water feature, entering the upper level over a bridge.

(b)

this concept into the design process should result in environments that meet everyone's needs in a seamless manner. In other words, the fact that the environment accommodates people with differing abilities does not have to be obvious.

Equal access in the United States to goods and services for all people is protected by Public Law 101-336: the Americans with Disabilities Act of 1990. The Americans with Disabilities Act Accessibility Guidelines (ADAAG) establish accessibility and physical design guidelines for commercial and public facilities. These guidelines should be viewed as minimums, and numerous state and federal agencies have established additional guidelines and requirements. Governing standards and regulations should be consulted prior to designing a project.

Retaining Walls

Retaining walls allow for the greatest vertical change in elevation in the shortest horizontal distance. They are also the most expensive method for accommodating grade changes, but they may be necessary where space is at a premium, such as at urban or small sites or where the use of walls is an integral part of the design concept.

Walls must be structurally designed to support the weight of the earth being retained. For a discussion of structural calculations and the sizing of retaining walls, see Munson (1974) and Sears (1988). Proper drainage of retaining walls is critical to their stability. There are two primary issues related to drainage. The first is the buildup of water pressure behind the wall, which, if not alleviated, will cause the wall to slide or overturn. To prevent the buildup of water pressure, drain holes, referred to as *weepholes,* are placed near the base of the wall, or a lateral drain pipe is installed behind the wall to collect and dispose of excess groundwater (Figure 3.30). The second issue is the saturation of the soil under the wall, which can cause overturning due to reduced bearing capacity. This is prevented

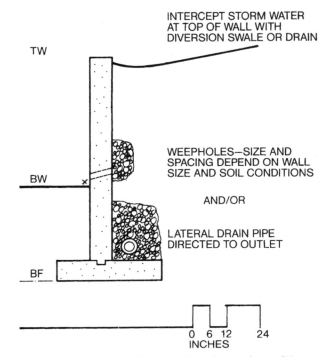

Figure 3.30. Retaining wall section. Depending on the conditions, weepholes, a lateral drain, or both may be required to prevent a buildup of water pressure behind a wall.

by intercepting storm runoff on the uphill side of the wall and can be accomplished through the use of swales or drains. Preventing runoff from flowing over the top of the wall also reduces potential staining of the face of the wall.

Figure 3.31 illustrates the drawing of contour lines where they intersect a vertical surface, such as a retaining wall. On a grading plan, the contour lines are drawn to the face of the wall but do not need to be drawn along the face, since they would not be visible. Top and bottom of wall spot elevations are typically indicated at the ends and corners of walls.

Several ways in which sloping ground and retaining walls may interface are illustrated in Figure 3.32. A slightly exaggerated pitch at the

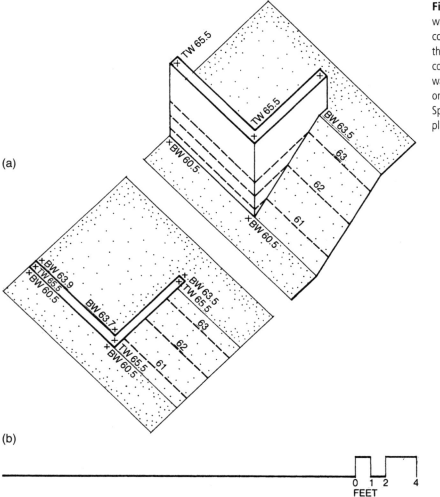

(a)

(b)

Figure 3.31. Contour lines at retaining walls. (a) Similar to curbs and stairs, the contour lines again follow along the face of the structure. (b) On construction drawings, contour lines are drawn to the edges of the wall. Since these lines are superimposed on the face of the wall, they are not seen. Spot elevations are indicated at appropriate places.

0 1 2 4
FEET

base of retaining walls to ensure positive drainage is indicated by the contour lines where they abut the wall. The condition illustrated in Figure 3.32e is unacceptable because of erosion, maintenance, and safety problems unless the wall is quite thick.

Slopes

Slopes are the least costly technique for changing grade but require more space than retaining walls.

To be visually significant, slopes should not be less than 5:1 (H:V). Generally, planted slopes should not exceed 2:1, but paved slopes may be 1:1 or greater. Mowed lawn areas should not exceed 3:1, although 4:1 is the preferred maximum. The use of slopes and the selection of a desired gradient are based on the design intent, soil conditions, susceptibility to erosion, and type of surface cover. All slopes must be stabilized by vegetative or mechanical means to reduce erosion potential.

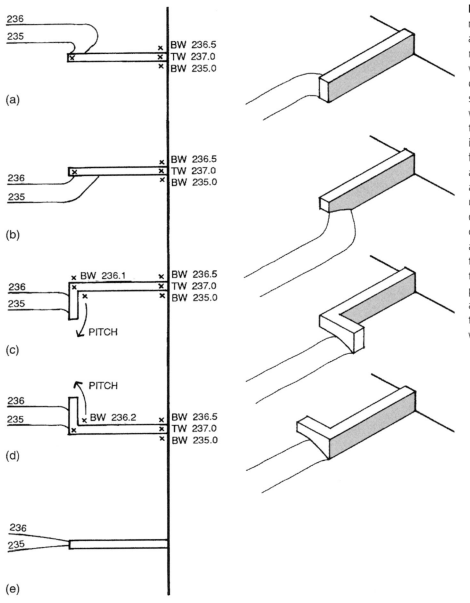

236
235

x BW 236.5
x TW 237.0
x BW 235.0

(a)

Figure 3.32. Grading options at retaining walls. (a) A slope is created along the uphill face of the wall, making the end of the wall more visually apparent. (b) A slope is created along the downhill face, somewhat reducing the scale of the wall visually. (c) The wall is shaped in the form of an L, with the L pointing in the downhill direction. A niche is formed on the downhill side, and again, the end of the wall protrudes, as in part a. (d) Again, the L form is used, but now pointing in the uphill direction. As a result, the outside corner of the L becomes more apparent. (e) Except for wide walls, this condition is unacceptable due to erosion, maintenance, and safety problems. In the options in parts c and d, the grading must be handled to prevent the trapping of storm water at the inside corner of the L.

x BW 236.5
x TW 237.0
x BW 235.0

236
235

(b)

x BW 236.1   x BW 236.5
                x TW 237.0
236   x BW 235.0
235

↙ PITCH

(c)

↖ PITCH
236
235   x BW 236.2   x BW 236.5
                       x TW 237.0
                       x BW 235.0

(d)

236
235

(e)

Terraces

Terraces provide a series of relatively flat intermediate levels to accommodate a change in grade. The reasons for terracing may be visual, functional, or structural. Terraces may be created by the use of slopes or walls or a combination of both (Figure 3.33). Where both the slope and the level portion, known as a *bench*, are relatively small in area and

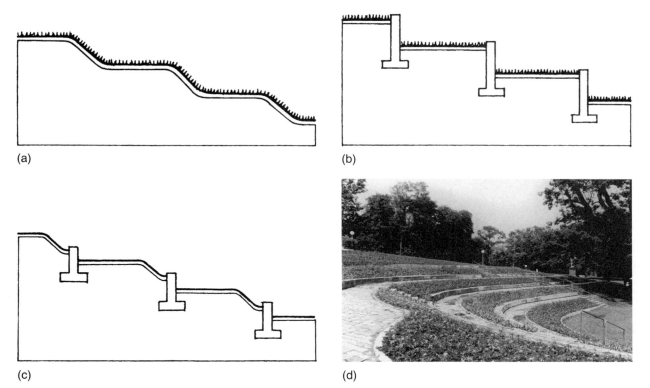

(a)

(b)

(c)

(d)

Figure 3.33. Terrace sections. (a) Terraces created by slopes. (b) Terraces created by retaining walls. (c) Terraces created by combining slopes and retaining walls. (d) An example of part c.

Figure 3.34. Drainage for slopes and terraces. (a) For relatively small terraces, the bench may be pitched in the downhill direction so that storm runoff flows across the slopes. (b) For large terraces, steep slopes, or easily erodible soils, the bench should be pitched back from the top of the slope. It is important, however, to prevent saturation of the bench by properly disposing of storm runoff.

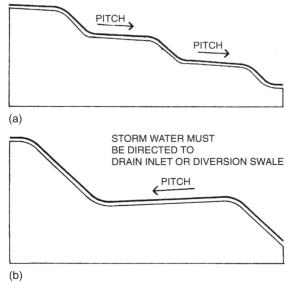

grade change, it is possible to pitch the bench in the downhill direction. However, where grade changes and area of slope are considerable, as in a highway cut or fill, the bench must be pitched back from the slope to reduce erosion (Figure 3.34). The storm runoff from the bench must be properly disposed of to prevent saturation of the toe of the uphill slope, which could cause the slope to slump.

Figure 3.35. The viewing platform suspended above the train tracks marks the terminus of the main waterfront street. In this image, note examples of the stairs, ramps, walls, and uniform slopes that comprise the design language of the site.

CASE STUDIES

Olympic Sculpture Park[1]

The Olympic Sculpture Park in Seattle, Washington, creates a sculpted urban setting for landscape-scale artwork. At the same time, it showcases a wide selection of grade change devices and contour signatures on its 9 ac (3.6 ha). This site, formerly a fuel storage and transfer site, occupies prime real estate on the downtown Seattle waterfront (Figure 3.35; see the Color Plates).

[1] Site Design / Architecture: Weiss/Manfredi Architects
Structural and Civil Engineering Consultant: Magnusson Klemencic Associates
Landscape Architecture Consultant: Charles Anderson Landscape Architecture
General Contractor: Sellen Construction
Geotechnical Engineering Consultant: Hart Crowser
Environmental Consultant: Aspect Consulting
Aquatic Engineering Consultant: Anchor Environmental

Evenly sloping faceted planes are composed to form precincts occupied by works of art and by landscapes characteristic of the Pacific Northwest—an evergreen-filled valley (Figure 3.36; see the Color Plates), steeply sloping meadows (Figure 3.37; see the Color Plates), aspen grove, and the shore. These areas are sewn together by a continuous path in the shape of a Z (Figure 3.38; see the Color Plates). This path simultaneously connects the three parcels that make up the site and, in two separate places, bridges over a well-trafficked street and an active rail line (Figure 3.39; see the Color Plates). This constant connects the city to Puget Sound while overcoming 40 ft (12 m) of elevation change from the top of the site to the shoreline (Figure 3.40; see the Color Plates).

The site required remediation from its industrial past before this vision could be enacted. Over 120,000 tons (108,862 metric tons) of contaminated soil were removed in the initial development of the site. The remaining contaminated soil was

Figure 3.36. A stone dust ramp and a terraced lawn descend into the "valley," the setting for Richard Serra's "Wake."

Figure 3.37. The "meadow" frames the arterial, ascending the uniform slopes on either side.

Figure 3.38. Alexander Calder's "Eagle" lies adjacent to the central leg of the Z as it crisscrosses the site. In the distance, the aspen grove is also perforated by the Z.

Figure 3.39. The wall in the foreground separates the aspen grove from the train tracks, while a rhythm of walls frames the meadow on the opposite side of the road in the background.

Figure 3.40. Mark DiSuvero's kinetic sculpture "Shubert Sonata" moves in the wind along the waterfront as the ramp descends to meet it.

capped by the new landform. Over 200,000 yd^3 (152,911 m^3) of clean fill were used to create the new park. Much of that fill came from excavation for an addition to the Seattle Art Museum's downtown building.

Gasworks Park[2]

The design of Gasworks Park, also in Seattle, Washington, set the precedent as a model for retrofitting abandoned industrial sites for recreational use. It also offers a great contrast in form to the Olympic Sculpture Park, which has built on its legacy. The gasworks facilities on the site were retained as an example of industrial archeology and as a giant play sculpture for children and adults. The site, dramatically located on Lake Union, commands

an excellent view of downtown Seattle. Landform was incorporated into the design of the park to take advantage of the view and waterfront location (Figure 3.41).

A knoll, called the Great Mound, was created at the water's edge to provide a vantage point for overlooking the park, Lake Union, and the city skyline. In a preliminary design scheme, a path spiraled up the knoll on the waterfront side of the landform. With this layout the view, which would be one of the primary reasons to climb to the top, would immediately be revealed to the park user; as a result, there would be little incentive for the user to climb to the top of the knoll. The path layout was refined to provide a choice. One route creates a series of switchbacks that progress up the landform on the side away from the water (Figure 3.42). With this configuration, the landform conceals the view as the pedestrian climbs up the hillside and

[2] Landscape Architect: Richard Haag

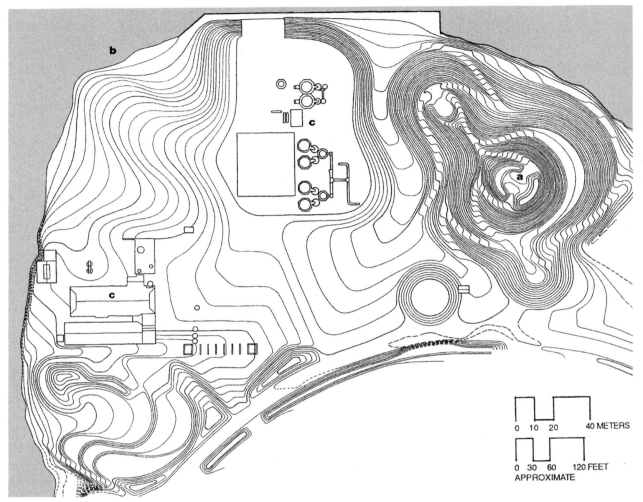

Figure 3.41. Site plan of Gasworks Park. (a) Great Mound. (b) Lake Union. (c) Industrial structures.

adds to the sense of anticipation and arrival once at the top. The second route cuts across the waterfront side of the Great Mound and leads to the shore of Lake Union and the top of the knoll (Figure 3.43). Berms placed at the top of the Great Mound create a crater-like form, define the entrances to the summit where a sundial is located, and provide a sense of enclosure (Figure 3.44).

Olympic Park[3]

Olympic Park is perhaps one of the most outstanding large-scale landform designs of the twentieth

[3] Architects: Günther Behnish & Partners
Engineer: Frei Otto
Landscape Architect: Günther Grzimek

Figure 3.42. Switchback paths traverse the landward slope of the Great Mound.

Figure 3.43. Path along the waterfront side of the Great Mound.

Figure 3.44. Summit of the Great Mound.

century. The design concept for the park is strongly defined through the use of grading and landform (Figure 3.45). The site selected for the 1972 Summer Olympics had been used as the dumping area for the rubble cleared from Munich, Germany, after the bombings of World War II. A decision was made to incorporate this material into the design rather than remove it from the site.

The design scheme for the Olympic athletic facilities and the surrounding park is an excellent example of how a complementary relationship can be achieved between building architecture and landscape architecture. There are three major components to the design: the structures for the sports facilities, a lake, and a "mountain." Conceptually, these elements are combined to create an illusion of a valley-like landscape. The walls of the valley are defined by landform (the Olympic mountain) on one side and by architecture (the tensile structures of the stadium, sports hall, and swimming pool) on the other. A lake establishes the valley floor between these major elements (Figure 3.46).

The large landform that creates the Olympic mountain is approximately 60 m (197 ft) at its highest point. It is traversed by an extensive system of walks and paths that, through changes in width, materials, steepness, and alignment, create a variety of experiences, from highly exposed to extremely intimate, for the pedestrian (Figure 3.47). Because of its size and uniqueness, particularly within the context of an urban setting, the park also provides a variety of recreational opportunities from skiing and sledding to flying model gliders (Figure 3.48). Although a grading plan was developed for the design of the mountain, it should be noted that creating a landform of this magnitude required a great deal of on-site direction and supervision during the earthmoving stage of construction to achieve the desired landscape and sculptural character.

The tent-like forms of the structures, particularly the stadium, create an illusion of mountains, which reinforce the landscape concept for the park. One side of the stadium has been

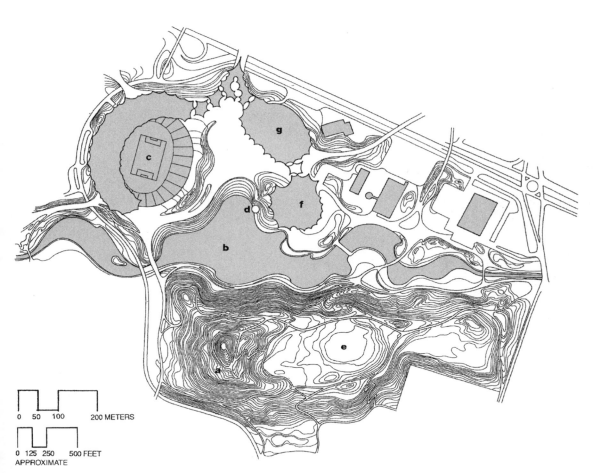

Figure 3.45. Plan of Olympic Park. (a) Olympic mountain. (b) Lake. (c) Stadium. (d) Amphitheater. (e) Plateau/upper meadow. (f) Pool. (g) Sports arena.

Figure 3.46. View of a model illustrating the valley-like form created by landform and architecture.

Figure 3.47. View of the Olympic mountain. The low height of the slope planting enhances the perceived size of the mountain landform.

65

Figure 3.48. Wind currents created by landform make Olympic Park an excellent place for flying model gliders.

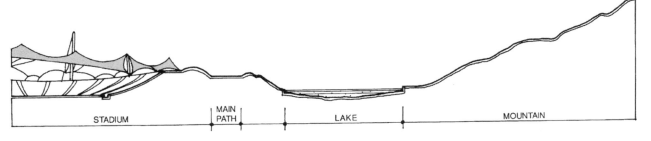

NOT TO SCALE

Figure 3.49. Section of Olympic Stadium, lake and landform.

tucked into the landform to reduce the apparent size of the structure so that it does not overpower the park landscape. From the park, the stadium appears much smaller than its capacity of 84,000, since it seems to sit in a "bowl" rather than pop out of a flat plane, which is typical of many stadiums (Figures 3.49 and 3.50). As discussed earlier, landform design and planting design should be coordinated to produce a unified design concept. Planting on the Olympic mountain is an excellent example of this complementary relationship. The perceived scale of this artificially created mountain-like landscape was an important criterion

in developing a planting scheme. The slope that defines one wall of the valley space is treated, for the most part, as a two-dimensional canvas on which plant material has been applied, since the steep slope is perceived as an edge or boundary rather than a space that can be traversed (Figure 3.47). Small-scale plant material was selected, because large-scale material (i.e., shade or canopy trees) would diminish the perceived height and overall visual impact of the landform. The grouping, scale, and texture of the plant material also create somewhat of a false perspective, thus making the slope appear larger than it is. The drama

Figure 3.50. The view across the lake illustrates the low profile of the Olympic Stadium.

Figure 3.51. The plateau provides a relatively flat area for more active play.

and sense of steepness might also have been lost if the slope had been overplanted.

A plateau, consisting of a large, open grass area, has been created as part of the mountain-like landform. The approach to the planting changes in this area, recognizing that both vegetation and landform are needed to define this landscape space. Masses of large trees are used to help define the edges and

spatial limits at one end of the plateau, while the summit of the mountain contains the space at the other end. The various types of landform (slopes, mountain, plateau), together with the different planting design treatments, add to the diversity of the park experience. The plateau also allows for a wide variety of activities and uses that could not otherwise be accommodated on the steep slopes (Figure 3.51).

Figure 3.52. People sitting on the slope are highly visible, yet removed from the mainstream of activity in the park.

Figure 3.53. Aerial view of the path system between the stadium and lakefront.

The height of the slope illustrated in Figure 3.52 demonstrates an interesting phenomenon. The people sitting on the slope are highly visible to surrounding park users. They can be seen easily while at the same time they command a panoramic view of the valley space. However, since they are also removed from the mainstream of activity, a personal level of privacy is achieved within this highly exposed, public landscape.

Landform has also been used to separate functions and activities. Large paved areas and wide walkways are needed to accommodate large crowds of people around the stadium. This extensive circulation system is separated from the lakefront and smaller-scale paths through the manipulation of landform (Figure 3.53). A berm and steep slopes completely block the view of the stadium from the walk in Figure 3.54. The terraces in Figure 3.55 create an amphitheater effect and provide an informal gathering and sitting space between the stadium and the lake. The stairs are sensitively placed into the terraced slopes with a staggered

arrangement emphasizing the curvilinear form of the terraces (Figure 3.56). Had the stairs simply cut across the terraces in a straight line, the curved geometry would have been interrupted, and the fact that there is only a small grade change across

Figure 3.54. View of the lakefront path illustrated in Figure 8.13. A steep slope separates the lakefront from the main walkway and stadium.

Figure 3.55. Grass terraces provide a transition between the lakefront and the large paved gathering space outside the stadium.

Figure 3.56. Aerial view illustrates the geometric progression created by the placement of the terrace stairs.

the terraces would have been more obvious. This condition is the opposite of the design of the stairs at Earthworks Park, which accentuates the grade change. The transition from steep slope (Figure 3.54) to grass terraces (Figure 3.55) to a formally defined amphitheater (Figure 1.29b) provides an interesting example of how a variety of grading techniques can be integrated to form a unified landscape setting.

One reason for creating the Olympic mountain was to establish a strong visual connection between park and city. Standing on top of the mountain provides a view to downtown Munich and surrounding urban neighborhoods, while the mountain is highly visible from these areas as well as from the clock tower of City Hall in the center of downtown.

(a)

(b)

(c)

(d)

Figure 1.30. Beebe Springs Creek Restoration, Chelan, Washington. (a) The channelized stream. (b) Oblique view of the project, showing the channelized stream still flowing in the upper right corner and the new channel still under construction below and to the left. (c) Heavy machinery was used to carve the new channel into the floodplain. (d) The resulting stream has a great deal of complexity and offers a much more habitable environment to salmon making the journey upstream. *(Photos: The Watershed Company)*

(a)

Figure 3.2. Two examples of lines of equal elevation in the landscape. (a) The edge of this detention pond defines a line of equal elevation. (b) The edges of these terraced rice patties also define lines of equal elevation.

(b)

◄Figure 3.13. The dots in this image show where contour lines would hit the horizon along this sloping lawn. Their even spacing denotes a uniform slope, as traced by the arrow above.

Figure 3.18. A small-scale urban ridge. Contours re delineated with black dashed lines, while white rrows show the direction of water flow.

Figure 3.19. A small-scale urban valley. Contours re delineated with black dashed lines, while white rrows show the direction of water flow.

▲ **Figure 3.20.** The Great Mound at Gasworks Park in Seattle, Washington, is a summit with complex curvilinear topography. For plan view contour drawings, see the site plan in Figure 3.41 on page 62.

▶ **Figure 3.21.** Steps act as contours tracing this depression in an urban plaza.

CONCAVE ⎪ CONVEX

▶ **Figure 3.22.** The profile of this hill in Gasworks Park contains both concave and convex slopes.

Figure 3.29. Accessible approaches. (a) This ADA accessible ramp was created as a sculptural entrance feature to a park that all users could enjoy. (b) This ADA accessible ramp provides those using it with a unique experience of the water feature, entering the upper level over a bridge.

◀Figure 3.35. The viewing platform suspended above the train tracks marks the terminus of the waterfront street. In this image, note examples of the stairs, ramps, walls, and uniform slopes that comprise the design language of the site.

▼ Figure 3.36. A stone dust ramp and a terraced lawn descend into the "valley," the setting for Richard Serra's "Wake."

▲ **Figure 3.37.** The "meadow" frames the arterial, ascending the uniform slopes on either side.

▶ **Figure 3.38.** Alexander Calder's "Eagle" lies adjacent to the central leg of the "Z" as it crisscrosses the site. In the distance, the aspen grove is also perforated by the "Z."

Figure 3.39. The wall in the foreground separates the aspen grove from the train tracks, while a rhythm of walls frames the meadow on the opposite side of the road in the background.

Figure 3.40. Mark DiSuvero's kinetic sculpture "Shubert Sonata" moves in the wind along the waterfront as the ramp descends to meet it.

Figure 9.4f. Retention basin (wet pond). (See pages 166–167 for Figures 9.4a–e.) (f) A well-designed retention basin, acting as a feature for the houses overlooking it and walking paths connecting the surrounding community to it.

▲ **Figure 9.7.** This rain garden is a simple depression with a drain at the lower left for overflow.

▶ **Figure 9.9b, c, and d.** Porous pavement. (See page 175 for Figure 9.9a.) (b) Pervious concrete pavement used as a sidewalk in a new residential community. (c) Open-gridded modular pavement infilled with sod. (d) Reinforced gravel paving.

(b)

Figure 9.11. Sculptural rainwater harvesting installation. The downspout from the building is considered part of the conveyance system. The corrugated steel is the cistern, and one of the sculptural half-pipes acts as an overflow for times when the cistern is full. The striped rod projecting from the center of the cistern is attached to a float insider that shows the amount of water in the cistern.

▲ **Figure 9.12.** Extensive green roof. Sedum plugs have been planted in an even spacing. The unplanted area is covered with a net straw blanket to keep the lightweight soil in place until the sedum grow to cover the entire roof area. *(Photo: Mathews Nielsen)*

▶ **Figure 9.13.** Intensive green roof. To allow for the greater soil depth of an intensive roof, soil is often placed in a raised planter or mounded to provide depth. This example shows both in a single composition.

(a)

Figure 9.27. The High Point NDS. (a) A grassed swale with cuts in the adjacent curb to collect street runoff. (b) A vegetated swale replacing a typical street-edge planter strip. (c) A gravel-lined swale running through the backyards of the community, with pervious concrete in the foreground. (d) Stepped infiltration basins along a more steeply sloping road in the neighborhood. (e) The detention pond is aerated by pumping water uphill to feed the constructed stream at the center of the image.

(b)

(c)

(d)

(e)

CHAPTER 4

Interpolation and Slope

TOPOGRAPHIC DATA

The previous chapter discussed contour lines from a descriptive viewpoint, that is, describing what contour lines portray. This chapter introduces the basic mathematical equations associated with plotting and manipulating contour lines.

In order to make informed design decisions as well as to execute construction drawings accurately, landscape architects require topographic data for all site development projects. This information is usually provided by a licensed land surveyor in the form of a topographic map or plan. However, there are occasions when a landscape architect may be required to gather topographic data or the data furnished by the surveyor are merely spot elevations, usually on a rectangular grid. This section discusses the latter two points.

Typically, topographic data are collected by laying out a grid pattern over the site to be surveyed.

The size of the grid selected depends on the extent of the area, the degree of topographic variation, and the purpose for which the survey will be used. Generally 20-, 25-, 50-, or 100-ft or 10-, 20-, or 30-m squares are used. For large rectangular areas, laying out the grid is a relatively simple task. Two rows of stakes may be placed along each of two sides of the rectangle, as illustrated in Figure 4.1, thus allowing the rod man to locate the remaining grid intersection points by aligning the leveling rod with two pairs of stakes. Leveling proceeds as in differential leveling, except that a number of foresights can be taken for each instrument setup. If the elevation of the area does not vary more than 10 or 12 ft (3.0 to 3.6 m), it may be possible to obtain all necessary data with one instrument setup. For referencing purposes, the grid intersections are labeled with letter and number coordinates.

For more complex sites, in configuration, topographic variety, or both, the same basic principles

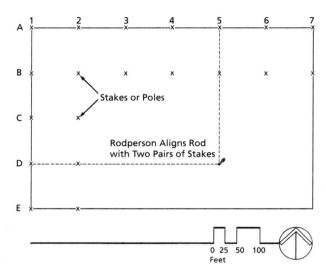

Figure 4.1. Plan of stake layout for collecting topographic data. As discussed in Chapter 9, the grid of spot elevations is particularly helpful when using the borrow pit method of determining cut-and-fill volumes. However, irregular grids or selected points may also be used to collect topographic data.

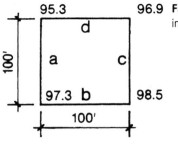

Figure 4.2. Sample grid cell in feet.

may be applied with modifications, such as additional setups, more foresights, or a grid geometry compatible with the shape of the site. Further foresights may be necessary where a high or low point exists between grid intersections, since, as discussed in the next section, the assumption is that there is a constant or uniform change in elevation from one grid corner to the next.

Once the elevations for each of the grid corners have been determined, they are plotted on a plan at a desired or specified scale. The next step in the process is to draw the contour lines (Figure 4.6), since, as discussed in Chapter 3, this allows for easier visualization and understanding of the three-dimensional form of the landscape. Before drawing the contour lines, however, it is necessary to introduce the concept of interpolation.

INTERPOLATION

Interpolation, by definition, is the process of computing intermediate values between two related known values. For the purpose of topographic surveys, interpolation is the process of locating whole number elevations (assuming that contour lines with a 1-ft or 1-m vertical interval are desired) between the elevations of the grid intersections. Interpolation may be performed by constructing a simple proportional equation

$$d/D = e/E$$

where

d = distance from one grid intersection to an intermediate point, in ft (m)

D = total distance between grid intersections, in ft (m)

e = elevation change between the same grid intersection and the intermediate point, in ft (m)

E = total elevation change between grid intersections, in ft (m)

■ EXAMPLE 4.1

The sample grid cell in Figure 4.2 and the accompanying calculations illustrate the process of interpolating between spot elevations. Locate the 96, 97, and 98 contour lines within this grid cell.

SOLUTION

The change in elevation along side a of the cell is from 97.3 to 95.3 for a total difference of 2.0 ft. Between these two points are the 97.0 and 96.0 elevations, which must be located in order to draw the whole-number contours for the cell. The difference in elevation from 97.3 to 97.0 is 0.3 ft. Together with the knowledge that the cell measures 100 ft on each side, three parts of the equation are known. Substituting into the proportional equation the unknown value, which is the distance d from the 97.3 spot elevation to the 97.0 spot elevation, can be calculated.

$$d/100 = 0.3/2.0$$

$$d \times 2.0 = 0.3 \times 100$$

$$d = \frac{0.3 \times 100}{2.0} = 15.0 \text{ ft}$$

Measuring 15.0 ft from 97.3 with the appropriate scale will locate the 97.0 elevation along side a.

The difference between 97.3 and 96.0 is 1.3 ft. Substituting into the equation the distance from the 97.3 spot elevation to the 96.0 spot elevation is 65.0 ft.

$$d/100 = 1.3/2.0$$

$$d \times 2.0 = 1.3 \times 100$$

$$d = \frac{1.3 \times 100}{2.0} = 65.0 \text{ ft}$$

Note that the distance also could have been determined from the 95.3 spot elevation. The difference in elevation from 95.3 to 96.0 is 0.7 ft, which computes to a distance of 35.0 ft, but now measured from the 95.3 intersection. As a check, the two distances calculated for the 96.0 spot elevation, when added together, must total the dimension of the side of the grid cell (65.0 + 35.0 = 100.0 ft).

The calculations for the remaining three sides are summarized below and the completed cell is shown in Figure 4.3.

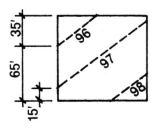

Figure 4.3. Sample grid cell with 1-ft contour lines located.

Side b:

98.5 – 97.3 = 1.2 ft (total elevation change, E)
98.5 – 98.0 = 0.5 ft (elevation change, e)

$$d/100 = 0.5/1.2$$

$$d = \frac{0.5 \times 100}{1.2} = 41.67 \text{ ft form the 98.5 intersection.}$$

Side c:

98.5 – 96.9 = 1.6 ft (E)
98.5 – 98.0 = 0.5 ft (e)
$$d/100 = 0.5/1.6$$

$$d = \frac{0.5 \times 100}{1.6} = 31.25 \text{ ft form the 98.5 intersection.}$$

98.5 – 97.0 = 1.5 ft (e)
$$d/100 = 1.5/1.6$$

$$d = \frac{1.5 \times 100}{1.6} = 93.75 \text{ ft from the 98.5 intersection.}$$

Side d:

96.9 – 95.3 = 1.6 ft (E)
96.9 – 96.0 = 0.9 ft (e)
$$d/100 = 0.9/1.6$$

$$d = \frac{0.9 \times 100}{1.6} = 56.25 \text{ ft from the 96.9 intersection.}$$

Rather than calculating each elevation, interpolation may be done graphically, as illustrated in Figure 4.4. Along side b of the grid cell there is a difference in elevation of 1.2 ft. By dividing the side into 12 equal spaces (each space representing 0.1 ft

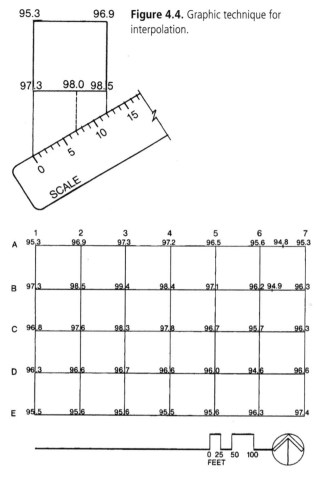

Figure 4.4. Graphic technique for interpolation.

Figure 4.5. Grid of spot elevations.

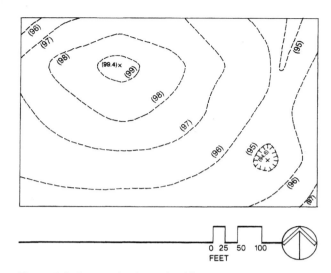

Figure 4.6. Contour plan interpolated from Figure 4.5.

for graphic proportioning and may be applied to the other three sides of the grid cell.

Figure 4.5 represents the completed grid for the layout illustrated in Figure 4.1. The process of interpolation may be applied to each of the grid cells to locate all the whole number spot elevations. (The sample grid cell is taken from the northwest corner of the grid.) Connecting the points of equal elevation may be left until the locations of all the whole number elevations have been determined for the entire grid, since contours are usually smooth curves rather than a series of straight line segments. The completed contour plan is shown in Figure 4.6. Construction lines, including the grid, commonly are not shown on the completed plan. The closed 95-ft contour in Figure 4.6 is a depression, which is depicted by the use of hachures, as illustrated.■

■ EXAMPLE 4.2

This example demonstrates that the interpolation process is the same whether the measurement units are in feet or meters. The spot elevations are in meters for the sample grid cell in Figure 4.7, and the cell measures 30.0 m on each side. Locate

of elevation change), counting either 7 spaces from the 97.3 spot elevation or 5 spaces from 98.5, the 98.0 spot elevation is located. The side of any grid cell may be divided into the desired number of *equal* spaces by placing a scale *at any angle* with the appropriate number of divisions (usually the same as the desired number of equal spaces) between perpendicular lines extended from the two end points of the side of the grid cell. From the appropriate point on the scale a line perpendicular to the side of the grid cell is extended back to the cell, thus locating the desired spot elevation. This is a common technique

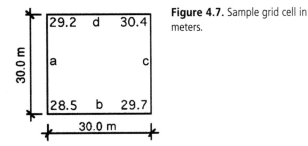

Figure 4.7. Sample grid cell in meters.

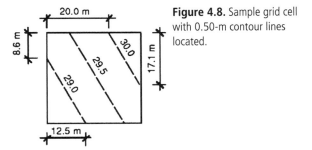

Figure 4.8. Sample grid cell with 0.50-m contour lines located.

the 29.0- and 30.0-m contour lines; then find the 29.5-m contour.

SOLUTION

As with Example 4.1, proceed around each side of the cell to locate the whole number spot elevations:

Side a (29.0 contour line):

$$d/D = e/E$$
$$d/30 = 0.2/0.7$$

$$d = \frac{0.2 \times 30}{0.7} = 8.578.6 \text{ m from the 29.2 spot elevation.}$$

Side b (29.0 contour line):

$$d/30 = 0.5/1.2$$

$$d = \frac{0.5 \times 30}{1.2} = 12.5 \text{ m from the 28.5 spot elevation}$$

Side c (30.0 contour line):

$$d/30 = 0.4/0.7$$

$$d = \frac{0.4 \times 30}{0.7} = 17.14 \approx 17.1 \text{ m from the}$$
$$\text{30.4 spot elevation}$$

Side d (30.0 contour line):

$$d/30 = 0.8/1.2$$

$$d = \frac{0.8 \times 30}{1.2} = 20.0 \text{ m from the 29.2 spot elevation}$$

The 29.5-m contour is located equidistant between the 29.0 and 30.0 contour lines. The completed grid cell is illustrated in Figure 4.8.

With practice, contour lines can be drawn quite rapidly on a grid, with much of the interpolation done mentally and visually. It should be noted here that computers in conjunction with digitizers and plotters may be used to generate contour plans, thus eliminating the need for tedious calculations or drafting time. ■

Interpolation Between Contour Lines

Interpolation may also be used to determine the elevation of points between contour lines. The information needed to compute these points includes the contour interval, the total distance between the contour lines, and the distance from one contour line to the point in question. With this information, the difference in elevation from the contour line to the point can be calculated by the following equation:

$$\frac{\text{distance from point to contour line}}{\text{total distance between contour lines}} \times \frac{\text{contour}}{\text{interval}} = \frac{\text{elevation}}{\text{difference}}$$

■ EXAMPLE 4.3

Determine the spot elevation for point A in Figure 4.9. The contour interval is 1 ft, and the distances are as indicated on the drawing.

SOLUTION

The difference in elevation between point A and the 67-ft contour line is calculated by substituting into the equation

$$4.0 \text{ ft}/10.0 \text{ ft} \times 1.0 \text{ ft} = 0.4 \text{ ft}$$

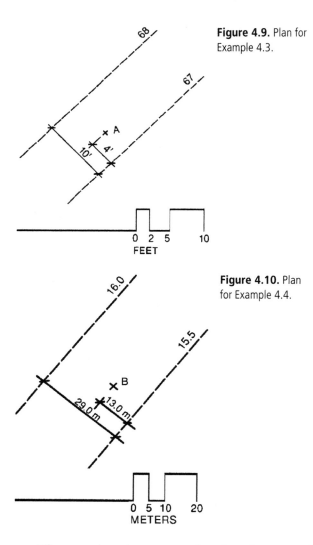

Figure 4.9. Plan for Example 4.3.

Figure 4.10. Plan for Example 4.4.

The spot elevation at point *A* is then determined by adding the elevation difference to the elevation of the contour line used as the point of reference:

$$67.0 + 0.4 = 67.4 \text{ ft (elevation point } A)$$ ■

■ EXAMPLE 4.4

Determine the spot elevation for point *B* in Figure 4.10. The contour interval is 0.5 m, and the distances are as indicated on the drawing.

SOLUTION

Using the same procedure as Example 4.3, the difference in elevation is calculated as follows:

$$13.0\,\text{m}/29.0\,\text{m} \times (16.0 - 15.5) = 13/29 \times 0.5$$
$$= 0.2241 \approx 0.2\,\text{m}$$

By adding the difference in elevation to the 15.5-m contour line, the spot elevation at point *B* is determined.

$$15.5 + 0.2 = 15.7 \text{ m (elevation point } B)$$

Finally, it must be emphasized that the interpolation process is valid only if there is a constant slope between two points, whether those points are contours or spot elevations. ■

CALCULATING SLOPE

Most often, changes in grade are described or discussed in terms of percentage of slope. Describing slope in this manner provides a common basis of understanding for the professionals associated with manipulating and changing the earth's surface, including landscape architects, engineers, and architects. Slope, expressed as a percentage, is the number of units (feet or meters) of rise or fall in 100 units (feet or meters) of horizontal distance. Note that the dimensional units must be consistent. In addition to being expressed as a percentage, slope may be described by decimal number. For example, a 12% slope may also be called a 0.12 slope but *not* a 0.12% slope. The terms *grade* and *gradient* are commonly used synonymously with *slope*.

A generalized definition of slope, then, is the vertical change in elevation (fall or rise in feet or meters) in a horizontal distance or $S = DE/L,$ where S is the slope and DE is the difference in elevation between the end points of a line of which the horizontal or map distance is L (Figure 4.11). To express S as a percentage, multiply the value by 100.

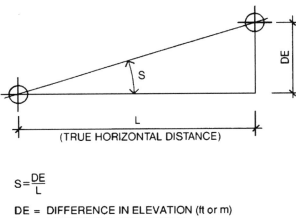

$$S = \frac{DE}{L}$$

DE = DIFFERENCE IN ELEVATION (ft or m)
L = HORIZONTAL DISTANCE (ft or m)
S = GRADIENT, EXPRESSED AS PERCENTAGE

Figure 4.11. Diagram of the slope formula.

One problem that commonly arises is that L is measured horizontally rather than along the slope. To reinforce this point, it should be remembered from surveying that all map distances are measured horizontally, not parallel to the surface of sloping ground. With the slope formula, three basic computations may be accomplished:

1. Knowing the elevations at two points and the distance between the points, slope S can be calculated.

2. Knowing the difference in elevation between two points and the percentage of slope, the horizontal distance L can be calculated.

3. Knowing the percentage of slope and the horizontal distance, the difference in elevation DE can be calculated.

The following sample problems illustrate the three basic applications of the slope formula.

▋ EXAMPLE 4.5

Two spot elevations are located 120 ft apart (measured horizontally). One spot elevation is 44.37 ft,

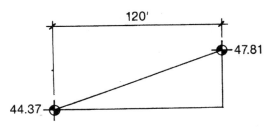

Figure 4.12. Section for Example 4.5.

while the other is 47.81 ft (Figure 4.12). Calculate the percentage of slope S.

SOLUTION
First, determine the difference in elevation DE between the spot elevations.

$$DE = 47.81 - 44.37 = 3.44 \text{ ft}$$

Then substitute the known values into the slope formula:

$$S = DE/L \qquad \qquad (4.1)$$

$$S = \frac{3.44}{120} = 0.0287 \text{ ft/ft} = 2.87\% \; ▋$$

▋ EXAMPLE 4.6

Determine the location of the whole number spot elevations (i.e., 45.0, 46.0, 47.0) in the previous problem.

SOLUTION
Since the horizontal distance L is the unknown, the slope formula may be rearranged as follows:

$$L = DE/S \qquad \qquad (4.2)$$

With S previously determined in Example 4.5, the next step is to calculate the difference in elevation between the known and desired spot elevations and substitute the values into the preceding equation (Figure 4.13).

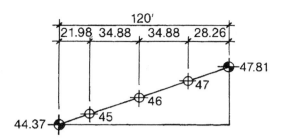

Figure 4.13. Section for Example 4.6.

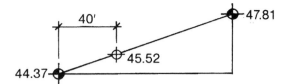

Figure 4.14. Section for Example 4.7.

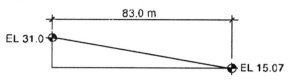

Figure 4.15. Section for Example 4.8.

$$DE = 47.81 - 47.00 = 0.81 \text{ ft}$$

$$L = \frac{0.81}{0.0287} = 28.26 \text{ ft}$$

$$DE = 47.00 - 46.00 = 1.00 \text{ ft}$$

$$= 46.00 - 45.00 = 1.00 \text{ ft}$$

$$L = \frac{1.00}{0.0287} = 34.88 \text{ ft}$$

$$DE = 45.00 - 44.37 = 0.63 \text{ ft}$$

$$L = \frac{0.63}{0.0287} = 21.98 \text{ ft}$$

As a check, the sum of the partial distances should equal 120 ft. (Note that in computing these distances, the value used for S was not rounded.)

$$28.26 + 34.88 + 34.88 + 21.98 = 120.00 \text{ ft} \blacksquare$$

■ EXAMPLE 4.7

Determine the spot elevation of a point 40 ft uphill from elevation 44.37. Use the slope calculated in Example 4.5.

SOLUTION

Since the difference in elevation DE is the unknown, the equation may be rearranged as follows:

$$DE = S \times L \qquad (4.3)$$

Therefore,

$$DE = 0.0287 \times 40 \text{ ft} = 1.15 \text{ ft}$$

The difference in elevation is then added to 44.37 to determine the desired spot elevation (Figure 4.14).

$$44.37 + 1.15 = 45.52 \text{ ft} \blacksquare$$

■ EXAMPLE 4.8

Two spot elevations are located 83.0 m apart (measured horizontally). The elevations, in meters, are as noted in Figure 4.15. Calculate the percentage of slope between the two points.

SOLUTION

Since S is the unknown, Equation 4.2 is the appropriate formula:

$$S = DE/L = (31.0 - 15.07)/83.0 = 15.93/83.0$$
$$= 0.1919$$

$$S \approx -19.2\%$$

Note that the direction of slope can be indicated as positive or negative for uphill or downhill, respectively. ■

SLOPES EXPRESSED AS RATIOS AND DEGREES

Often slopes are expressed as ratios such as 4:1. This means that for every 4 units (feet or meters) of

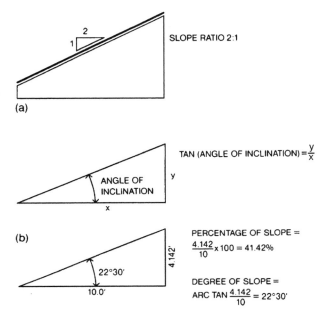

Figure 4.16. Alternative methods of expressing slope. (a) As a ratio. (b) In degrees.

horizontal distance there is a 1 unit (foot or meter) vertical change either up or down. On construction drawings, particularly sections, ratios may be shown graphically using a triangle, as illustrated in Figure 4.16a. In expressing ratios, the horizontal number should always be placed first. Conversely, ratios may be expressed by their percentage equivalents. A 4:1 ratio is equivalent to a 25% slope (e.g., a 25-ft vertical change in 100 ft).

Civil engineers and surveyors may express slope in degrees rather than percentage, although this terminology is rarely used by landscape architects. However, the conversion from one system to the other is quite simple, since the slope formula is a basic trigonometric function. The percentage of slope is actually the tangent of the angle of inclination, as illustrated in Figure 4.16b. It should be noted that the rate of change between percentage and degrees is not arithmetically constant. For example, a 100% slope equals 45°, whereas a 50% slope equals 26°34′. It is important to note that

percentage of slope, slope ratios, and slope angles are dimensionless and are not affected by U.S. Customary or metric units as long as consistent dimensional values are used.

SLOPE ANALYSIS

To determine the best areas for placing buildings, roads, parking lots, and other uses on a particular site, landscape architects often conduct an analysis of the steepness of the terrain. This process, commonly referred to as *slope analysis,* provides information that can be used in conjunction with other considerations such as economics, vegetation, drainage, soils, etc., in making site planning decisions.

In order to conduct a slope analysis on a map, the following information is required: horizontal scale, contour interval, and percentage of slope categories.

The scale and contour interval are established by the contour map used for the analysis. The slope categories are selected by the evaluator based on the amount of change in elevation, the complexity of the landforms, and the types of activities to be accommodated. An example of slope categories can be found in the soil classification system of the U.S. Department of Agriculture (USDA) Natural Resources Conservation Service (NRCS, formerly the Soil Conservation Service) for land use.

▓ EXAMPLE 4.9

The task for this problem is to analyze the slopes illustrated by the contour plan in Figure 4.17. The scale is noted on the figure, and the contour interval is 2 ft. The slope categories are divided into three groups: less than or equal to 5%, greater than 5% but less than 15%, and equal to or greater than 15%. To perform the analysis, the allowable horizontal distance between contours for each slope category must be determined.

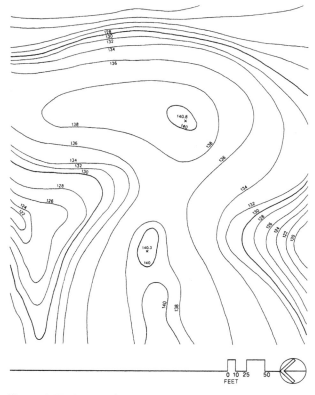

Figure 4.17. Contour plan.

SOLUTION

For the first category the range is from 0 to 5%. The unknown variable in the slope formula is the distance L, whereas the known variables are the difference in elevation (the contour interval, or 2 ft) and the slope, in this case the range from 0 to 5%. Substituting into the slope formula $L=DE/S$, at 0% the contours must be infinitely far apart, while at 5% the distance between contours equals 40 ft.

$$L = 2.0/0.05 = 40 \text{ ft}$$

Therefore, any adjacent contours closer than 40 ft represent a slope greater than 5%.

For the next category, greater than 5% and less than 15%, the maximum distance between adjacent contours is the 40 ft already determined by the first category. The minimum distance, or the steepest slope, is determined by substituting the upper limits of the category (15%) into the formula.

$$L = 2.0/0.15 = 13.3 \text{ ft (or 13 ft)}$$

Thus, slopes ranging from greater than 5% to less than 15% are represented by contours that range from 13 to 40 ft apart. (Due to the small map scale, the 13.3 ft may be rounded to 13 ft.)

The third category, slopes equal to or greater than 15%, is represented by adjacent contours that are less than 13 ft apart.

A simple technique to determine the percentage of slope between contours is to construct a wedge-shaped piece of paper indicating the critical dimensions between slope categories drawn to the proper map scale.

The wedge in Figure 4.18 is a graphic interpretation of the information illustrated by the scales to the right. By moving the wedge over the contour map, it is easy to determine the distance between adjacent contours and the corresponding slope category. For ease of visualization and evaluation, the slope analysis is usually presented graphically on the topographic map, as in Figure 4.19. ■

Computers and Terrain Analysis

Computers can be useful tools in the analysis of topography. Digital elevation data, consisting of elevation values at the intersections of a regular grid or other specified sampling interval, can be used to create contour maps, elevation maps, and three-dimensional views. Digital elevation model (DEM) data, based upon different geographic reference systems, sampling spacing, and levels of accuracy, are available from the U.S. Geological Survey. The data can be manipulated to perform tasks like analyzing slope and aspect (slope orientation), creating cross sections, and calculating cut and fill volumes.

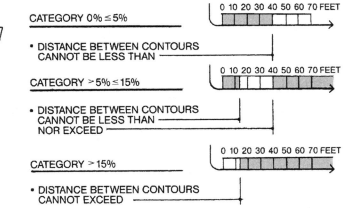

Figure 4.18. Wedge and graphic scales for conducting slope analysis.

CATEGORY 0% ≤ 5%

0 10 20 30 40 50 60 70 FEET

• DISTANCE BETWEEN CONTOURS CANNOT BE LESS THAN

CATEGORY > 5% ≤ 15%

0 10 20 30 40 50 60 70 FEET

• DISTANCE BETWEEN CONTOURS CANNOT BE LESS THAN NOR EXCEED

CATEGORY > 15%

0 10 20 30 40 50 60 70 FEET

• DISTANCE BETWEEN CONTOURS CANNOT EXCEED

40'

13'

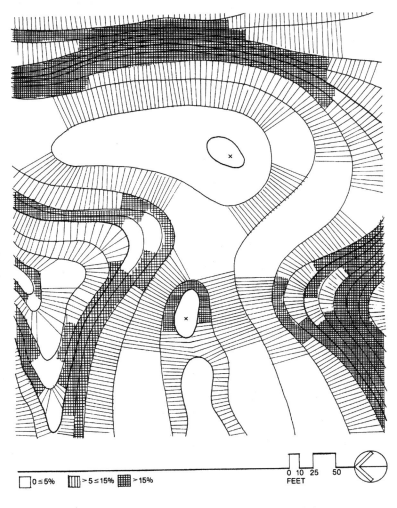

Figure 4.19. Graphic presentation of slope analysis.

0 ≤ 5%   > 5 ≤ 15%   > 15%

0 10 25   50
FEET

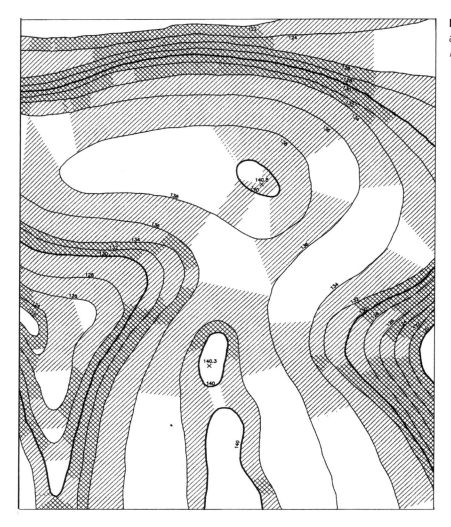

Figure 4.20. Computer-generated slope analysis. *(Software: Softdesk Civil/Survey Pack Version 7.20)*

☐ 0≤5%　▨ >5≤15%　▨ >15%

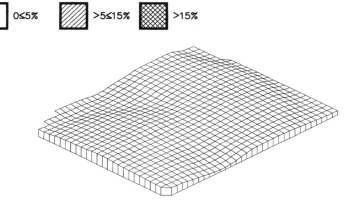

Figure 4.21. DTM of the contour plan in Figure 4.17. *(Software: Softdesk Civil/ Survey Pack Version 7.20)*

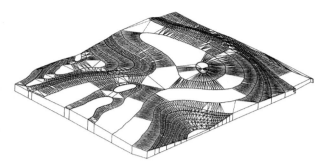

Figure 4.22. DTM with slope analysis. *(Software: Softdesk Civil/ Survey Pack Version 7.20)*

Digital terrain models (DTMs) provide a three-dimensional representation of the ground surface and facilitate the visualization and interpretation of landform. Digital terrain programs also allow for changing the direction, as well as the angle, of view so that a more complete understanding of the landform can be achieved.

The slope analysis depicted in Figure 4.20 is the same as Figure 4.19. However, the analysis drawing has been computer generated. Figure 4.21 is a DTM of the topographic map illustrated in Figure 4.17. In Figure 4.22 the slope analysis has been combined with the DTM.

CHAPTER 5

Grading of Simple Design Elements

The purpose of this chapter is to demonstrate, by example, the various uses of the slope formula while grounding that information in a graphic understanding of how slope information is conveyed. Several problems are presented, which, in addition to illustrating the mechanics of manipulating the formula, introduce concepts that are basic to the grading process.

GRADING OF LINEAR ELEMENTS

One of the most basic components encountered by designers in grading problems are linear elements such as pathways, roads, sidewalks, and so on. These elements represent a microcosm of most grading problems found in landscape architecture. These include ridges (crowns), valleys (swales), slopes in two directions (cross slopes), and vertical planes (curbs). Developing the ability to grade

these elements and to visualize this process in three dimensions will measurably improve one's understanding of manipulating contours.

Contour Signatures of Linear Elements

Before introducing the design of these elements, it is worthwhile to look at contour signatures and understand the experience of these elements. Figure 5.1 shows six models of landforms along a linear path and their accompanying contour signatures, which should be familiar from Chapter 1.

The first three models show pathways set in a valley, with the adjacent conditions changing. Being in a valley, the paths all provide a sense of enclosure, but the feeling of that enclosure changes. In Figure 5.1a, the concave slope provides a more open sense of enclosure than the convex slope in Figure 5.1b, which would feel more constricted. Figure 5.1c makes drainage apparent in the swales

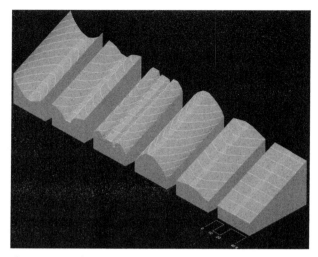

Figure 5.1. Path experience models. Note that all paths are on a 10% longitudinal slope,[1] that the path is cross-sloped at 2%, and that the models are all vertically exaggerated 5x. (a) Path along a valley with concave slopes leading away. (b) Path along a valley with convex slopes leading away. (c) Path with swales on both sides and berms beyond. (d) Path along a ridge with convex slopes leading away. (e) Path along a ridge with uniform slopes leading away. (f) Path down a uniform slope.

adjacent to the path, and the low height of the berms implies a separation from the landscape beyond, with less enclosure than either of the first two models.

The next three models show pathways on a successive range of conditions from a dramatic ridge to a path along a uniform plane. The convex slopes in Figure 5.1d make the path feel more dramatically elevated from the surroundings because the contours steepen more quickly farther away from the path. By contrast, the contours of Figure 5.1e provide a simplified elevation along a ridge with the

---

[1] Though 10% slopes are on the extreme end of slopes used for pathways, especially given ADA constraints, they were used in this model because they show the contour signature in model form more readily than lower slopes.

contours sloping away uniformly. Figure 5.1f shows the path as if it was within a uniformly sloping open field. This path provides neither prominence above the surroundings nor enclosure within, but it does make the user feel part of an expansive landform.

Now that the experience of linear spaces and their associated contour signatures have been explored, learning how to cross-slope a pathway is the next step in understanding the process of grading a linear element.

Path Cross-Slope Grading

Providing cross slopes, slopes across a structure, on pathways, drives, roads, and other flat linear surfaces, is done to allow for positive drainage and to prevent ponding within the paved area. This is also undertaken in the design of roads and paths to shed water to gutters or into the grass to keep the higher central surface from becoming inundated with water. The slope perpendicular to traffic is typically graded at 2%. Remember that as the longitudinal slope changes, the look of the cross slope changes as well. In Figure 5.2, note that because the cross slope and the longitudinal slope are equal, the contour line crosses the path at a 45 degree angle and as the longitudinal slope increases, that angle lessens.

■ Example 5.1

In Figure 5.3, the objective is to grade the 10-ft-wide linear pathway so that it slopes evenly between the two given elevations and has a 2% cross slope toward the bottom of the image.

SOLUTION

The first step is to find out what the longitudinal slope created by the given elevations is using Equation 4.1 ($S = DE/L$).

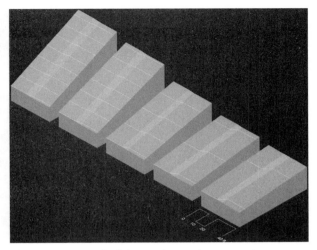

Figure 5.2. Longitudinal slope and cross-slope comparison models. Note that the model has been vertically exaggerated 5× and the path is cross-sloped at 2% in each model; only the longitudinal slope changes. (a) A 10% longitudinal slope. (b) A 8.33% longitudinal slope. (c) A 5% longitudinal slope. (d) A 3% longitudinal slope. (e) A 2% longitudinal slope.

This is done by first determining the difference in elevation, *DE*, between the spot elevations:

$$DE = 118.00 - 113.00 = 5.00 \text{ ft}$$

L is then measured from the drawing to be 166.67 ft. These known values can now be substituted into Formula 4.1:

$$S = DE/L$$

$$S = 5/166.67 = 0.0300 \text{ ft/ft} = 3.00\%$$

Using this longitudinal slope information, locations where the other contour lines contact the path can be found using Formula 4.2. Because the intent is to find evenly spaced contours 1 ft apart in elevation, the *DE* will be 1 ft. *S* was the result of the first step, 3.00%. Those values are plugged into the following formula:

$$L = DE/S = 1/0.03 = 33.33 \text{ ft}$$

L can now be used to locate where the other contour lines will intersect the path (Figure 5.4a).

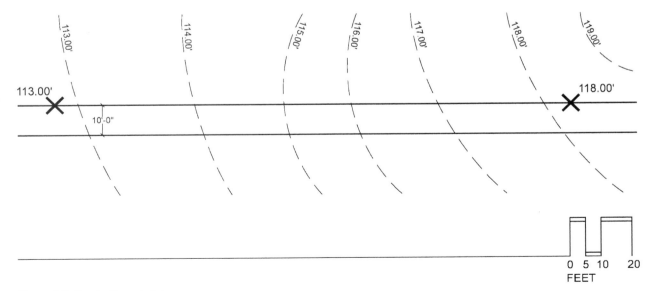

Figure 5.3. Plan for Example 5.1.

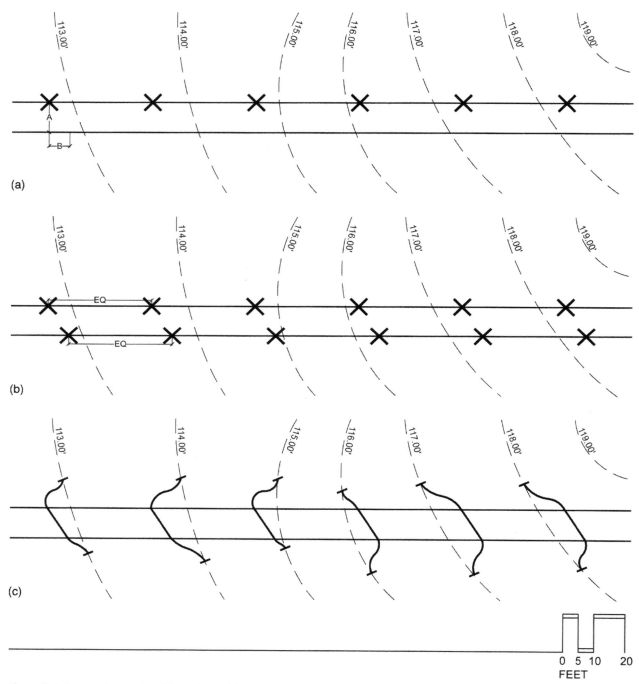

Figure 5.4. Steps to the solution of Example 5.1. (a) Locating points of even contours along the path after determining the longitudinal slope. (b) Locating points along the bottom side of the path after determining the cross slope. EQ indicates that the dimensions are equivalent. (c) The solution connecting the existing contours to the proposed elevations along the path.

These first steps have established the longitudinal slope and the locations where other contours contact the path. The next steps deal specifically with finding the cross slope from these points.

Given that the path is 10 ft wide and the cross slope is to be 2%, these values can be plugged into Formula 4.3 to find out what the difference in elevation is across the pathway ("A" in Figure 5.4a).

$$DE = S \times L = 0.02 \times 10 = 0.2 \text{ ft}$$

With the cross slope being directed toward the bottom of the page, the pathway is 0.2 ft lower in that direction. The next step is to find where the 113.00 contour will hit the lower side of the path. This can be accomplished using the change in elevation just calculated and the original longitudinal slope, because the change in elevation is being measured along the length of the pathway ("B" in Figure 5.4a). Because DE and S are given, Formula 4.2 will be used to find L.

$$L = DE/S = 0.2/0.03 = 6.67'$$

"B" in Figure 5.3a will be measured as 6.67′ (Figure 5.4b). Notice that this measurement is being taken to the right of the page because the cross slope sloped down across "A" in Figure 5.3a, so to locate the 113.00 contour, the measurement needs to be taken in the direction of the higher elevation contours.

Note that the previous two steps could be combined into one step using the following formula:

L = [path width (L) × cross slope (S)]/longitudinal slope (S) **(5.1)**

With the slope dropping evenly, the elevation points for the other contours can be laid out using the 33.33 ft spacing calculated earlier for the other side of the path (Figure 5.4b). Now the contour lines can be drawn in and tied back into the existing contours using smooth transitions (Figure 5.4c). ▪

Path Layout with a Maximum Gradient

Approaching the challenge of grading a linear feature from a different angle, often the design of roads, walks, and paths may not exceed a specified gradient or slope. Slope criteria may be established by building and zoning codes, highway departments, accessibility for the handicapped, or commonsense constraints such as climatic conditions and the age of anticipated users. The following example illustrates, within a natural landscape, how a path may be designed not to exceed a specified gradient while at the same time minimizing the amount of grading required.

▪ EXAMPLE 5.2

In Figure 5.5 the objective is to construct a path from the road pull-off to the lake dock at a desired maximum slope of 4%. Both the horizontal scale of the plan and the contour interval must be known in order to solve the problem. In this example the scale is shown on the figure, and the contour interval is 1 ft. The path begins at point A along the 238-ft contour line.

SOLUTION

First, the known values must be substituted into the equation $L = DE/S$ to determine the length of the path between adjacent contours in order to satisfy the 4% criterion.

$$L = 1.0/0.04 = 25 \text{ ft}$$

By drawing an arc with a radius of 25 ft at the proper scale with point A as its center, two intersection points are obtained along the 237-ft contour line. A line drawn from point A to either of these two points will have a gradient of 4%. Any line drawn within the shaded triangle formed by the two path alternatives will be shorter than 25 ft and therefore steeper than 4%. Conversely, lines

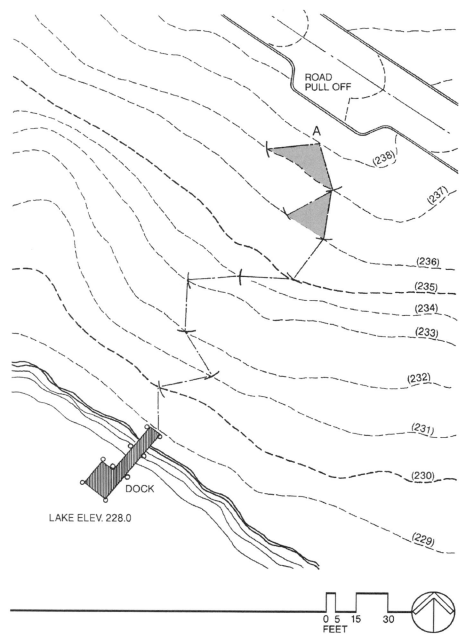

Figure 5.5. Plan for Example 5.2.

drawn beyond the boundaries of the triangle will be less than 4%. Selecting one of the previously established points on the 237-ft contour line as the center point, another arc is drawn with a radius of 25 ft. This arc intersects the 236-ft contour line at two points. Deciding which path direction to select is based on a number of considerations, such as overall design intent, views, location of trees, soil stability, and so on. Progressing downhill on a contour-by-contour basis, the entire alignment for the path sloping at 4% may be established.

An alternative to the process described above is to take the difference in elevation between point A and the lake dock. By dividing by the desired percentage of slope, the total length of the path is determined. Assuming constant gradients, a path of shorter length will exceed 4%, while a longer path will be less than 4%.

$$238 - 229 = 9 \text{ ft}$$

$$9/0.04 = 225 \text{ ft}$$

Thus, any combination of curves and straight lines with a total length of 225 ft and a constant gradient will meet the desired 4% criterion. However, this method does not necessarily relate as well to the natural topography of the land as the first method does. ■

Road Grading Definitions

Grading a road and its attending structures adds another level of complexity to the understanding of grading linear elements. However, before discussing how to grade a road, it is necessary to define the terminology associated with road construction.

Crown

Crown is the difference in elevation between the edge and the centerline of a roadway. The primary purpose is to increase the speed of storm runoff

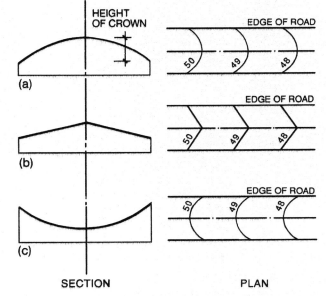

Figure 5.6. Road crowns. (a) Parabolic section. (b) Tangential section. (c) Reverse crown.

from the road surface. A secondary purpose is to visually separate opposing lanes of traffic. Crown height may be expressed in inches or inches per foot. In the latter case, the total crown height is calculated by multiplying half of the road width by the rate of change. For example, the crown height for a 24-ft-wide road with a crown of ¼ in./ft is 3 in. (12 ft × ¼ in./ft = 3 in.) There are three basic types of road crown sections (Figure 5.6).

Parabolic Section. A parabolic crown is commonly used in asphalt construction. The change in slope direction at the roadway centerline is achieved by a rounded transition. Contour lines point in the downhill direction (similar to a ridge contour signature).

Tangential Section. A tangential crown is most often found with concrete surfaces, since it is easier to form. The centerline of the roadway is visually emphasized due to the intersection of the sloping

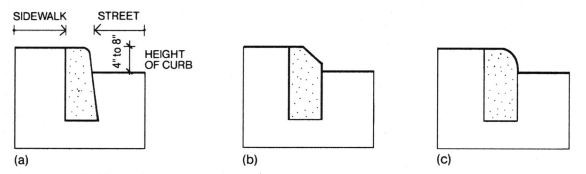

Figure 5.7. Curbs. (a) Batter-faced section used for typical street curb. (b) Beveled section. (c) Rounded section. Both b and c are referred to as *mountable curbs.*

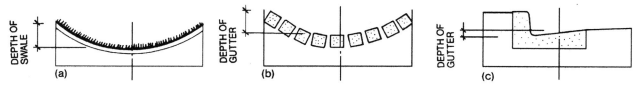

Figure 5.8. Swales and gutters. (a) Vegetated parabolic swale. (b) Paved gutter. (c) Combination curb and gutter.

planes along this line. Again, the contour lines point in the downhill direction, but are **V**-shaped rather than rounded in appearance.

Reverse Crown. A reverse crown may be either parabolic or tangential in section. It is typically used where it is not desirable to direct storm runoff to the edge of the road or in restricted conditions such as urban alleys. Its contour signature is similar to that of a valley.

It should be noted that not all roads have crowns. Some roads are cross-sloped: in other words, storm runoff is directed from one side of the road to the other. This type of road section is also used to bank road curves to counteract overturning forces (see Chapter 15).

Curb

A curb is a vertical separation at the edge of the roadway. It is usually 6 in. (150 mm) high but may range from as low as 2 in. (50 mm) to as high as

8 in. (200 mm). Curbs are used to direct and restrict storm runoff and to provide safety for pedestrians along the road edge. In addition to vertically faced curbs, beveled or rounded cross sections may be used (Figure 5.7).

Swale

A swale is a constructed or natural drainage channel that has a vegetated surface (usually grass). A *gutter* is a paved swale. The depth of swales (but not necessarily of gutters) is usually measured as the difference in elevation between the centerline and a point at the edge of the swale on a line taken perpendicular to the centerline (Figure 5.8). Since swales are depressions similar in form to valleys, the contour signatures are also similar. Swales are commonly used to intercept, direct, and control storm runoff, which will be discussed in Chapter 13.

However, it is important to understand how swales are represented by contour lines. Figure 5.9

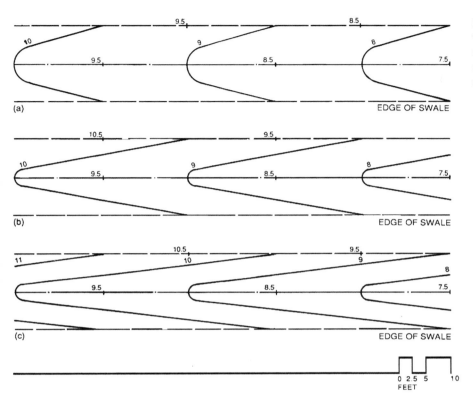

(a)

EDGE OF SWALE

(b)

EDGE OF SWALE

(c)

EDGE OF SWALE

0 2.5 5   10
FEET

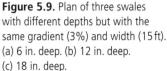

Figure 5.9. Plan of three swales with different depths but with the same gradient (3%) and width (15 ft). (a) 6 in. deep. (b) 12 in. deep. (c) 18 in. deep.

illustrates three swales of different depths but with the same width and longitudinal gradient. Often the high point of a swale is the dividing point for two swales sloping in opposite directions. This point is referred to as a *saddle,* since it is simultaneously a high point (parallel to the direction of the swales) and a low point (perpendicular to the direction of the swales). This phenomenon is illustrated in Figure 5.10.

EXAMPLE 5.3

Figure 5.11 illustrates, in plan and section, a variety of conditions found in conjunction with roads and streets, including crown, curb, sidewalk, and swale. From the established spot elevation of 25.42

ft at point A, the location of the 25-ft contour line is to be determined based on the following criteria: a 6-in. crown height, a 6-in. curb height, a 4-in. swale depth, a 3% slope parallel to the direction of the street, and a 2% slope across the sidewalk perpendicular to and downward toward the street. The process of locating the 25-ft contour line is explained in this example.

SOLUTION
The first step is to locate the 25.0-ft spot elevation along the road centerline. Since the difference in elevation is 0.42 ft and the slope is given as 3%, the distance between 25.42 and 25.0 spot elevations equals 14.0 ft (0.42/0.03 = 14.0 ft). Based on the stated criteria, the crown height is 6 in.

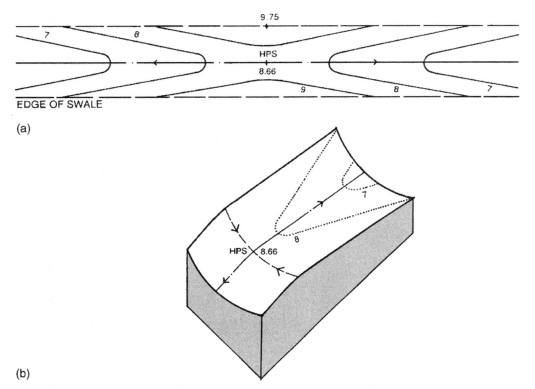

(a)

(b)

Figure 5.10. Saddle created by the high point of two swales sloping in opposite directions. (a) Plan. (b) Axonometric.

Therefore, the spot elevation at the edge of the road opposite the 25.0-ft spot elevation is 6 in. (0.5 ft) lower than the centerline, or 24.5 ft. The 25.0-ft spot elevation at the edge of the road is located uphill from this point. The difference in elevation is 0.5 ft; therefore, the distance from 24.5 to 25.0 is 16.7 (0.50/0.03 = 16.7 ft).

On the east side of the road, the edge is a 6-in. high curb. This means that the elevation at the top of the curb is always 0.5 ft above the elevation of the edge of the road pavement. Where the edge of the road is elevation 25.0 ft, the top of the curb is 25.5, and where the road is 24.5 ft, the top of the curb is 25.0. Therefore, the 25.0 contour line follows along the face of the curb until it emerges

at the 25.0-ft spot elevation, as illustrated in plan (Figure 5.11) and isometric (Figure 5.12).

Adjacent to the curb is a sidewalk that slopes toward the road at 2% while at the same time sloping 3% parallel to the direction of the road. As a result, the far edge of the sidewalk is higher than the edge along the curb. The difference in elevation between the two edges of the walk is the width, 6 ft, multiplied by the slope, 2%, or 0.12 ft. Thus, the elevation at the far edge of the sidewalk directly opposite the 25.0-ft spot elevation at the top of the curb is 25.12 ft. The 25.0-ft spot elevation along this edge is located downhill, parallel to the direction of the road at a slope of 0.03. The distance is computed by dividing the difference in elevation, 0.12 ft, by the

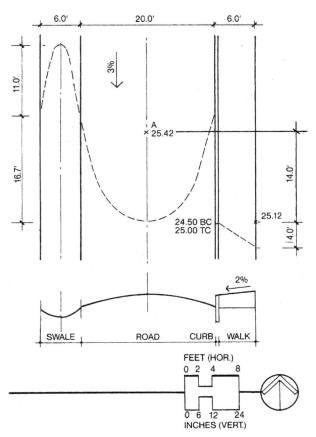

Figure 5.11. Plan and section for Example 5.3.

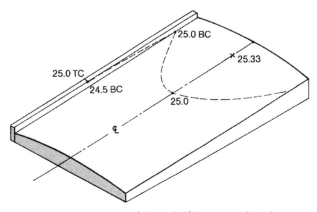

Figure 5.12. Axonometric of the path of the contour line along face of curb.

slope, 3% (0.12/0.03 = 4.0 ft). Therefore, the 25.0 spot elevation is located 4.0 ft from the 25.12-ft spot elevation in the downhill direction. The 25 ft-contour line is constructed across the sidewalk by connecting the 25.0-ft spot elevation at the top of the curb with the 25.0-ft spot elevation at the edge of the sidewalk.

On the west side of the road is a swale that is 6 ft wide and 4 in. deep. Therefore, the centerline of the swale is 4 in. or 0.33 ft lower than the two edges. As a result, where the edge of the road is at elevation 25.0 ft, the elevation at the centerline of the swale is 24.67 ft. The 25.0-spot elevation along the swale center-line is located by dividing the difference in elevation, 0.33 ft, by the slope of the swale centerline, which is the same as that of the road, 3% (0.33/0.03 = 11.0 ft). Measuring 11 ft uphill along the centerline from the 24.67-ft spot elevation locates the 25.0-ft spot elevation. The 25-ft contour line is constructed as shown in Figure 5.8. Note that the crown of the road and the bottom of the swale are indicated by rounded contours that reflect the rounded shape of these elements in section. Both are also shown sym-metrically about their respective centerlines. ■

Road Grading Process

I. Set grades along the centerline of the road after establishing a desired slope.

    A. Find Slope (S) by measuring the length of road to be graded and noting change in elevation (DE) across that distance (L).

        i. Note that this is for a simple, evenly sloping road. More complex geometries and their calculation will be discussed in Chapters 15 and 16.

II. Measuring perpendicular to the centerline, set the cross slope, crown, and swale spot elevations.

    A. If given a cross-slope percentage for the crown, find the change in elevation (DE)

for the given slope (S) and distance (L) (from the crown to the curb).

B. If given an elevation for the crown, turn that height into decimal feet (3 in. is equal to 0.25 ft) and use that as the change in elevation (DE) that will provide the elevation at the curb.

III. Work from the spots to even elevations to set the first continuous new contour line.

IV. Copy these points at the given contour interval using the slope established in part I to the pertinent important points of elevation, centerlines of swales and roads, and edges of roads, and sidewalks.

V. Draw in contours from guiding spot elevations and provide smooth transitions to the existing landform.

GRADING BY PROPORTION

Grading a road provides an excellent opportunity for illustrating the use of visual and graphic techniques to locate proposed contour lines. The key to this process is to remember that there is a direct proportional relationship between change in elevation and horizontal distance between contour lines. This is demonstrated in Example 5.3, where a 1.0-ft change in elevation at a 3% slope requires a distance of 33.3 ft. For a 0.5-ft change in elevation, only one-half of that distance is required, or 16.7 ft, while a 0.33-ft change requires one-third of the distance, or approximately 11 ft.

Figure 5.13 outlines a graphic technique that may be used to lay out the contour lines for a symmetrical road crown. Once this technique is fully understood, it can be applied to *any* grading situation and can facilitate a quick visual approach to solving grading problems.

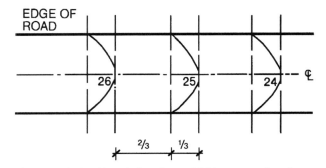

Figure 5.13. Graphic technique for establishing contour lines for crowned roads. Step 1: Locate whole number spot elevations along the road centerline. Step 2: Express crown height as a fraction of a foot (e.g., 6 in. = 1/2 ft, 4 in. = 1/3 ft). Step 3: Divide the space between the whole spot elevations according to fraction. Step 4: Draw a smooth curve from the spot elevation to the place where fraction lines cross the edge of the road.

■ EXAMPLE 5.4

This example combines several of the points made in previous examples. For this problem, only a portion of a proposed road and grading solution is illustrated in Figure 5.14. The objective of the problem is to locate and draw the proposed contour lines with a 1-ft interval according to the given criteria and to connect the corresponding proposed and existing contour lines where appropriate. The design criteria are as follows: a 4% slope toward the south parallel to the direction of the road; a 4-in. crown height; a 6-ft-wide swale along the west edge of the road, 6 in. deep and also sloping at 4%; a 6-ft-wide shoulder along the east edge that slopes at 2% perpendicular to and away from the road; and side slopes perpendicular to the centerline of the road at a ratio of 3:1 in cut and fill. The spot elevation at point A has been established as 69.0 ft.

SOLUTION

The first step is to locate the whole number spot elevations along the road centerline. From the equation $L = DE/S$ the distance required for a 1.0-ft change

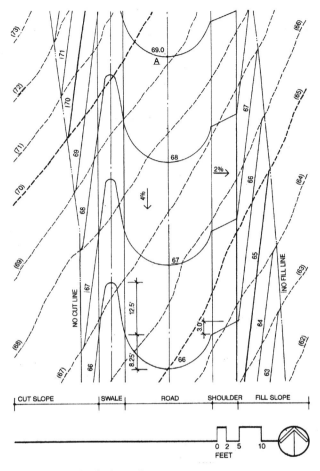

Figure 5.14. Plan for Example 5.4.

in elevation at 4% is 25 ft. Spot elevations 68.0, 67.0, and 66.0 are marked off along the centerline at 25-ft intervals. Because of the crown, points on both edges of the road on a line perpendicular to the centerline will be 4 in., or 0.33 ft, lower than a point at the center. Thus, each whole number spot elevation at the edge will be located 8.25 ft in the uphill direction from the same elevation at the center of the road. This distance was calculated by dividing the difference in elevation, 0.33 ft, by the slope, 4% (0.33/0.04 = 8.25 ft). From this information, spot

elevations 69.0, 68.0, 67.0, and 66.0 can be located on both edges of the road.

By examining the existing grades and the proposed spot elevations, it is determined that the west edge of the road is in cut and the east edge is in fill. The swale that has been proposed along the west edge is necessary in order to intercept the storm runoff from the cut slope. The swale is 6 in. (0.50 ft) deep, which means that a point on the centerline of the swale is 0.50 ft lower than the edge of the road. Each whole foot spot elevation along the swale centerline is 12.5 ft uphill from the corresponding elevation at the road edge (0.50/0.04 = 12.5 ft). The whole foot spot elevation along the far edge of the swale is opposite the whole foot spot elevation at the edge of the road.

A 6-ft-wide shoulder, which slopes away from the road, is proposed along the east edge. The far edge of the shoulder is 0.12 ft *lower* than the edge of the road. This is determined by multiplying the slope by the shoulder width (0.02 × 6 ft = 0.12 ft). Again, the whole foot spot elevation at the edge of the shoulder must be located in the uphill direction from the whole foot spot elevation at the edge of the road. The distance uphill is calculated by dividing the difference in elevation, 0.12 ft, by the slope, 4%, which equals 3.0 ft.

The 3:1 side slopes begin at the outside edges of the swale and the shoulder. Lines are drawn perpendicular to the road centerline through the full-foot spot elevations at the outside edges of the swale and the shoulder. Beginning at the respective edges, points are located at 3-ft intervals along the lines, since each 3-ft horizontal distance results in a 1-ft change in elevation. The proposed contour lines are located by connecting all the points of equal elevation determined in each of the previous steps. The proposed contour lines are drawn to the point where they intersect the corresponding existing contour lines. This is the point of no cut or fill, since beyond this point the existing contour line does not change. ■

VISUALIZING TOPOGRAPHY FROM CONTOUR LINES

Occasionally, it may be somewhat confusing to interpret contour maps or to construct new contour lines for proposed grading projects. One of the most common problems among students is drawing contour lines in the proper direction for proposed crowns, curbs, and swales. The following simple technique provides a visual aid in these situations.

By turning the plan so that the viewer is looking in the downhill direction (i.e., the higher elevations are closer to the eye than the lower elevations), the proposed contour lines, if drawn correctly, resemble the proposed profile: that is, a cross section with an exaggerated vertical scale. Using Figure 5.14 as an example, turn the page so that the plan is viewed from the north. Following the proposed 67-ft contour line, it can be seen that the contour plan of each of the proposed components reflects its respective cross section: the swale looks like a valley, the crown looks like a ridge, and the shoulder slopes away from the road. The existing contour slopes down toward the swale on the right (west), indicating cut, and slopes away from the shoulder on the left (east), indicating fill.

GRADING OF PLANAR AREAS

Contour Signatures of Planar Areas

Earlier in the chapter, linear elements were examined for the experience of spaces created by different contour signatures. A similar exploration of planar area grading will expand the palette of contour signatures that might be employed in the design of different landscape areas. Five sets of models have been created to investigate the range of approaches to the grading of planar areas.[2]

---

[2] Model graphics for Figures 5.15, 5.16, 5.17, 5.18, and 5.19 have been adapted from Harris and Dines, *Time-Saver Standards for Landscape Architecture* (1988).

In Figure 5.15 are the most simplified scenarios for grading an area. More complex versions that better take into account the surrounding context can be found in Figures 5.18 and 5.19. Figure 5.15a shows a uniform slope draining from a ridge. Figure 5.15b is the inverse, with uniform slopes draining to a valley of equal elevation. With the bottom of the valley at an equal elevation, a trench drain with a sloping bottom would be required to provide proper drainage of the area. Figure 5.15c shows a single sloping plane draining the same area as the first two models. Note that it takes twice as much elevation change to drain the same area in this condition.

The models in Figures 5.16 and 5.17 are studies of opposite approaches to drainage. In Figure 5.16, water is being drained from high points in both models evenly to the edges of the area. The model in Figure 5.16b shows what this condition will look like if the high point has been elongated into a ridge, defined by two high points. In Figure 5.17, the different models show water being drained evenly to low points within the area. Notice that the more low points there are, the smaller the grade change required to provide proper drainage. At the

Figure 5.15. Uniform slopes with one or two level edges. (a) A ridge sloping to two level edges. (b) Two level edges sloping to a trench drain. (c) One level edge sloping uniformly.

same time, be aware that the more low points there are, the more catch basins will be required, which typically makes the design more expensive.

In Figures 5.18 and 5.19, the models take principles modeled in Figures 5.15, 5.16, and 5.17 and combine them to show more complex solutions to the problem of sculpting areas to drain. Figure 5.18 is a study in moving high points to different locations in an area and sloping evenly away from them. At a small scale, Figure 5.18a is similar to the start of a swale, while Figure 5.18b is similar to when the ends of two swales meet (as in Figure 5.10). Figures 5.18c–e are updated versions of the models in Figures 5.15 and 5.16. The contours have been rounded, and slopes at the perimeter of the area have some variability to show how they might tie into the surrounding grade. Figure 5.19a shows a scenario that will be discussed in greater detail later in this chapter: grading a sloping terrace and using swales to divert runoff from the terrace. A similar condition is shown in Figure 5.19b, but instead of a swale, a ridge is used to divert runoff from the terrace. Draining diagonally is introduced in Figure 5.19c and warped in Figure 5.19d, with the contours on the right side of the model sloping more steeply than those on the left side.

Now that a range of contour signatures for draining planar areas have been explored, it is appropriate to begin applying that understanding to a range of problems with growing complexity.

Slopes for Surface Drainage

One primary objective in grading, in most instances, is to slope the ground surface away

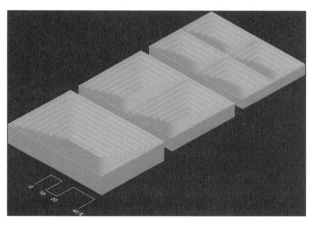

Figure 5.17. Perimeter edge level and sloping to low points. (a) Sloping to a single low point. (b) Sloping to two low points. (c) Sloping to four low points.

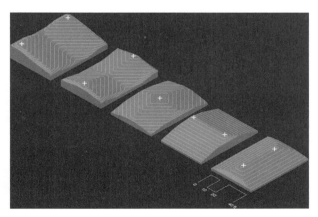

Figure 5.18. Sloping evenly from high points, marked by "+" signs. (a) Two high points in corners along the same edge, sloping in a "V" pattern. (b) Two high points midway along opposite edges, forming a saddle. (c) One high point in the center of the area, sloping evenly away. (d) A ridge crossing the short dimension and draining to the ends. (e) A ridge crossing the long direction and draining to the ends.

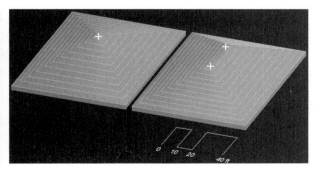

Figure 5.16. Perimeter edge level and sloping from high points marked by "+" signs. (a) Sloping from a single high point. (b) Sloping from a ridge, defined by two high points.

Figure 5.19. Sloping planes. (a) Evenly sloping plane, with a swale to direct runoff around the area. (b) Evenly sloped plane topped by a ridge. (c) Evenly sloping diagonal plane from one corner to another. (d) Warped plane, with two sides sloping steeply and two sloping shallowly.

from buildings to ensure proper drainage of storm water. Storm water is directed away from buildings to avoid potential leakage into interior spaces, the saturation of soils that reduces bearing capacity, and potential adverse effects of moisture on building materials.

■ EXAMPLE 5.5

To illustrate the concept of drainage away from a structure, often referred to as *positive drainage,* the rectangle in Figure 5.20 represents a building measuring 30 ft by 50 ft. The objective of the problem is to locate and draw the 25- and 26-ft contour lines so that a 3% slope away from the building is achieved. The spot elevations at the exterior corners of the building are as indicated.

SOLUTION

The first step in the solution is to determine the distance from the spot elevations to the whole number contour lines. Along the south face of the building there is a change in elevation from

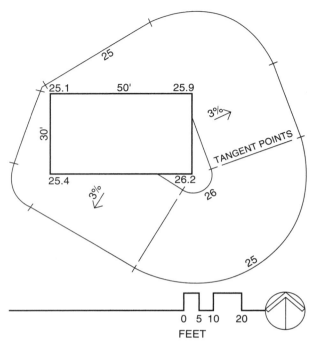

Figure 5.20. Plan for Example 5.5.

25.4 to 26.2. Thus, a 26.0-ft spot elevation exists between these points and is easily located using the following proportion:

$$\frac{x \text{ (hor. dist. from 26.2 to 26.0)}}{50 \text{ (hor. dist. from 26.2 to 25.4)}} = \frac{0.2 \text{ (elev. change from 26.2 to 26.0)}}{0.8 \text{ (elev. change from 26.2 to 25.4)}}$$

$$\frac{x}{50} = \frac{0.2}{0.8}$$

$$x = \frac{0.2 \times 50}{0.8} = 12.5 \text{ ft}$$

Therefore, the 26.0-ft spot elevation is located 12.5 ft (or ¼ the length of the south face) from the southeast corner.

The same process is applied to the east face, again to locate the 26.0-ft spot elevation.

$$\frac{x \text{ (hor. dist. from } 25.9 \text{ to } 26.0)}{30 \text{ (hor. dist. from } 25.9 \text{ to } 26.2)} = \frac{0.1 \text{ (elev. change from } 25.9 \text{ to } 26.0)}{0.3 \text{ (elev. change from } 25.9 \text{ to } 26.2)}$$

$$\frac{x}{30} = \frac{0.1}{0.3}$$

$$x = \frac{0.1 \times 30}{0.3} = 10 \text{ ft}$$

As a result, the 26.0-ft spot is located 10 ft, or one-third of the distance, from the northeast corner.

The next step is to determine the distance that the 26-ft contour line must be located in any direction from the southeast corner in order to fulfill the requirement of a 3% slope away from the building. The known values are $S = 0.03$ and $DE = 0.2$ ft, which may be substituted into the equation $L = DE/S$ or $L = 0.2/0.03$. The computed distance is 6.67 ft or approximately 6.7 ft. An arc with a radius of 6.7 ft is constructed to the proper scale around the southeast corner, and lines are drawn tangent to this arc from the previously determined 26-ft spot elevations. The 26-ft contour line is now complete.

The same method described above is used to compute the distance from each of the four corners to the 25 ft contour line. These computations are as follows:

Northeast corner: 0.9/0.03 = 30 ft
Southeast corner: 1.2/0.03 = 40 ft
Southwest corner: 0.4/0.03 = 13.3 ft
Northwest corner: 0.1/0.03 = 3.3 ft

Using these distances as radii, arcs are constructed around the appropriate corners and the 25-ft contour line is completed by connecting the arcs with tangent lines, as illustrated in Figure 5.20. ■

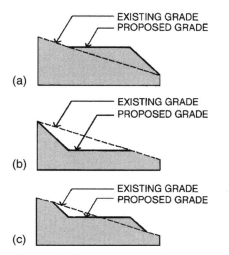

Figure 5.21. Terrace sections. (a) Terrace constructed on fill. (b) Terrace constructed in cut. (c) Terrace constructed partially on fill and partially in cut.

Terrace Grading

Another common grading problem is the construction of relatively level areas, or terraces, on sloping terrain. Most hillside development, whether it be for outdoor living areas, recreation facilities, or circulation systems, requires some form of terracing. In section, terraces may be graded in one of three ways: completely on fill, completely in cut, or partially on fill and partially in cut. *Fill* is soil that has been added to raise the elevation of the ground, while *cut* is a surface from which soil has been removed to lower the ground elevation. For further discussion see Chapter 8, particularly Figure 8.2. The three terrace conditions are illustrated in Figure 5.21. A grading technique for the first two conditions is explained in the next two examples.

■ EXAMPLE 5.6: TERRACE ON FILL

A terrace measuring 25 ft by 40 ft is to be constructed with its south edge at elevation 220.0, as shown in Figure 5.22. The terrace will slope

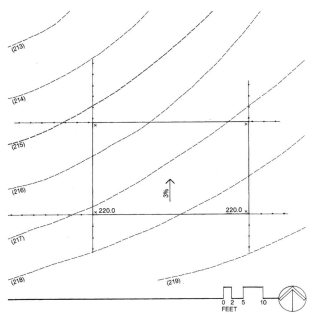

Figure 5.22. Plan for Example 5.6.

downward at 3% toward the north for drainage, and the side slopes will be graded at a ratio of 3:1 (1-ft drop in 3-ft horizontal distance). The purpose of making the side slopes quite steep is to return to the existing grade in the shortest distance possible. This reduces the amount of disturbance caused by grading and reduces the cost. From the information provided, draw the proposed contour lines.

SOLUTION

The first step in solving this problem is to determine the elevation along the north, or lower, edge of the terrace. From the equation $DE = S \times L$, the north edge is 0.03×25 ft $= 0.75$ ft lower than the south edge, or 219.25 ft (220.0 − 0.75).

The next step is to determine the distance from the north edge of the terrace to the 219-ft contour line. Since the side slopes are to be graded at 3:1, the horizontal distance from the terrace edge to the

219-ft contour line is 0.75 ft, as calculated by the following proportion:

$$\frac{x \text{ (horizontal distance from 219.25 to 219.0)}}{0.25 \text{ (elevation difference from 219.25 to 219.0)}} = \frac{3}{1} \text{(proposed ratio)}$$

$$x = \frac{0.25 \times 3}{1}$$

$$= 0.75 \,\text{ft}$$

This distance is marked off along lines drawn perpendicular to the terrace at the northeast and northwest corners, as shown in Figure 5.22. (It is advisable to study Figures 5.22 and 5.23 carefully while following the procedure outlined in the text.) From the point of the 219-ft spot elevation, the remaining whole number spot elevations (218, 217, 216, etc.) can be located by progressing along the line in 3 ft-increments, since for every 3 ft of horizontal distance there is a 1-ft vertical drop. These points are used for the construction of the proposed contour lines.

The same procedure is followed at the south edge of the terrace, where, again, lines are drawn perpendicular to the terrace at the southeast and southwest corners. Since the elevation of the south edge is already a whole number (220), the remaining whole number spot elevations can be located by progressing out from the edge in 3-ft increments.

Beginning with the 219-ft contour line, draw straight lines through the 219-ft spot elevations until the lines of adjacent sides intersect. The proposed 219-ft contour line is a closed contour, since it never intersects with the 219-ft contour line already existing on the site. Proceeding with the proposed 218-ft contour line and following the same technique, the new 218-ft contour line intersects the existing 218-ft contour line at two points. To continue the proposed contour line

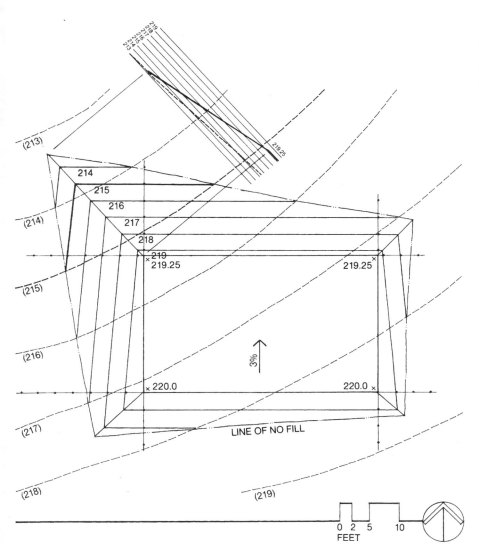

Figure 5.23. Completed contour plan. The section is used to determine the location of the no cut–no fill line between contour lines 214 and 213.

beyond the intersection point would result in cut that is unnecessary, since the terrace is entirely on fill. Therefore, the new contour lines are drawn only to the point where they intersect the corresponding existing contour lines. This is the point at which the grade returns to the original or existing ground surface. This is referred to as the *point of no fill* (or *no cut*). The procedure is continued

for successively lower contour lines (217, 216, 215, etc.) until the point is reached where existing contours are no longer disturbed, as shown in Figure 5.23.

Frequently, the points of no fill (or no cut) are delineated by a line that also serves as the limit line for the grading contractor's work. Where there is no intersection of existing and proposed contour

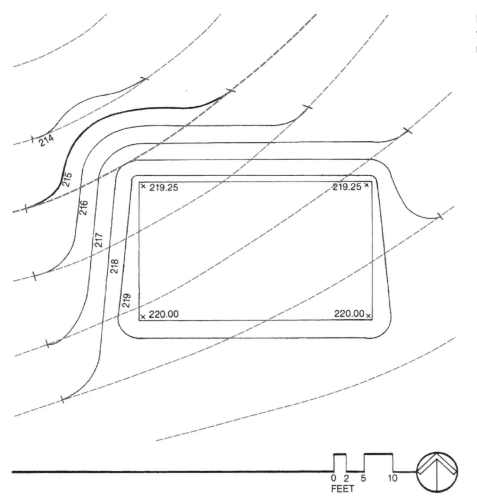

Figure 5.24. Contour lines adjusted to provide a smoother and more rounded appearance.

lines of equal elevation to delineate the no fill (or no cut) line easily, a section showing the proposed and existing grade lines may be constructed. The point of no fill (or no cut) occurs where the two grade lines intersect. With regard to the shape of the side slopes constructed in this example, two points must be made. First, the side slopes in plan view form planes with distinct intersections. This is difficult to construct and maintain and, within a natural context, usually does not blend well with

the surrounding landscape. For these reasons, the contours are given a smoother and more rounded appearance, as shown in Figure 5.24.

The second point pertains to the relationship of the rather steep side slopes to the edge of the terrace and where the side slopes meet existing grade. As constructed, there is an abrupt change in grade at top and bottom of slope, as shown in section in Figure 5.25a. Again, not only is this condition difficult to maintain, it is also subject

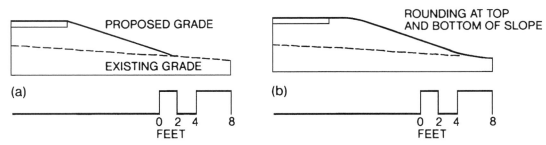

Figure 5.25. Slope sections. (a) Abrupt transition at top and bottom of slope. (b) Rounded transition at top and bottom of slope. Note that providing a transition area requires additional horizontal distance.

to erosion, particularly at the top of the slope. An alternative is to provide additional space at the top and bottom of the slope to allow for a smoother transition, as illustrated in Figure 5.25b. ■

■ EXAMPLE 5.7: TERRACE IN CUT

A terrace measuring 8.0 m by 10.0 m is to be built with the southern, or higher, edge at elevation 108.1 m, as shown in Figure 5.26. The surface of the terrace will slope toward the north at 3%. The proposed side slopes, which are in cut, will have a 3:1 slope. From the information given, locate the proposed contour lines.

SOLUTION

The procedure for solving this problem is similar to that in the previous example. First, the elevation of the northern edge of the terrace is determined to be 107.86 m ($0.03 \times 8.0 = 0.24$ m and $108.1 - 0.24 = 107.86$ m). Analysis of the relationship between the existing and proposed elevations shows that, essentially, grading is not required along the northern edge, since the proposed and existing grades correspond. Along the southern edge there is between 0.7 and 1.0 m of cut. This means that the ground must slope uphill from this edge at the proposed 3:1 ratio in order to return to the existing or original grade. The solution is shown in Figure 5.27.

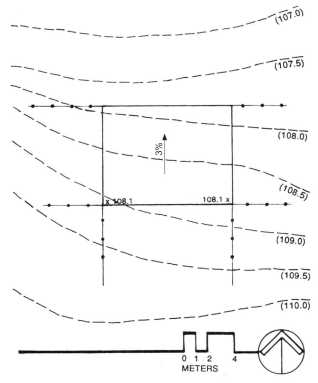

Figure 5.26. Plan for Example 5.7.

Applying the 3:1 ratio to the contour interval of 0.5 m, the distances marked off along the lines drawn perpendicular to the edges of the terrace at the southeast and southwest corners are 3 × 0.5 m, or 1.5 m. The elevation difference from the southern edge to the next contour line is 0.4 m (108.5 − 108.1). Therefore, the first mark is 1.2 m (3 × 0.4) from the southern corners.

The completed contour plan in Figure 5.27 contains the same problems created by intersecting planes that were discussed in relation to Figures 5.24 and 5.25, and the same principles should be applied in refining this proposed grading plan. The terrace in cut points out an additional problem. If the terrace created in Example 5.7 were a structure like a building or pavement, the storm water from the side slopes would be directed toward the structure. This condition is contrary to positive drainage, as presented in Example 5.5. In order to prevent this condition, the storm water runoff must be intercepted and diverted around the structure, usually by the use of a swale. Swales are discussed more completely in a subsequent section of this chapter, and an alternative solution to Example 5.7 is presented in Example 5.8. ∎

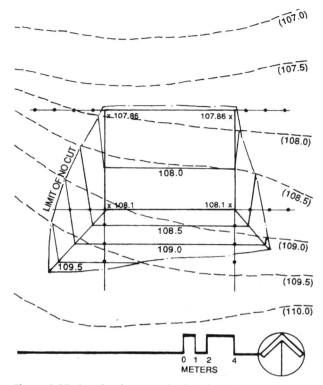

Figure 5.27. Completed contour plan based on criteria.

SWALES TO DIVERT RUNOFF

The purpose of the last example in this chapter is to introduce the concept of *diversions* to direct storm runoff around a structure. A diversion is a channel with a supporting ridge on the lower side constructed across a slope to a suitably stable outlet. Diversions are used to protect structures, streets, low-lying areas, steep or easily erodible slopes, and exposed soils during construction from storm water runoff.

∎ EXAMPLE 5.8

This example is the same as Example 5.7 except that diversions are used to divert storm runoff around the terrace. Design criteria for the diversions include a 2.0-m width, 0.2-m *minimum* depth, and slope along the centerline *not to exceed* 4%. The side slopes, which begin at the outside edge of the swale, are 3:1.

SOLUTION

To divert the water around the terrace, two swales sloping in opposite directions (similar to Figure 5.10) will be most effective given the existing topographic condition. The first step is to locate the saddle point between the proposed swales and determine its elevation. The centerline for each swale is located 1.0 m from the edge of the terrace. As a starting point, the midpoint of the south

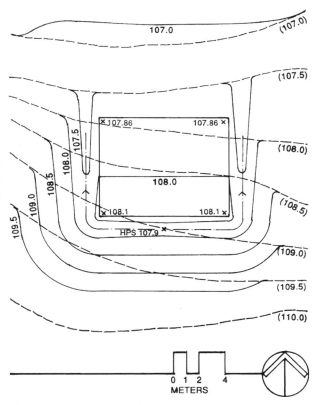

Figure 5.28. Plan for Example 5.8.

side of the terrace is selected as the dividing point between the swales. The proposed elevation of the saddle point is 107.9 m [108.1 m (elevation at south edge of terrace) − 0.2 m (minimum depth of swale) = 107.9 m].

The maximum slope along the centerline of the swale is 4%. Therefore, the 107.5-m spot elevation cannot be closer than 10.0 m from the saddle point measured along the centerline of the swale (107.9 m − 107.5 m = 0.40 m and 0.40 m/0.04 = 10.0 m). Because the elevation of the south edge of the terrace remains constant while the centerline of the swale slopes, the swales become deeper than 0.2 m as they progress downhill. The solution, as

illustrated in Figure 5.28, maintains the outside edge of the swales at the same elevation as the edge of the terrace. As presented, the solution is still a mechanical interpretation of the criteria. The proposed contours could be adjusted to blend the new grades with the existing grades. ■

AREA GRADING PROCESS

I. Examine the given topography.

    A. The goal of developing grading plans for confined areas is often to work closely with the existing topography.

        1. The geometries shown in Figures 5.15 through 5.19 are a good starting point when trying to match a geometry to an existing condition.

II. Select a geometry to test from that group and decide where to slope the area and, ultimately, where to collect the water before it leaves that area.

    A. Note that some areas will make up entire sites, while other sites may have to be broken into smaller areas.

    B. It is generally important to minimize the distance that a water sheet flows across any area before it is picked up in a conveyance, either a swale or a catch basin.

    C. With respect to methods of conveyance, catch basins are expensive and imply the need for plumbing underground. A good goal is to minimize the number of catch basins, using swales to convey water through the site where possible.

III. Test elevations and maximum and minimum allowed cross slopes across the longest runs in your area.

A. This is done to ensure an awareness of whether the situation will require a large amount of cut or fill.

IV. Start sketching in the geometry using the successfully tested slopes, making sure that the transitions between different slopes are gradual and not jarring.

V. Tie back into existing grades smoothly, as shown in Figures 5.24 and 5.28.

CHAPTER 6

Grading Process

INTRODUCTION

The grading procedure presented in this book is best described as a *controlled intuitive process.* Unfortunately, there is no precise sequence to follow in order to arrive at a correct grading solution, since every grading problem is different and, in most cases, there is more than one appropriate solution to a particular problem. This lack of precision is often a source of frustration to students. This frustration may be reduced through continued practice and by following a generalized three-phased approach. These phases include:

An inventory and analysis of the site and development program

Design development

Design implementation

Phase 1: Inventory and Analysis

The initial phase of any landscape architectural design project is to inventory the existing physical and cultural conditions of the site and its surroundings. Both the inventory and the development program (i.e., what is to be placed on the site) are analyzed and evaluated to identify conflicts, constraints, and opportunities that will guide the design development and the proposed grading scheme. This phase relates directly to the discussion in Chapter 2.

Phase 2: Design Development

During this phase, the observations and evaluations of the first phase are synthesized into a design concept that may generate one or more design solutions. As a result of the compartmentalization of the educational system, which typically separates courses in grading technology from courses in design, the integration of site design and engineering is often overlooked by students. From experience and observation, many students wrongly conclude that, because grading is taught as an engineering subject, design is of secondary importance. The reverse situation is commonly found in the design studio.

With regard to grading and design, three points must be emphasized: First, grading and site design are two highly related and dependent processes. To achieve an appropriate as well as successful final product, both types of design must be integrated in a holistic manner at the outset of the project. Second, before manipulating contours on a grading plan, it is important to have a clear understanding of the form of the desired final product. Without this knowledge, the manipulation of contours is aimless and futile. To reinforce this point, any appropriate three-dimensional form can be expressed by contours on a grading plan. However, without a preconception of what that form should be, it can never be attained. Finally, a change in grade must be purposeful, whether for functional or aesthetic reasons, and not arbitrary. The intent to change a grade 2 in. is no less important than the intent to change a grade 20 ft.

Phase 3: Design Implementation

At this point, the design solution is translated into a workable and buildable scheme through the development of construction drawings and specifications. Although not always applicable or necessary, four steps may be followed to make the task of developing accurate, concise, and correct grading plans easier. Based on a process developed by David Young and Donald Leslie at Pennsylvania State University, these steps include (1) development of section criteria, (2) application of section criteria, (3) development of slope diagrams, and (4) evaluation of slope diagrams.

Since grading is the change upward or downward of the ground surface, plans alone are normally inadequate to study vertical relationships properly. Therefore, sections should be drawn at critical points and section criteria developed to establish relative vertical relationships, approximate slopes,

and select appropriate grade change devices, such as walls, slopes, and steps. Once the section criteria have been developed, they may be applied to the plan in order to establish key spot elevations.

The purpose of slope diagrams is to outline the extent of areas to be graded, to relatively the same slopes; indicate the direction of proposed slopes, establish drainage patterns by outlining proposed drainage areas and locating proposed high points and collection points; and, finally, establish spot elevations at critical points, such as building corners and entrances, top and bottom of stairs and walls, and high points of swales. For evaluation purposes, a checklist may be established to determine whether the slope diagrams maintain the integrity of the overall design concept; respond appropriately to identified constraints; provide positive, efficient, and ecologically sensitive drainage; and maintain a relative balance between cut and fill, if possible. Slope diagrams should be revised where problems or conflicts are identified.

It should be noted that in the steps outlined, no contour lines have been manipulated or drawn. Only areas to be regraded, approximate slopes, and critical spot elevations have been determined. These now provide a controlled framework within which the proposed contour lines may be located.

It is important to realize that very rarely is a grading plan completely correct or appropriate on the first try. The development of a grading plan is to some degree a trial-and-error process often requiring numerous adjustments. These adjustments are usually minor; however, in some instances, the entire grading approach may need to be reexamined. Finally, although the overall design concept is established during the design development phase, many detailed design decisions made at the implementation phase will contribute to the ultimate success of a project.

APPLYING THE GRADING PROCESS

■ Example 6.1

The following example is presented to illustrate a typical sequence of events associated with a grading design problem. In this problem a small, L-shaped office building with a slab foundation is to be constructed on a suburban corner lot. The development program requires a seven-car parking area with potential for expansion, an entrance court, and handicapped access. The site is to be designed and the grading plan developed.

Site Analysis

As can be seen in Figure 6.1, there are no major natural constraints on the site. The high point located in the northeast corner is at elevation 44.8 ft, while the low point, elevation 35.8 ft, is located on the property line in the southwest corner. The steepest slope is approximately 10%, with the average slope across the site approximately 6%. The existing surface drainage pattern is primarily sheet flow, with approximately half directed toward Third Street and half toward Oak Street. The most significant feature on the site is the grove of mature red oak trees.

The adjacent land uses include a bank on the north to a single-family residence on the east. The residence is screened from the property by a hemlock hedge. The heaviest vehicular traffic is along Oak Street, while most pedestrians will approach the site from the southwest.

Design Development

As shown in Figure 6.2, both the building and the parking area are located as far from the oak trees as possible to ensure the preservation of the trees. The building is placed with the open part of the L toward the street corner in order to orient the building entrance toward the primary pedestrian approach and to maximize the amount of glazing facing south to increase energy efficiency, as this site is located in a cold climate region. The entrance court is developed within the open space of the L. The parking area is located in order to maximize the distance between the driveway entrance and the street intersection and to take advantage of the visual screen already provided by the adjacent hedge. The parking entrance is not located on Oak Street in order to preserve the existing oak grove and to avoid possible conflicts with the bank traffic.

Design Implementation

In developing the grading plan, the four major elements of the design, including the parking area, building, entrance court, and oak grove, are analyzed. Where appropriate, section criteria and grading diagrams are developed for each component, and alternative solutions are presented and explored.

Parking Area

The existing grade slopes downward toward Third Street along the longitudinal axis of the parking area. To be consistent, the proposed grading for the parking area should slope in the same direction. There are four basic approaches to grading the parking area, as illustrated by the sections and slope diagrams in Figure 6.3. The first is to cross-pitch the pavement toward the building and collect the storm water runoff in the southwest corner of the lot. The second is to cross-pitch the pavement away from the building and collect the runoff in the southeast area of the lot. The third combines the first two options, resulting in a valley down the center of the parking area. The fourth alternative combines the first two options

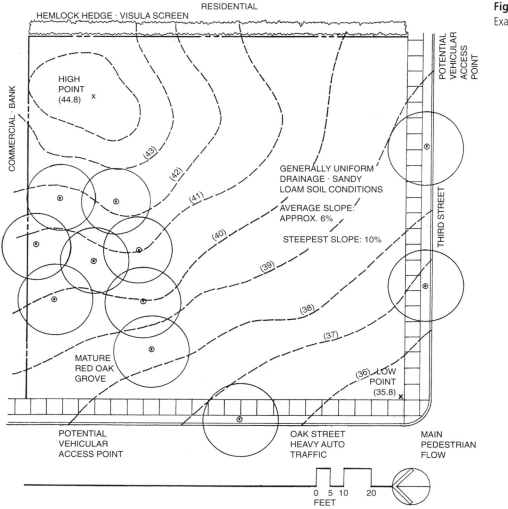

Figure 6.1. Site analysis for Example 6.1.

to create a ridge along the center of the parking area. Runoff is collected in both the southeast and southwest corners of the lot.

Generally, cross-sloping small parking areas in one direction is the most efficient and visually least disturbing method of grading. However, in working through the four options for this problem, it was determined that pitching toward the center was the best alternative. Cross-pitching the parking area toward the building placed the catch basin too close to the building and in an inconvenient location for pedestrians, particularly if it clogged. Cross-pitching away from the building resulted in more cut in the northeast corner of the lot. The ridge alternative did not result in significant grading advantages and would be more costly because

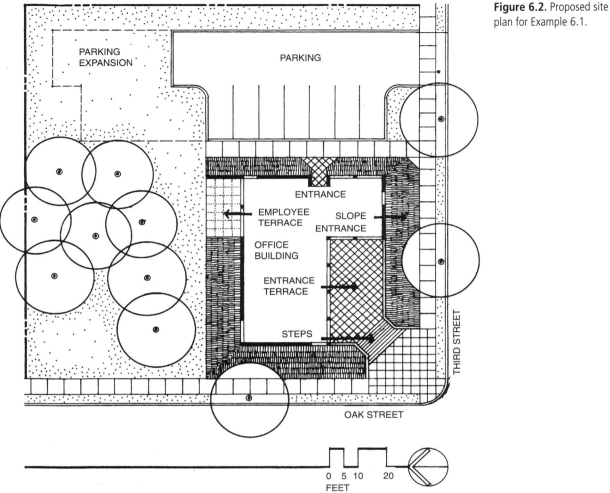

Figure 6.2. Proposed site plan for Example 6.1.

PARKING EXPANSION

PARKING

ENTRANCE

EMPLOYEE TERRACE

SLOPE ENTRANCE

OFFICE BUILDING

ENTRANCE TERRACE

STEPS

THIRD STREET

OAK STREET

0 5 10 20 FEET

of the additional storm drainage structure. Other factors that influenced this decision are the accessibility for the disabled at this end of the building and the limited change in grade that can occur along the face of the building caused by the slab construction. The controls for selecting the proposed elevations and gradients within the parking area are based on these factors in conjunction with the existing grades along the east property line and at the entrance to the parking area.

Building

Several concerns must be addressed in establishing a finished floor elevation for the building. First, positive drainage away from the building must be maintained on all sides. A second concern is the

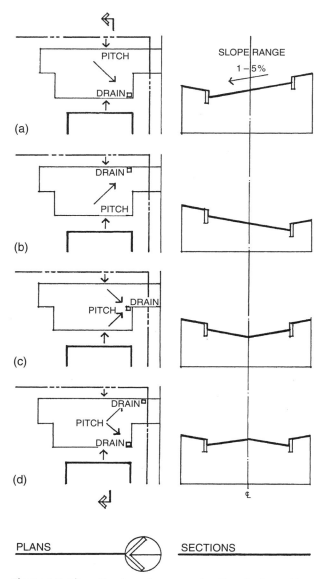

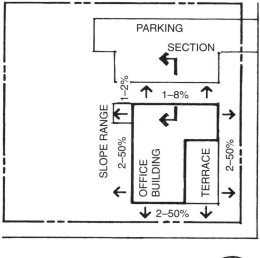

PLANS ⊙ SECTIONS

Figure 6.3. Alternative slope diagrams and sections for the parking area. (a) Cross-pitched toward the building. (b) Cross-pitched away from the building. (c) Pitched to the center, creating a valley. (d) Pitched to the edges, creating a ridge.

Figure 6.4. Slope diagram for the building. The primary objective is to maintain positive drainage away from the building. Except for the east side, where handicapped access must be maintained, there are very few slope restrictions.

elevation of the east entrance and its relationship to the proposed parking lot grades. The elevation of the southwest entrance and its relationship to existing sidewalk grades must also be considered. In addition, the proposed finished floor elevation must be evaluated. A basic slope diagram for the building is shown in Figure 6.4.

In examining the relationship of the building to the existing grades, a finished floor elevation of approximately 38 ft would seem appropriate, since the 38-ft contour line roughly bisects the building. This is a typical strategy, since it strikes a balance in the grade change from one end of the building to the other and potentially produces a more balanced cut-and-fill condition. However, when examining the relationship of the east entrance to

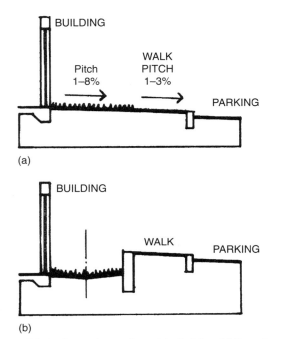

(a)

(b)

Figure 6.5. Section at the east face of the building. (a) Floor elevation set higher than parking lot elevation. (b) Floor elevation set lower than parking lot elevation.

the parking area, there are two basic alternatives. The first is to create a positive drainage condition; thus, the elevation at the edge of the building must be higher than the elevation at the top of the curb at the edge of the parking lot, as shown in Figure 6.5a. If the finished floor elevation is established at 38 ft, the elevation of the parking lot adjacent to the east entry must be lower than 38 ft. This results in approximately 2 ft of cut in the parking lot. A second alternative would be to construct the walk edge of the parking area at an elevation above the finished floor elevation, as illustrated in Figure 6.5b. This results in more costly construction and may cause drainage problems, since a low area is created directly adjacent to the building.

In the third and final analysis, perhaps the finished floor elevation (FFE) should be raised above 38 ft, thus ensuring good drainage, reducing cut, and reducing construction costs. In raising the elevation of the building, however, most of the foundation slab will be placed on fill. Purchasing and properly placing the fill material can add to the cost of the project. Also, if the foundation slab is not constructed properly, future soil settlement may cause cracking and structural problems within the building. As can be seen from these three conditions, a number of factors must be explored and assessed in making grading decisions. In this case, since the scale of the building is small, it is felt that raising the FFE represents the best option and could be properly constructed.

Entrance Court

There are several ways in which the entrance court could be designed, each directly related to grading decisions. Three schematic plans and accompanying sections are illustrated in Figure 6.6. If the FFE is established above 38 ft, it is necessary to provide stairs at the southwest entrance. Also, along the south and west faces of the building, slopes are needed, since the floor elevation is above the existing grades of the sidewalk. The three solutions illustrated respond to these conditions. It should be noted that these solutions were studied during the design development phase in order to reach a design decision. There is not always a distinct separation between the work to be performed in each of the phases. The third option (Figure 6.6c) was selected for several reasons. The entrance courts in Figure 6.6a and b were considered too large in relation to the size of the building. The option in Figure 6.6c provides a transitional space between the street corner and the

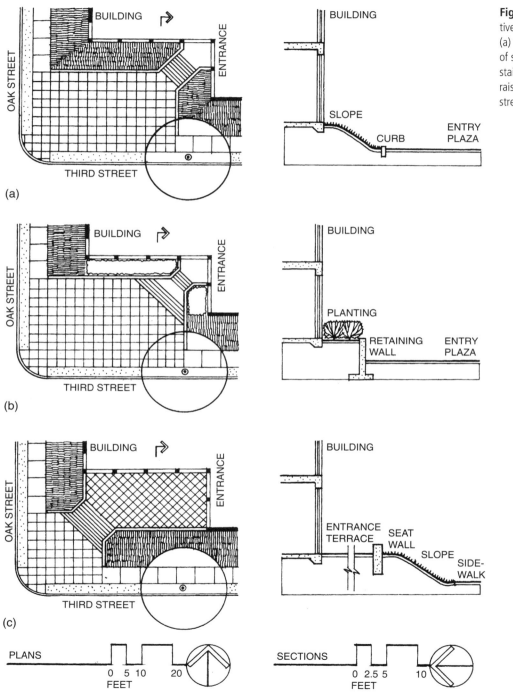

Figure 6.6. Design alternatives for an entrance terrace. (a) Terrace with a simple set of stairs. (b) Terrace with stairs as a feature. (c) Terrace raised above surrounding street and sidewalk.

building entrance, and by continuing the slopes along the edges of the entrance court, the relationship of the building to the street corner is more clearly defined. The other two solutions are also correct and could be implemented if different design objectives were desired.

Oak Grove

In order to preserve the oak grove, there should be as little regrading and soil disturbance as possible within the drip line of the trees. Minimizing grading restricts the extent to which the existing contour lines may be altered on the north side of the building. As a result, the intent is to return to the existing grade in as short a distance as possible beyond the building. To be consistent with the treatment of the south and west sides, a slope is used along this edge of the building.

Synthesis

The rationale and criteria presented in the previous sections are synthesized into a final grading plan. Figure 6.7 illustrates the placement of critical spot elevations and proposed gradients, while Figure 6.8 illustrates the final grading plan. From this drawing, a grading contractor should be able to execute this portion of the project. Again, it must be emphasized that this is *a* solution, not *the* solution, to this problem. ▪

GRADING PLAN GRAPHICS

There are two basic types of grading plan. The first is the conceptual grading plan that communicates the design intent but is not usually an accurate or engineering representation of the ground form (Figure 6.2). The audience for this plan is normally the client, who may be an individual, an architect, or a public agency, and its purpose is to make the proposed concept easily understandable. The second is the grading plan executed as part of a set of construction documents (Figure 6.8). The purpose of this plan is to interpret accurately the design intent and communicate this information effectively to the grading contractor. The plan, in conjunction with the technical specifications, must provide complete instructions concerning the nature and scope of the work to be performed as well as a solid basis for estimating the cost involved. The success of a project depends on the *accuracy, completeness,* and *clarity* of the construction drawings.

Construction Grading Plan

The grading plan should show all existing and proposed features of the site. This includes all buildings; structures, such as walls, walks, steps, and roads; utilities, such as water, sewer, storm drainage, and electrical lines; utility structures, such as manholes, meter pits, and junction boxes; and underground structures, such as vaults, septic systems, and fuel storage tanks. Proposed features are normally drafted as solid lines, and the existing features are shown as dashed lines or are photographically screened to appear lighter. In addition, of course, both existing and proposed contour lines and spot elevations are shown.

Spot elevations are used to supplement contours in the following situations:

1. To indicate variations from the normal slope or gradient between contour lines
2. To indicate elevations of intersecting planes and lines, such as corners of buildings, terraces, and walks
3. To indicate elevations at top and bottom of vertical elements, such as walls, steps, and curbs
4. To indicate floor and entrance elevations

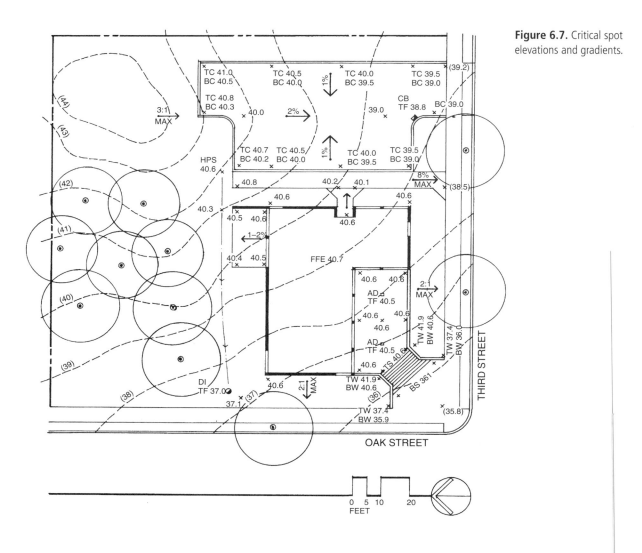

Figure 6.7. Critical spot elevations and gradients.

5. To indicate elevations of high and low points

6. To indicate top of frame (rim) elevations and inverts for utility systems

With the preceding list in mind, examine the use of spot elevations in Figure 6.8. In some cases, only spot elevations are shown on highway plans and contour lines are omitted.

The following elements should appear on all grading plans:

1. *Written and/or Graphic Scale.* The scale at which a grading plan is drawn depends on the scope of the project and the nature of the available topographic data. Scales for site plans usually range from $\frac{1}{8}$ in. = 1 ft to 1 in. = 40 ft in

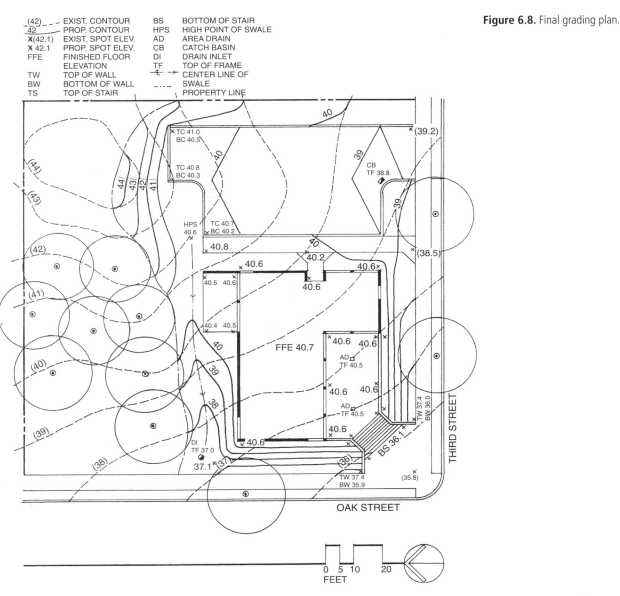

Figure 6.8. Final grading plan.

the U.S. Customary system and from 1:100 to 1:500 in the metric system.

2. *North Arrow.* A north arrow is provided for orientation purposes. It should be indicated whether this is assumed, magnetic, or true north.

3. *Notes.* Notes include general or explanatory information as well as descriptions of any unique conditions of the plan. All plans should contain a note describing the source from which the existing conditions were taken as well as benchmarks and reference datum.

_(24)_ _ _ _ _ _	EXISTING CONTOUR	⎤ LABEL UPHILL-SIDE/EVERY 5TH OR
24	PROPOSED CONTOUR	⎦ 10TH CONTOUR LINE HEAVIER
x (24.21)	EXISTING SPOT ELEVATION	⎤
x 24.71	PROPOSED SPOT ELEVATION	
FFE	FINISHED FLOOR ELEVATION	
TW/BW	TOP OF WALL/BOTTOM OF WALL	
TC/BC	TOP OF CURB/BOOTM OF CURB	
TS/BS	TOP OF STAIR/BOTTOM OF STAIR	INCLUDE SPOT
BF	BOTTOM OF FOOTING	ELEVATION
HP/LP	HIGH POINT/LOW POINT	
HPS	HIGH POINT OF SWALE	
TF or RE	TOP OF FRAME OR RIM ELEVATION	
INV. EL.	INVERT ELEVATION	⎦
☐ CB	EXISTING CATCH BASIN	⎤
◪ CB	PROPOSED CATCH BASIN	
○ DI	EXISTING DRAIN INLET	REQUIRE TOP OF
◑ DI	PROPOSED DRAIN INLET	FRAME AND INVERT
○ MH	EXISTING MANHOLE	ELEVATIONS
● MH	PROPOSED MANHOLE	⎦
◑ AD	PROPOSED AREA DRAIN	⎤ REQUIRES TOP OF ⎦ FRAME ELEVATION
CIP	CAST IRON PIPE	⎤
RCP	REINFORCED CONCRETE PIPE	
CMP	CORRUGATED METAL PIPE	INCLUDE PIPE SIZE
VCP	VITRIFIED CLAY PIPE	
PVC	POLYVINYL CHLORIDE (PLASTIC) PIPE	⎦
STA. 0+00	STATION POINT	
P̶L̶ _ _	PROPERTY LINE	
CLL _ _	CONTRACT LIMIT LINE	
℄ _ . _	CENTER LINE	
℄ _ . _→	CENTER LINE OF SWALE	⎤ INDICATE FLOW DIRECTION ⎦

Figure 6.9. Typical grading plan symbols and abbreviations.

4. *Legend.* All symbols and abbreviations used on the drawing should be identified in a legend. Examples of typical symbols and abbreviations are presented in Figure 6.9. It should be noted that convention varies in different regions of the country and even between design offices within the same region. This fact only reinforces the need for a legend. The conventions used in this book include dashed lines for existing contours, solid lines for proposed contours, parenthetic labels for both existing contours and existing spot elevations, labeling contours on the *uphill* side, and use of a wider line for every fifth or tenth contour line. Generally, contour lines are drawn freehand for unpaved areas and drafted for paved areas.

5. *Title Block.* Information such as project name, location of project, name of client, name of design firm, drawing title, drawing number, scale, and date should be arranged in an orderly and easy-to-read manner, normally in the lower-right-hand corner of the sheet.

The readability of construction drawings is dependent on the clarity and legibility of the graphic technique. Variations in line thickness (referred to as *line weight*) and line type (e.g., solid, dashed, and dotted) are used to indicate a hierarchy of importance, a change in level, or a change in material. The organization of the information also contributes to the readability of a drawing. Development of a consistent, clear lettering style will add to the quality of the drawing.

CHAPTER 7

Soils in Construction

Soil structure and composition need to be considered in many aspects of site development. This chapter focuses on the use of soil as a construction material and provides an overview of how physical and engineering properties vary with soil type.

ROLE OF SOIL IN SITE PLANNING

Site planning requires an understanding of soils and how they affect hydrology, construction, erosion control, and plant growth. The surface condition and structure of a soil largely influence how much runoff will result from precipitation. Soil, therefore, is an important factor considered in the design of storm water management facilities. In grading activities, soil is a construction material with engineering properties that can vary greatly, depending on physical parameters such as texture, gradation, and water content. Soil also serves as a foundation material, providing support for buildings and other structures. Location of new site elements and the details of the element's construction, can be impacted by

the location of different soil types on a site. When soils are exposed during construction, they are highly susceptible to the erosive forces of wind and water. The nature of the soil on a site will, in part, determine the type and extent of the erosion and sediment control measures to be applied. Decisions on the final stabilization of a site through revegetation and plant establishment will again involve consideration of soil conditions. Organic matter and nutrient content, along with pH, density, and the water-holding capacity of the soil, are evaluated to determine the supplements that may be necessary to improve the growing environment.

IMPLICATIONS OF SOILS FOR SITE CONSTRUCTION

Earthwork

Almost all development involves altering the existing site topography. Excavation for utilities, grading for roadways, and general reshaping of the landscape to accommodate structural features are typical earthwork activities (Figure 7.1). The steepness to which a slope may be graded without construction of a retaining wall is dependent upon the shear strength of the exposed soils, maintenance considerations, and stabilization techniques. Where retaining walls are necessary, their design will be based on the engineering properties of the soil and on the presence or absence of additional groundwater or pore water pressures. Fill operations, including the method of soil placement and the type of compaction equipment, are specified according to the soil types to be handled. Soil conditions are also evaluated in determining the need for bracing or shoring of temporary excavations or for establishing slopes and benches for sidewalls when excavating trenches. Procedures and operations may vary on a construction site where soil conditions vary.

Footings and Foundations

The weight of a building or structure is supported by the soil beneath. Footings serve to transfer this weight or load safely to the soil. The design of a footing depends on the applied load and the nature of the underlying soil. Shallow foundations, including

Figure 7.1. Rough grading for a parking lot performed by a small bulldozer.

wall or spread footings, are generally used where firm soils are present or where light structures are to be supported. Deep foundations, including piles or caissons, are used where weaker surface soils are underlain by more stable soils or bedrock. *Piles* are vertical structural members made of steel or concrete, which are driven into the ground by a pile driver until there is significant resistance or bedrock is reached to support the intended load. *Caissons* are similar to piles. However, rather than being driven, caissons are constructed by drilling holes in the ground and filling them with concrete. Caissons are also constructed either to bedrock or to a depth where the bearing capacity of the soil is suitable to carry the structural load.

The prominent buildings on the New York City skyline are possible because massive foundations are supported on sound bedrock. Without such conditions, building weight and height would be limited. The Bell Tower of Pisa is a classic example of construction on poor foundation soils. The 16,170-ton (14,700-metric ton) structure was constructed on soft, marshy deposits of sandy and clayey silts. Because the deposits on the southern side of the tower contain more clay, the structure began to settle unevenly and lean even before construction was completed. Recently, through the controlled extraction of soil from the northern side of the tower, further movement has been halted and the angle of lean has been somewhat corrected.

Foundation walls that extend below the ground surface are designed for the soil loads exerted on them. Permissible loads vary with soil type and are increased where water may saturate the soil pores. Frequently, foundations and retaining walls must carry additional loads, or *surcharges*, in addition to the earth behind the walls. These surcharges exert additional pressure through the soil to the walls and must also be evaluated in the structural design. Examples of surcharge loads include slopes, stepped terracing, structures, and vehicular traffic.

Figure 7.2. The Leaning Tower of Pisa: an example of uneven settling due to contrasting soil conditions. *(photo: Corrie Rosen.)*

Drainage Requirements

Site drainage includes management of both surface and subsurface water. The relationship between water and soil needs to be understood for that management to be successful. Sandy,

noncohesive soils tend to be more erodible, more permeable, and easier to drain. Clayey soils tend to be more erosion resistant, less permeable, and more difficult to drain. Stratified soils that are composed of layers of both coarse- and fine-grained soils may present complex conditions that need to be evaluated in site design. For example, a sandy layer that is underlain by a less permeable silt or clay soil may hold water or transmit water laterally. If this layer is intercepted by the excavation of a building foundation, the seepage or flow of water out of the sandy layer may create undesirable effects unless drainage measures are provided.

GEOTECHNICAL EXPLORATION AND SOIL INVESTIGATION

Land Use Feasibility

Today, site planners have a large amount of information about natural resources available, which can aid in the evaluation of the suitability of a site for a particular land use. Topographic maps, geologic maps, hydrology and soil surveys have been prepared for many areas. For some locations, environmentally sensitive areas such as wetlands and floodplains have been delineated. With this resource information, planners can begin their feasibility assessment. Many county-based soil surveys published by the USDA contain soil suitability information for typical site development activities (Figure 7.3). By generally identifying the portions of a site that are suitable or unsuitable for development, the planner can prepare a conceptual site plan. This conceptual plan, along with the general resource information, serves as the basis for formulating the detailed geotechnical exploration and soils investigation plan needed to verify on-site conditions.

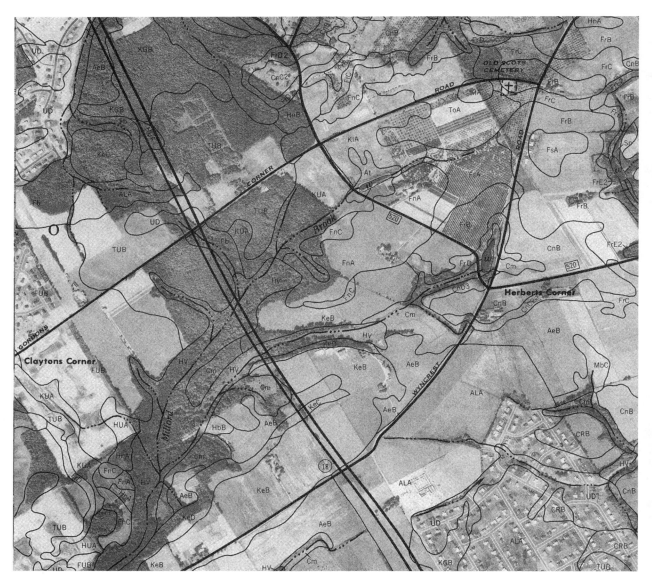

Figure 7.3. Example of a soil survey map. Soil series boundaries (referred to as *soil map units*) are delineated. Soil surveys are intended for a diverse audience ranging from farmers and foresters to planners and conservationists. To serve this broad spectrum of users, soil surveys provide extensive information in terms of soil properties, use, and management. Source: *Soil Survey of Monmouth County New Jersey, NRCS, USDA.*

Site-Specific Investigations

General resource information is typically prepared at a scale sufficient to broadly characterize an area. For example, the USDA soil delineation maps identify major soil series that may contain small areas that differ in physical properties. If these differing properties could impact the design or function of the planned improvements, their precise location needs to be determined through a detailed site-specific investigation. Geotechnical explorations are conducted to identify subsurface conditions and to gather samples for laboratory testing when data are needed by the structural designer. After review of the detailed investigation, the conceptual site plan is often refined to improve its feasibility. Structure locations may be adjusted or roadways realigned to better fit site conditions.

Critical Conditions

It is important to identify, through general inventories and detailed investigations, any critical conditions that could adversely impact the construction or integrity of the planned improvements. Critical conditions may include features unique to a particular region, such as acid soils, limestone sinkholes, perched groundwater tables, peat deposits, or organic soil deposits. Often these and other critical features are known to exist in an area, and it is important for the site investigation to be detailed enough to determine their presence and extent. It is far easier to accommodate critical conditions in planning than after construction has begun.

SOIL CHARACTERISTICS

Soil Phases

From the geotechnical or engineering viewpoint, soil may be defined as an accumulation of solid particles generated from the physical and chemical weathering of parent rock containing a network of voids that may be filled with either gas (air) or fluid (water). Soil, therefore, contains three phases: solids, water, and air. By separating soil into its three phases with a phase diagram, as shown in Figure 7.4, some general relationships may be illustrated. The total volume (V) of soil is equal to the volume of solids (V_s) plus the volume of voids (V_v). The volume of voids is equal to the volume of water (V_w) plus the volume of air (V_a). The total weight (W) of the soil is equal to the weight of solids (W_s) plus the weight of water (W_w) only, since the weight of air in the voids is considered negligible. From these relationships, several useful physical properties can be derived.

Physical Properties

There are many physical properties of a natural or in-situ soil that can be evaluated by soil experts to help determine the soil's suitability for various purposes. These properties can include particle size, shape, and mineralogy, along with structure, texture, color, organic matter content, pH, and others. Physical properties such as density, moisture content, and specific gravity provide useful information to geotechnical experts and reveals how the soil will behave or perform as a construction material.

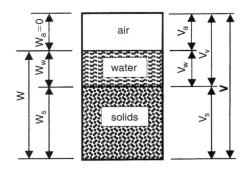

Figure 7.4. Soil phase diagram with basic volume and weight relationships.

Unit Weight and Bulk Density

The *unit weight* or *bulk density* of a soil is defined as the weight of the soil divided by its volume and is expressed in grams per cubic centimeter or pounds per cubic foot.

Water Content

The amount of water contained in the soil will influence the degree to which it can be worked or compacted in grading operations. As the water content, or moisture content, increases, soil will move from a solid state, through a semisolid state and a plastic state, to a liquid state. When all of the voids in a soil are filled with water, the soil is saturated.

Specific Gravity

The ratio of the unit weight of soil solids to the unit weight of water is defined as the *specific gravity* of the soil solids. Values range between 2.5 and 2.8, depending on the soil mineralogy, with a typical value of 2.65.

SOIL CLASSIFICATION

Classification Systems

Several classification systems have been developed to aid in identifying soils with similar characteristics or properties. The criteria and designations used within a particular system reflect the purpose for which the classification system was developed. For example, the American Association of State Highway and Transportation Officials (AASHTO) classification system groups soils based on suitability for roadway subgrades. Landscape architects are concerned with both the agronomic and engineering aspects of soil. Two important classification systems with which they should be familiar are the USDA Textural Classification System and the Unified Soil Classification System (USCS) as defined by the American Society for Testing and Materials (ASTM D-2487).

USDA Textural Classification System

The USDA system was first developed to describe soils for agricultural purposes. Textural designations are based on three major particle size groups: sand, silt, and clay. Sand is defined as particles ranging from 2.0 to 0.05 mm in diameter, silt from 0.05 to 0.002 mm, and clay as less than 0.002 mm. Based on the percentage of sand, silt, and clay in the soil mixture, there are 12 textural designations, as indicated by the textural triangle in Figure 7.5.

USCS (ASTM D-2487)

The USCS distinguishes soils based on their engineering performance as a construction material, and it considers texture, gradation, plasticity, and organic matter content. Broadly, soils are classified as coarse-grained, including gravels and sands; fine-grained, including silts and clays; or organic. Gravels and sands having little or no fines (particles less than 0.074 mm in size) are further described

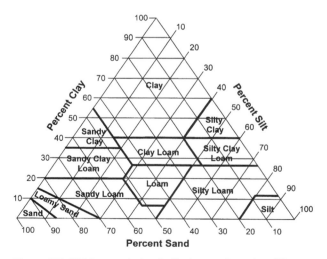

Figure 7.5. USDA textural triangle. The intersection point of lines drawn from each side of the triangle determines the soil texture classification. For example, a soil with 60% sand, 30% silt, and 10% clay is classified as a sandy loam.

Table 7.1 USCS Basic Soil Groups (ASTMD 2487)

Major Soil Division			Group Symbol	Group Name
Coarse-grained soils (more than 50% retained on No. 200 sieve)	Gravel (more than 50% of coarse fraction retained on No. 4 sieve)		GW	Well-graded gravel
			GP	Poorly graded gravel
			GM	Silty gravel
			GC	Clayey gravel
	Sands (50% or more of coarse fraction passes the No. 4 sieve)		SW	Well-graded sand
			SP	Poorly graded sand
			SM	Silty sand
			SC	Clayey sand
Fine-grained soils (50% or more passes the No. 200 sieve)	Liquid limit less than 50		CL	Lean clay (low plasticity)
			ML	Silt
			OL	Organic clay or silt
	Liquid limit 50 or more		CH	Fat clay (high plasticity)
			MH	Elastic silt
			OH	Organic clay or silt
Highly Organic Soils			PT	Peat

as well graded or poorly graded. Well-graded gravel and sands have a wide range of particle sizes, and poorly graded types have a very narrow range of particle sizes. Coarse-grained soils with fines and fine-grained soils are also subdivided according to the plasticity of the fine-grained fraction. The three major soil divisions of the USCS are divided into 15 basic soil groups, each indicated by a group symbol. These 15 soil groups are summarized in Table 7.1.

Grain Size Analysis

Classification systems generally describe soil particles as cobble, gravel, sand, silt, and clay, based on size. Although all systems do not include the full range of designations or have the same size criteria (Table 7.2), cobbles are typically particles larger than 76 mm (3 in.), gravel and sand are particles as small as 0.074 mm (No. 200 sieve) in size, and silt and clay are less than 0.074 mm in size.

Table 7.2 Comparison of Particle Size Classes (size in mm)

	USCS	USDA	AASHTO
Cobbles	76–300	76–250	—
Gravel	4.750–76.0	20.–76.0	2.0–76
Sand	0.075–4.750	0.05–2.0	0.075–2.0
Silt	<0.075	0.002–0.05	0.005–0.075
Clay	<0.075	<0.002	<0.005

Source: Adapted from USDA-NRCS, *Field Book for Describing and Sampling Solis.* (2002)

Particle sizes within a soil sample are determined through grain size analysis. Sieves with standard mesh openings are used for determining the grain size distribution of the sand and gravel fraction, and hydrometers are used to analyze the fines (silts and clays). Grain size distribution curves typically are plotted on the basis of the percentage of material by weight passing a particular sieve size.

Fine-Grained Soil Analysis

The engineering properties of coarse-grained soils having few fines can be largely ascribed to interparticle contact. As the percentage of fines increases, the plasticity characteristics of the finer fraction have a greater influence on these properties. Therefore, an additional analysis for fine-grained soils is necessary for classification with the USCS.

The consistency and behavior of fine-grained soils are affected by moisture content. Albert Atterberg, a Swedish soil scientist of the late 1800s and early 1900s, defined four states of consistency for a soil—solid, semisolid, plastic, and liquid—listed in order of increasing water content. The boundaries between these different soil states are referred to as the *Atterberg limits*, which are expressed in terms of moisture content. The *liquid limit* (LL) is the boundary between the plastic and liquid states. The *plastic limit* (PL) is the boundary between the semisolid and plastic states, and the *shrinkage limit* is the boundary between the solid and semisolid states. Detailed testing methods for determining the Atterberg limits have been established by ASTM D-4318: Standard Test Methods for Liquid Limit, Plastic Limit, and Plasticity Index of Soils, and standard testing procedures can be found in soil laboratory manuals.

ENGINEERING PROPERTIES OF SOILS

The properties that relate to a soil's suitability as a construction material are often termed *engineering properties*. Mineralogy, composition, structure, and moisture combine to influence the strength, permeability, and compressibility of a soil, which in turn will determine its performance as an engineering material.

Bearing Capacity

Bearing capacity is defined as what a soil is able to support. It is expressed in pounds per square foot or Newtons per square meter. Hard, sound rock has the highest bearing capacity, while saturated and organic soils have the lowest. If the bearing capacity of an existing soil cannot support the proposed load or structure, the soil must be removed and replaced with a suitable material or other engineering measures must be taken. Such measures include the use of piles, spread footings, floating slabs, and other structural techniques. Local building codes often prescribe allowable (or presumptive) bearing capacities for regional soil conditions (Table 7.3).

Shear Strength

Shear strength determines the stability of a soil and its ability to resist failure under loading. Shear strength is the result of internal friction and cohesion. *Internal friction* is the resistance to sliding between soil particles, and *cohesion* is the mutual attraction between particles due to moisture content and molecular forces. Under typical conditions, sand and gravel are considered cohesionless. Clay soils have high cohesion but little internal friction. As a general rule, the landforms constructed on cohesive (clay) soils require the use of lower slopes as the height of the form increases. Because of their internal friction, the shear strength of sand and gravel increases in relation to increased normal pressure; therefore, the angle of slope need not decrease with increased height.

Table 7.3 Presumptive Allowable Bearing Stress Values

Foundation Description	Allowable Stress
Crystalline Bedrock	12,000 psf
Sedimentary Rock	6,000 psf
Gravel or Sandy Gravel	5,000 psf
Sand, Silty Sand, Clayey Sand, Silty Gravel, Clayey Gravel	3,000 psf
Clay, Sandy Clay, Silty Clay, Clayey Silt	2,000 psf

Source: Building Officials and Code Administrators, Inc. (BOCA), *Basic Building Code*, 12th ed. (1993).

Slope failure occurs when shear stress exceeds shear strength. The reason for failure is either increased stress or decreased strength brought about by natural or human-induced activity. Examples of increased stress are situations in which the load at the top of a slope is increased or the lateral support at the base of a slope is removed through excavation or erosion. Decreased strength, as well as increased stress, occurs when the moisture content of the soil is increased. Care must be taken when construction takes place at the top or bottom of a relatively large slope, and particular attention must be given to the handling of storm runoff.

Frost Penetration

In northern climates, silty soils and soils with a wide, fairly evenly distributed range of particle sizes, referred to as *well-graded soils*, are subject to frost action. Damage to structures and roads due to frost action is caused by the movement of soil as it freezes and the loss of bearing capacity as it thaws. The soil expands as capillary water in the soil freezes, forming ice lenses. As the soil thaws, it becomes saturated and its strength decreases. The depth to which the soil will freeze depends on temperature, soil structure, and the presence of capillary water. Local building codes typically specify a minimum footing depth that is deeper than the expected maximum frost penetration for the region.

Shrinkage and Swell

Clay soils and soils containing clayey fines tend to shrink as they dry and expand as moisture content increases. The degree of volume change will depend on the mineralogy of the clay particles and the degree of moisture change. Highly plastic clays with very fine, or colloidal, particles that exhibit significant volume change are termed *expansive clays*. Where structural loadings are not high enough to

restrain swelling and movement, alternate cycles of shrink–swell can be damaging to foundations. The expansive properties of certain clays can be beneficial, however, when used to seal reservoirs or waste containment areas. The clay particles adsorb water, forming weak bonds with water molecules, and *swell* to fill voids and block free water movement.

STRUCTURAL SOILS

As pointed out in Chapter 2, soil as a biological medium has very different characteristics in terms of pore space and organic content than soils used for structural purposes. These disparate conditions come into conflict, particularly in urban settings such as plazas and streetscapes, where plantings, sidewalks, and other load-bearing pavements coexist. An additional problem in urban areas is the lack of adequate soil volumes to support the growth and health of trees.

An innovative approach, using what is referred to as *structural soil*, has been developed by the Urban Horticulture Institute at Cornell University to address load-bearing requirements, root growth, and adequate soil volumes. *Structural soil* is a mix of gap-graded angular crushed stone, clay loam soil, and hydrogel as a binding agent. *Gap-graded* means that the mix lacks stone in the midrange size (Figure 7.6). The crushed stone can be compacted to meet the necessary loading requirements, and the clay loam soil fills the large pore spaces. Plant roots are able to penetrate the pore spaces to access air and water, which promotes healthy root development.

Typically, trees are planted in isolated planting pits with a limited amount of soil. Structural soil allows a different approach to planting in the urban environment. With structural soil, the entire paving base course becomes a suitable medium for root growth development and thus significantly increases the soil volume available for planting.

Figure 7.6. Image of structural soil. Note the absence of sand, or midrange aggregate, in the soil mixture. *(Photo: Mathews Nielsen)*

Figure 7.7. Image of a lightweight soil-less growing medium for use in a rooftop sedum planting. Note the minimal organic content and the pores in the pumice stone that will help capture and retain moisture. *(Photo: Mathews Nielsen)*

LIGHTWEIGHT SOILS

As cities have become more densely developed, designers and planners have sought ways to make it possible to provide lushly planted landscapes throughout the urban environment. One of the major challenges to realizing this goal has been the expense of supporting dense moisture-retaining soils along with the loading of the plants themselves over structure. These structures can include existing buildings or piers, or new construction on structures ranging from housing to transportation infrastructure. Lightweight soils have been developed to support a range of plant life while minimizing the cost of structures required to support planting on structure.

Lightweight soils can be fabricated from a range of components, depending on the weight limitations of the structure or the goals for types of plant life the design hopes to support. For the lightest-weight installation, the growing medium is truly soil-less and is comprised of lightweight aggregate that might include pumice, expanded slate, vermiculite, or perlite, with a negligible organic component. This growing medium is best suited for plants adapted to rocky alpine conditions, like sedum. In installations where a greater load can be supported and a broader palette of plants is desired, other components are added, including sand, slow-release fertilizers, lime, and a range of organic components which might include regular topsoil, peat moss, composted bark mulch, and composted manure. The range of saturated soil weights can vary greatly, depending on the design, which is usually undertaken with a qualified soil scientist, from around 40 to over 100 lb/ft^3, depending on the soil mix.

Lightweight soil will be discussed in context as part of a green roof, or planting on structure, system in Chapter 9.

GEOTEXTILES

Types of Geotextiles

Geotextiles are synthetic fabrics with physical and engineering properties that are used to enhance soil properties or to improve structural performance. Geotextiles are a subset of *geosynthetics,* which also include geogrids (plastic nets or grids used for soil reinforcement), geomembranes (impervious rubber or plastic sheets used for water or vapor barriers), and geocomposites (a combination of a fabric, grid, or membrane, an example of which can be found in Figure 9.15). Geotextiles are woven or nonwoven (spun) fabrics of synthetic polymer fibers. Typical properties important to their use in construction include tensile strength, elongation, puncture resistance, and resistance to deterioration under ultraviolet light. For compatibility with the base soil in terms of water movement, apparent opening size and permeability of the fabric are also important properties.

Geotextile Applications

Geotextiles have many different applications in construction. The type of material selected should be based on the application, soil conditions, and expected loadings. The four functional applications for geotextiles are drainage, filtration, reinforcement, and separation.

Drainage denotes the ability of the geotextile to convey water within the plane of the fabric. Thicker nonwoven fabrics are suited to this purpose but woven fabrics are not. Geotextiles may be placed in layers of fine-grained soils to help remove or intercept excess soil water.

Filtration is the ability of the geotextile to allow water movement through the plane of the fabric while preventing the movement of soil particles. Both the apparent opening size of the fabric and permeability are important considerations. If the openings are too small, the geotextile may clog with soil particles and become a barrier to water movement. Gravel-filled drainage trenches may be lined with a geotextile that allows water to pass into the trench but prevents soil movement.

Reinforcement indicates the ability of the geotextile to distribute imposed loadings to the underlying soil, such as in road construction, where soft foundation soils are present.

Separation is the ability of the geotextile to prevent the mixing of two different materials during installation or is used where mixing would be detrimental. Geotextiles are sometimes placed over gravel on which concrete will be placed to prevent the movement of the cement paste into the voids while still permitting the movement of water.

Many applications for geotextiles involve a combination of two or more of these functions. For example, a geotextile may be placed under rock riprap along a stream bank to provide filtration (allowing water movement from the soil into the stream) and separation (preventing the mixing of the rock with the base soil).

CONSTRUCTION SEQUENCE FOR GRADING

There are four general phases to earthwork activities during construction of a project: (1) site preparation, (2) bulk excavation or rough grading, (3) backfilling and fine grading, and (4) finish surfacing. Some or all of these phases may be necessary, depending on site conditions and the scope of the project.

Site Preparation

The four areas of concern in preparing a site for grading are protection of the existing vegetation and structures that are to remain, removal and storage of topsoil, erosion and sediment control, and clearing and demolition. Of course, not all four procedures may apply to every project.

Protection of Vegetation

For the most part, this phase of preparation is self-explanatory. However, as pointed out earlier, any disturbance within the drip line of trees that are to remain should be avoided. This refers not only to cutting and filling, but also to the storage of materials and movement of equipment, since this will result in increased compaction and reduced aeration of the root zones of trees and shrubs.

Topsoil Removal

The upper soil layer usually contains substantial amounts of organic matter and nutrients resulting from biological activity and the decay of vegetation. Because of its value to plant reestablishment, topsoil is usually stripped from areas where the layer is of sufficient thickness and saved in stockpiles for use in finish grading. Stripping should occur only within the limits of the construction area. If the topsoil is to be stockpiled for an extended period, it should be seeded with an annual grass to reduce loss resulting from erosion. Under ideal conditions, the topsoil will not be stockpiled for longer than 6 months and will not be piled higher than 4 ft (1.3 m).

Erosion and Sediment Control

Many states have enacted standards for soil erosion and sediment control, particularly for new construction. Temporary control measures, which are discussed further in Chapter 10, should be used as appropriate to divert runoff away from disturbed areas, to provide surface stabilization, and to filter, trap, and collect sediment. These measures should comply with all regulatory requirements and standards.

Clearing and Demolition

Buildings, pavements, and other structures that interfere with the proposed development must be removed prior to the start of construction. The same is true for interfering trees and shrubs as well as any debris that may be found on the site.

Placement of Grade Stakes

The last step in preparing a site for excavation is the placement of grade stakes. Grade stakes indicate the amount of cut or fill necessary to achieve the proposed subgrade.

Bulk Excavation

The bulk excavation or rough grading phase is the stage at which major earthmoving and shaping takes place (Figure 7.8a). The extent to which bulk excavation is necessary depends on the scale and complexity of the project. Bulk excavation includes shaping of the basic earth form along with providing footing and foundation excavations for all structures. In some projects, structure excavation may be identified as a separate item if specialized construction equipment, different from the bulk excavation equipment, is required.

Backfilling and Fine Grading

Once the rough grade has been achieved and structures have been built, backfilling and fine grading may proceed (Figure 7.8b). Activities include backfilling excavations for structures, such as retaining walls and building foundations, and filling utility trenches for water mains, sewer lines, and so forth. All backfills must be properly compacted to minimize future settlement problems and must be executed in a manner that does not damage utilities or structures. Fine grading is conducted to ensure that the earth forms and surfaces have been properly shaped and that the subgrade has been brought to the correct elevation (Figure 7.9).

Finish Surfacing

To complete the project, the surfacing material is installed (Figure 7.8c). Usually, the hard surfaces,

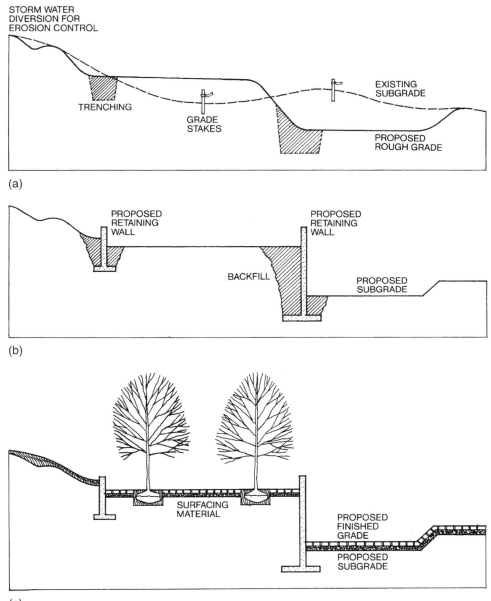

Figure 7.8. Grading sequence. (a) Rough grading is the phase in which major earth shaping and excavation occur. (b) All utility trenches and structures are backfilled and the subgrade is brought to the proper elevation during the backfilling and fine grading phases. (c) Under the finished grading phase all surfacing materials, such as pavements and topsoil, are placed.

Figure 7.9. The prepared base course establishes the subgrade for asphalt pavement that will become the surfacing material.

Figure 7.10. Highly controlled fill. Poor-quality soil has been removed and replaced with granular soil (predominantly sand) with a high load-bearing capacity for an entry drive and a parking lot.

like pavements, are installed first, and then the topsoil is placed. Salvaged and, if necessary, new topsoil is spread in areas to be revegetated. The subsoil is typically roughened or scarified to allow the topsoil to bond better to the surface and to promote root growth between the soil layers. Since topsoil and pavements represent finish material, the final grade of the surface of these materials must agree with the proposed finished grades (contours and spot elevations) indicated on the grading plan.

PLACING AND COMPACTING SOILS

Fill Materials

The equipment and procedures used in the placement of fill may vary, depending on the type of material and the purpose of the fill. Where a fill area is to serve as the subgrade for a structure or roadway, placement is closely controlled to ensure a stable foundation and to avoid differential settlement (Figure 7.10). Fill is spread in uniform layers of a specified thickness, called *lifts*, with each layer compacted by equipment best suited for the

fill material. The material itself is usually held to a uniform consistency and moisture content. Bulk or uncontrolled fill placement may be acceptable in certain locations, depending on the future use of the area.

Compaction

Many of the engineering properties of soil related to the stability of structures are enhanced through *compaction*, which is the densification of soil by decreasing the voids. Increasing the density of a soil through compaction increases its bearing capacity and shear strength.

Moisture content plays a significant role in determining the degree to which a soil can be compacted. If the same compaction effort is applied to three samples of the same soil—one dry, one moist, and one saturated—three different densities will likely result. In a dry sample, particles must be crushed and rearranged to reduce or fill void space. In a saturated sample, water fills the voids and, since it is incompressible, limits compaction. In a moist soil, there is enough water to facilitate the movement of particles without filling all of the voids. For each soil type there is an optimum moisture content and a maximum density that can be achieved for a given compaction effort. Two standardized test procedures are commonly used to determine soil density: the Standard Proctor Test (ASTM D 698) and the Modified Proctor Test (ASTM D 1557). The tests differ in the amount of energy applied to the soil; higher energy and higher degrees of compaction are achieved with the Modified procedure.

Equipment used to compact soil varies with the soil type. Vibratory steel drum equipment is used to compact most sandy soils (Figure 7.11). Vibration helps to shake and rearrange particles to reduce void space. Fine sands and nonplastic silts are compacted with the use of heavy rubber-tired rollers. Clayey soils are best compacted by kneading, which is accomplished with the use of a sheeps-foot roller.

Although necessary for the structural improvements at a site, compaction can adversely impact landscape features. Often the density necessary for a sound foundation is restrictive to root growth (Table 7.4). Fills and areas traversed by heavy construction equipment must be scarified or reopened to the expected rooting depth of the vegetation to be established at the end of construction. Reopening the soil improves permeability and aeration, both necessary for healthy vegetation. Good construction management and the prohibition of construction equipment and vehicles at areas to be planted will help to avoid unnecessary problems.

Figure 7.11. Earthmoving and compacting equipment. The tractor-scraper has self-loading, hauling, and spreading capabilities. Dozers are used for clearing, rough grading, cutting, and filling. Steel-wheeled rollers are used to compact coarse materials, such as sand and crushed stone, and asphalt pavement.

removal of topsoil through its final placement may be included in a single specification. Where earthwork is a critical or major component, there may be a detailed specification developed for each phase: topsoil removal, bulk excavation, structure excavation, earth fill, structure backfill, final shaping and grading, and so on. Generally, the specifications should define the scope of the work; describe the limits of excavation and identify the use or disposal of the materials; characterize suitable fill materials, whether from on-site or off-site sources, along with placement and compaction requirements; and describe the finish grading requirements. Many specifications also define how the features of the work will be evaluated as the basis for approval and payment.

EARTHWORK SPECIFICATIONS

Content

Earthwork specifications must adequately describe the materials and placement procedures necessary for a project. Where earthwork is a minor component of the overall work, all phases from initial

Critical Issues

Specifications should address both performance and safety concerns. Where materials must perform within certain tolerances, such as fill that will support a building foundation, it is important that

Table 7.4 General Relationship of Soil Bulk Density to Root Growth Based on Soil Texture

Soil Texture	Ideal Bulk Densities (g/cm³)	Bulk Densities That May Affect Root Growth (g/cm³)	Bulk Densities That Restrict Root Growth (g/cm³)
Sands, loamy sands	<1.60	1.69	>1.80
Sandy loams, loams	<1.40	1.63	>1.80
Sandy clay loams, loams, clay loams	<1.40	1.60	>1.75
Silts, silt loams	<1.30	1.60	>1.75
Silt loams, silty clay loams	<1.10	1.55	>1.65
Sandy clays, silty clays, some clay loams (35–45% clay)	<1.10	1.49	>1.58
Clays (>45% clay)	<1.10	1.39	>1.47

Source: NRCS Soil Quality Institute, *Soil Quality Test Kit Guide*. USDA, Agricultural Research Service and NRCS (1999).

the specifications detail the construction requirements that must be met, such as density, moisture content, bearing capacity, and the like. Provisions requiring that on-site testing be conducted to verify compliance should be incorporated into the specifications. Where appropriate, reference standards and specifications, such as those of the American Society for Testing and Materials (ASTM) and the state departments of transportation (DOT), should be used to establish the nature and quality of materials and the standard testing methods and criteria. Specifications must address safety requirements as well. Construction sites, particularly those involving open excavations or trenching, can pose hazards to workers and the public. As a minimum, most specifications address safety issues by incorporating references to standards published by the Occupational Safety and Health Administration (OSHA).

CHAPTER 8

Earthwork

This chapter is concerned with grading operations and the calculation of cut-and-fill volumes. Methods of earthmoving and earthmoving equipment are not discussed. The following section defines

the basic terminology associated with earthwork (Figure 8.1).

DEFINITIONS

Finished Grade

The final grade after all landscape development has been completed. It is the top surface of lawns, planting beds, pavements, and so on, and is normally designated by contours and spot elevations on a grading plan.

Subgrade

The top of the material on which the surface material, such as topsoil and pavements (including base material), is placed. Subgrade is represented by the top of a fill situation and the bottom of a cut excavation. *Compacted subgrade* refers to a subgrade that must attain a specified density, whereas

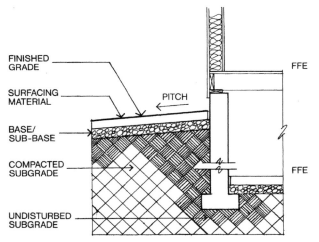

Figure 8.1. Grading terminology.

undisturbed subgrade indicates a soil that has not been excavated or changed in any way.

Base/Sub-base

Imported material (normally coarse or fine aggregate) that is typically placed under pavements.

Finished Floor Elevation

Usually the elevation of the first floor of a structure but may be used to designate the elevation of any floor. The relationship of the finished floor elevation to the exterior finished grade depends on the type of construction.

Cut/Cutting

The process of removing soil. Proposed contours extend across existing contours in the uphill direction.

Fill/Filling

The process of adding soil. Proposed contours extend across existing contours in the downhill direction. When the fill material must be imported to the site, it is often referred to as *borrow* (Figure 8.2).

Compaction

The densification of soil under controlled conditions, particularly a specified moisture content.

Topsoil

Normally the top layer of a soil profile, which may range in thickness from less than 1 in. (25 mm) to more than 1 ft (300 mm). Because of its high organic content, it is subject to decomposition and therefore is not an appropriate subgrade material for structures.

GRADING OPERATIONS

There are two basic ways in which a proposed grading plan may be achieved. The first is to balance

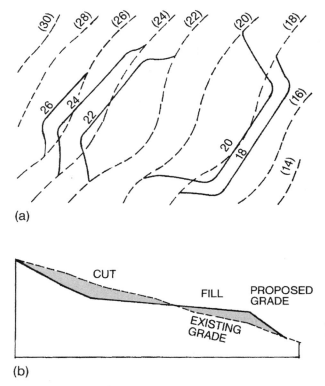

(a)

(b)

Figure 8.2. Cut and fill. (a) Plan indicating existing and proposed contour lines. Cutting occurs where the proposed contours move in the uphill direction, while filling occurs where they move in the downhill direction. (b) Section showing where there is a change from cut to fill and where proposed grades return to existing grades. Both of these conditions are referred to as *no cut–no fill.*

the amount of cut and fill required on the site. This may be accomplished by cutting and filling in the same operation—in other words, excavating or scraping, moving, and depositing the soil in one operation. An alternative method, which may be necessary, depending on the scale and complexity of the project, is to stockpile the cut material and then place it in the fill areas as required. In either case, the cut material must be suitable as fill.

The second method is to import or export soil to satisfy the cut and fill requirements. This results when cut and fill do not balance on the site or when the cut material is unsuitable as fill material. Obviously, balancing cut and fill on site is the less costly option and normally the most energy efficient.

If it is not possible to balance cut and fill on a site, the question arises as to which is more desirable: importing fill material (*borrow*) or exporting cut material. There is no general consensus among professionals, and the answer is somewhat dependent on location, scale of the project, and soil conditions. However, the authors feel that it is preferable to export soil for the following reasons.

First, importing soil tends to be more expensive, since it requires purchasing the material, hauling it to the site, and then placing and properly compacting it. Second is the condition that importing material indicates: more of the site is in fill than in cut. This is important because a fill condition is generally structurally less stable than a cut condition and is more susceptible to erosion and settlement. To reduce the potential for settlement, costly compaction methods may be necessary or, in critical situations, special footings may have to be used for structures. Other factors influencing the cost of grading are the size and shape of the site, intricacy of the grading plan, and types of soil. The size, shape, and scale of a project influence labor and equipment requirements, whereas earth forms and grading tolerances influence the amount of detail and accuracy necessary in executing the design. Soil conditions will also affect the type of equipment used and the suitability of the soil for the proposed uses.

COMPUTATION OF CUT-AND-FILL VOLUMES

Estimates must be made of cut and fill volumes to establish construction costs and to determine whether the volumes balance or whether more cut or fill will be required. There are several methods for calculating volumes, three of which are the average end area, contour area, and borrow pit (grid) methods. All the methods provide only an *approximation,* since actual cut-and-fill volumes are rarely the straight-edged geometric solids on which the computations are based. It should also be noted that computer programs exist for each of these methods.

Average End Area Method

The average end area method is best suited for lineal construction, such as roads, paths, and utility trenching. The formula states that the volume of cut (or fill) between two adjacent cross sections is the average of the two sections multiplied by the distance between them.

$$V = [(A_1 + A_2) / 2] \times L \qquad (8.1)$$

where
A_1 and A_2 = end sections, in ft^2 (m^2)
V = volume, in ft^3 (m^3)
L = distance between A_1 and A_2, in ft (m)

To apply the method, cross sections must be taken at selected or predetermined intervals. The shorter the interval between sections, the more accurate the estimate will be. Each cross section indicates the existing and proposed grades. Typically, the sections are drawn with the vertical scale exaggerated 5 to 10 times the horizontal scale. The area between the existing and proposed grades is measured, keeping cut separate from fill. Methods for measuring areas include planimeter, digitized computer-aided design (CAD) information, geometry, and grids. The last step is to average the area of the two adjacent sections and then multiply by the distance between them to determine the volume in cubic feet or cubic meters. To convert to cubic yards—the standard unit of measurement for earthwork volumes in the U.S. Customary

Table 8.1 Data for Example 8.1

Station	Area (ft²)	Average (ft²)	Distance (ft)	Volume (ft³)
2+00	0			
2+50	101	50.5	50	2,525
3+00	40	70.5	50	3,525
3+25	0	20.0	25	500
				6,550

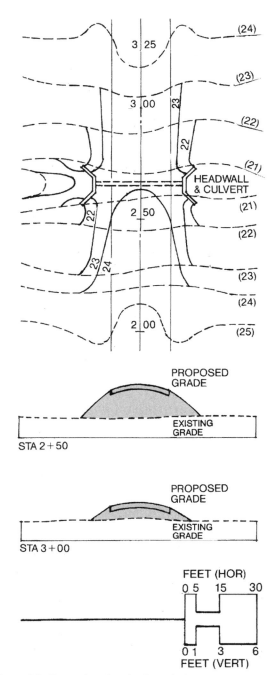

system—cubic feet must be divided by 27 ft³/yd³. The information is usually organized in tabular form, as illustrated in Table 8.1.

▪ EXAMPLE 8.1

A portion of an existing road is to be regraded to accommodate a new inlet, as illustrated in Figure 8.3. Determine the volume of fill required. For the purpose of this problem, stations 2+00 and 3+25 are considered points of no cut–no fill.

SOLUTION

The first step is to select an interval between cross sections and to locate the sections on the plan. An interval of 50 ft is selected for this example, and sections are taken at stations 2+50 and 3+00. The sections are drawn indicating the existing and proposed grades, with the vertical scale exaggerated five times. Next, the areas of the sections are measured. Usually areas are measured in square inches and then converted to square feet based on the horizontal and vertical scales of the drawing. In this case, 1 in.² = 30 ft × 6 ft = 180 ft². Since there is no cut or fill at station 2+00, the average sectional area between stations 2+00 and 2+50 is

$$\frac{0 + 101 \text{ ft}^2}{2} = 50.5 \text{ ft}^2$$

Figure 8.3. Plan and sections for Example 8.1.

The volume is now determined by multiplying the average area by the distance between the sections:

$$50.5 \text{ ft}^2 \times 50 \text{ ft} = 2{,}525 \text{ ft}^3$$

The volume between stations 2+50 and 3+00 is

$$\frac{101 + 40}{2} \times 50 = 3{,}525 \text{ ft}^3$$

The last volume to be calculated is between stations 3+00 and 3+25. Again, there is no change in grade at station 3+25.

$$\frac{40 + 0}{2} \times 25 = 500 \text{ ft}^3$$

Notice that the interval between the last two sections is only 25 ft. The data for this example are summarized in Table 8.1.

The result obtained in Example 8.1 significantly overestimates the total volume. This is true because the two end sections are actually conical or pyramidal, for which the volume is $A/3 \times L$, rather than $(A_1 + A_2)/2 \times L$. A difference of 50% for the end volumes is caused by the simplification. When the conical (or pyramidal) formula is used, the volumes for Example 8.1 become 1,683, 3,525, and 333 ft^3 for a total of 5,541 ft^3. Note that the previously computed end volumes of 2,525 and 500 ft^3 are 1.5 times 1,683 and 333 ft^3, respectively.

When a project has many sections, this detail is usually disregarded because of the inherent inaccuracy of volume computations. However, where only a few sections are needed (as in the example), it is advisable to use the conical formula.

Regardless of the formulas used, the average end area method tends to overestimate volumes. ■

■ EXAMPLE 8.2

The plan for Example 8.1 has been converted to metric measurements for Example 8.2. (Figure 8.4).

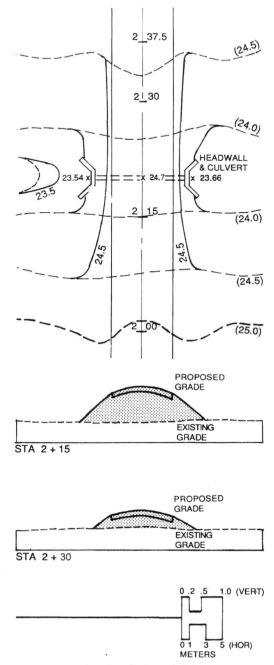

Figure 8.4. Plan and sections for Example 8.2.

Table 8.2 Data for Example 8.2

Station	Area (m²)	Average (m²)	Distance (m)	Volume (m³)
2+00	0			
2+15	9.38	4.69	15	70.35
2+30	3.72	6.55	15	98.25
2+37.5	0	1.86	7.5	13.95
				182.55

Computations, based on 30.0-m stations and fractions thereof, are summarized in Table 8.2.

Since the calculations in Table 8.2 are based upon 30.0 m (98.43 ft), the volumes in Examples 8.1 and 8.2 cannot be directly compared. However, in examining the process, the following comparison can be made of the results. First the volumes must be converted to similar units. The conversion is computed as follows:

$$182.55 \, \text{m}^3 \times 35.315 \, \text{ft}^3/\text{m}^3 = 6,446.75 = 6,447 \, \text{ft}^3$$

The 15.0-m interval represents 98.43% (49.215/50 = 0.9843) of the original dimension of 50 ft used in Example 8.1. If the volume determined in Example 8.1 is adjusted by this percentage, a reasonable comparison can be achieved with results of Example 8.2 (6,550 × 0.9843 = 6,447 ft³). ■

Contour Area Method

This method is appropriate for large, relatively uncomplicated grading plans and may also be used to calculate volumes of water in ponds and lakes. To apply this method, the first step is to establish the no cut–no fill line and then to separate the area of cut from the area of fill. The next step is to measure the horizontal area of change for *each* contour line within the no cut–no fill limit, keeping areas of cut separate from areas of fill. In other words, measure the area bounded by the same numbered existing and proposed contour lines. Finally, the

Table 8.3 Contour Area Measurements

Contour Number	Area of Cut (ft²)	Area of Fill (ft²)
67	0	64
68	0	176
69	0	376
70	0	460
71	0	748
72	284	1,056
73	360	336
74	464	0
75	172	0
Total	1,280	3,216

volumes of cut and fill can be calculated by applying the following formula:

$$V = A_1 h/3 + (A_1 + A_2)h/2$$
$$+ \cdots (A_{n-1} + A_n)h/2 + A_n h/3 \quad \textbf{(8.2)}$$

where
A_1, A_2, A_n = area of horizontal change for each contour in ft²(m²)

h = vertical distance between areas in ft (m)

The first and last terms on the right-hand side of the equation are considered conical or pyramidal solids, as shown by the shaded areas in section in Figure 8.5. The volume of such a solid $(A/3)h$ was given in the preceding example. If the altitude h is equal to the contour interval i, the equation can be simplified as follows:

$$V = i(5/6A_1 + A_2 + A_3 + \cdots 5/6A_n) \quad \textbf{(8.3)}$$

Because of the approximate nature of computing earthwork, the equation can be further simplified to:

$$V = i(A_1 + A_2 + A_3 + \cdots A_n) \quad \textbf{(8.4)}$$

However, using this final form of the equation will result in overestimated earthwork volumes. For ease of computation, the information should be organized as shown in Table 8.3.

■ EXAMPLE 8.3

Figure 8.5 illustrates a slope that has been regraded to accommodate a small plateau area. Using the contour area method, calculate the volumes of cut and fill required.

SOLUTION

As noted, the first step is to delineate the extent of the earthwork by a no cut–no fill line and to separate the area of cut from the area of fill, followed by measuring the area of change for each contour line. This

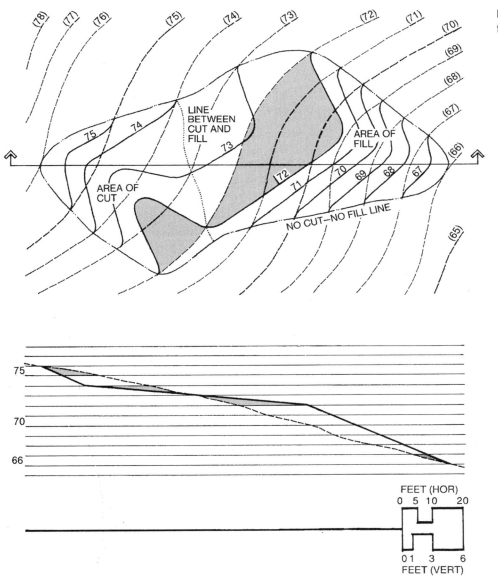

Figure 8.5. Plan and sections for Example 8.3.

is demonstrated by the shaded areas for the 72-ft contour line. The areas for each contour line are recorded in Table 8.3. The last step is to multiply the total areas by the contour interval, in this case 1 ft, and divide by 27 ft³/yd³ to convert the volumes to cubic yards, as shown in the examples below:

1,280 × 1/27 = 47.41 yd³ cut
3,216 × 1/27 = 119.11 yd³ fill ■

Borrow Pit Method

The borrow pit method, sometimes referred to as the *grid method*, is appropriate for complex grading projects and urban conditions. Existing elevations are determined at each grid intersection on the site by borrow pit leveling normally done in preparation for contour mapping, as described in Chapter 4. If such elevations are not available but a contour map of the project site has been prepared, a grid is placed over the area to be regraded. Care must be taken in determining the size and location of the grid on the site. The estimate becomes more accurate as the size of the grid decreases, and in some cases it may even be appropriate to break up the area into two or more parts, each with a different-sized grid. Existing and proposed grades are determined at each grid intersection by inter-polation and the difference between elevations calculated. A notational system should be used to distinguish fill from cut, such as *F* and *C*. From this point there are two ways to proceed.

The first approach is to apply the borrow pit method on a cell-by-cell basis. An average change in elevation is calculated for each cell by determin-ing the difference in elevation for all four corners of each cell, as illustrated in Figure 8.6, adding all four differences and dividing by 4. The volume is calculated by adding all the averaged values together, keeping cut and fill separate, and multi-plying by the area of one grid cell.

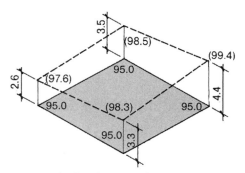

Figure 8.6. Example of single grid cell for the borrow pit method. Plans for a borrow pit grid are illustrated in Figures 4.5 and 8.7.

■ EXAMPLE 8.4

The grid of spot elevations illustrated in Figure 4.5 is shown in Figure 8.7a with the resulting contour lines. For this problem, a rectangular area bounded by corners B2, B5, D2, and D5 is to be excavated with vertical sides to a finished elevation of 95.0. Calculate the volume of the excavation using the borrow pit method. For identification purposes the six cells are numbered in Figure 8.7a.

SOLUTION

The first step is to determine the difference in eleva-tion between the existing and proposed grades. This is demonstrated (Figure 8.6) for cell No. 1 as follows:

Corner: B2 98.5 − 95.0 = 3.5 ft
　　　　 B3 99.4 − 95.0 = 4.4 ft
　　　　 C2 97.6 − 95.0 = 2.6 ft
　　　　 C3 98.3 − 95.0 = 3.3 ft

Next, the differences are totaled and divided by 4 to calculate the average:

$$\frac{3.5 + 4.4 + 2.6 + 3.3}{4} = \frac{13.8}{4} = 3.45 \text{ ft avg.}$$

The same procedure is applied to the remain-ing five cells with the following results:

Cell No. 2: 3.475 ft avg.
Cell No. 3: 2.50 ft avg.

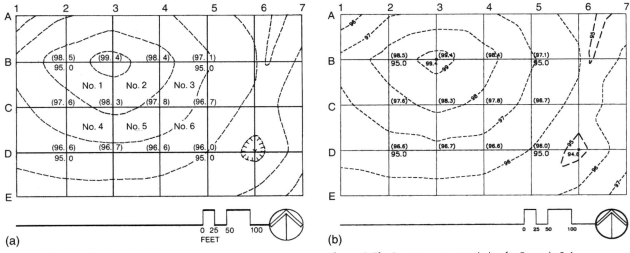

Figure 8.7a. Plan for Example 8.4.

Figure 8.7b. Computer-generated plan for Example 8.4.

Site Volume Table: Unadjusted							
Site	Stratum	Surf1	Surf2	Cut yards	Fill yards	Net yards	Method
SITE1							
	SITE	EG	EG1				
				5607	0	5607 (C)	Grid
				5877	0	5877 (C)	End area
				5851	0	5851 (C)	Prismoidal

(c)

Figure 8.7c. Summary of earthwork volumes calculated by computer. *(Software: Softdesk Civil/Survey Pack: Earthworks Version 7.21)*

Cell No. 4: 2.30 ft avg.
Cell No. 5: 2.35 ft avg.
Cell No. 6: 1.775 ft avg.

The final step is to add up the averages for all the cells and to multiply by the area of one cell (100 ft × 100 ft = 10,000 ft²).

$$3.45 + 3.475 + 2.50 + 2.30 + 2.35 + 1.775$$
$$= 15.85 \text{ ft}$$

$$15.85 \times 10,000 = 158,500 \text{ ft}^3$$

$$158,500/27 = 5,870.37 \text{ yd}^3$$

Since earthwork computations are only approximate, this may be rounded to 5,900 yd³.

Figure 8.7b is the same as Figure 8.7a except that the interpolation process and resulting contour lines have been done by computer. Notice that there are some minor discrepancies between the two contour plans. This variation may be attributed to the interpolation routines of the computer software.

From the digital data input for Figure 8.7b, unadjusted cut volumes were calculated by computer using three different methods: grid, end area, and prismoidal. The computer output is summarized in Figure 8.7c. The differences in volume for the three methods reinforce the fact that these values are estimations and that different methods will yield different results. The variation between the computer and noncomputer values for the grid method may be attributed partially to the difference in the interpolation for the contour plans.

The second approach is derived by simplifying the equation of the first approach by common factoring. The advantage of this procedure is that it reduces the number of calculations required.

$$V = \frac{A}{4} \times (1h_1 + 2h_2 + 3h_3 + 4h_4) \quad \textbf{(8.5)}$$

where

V = volume of cut (or fill) in ft³(m³)
A = area of one grid cell in ft²(m²)
h_1 = sum of the cuts (or fills) for all grid corners common to one grid cell
h_2 = sum of the cuts (or fills) for all grid corners common to two grid cells
h_3 = sum of the cuts (or fills) for all grid corners common to three grid cells
h_4 = sum of the cuts (or fills) for all grid corners common to four grid cells

This process is demonstrated in the following example. ■

■ **EXAMPLE 8.5**

Using Example 8.4, the volume of excavation is now calculated by the simplified equation.

SOLUTION

There are four corners that appear in only *one* grid cell of the area to excavated: B2, B5, D2, and D5. The depth of cut for these corners is obtained by subtracting the proposed finished elevation from the existing elevation: 98.5 – 95.0 = 3.5 ft for B2. The

remaining three cuts are 2.1, 1.6, and 1.0. The sum of h_1 is 3.5 + 2.1 + 1.6 + 1.0, which equals 8.2 ft.

Proceeding clockwise, the corners common to two grid cells of the excavated area are B3, B4, C5, D4, D3, and C2. The depths of cut for these corners are 4.4, 3.4, 1.7, 1.6, 1.7, and 2.6, again obtained by subtracting the proposed finished elevation, 95.0 ft, from the existing grades. The sum of h_2 is 15.4 ft.

There are two corners common to four grid cells within the area to be graded: C3 and C4. The sum of h_4 is 3.3 + 2.8, which equals 6.1 ft. There are no corners common to three grid cells. Since all 12 corners of the grid have been accounted for, the values may be substituted into the formula. Again, each cell measures 100 ft × 100 ft; therefore, the area of each cell equals 10,000 ft².

$$V = \frac{A}{4}(1h_1 + 2h_2 + 3h_3 + 4h_4)$$
$$= \frac{10,000}{4}(1 \times 8.2 + 2 \times 15.4 + 3 \times 0.0 + 4 \times 6.1)$$
$$= 2500(8.2 + 30.8 + 0.0 + 24.4)$$
$$= 158,500 \text{ ft}^3$$
$$= \frac{158,500}{27} = 5,870.37 \text{ yd}^3$$

For estimating purposes this may again be rounded upward to 5,900 yd³.

The method works the same way for fill, except that the height of fill required for each corner is determined by subtracting the existing elevation from the proposed finished elevation. Where a project consists partially of cut and partially of fill, the cut and fill are determined separately and the net volume of cut or fill can then be computed. ■

Adjusting Cut-and-Fill Volumes

Two adjustments must be made in determining cut-and-fill volumes. The first is concerned with surface materials, while the second involves the compaction and shrinkage of soil volumes.

For estimating purposes, cut-and-fill volumes are determined between existing and proposed subgrades, *not* between existing and proposed finished grades. However, contour lines and spot elevations on grading plans and topographic surveys usually indicate finished grade conditions. As a result, compensation must be made for both the existing surface material to be removed and the proposed surfacing material to be installed. This may be accomplished in a variety of ways, a few of which will be discussed. It is important, however, to understand the following basic principles:

1. In cut, proposed surfacing material (including pavement and topsoil) *increases* the amount of excavation required.

2. In fill, proposed surfacing material *decreases* the amount of borrow required.

3. In cut, the removal of existing pavement or the stripping of topsoil *decreases* the volume of soil to be removed.

4. In fill, the removal of existing pavement or the stripping of topsoil *increases* the volume of soil to be placed.

These principles are illustrated in Figure 8.8. It should be noted that where the depths of the proposed and existing surface materials are the same, they are self-compensating and no adjustment is required. With both the average end area and borrow pit methods, it is possible to incorporate the adjustment directly into the volume calculations. For the average end area method, the cross sections may be drawn indicating the existing and proposed subgrades rather than finished grades. For the borrow pit method, the spot elevations indicated at the grid corners could be based on the proposed and existing subgrades.

Another alternative is simply to measure the plan area of the surface material, keeping areas within cut separate from areas within fill, and multiply by the depth of the material to calculate

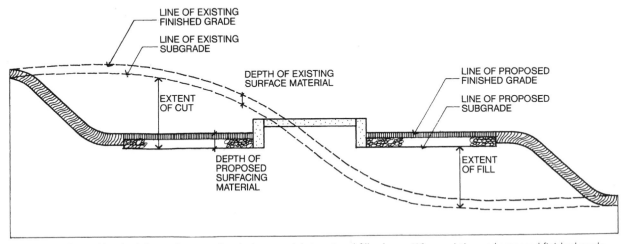

Figure 8.8. Relationship of existing and proposed surfacing materials to cut-and-fill volumes. Where existing and proposed finished grade elevations, rather than subgrade elevations, are used to compute volumes, make the following adjustments: Gross cut volume − existing surfacing material volume + proposed surfacing material volume = Adjusted cut volume. Gross fill volume + Existing surfacing volume − proposed surfacing material volume = Adjusted fill volume.

the volume. The volume may be added to or subtracted from the cut or fill volumes as described in the principles above. This technique is illustrated in Example 8.6.

◼ EXAMPLE 8.6

Again, using the data from Example 8.4, the volume of excavation is to be adjusted based on the following information. There is an existing 6-in. layer of topsoil that must be stripped before excavation can begin. The proposed 95.0-ft finished elevation is the top of a 6-in. concrete slab with a 4-in. gravel base.

SOLUTION

The topsoil to be stripped reduces the gross volume of excavation. The volume of topsoil is the area (60,000 ft^2) multiplied by the depth (0.5 ft).

$$60,000 \times 0.5 = 30,000 \text{ ft}^3$$

$$30,000/27 = 1,111.11 \text{ yd}^3 \text{ or } 1,110 \text{ yd}^3$$

On the other hand, the depth of the excavation must be increased by 10 in. (0.83 ft) to accommodate the concrete slab and base course. The resulting increased cut volume is

$$60,000 \times 0.83 = 49,800 \text{ ft}^3$$

$$\frac{49,800}{27} = 1,844.44 \text{ yd}^3 \text{ or } 1,840 \text{ yd}^3$$

The final adjusted volume is determined as follows:

5,900 yd^3(gross cut) + 1,840 yd^3(proposed surfacing) − 1,110 yd^3(existing topsoil) = 6,630 yd^{3}adjusted volume

The second factor affecting cut-and-fill volumes is the change in soil volume as a result of compaction and shrinkage. Usually *in-place* volumes of cut, referred to as *bank yards*, will yield less than their volume in fill by 10 to 20%, depending on soil type and compaction techniques. This means that 100 yd^{3}of cut will yield approximately only 80 to 90 yd^{3}of fill. Therefore, to balance cut and fill on a site, a 100-yd^{3}fill would require approximately 110 to 125 yd^{3}of cut. For cost estimating purposes, fill volumes, referred to as *compacted yards*, should be increased by 10 to 20%, depending on the soil to determine the actual quantity of borrow required. ◼

Calculating Cut-and-Fill Volumes by Computer

Through the use of computers and digital data, the task of calculating cut-and-fill volumes has been greatly simplified. Programs exist for the average end area, contour area, and borrow pit methods. Furthermore, developing designs using standard computer software allows for the integration of CAD, DTM, and visualization programs to create three-dimensional models of proposed landscapes. Combining existing and proposed elevation data, the DTM can be used to construct profiles that allow for the computation of cut-and-fill volumes using the average end area method.

Balancing Cut-and-Fill Volumes

On some projects it may be desirable, or even required, that all grading be self-contained on the site so that no soil can be imported to or exported from it. On such projects, the line of no cut–no fill on the grading plan will result in areas with shapes other than square or rectangular. The borrow pit method described earlier can be applied only when all grid cells are identical squares or rectangles. Where the areas of the cells are not equal, the volume for each area must be determined separately.

The basic approximation for computing cut or fill is that the volume is the product of the mapped (horizontal) area multiplied by the average of the cuts (or fills) at each corner of that area. Some of these cuts (or fills) may be zero, but they must be

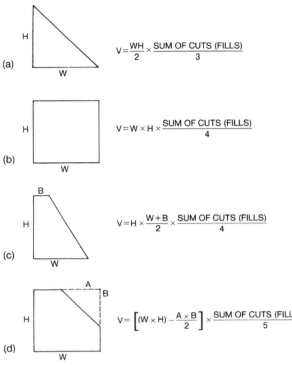

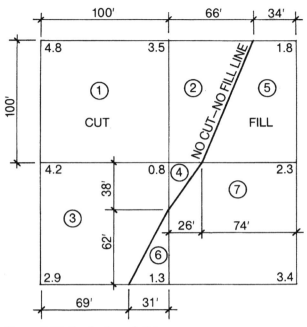

Figure 8.10. Plan for Example 8.7.

Figure 8.9. Borrow pit volume formulas. (a) Triangular areas. (b) Square and rectangular areas. (c) Trapezoidal areas. (d) Pentagonal areas.

included in averaging. Figure 8.9 illustrates the variety of geometrical areas that may occur on a grading plan and formulas for the corresponding volumes.

■ EXAMPLE 8.7

Figure 8.10 represents a project that will be partially in fill and partially in cut. The number at each corner indicates the height of fill or the depth of cut required. Determine the volume of fill and cut for each area and the total volumes of fill and cut. All distances are as shown on the plan.

SOLUTION

Volumes 1, 2, 3, and 4 are in cut and 5, 6, and 7 are in fill. The volumes for each area will be computed

separately according to the formulas given in Figure 8.9.

$$\text{Volume No.} 1 = W \times H \times \frac{\text{sum of cuts}}{4}$$

$$= 100 \times 100 \times \frac{4.8 + 3.5 + 0.8 + 4.2}{4}$$

$$= \frac{10,000 \times 13.3}{4} = 33,250 \text{ ft}^3$$

$$= \frac{33,250}{27 \text{ ft}^3/\text{yd}^3} = 1,231.48 \text{ yd}^3$$

$$\text{Volume No.} 2 = H \times \frac{(W + B)}{2} \times \frac{\text{sum of cuts}}{4}$$

$$= 100 \times \frac{66 + 26}{2} \times \frac{3.5 + 0 + 0 + 0.8}{4}$$

$$= \frac{4,600 \times 4.3}{4} = 4,945 \text{ft}^3 = 183.15 \text{ yd}^3$$

Note that the zeros used in the sum of the cuts represent the corners at the no cut–no fill line.

$$\text{Volume No. 3} = \left[\frac{(W \times H) - (A \times B)}{2}\right] \times \frac{\text{sum of cuts}}{5}$$

$$= \left[(100 \times 100) - \frac{(62 \times 32)}{2}\right]$$

$$\times \frac{(4.2 + 0.8 + 0 + 0 + 2.9)}{5}$$

$$= \frac{9,039 \times 7.9}{5} = 14,281.62\,\text{ft}^3$$

$$= 528.95\,\text{yd}^3$$

$$\text{Volume No. 4} = \frac{(W \times H)}{2} \times \frac{\text{sum of cuts}}{3}$$

$$= \frac{(26 \times 38)}{2} \times \frac{0.8 + 0 + 0}{3}$$

$$= \frac{494 \times 0.8}{3} = 131.73\,\text{ft}^3 = 4.88\,\text{yd}^3$$

Similarly, the volumes of fill are computed as follows:

Volume No. 5 = 5,400 × 4.1/4
= 5,535 ft³ = 205.00 yd³
Volume No. 6 = 961 × 1.3/3
= 416.43 ft³ = 15.42 yd³
Volume No. 7 = 9,506 × 7.0/5
= 13,308.4 ft³ = 492.90 yd³

The total volume of the cut is 1,231.48 + 183.15 + 528.95 + 4.88 = 1,948.46 yd³, which may be rounded to 1,950 yd³. The volume of fill is 205.00 + 15.42 + 492.90 = 713.32 yd³, which is approximately 710 yd³.

It may be noted that the volume of cut is 1,950/710, or over 2.7 times the volume of fill, which in engineering usage is stated as a cut-to-fill ratio of 2.7. Even considering shrinkage (settling and compaction), it is evident that there will be a considerable amount of extra soil. A ratio of 1.1 to 1.2 ft³ of cut to each ft³ of fill required is often used where a balance of volumes is desired. The next example will demonstrate how this may be accomplished. ∎

■ EXAMPLE 8.8

Assuming that the desired final grade of the project in Figure 8.10 is to be level, adjust all cuts and fill heights to achieve a cut-to-fill ratio of 1.2.

SOLUTION
To achieve a 1.2 cut-to-fill ratio requires basically a trial-and-error procedure. Since there is an excess of cut (or since the proposed grade is too low), the final grade must be raised, resulting in less cut and more fill. As a result, the *area* of cut will decrease, while the *area* of fill will increase. Also, for every 0.1 ft that the final grade is raised, 0.1 ft must be subtracted from each cut depth and added to each fill height.

For a preliminary estimate of volumes, it can be assumed that the cut (or fill) occurring on an outside corner is the average cut (or fill) for one-quarter the area of a grid square. The cuts (or fills) common to two grid squares may be assumed to be the average cuts (or fills) for two-quarters or one-half of the area of a grid square; the cuts (or fills) common to three squares account for three-quarters of a grid square; and the cuts (or fills) common to four grid squares may be averaged over four-quarters of the area or one full grid square. This is illustrated in Figure 8.11. These assumptions

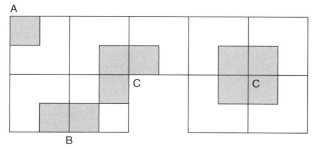

Figure 8.11. Approximate average cut-and-fill values. Rather than average the corner values for each grid cell, the cut or fill value at each grid intersection may be assumed to be the average value for the adjacent grid cell area. Thus, point *A* is the average for one-quarter of a cell, *B* is the average for one-half of a cell, *C* is the average for three-quarters of a cell, and *D* is the average for one full cell.

make it possible to do preliminary computations with new trial cut depths or fill heights without actually computing volumes, which would be more laborious. Also, as a result of the change in cut-and-fill *areas,* the actual location of the final no cut–no fill line is not yet known. In the preliminary computations, each cut (or fill) on an outside corner will have one-quarter weight, each one common to two grid squares will have one-half weight, each one common to three grid squares will have three-quarters weight, and each one common to four grid squares will have one full weight.

For a trial grade the weighted cuts and fills are determined. The sum of the weighted cuts is compared to the sum of the weighted fills. When the ratio of these sums is close to the desired cut-to-fill ratio, actual volumes are computed.

In this example, since there is such a large excess of cut, the first trial will raise the proposed grade 0.6 ft, so that each cut will be 0.6 ft less and each fill 0.6 ft more, as shown in Figure 8.12. The sum of the

weighted cuts is $4.2/4 + 2.9/2 + 3.6/2 + 0.2 + 2.3/4 = 5.075$ ft. The sum of the weighted fills is $2.4/4 + 2.9/2 + 1.9/2 + 4.0/4 = 4$. Therefore, the trial cut-to-fill ratio is $5.075/4 = 1.27$. This is close enough to the desired 1.2 ratio to compute the actual volumes.

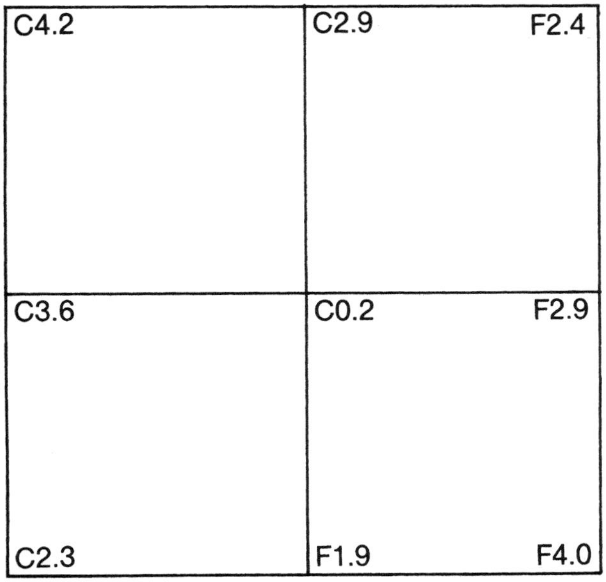

To do this, the first step is to locate the no cut–no fill line wherever there is a change from cut to fill. The point at which the no cut–no fill line crosses a grid line can be determined by the following proportion:

$$\frac{d_1}{L} = \frac{C}{C + F} \tag{8.6}$$

also

$$d_2 = L - d_1 \tag{8.7}$$

where

d_1 = distance to the point of no cut–no fill from the grid corner in cut
L = distance between grid corners (100 ft in this example)
C = depth of cut
F = fill height
d_2 = distance to the point of no cut–no fill from the grid corner in fill

If it is more convenient to proceed from the grid corner that is in fill, the relationship can also be expressed as follows:

$$\frac{d_2}{L} = \frac{F}{F + C} \tag{8.8}$$

and

$$d_1 = L - d_2 \tag{8.9}$$

Using these relationships, the distance for the lower left is computed as follows:

$$\frac{d_1}{100} = \frac{2.3}{2.3 + 1.9}$$

$$d_1 = 100 \times 2.3/4.2 = 54.76 \text{ or } 55 \text{ ft}$$

$$d_2 = 100 - 55 = 45 \text{ ft}$$

C4.2	C2.9	F2.4
C3.6	C0.2	F2.9
C2.3	F1.9	F4.0

Figure 8.12. Plan for trial 1, Example 8.8.

Similarly, the other distances are determined as follows:

$$d_2 = 100 \times \frac{1.9}{1.9 + 0.2} = 90 \text{ ft } (d_1 = 10 \text{ ft})$$

$$d_1 = 100 \times \frac{0.2}{0.2 + 2.9} = 6 \text{ ft } (d_2 = 94 \text{ ft})$$

$$d_1 = 100 \times \frac{2.9}{2.9 + 2.4} = 55 \text{ ft } (d_2 = 45 \text{ ft})$$

The location of the no cut–no fill line is shown in Figure 8.13. The line has shifted to the left and, as previously noted, the area of cut has been reduced and the area of fill has increased. The

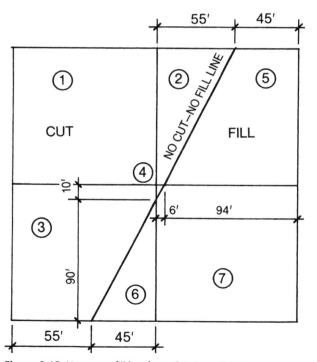

Figure 8.13. No cut–no fill line for trail 1, Example 8.8.

volume of cut and fill are computed as before, with the following results.

Cut

$$\text{Volume No. 1} = 100 \times 100 \times \frac{10.9}{4}$$
$$= 27,250 \text{ ft}^3 = 1,009.26 \text{ yd}^3$$

$$\text{Volume No. 2} = 100 \times \frac{55 + 6}{2} \times \frac{3.1}{4}$$
$$= 2,363.75 \text{ ft}^3 = 87.55 \text{ yd}^3$$

$$\text{Volume No. 3} = \left[(100 \times 100) - \frac{90 \times 45}{2} \right] \times \frac{6.1}{5}$$
$$= 9,729.5 \text{ ft}^3 = 360.35 \text{ yd}^3$$

$$\text{Volume No. 4} = \frac{6 \times 10}{2} \times \frac{0.2}{3} = 2.0 \text{ ft}^3 = 0.07 \text{ yd}^3$$

Fill

$$\text{Volume No. 5} = 6.950 \times \frac{5.3}{4}$$
$$= 9,208.75 \text{ ft}^3 = 341.06 \text{ yd}^3$$

$$\text{Volume No. 6} = 2,025 \times \frac{1.9}{3}$$
$$= 1,282.5 \text{ ft}^3 = 47.5 \text{ yd}^3$$

$$\text{Volume No. 7} = 9,970 \times \frac{8.8}{5}$$
$$= 17,547.2 \text{ ft}^3 = 649.9 \text{ yd}^3$$

$$\frac{\text{Total Volume of Cut}}{\text{Total Volume of Fill}} = \frac{1,457.23 \text{ yd}^3}{1,038.46 \text{ yd}^3} = 1.4$$

This is more than the preliminary ratio of 1.27 and is still too great. The final grade will be raised again by 0.1 ft, as shown in Figure 8.14. The resulting volumes are as shown on the following page:

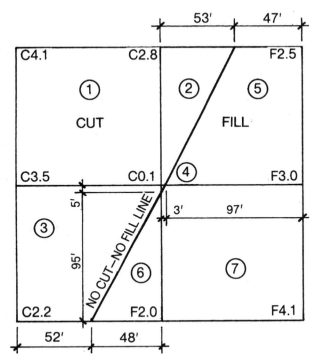

Figure 8.14. Plan for trial 2, Example 7.8.

Cut

Volume No. 1 = 972.22 yd³
Volume No. 2 = 75.19
Volume No. 3 = 331.67
Volume No. 4 = 0.01
Total Cut = 1,379.09 yd³

Fill

Volume No. 5 = 366.67 yd³
Volume No. 6 = 56.30
Volume No. 7 = 673.57
Total Fill = 1,096.54 yd³

The cut-to-fill ratio is now 1.26, which is still a little high. However, raising the final grade another 0.1 ft results in a cut-to-fill ratio of 1.06. Therefore, the 1.26 ratio is accepted, since it is very difficult to grade to tolerances of less than 0.1 ft. ■

While the desired final surface was to be level in Example 8.8, the method used can be applied to any required final plane surface, level or sloping. The mapped (horizontal) distances should be used to determine the areas for volume computations and to locate the no cut–no fill lines.

Another point that aids in achieving a balance is to understand the relationship of volume to depth and area. Raising or lowering large areas only a few inches may significantly change cut-and-fill volumes. For instance, if the grade over a 1-acre area is raised or lowered by 4 in., the change in volume is greater than 500 yd³. A grade change of 0.20 m over an area of 0.50 ha results in a volume change of 1,000 m³. Establishing simple area-to-volume relationships for different depths will make the task of balancing cut and fill easier.

CHAPTER 9

Storm Water Management

STORM RUNOFF

Storm or *surface runoff* is storm water that moves on the ground by gravity and flows into streams, rivers, ponds, lakes, and oceans. For impervious surfaces, such as pavements and roofs, runoff occurs almost immediately. For pervious surfaces, the intensity of precipitation must exceed the infiltration rate, that is, the surface must be saturated before runoff will occur. *Subsurface runoff* is storm water that infiltrates and moves through the soil both horizontally and vertically. The rate of movement is influenced by soil permeability and usually occurs at a much slower rate than surface runoff.

As noted in Chapter 2, the acts of grading and controlling and managing storm water runoff are inextricably linked. Almost all site development projects result in the remolding and sculpting of the earth's surface as well as changes in surface character. These changes may significantly alter storm runoff patterns in terms of rates, volumes, and direction. Landscape architects and site planners must understand the consequences if these changes are to be effected in a safe, appropriate, and ecologically sensitive manner. This chapter provides an introduction to basic management principles and techniques as well as potential problems caused by storm water runoff. The proper design of any management system requires an interdisciplinary approach including professional expertise in ecology, engineering, hydrology, and landscape architecture.

It cannot be stressed enough that all storm water management practices must be *site, region,* and *climate specific.* In addition, legislative controls in terms of runoff, erosion, sedimentation, and water quality have become increasingly common at federal, state, and local levels. It is imperative that regulatory requirements be reviewed before beginning a site development project and that appropriate measures be taken to comply with or attempt to modify these requirements.

HYDROLOGIC CYCLE

The hydrologic cycle is a natural, dynamic process, which is diagrammatically illustrated in Figure 9.1. Within a natural system, changes such as the creation of river valleys, the redirection of a stream channel, or erosion and sedimentation usually occur slowly over long periods of time. Generally, site development disrupts the natural hydrologic cycle by accelerating runoff and reducing the proportion of precipitation that infiltrates the ground or is taken up by vegetation. It is the role of the site planner to minimize, mitigate, or ameliorate these disruptions to the natural system through appropriate storm water management and sound land use practices.

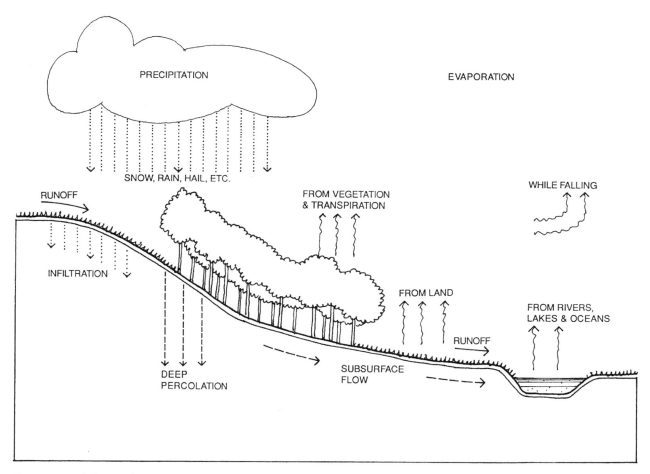

Figure 9.1. Hydrologic cycle.

NATURE OF THE PROBLEM

Urbanization has a profound impact on existing natural and constructed drainage systems. Development typically results in an increased amount of impervious surfaces, such as roofs, streets, parking lots, and sidewalks. The consequences of these surface changes are numerous but are primarily rooted in the fact that developed sites lose much of their natural storm water storage capacity. The loss of vegetation, organic litter, and changes in surface characteristics, such as roughness and perviousness, result in the rapid conversion of rainfall to storm water runoff. Often the increased rate and volume of runoff become too great for existing drainage systems to handle. In order to accommodate the increases, drainage systems are structurally altered through the use of curbs, gutters, channels, and storm sewer pipes to direct and convey runoff away from developed areas.

There are several environmental impacts that may result from changes in the storm drainage pattern. These include increased flood potential due to increases in peak flow rates; decreased groundwater supply caused by reduced infiltration; increased soil erosion and sedimentation brought about by greater runoff volumes and velocities; increased petrochemical pollution from street and highway runoff; and the contamination of winter runoff by salt and sand in colder regions. Addressing these and other issues in the design and implementation phases will result in a more environmentally responsive management system.

Hydrologic Changes

There are a variety of changes in stream hydrology that result from development. Peak discharges, which can be as much as two to five times the predevelopment rate, generally increase the frequency and severity of flooding. Development that

had once been considered above flood level may become subject to flood damage. In addition to increased rates of runoff, the volume of runoff may be increased as a result of reduced infiltration and storm water storage capacity. Higher runoff velocities, which also reduce the time it takes the peak discharge to reach a stream or drainage channel, result from smoother surfaces, such as pavements, which create less friction to slow runoff flow. Increased velocities and/or shorter overland travel times also provide less opportunity for infiltration. Higher velocities coupled with increased imperviousness may also result in reduced stream flow during extended dry periods caused by reduced infiltration. Groundwater that would normally be recharged during wet periods and released slowly from soil during dry periods is lost as surface runoff (Figure 9.2).

Stream geometry also changes. Streams are widened due to increased volume and velocity, which results in increased stream bank erosion. Usually the stream bank is undercut, destabilizing vegetation and, in turn, exacerbating the erosion problem. Eroded material is deposited in stream channels as sediment, which reduces stream flow capacity. Flood elevations are raised; as noted, this phenomenon increases the extent of the area at risk of flood damage.

The quality of storm water is also degraded as a result of development. Pollutants are accumulated on paved surfaces and are flushed from these surfaces during a rainstorm. Not only do developed or urbanized landscapes increase the ease with which pollutants can be collected and concentrated, but they also increase their sources. Contaminants may be released through corrosion, decay, oil and fuel leaks, leaching or wearing away of construction materials and coatings, brake linings, tires, and catalytic converters. Developed areas, as well as agricultural areas, contribute herbicides, pesticides, and fertilizers, which

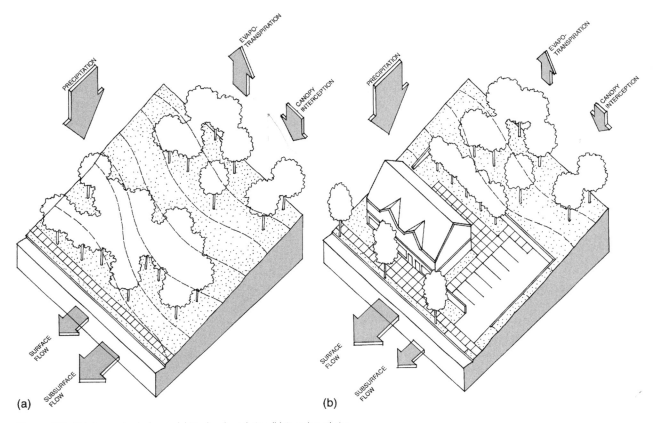

Figure 9.2. Relative water balance. (a) Undeveloped site. (b) Developed site.

stimulate algal growth and reduce the availability of oxygen in water. Fallen leaves and animal droppings that would normally decompose in undeveloped or low-density settings are more easily washed from paved surfaces, further increasing nutrient and bacteria levels in streams, ponds, and lakes.

Changes in stream hydrology and geometry, combined with reduced water quality, decrease the value of aquatic, stream bank, and floodplain habitats. Not only are stream channels and flows altered and pollution levels raised, but these conditions are further exacerbated by low summer flows and higher water temperatures.

MANAGEMENT PHILOSOPHY

Historically, the primary concern in dealing with storm water runoff was to remove it as quickly as possible from a developed site to maximize local convenience and protection. Traditionally, this was accomplished by conveying runoff by storm sewers, swales, gutters, and channels to the nearest water body, usually a stream or river. Little consideration was given to potential off-site impacts. This practice has had a cumulative effect on environmental and water quality.

More recent storm water management practices have recognized the need for controlling off-site impacts caused by increased runoff volumes and peak discharge rates. The objectives of these revised practices have been twofold: first, to reduce downstream flooding through the use of detention facilities that store and release runoff at a controlled rate and, second, to reduce flooding damage by restricting floodplain development. Most legislation at either the state or local level states that the peak rate of runoff after development cannot exceed the rate prior to development. In some cases, the peak development rate must be even less than the predevelopment rate. However, such practices, when executed on a site-by-site basis, may in fact still not solve regional flooding problems and fail to address water quality and habitat issues. To address this challenge, a site should always be considered in the context of its watershed.

The most recent philosophy with regard to storm water management is to develop a comprehensive, integrated approach that addresses water quality in addition to the volume and rate of runoff. One of the primary management objectives is to deal with runoff on-site rather than transporting the problems off-site. A basic objective of any site design should be to minimize hydrologic problems by preserving and maintaining the predevelopment drainage patterns to the greatest extent possible. Combined with appropriate management techniques, including detention, storage, and infiltration, proposed drainage system costs can be reduced by minimizing the need for piping and drainage structures.

For a variety of reasons, however, the site-by-site approach to storm water management with heavy reliance on structural measures has not been as effective as anticipated. This approach has also fostered the idea that larger volumes of runoff are an inevitable and unavoidable consequence of site development. This is analogous to treating a disease rather than seeking a cure. Contemporary storm water management and associated erosion and sedimentation control philosophies are oriented toward the *prevention* of excessive storm water runoff through innovative planning and site design.

STORM WATER MANAGEMENT STRATEGIES

Although this book focuses primarily on site engineering for the site-scale development project, it must be realized that individual projects, when aggregated, have environmental, social, and regional impacts such as those on water quality, energy consumption, and traffic. Storm water management is an excellent example of an issue that requires consideration at the regional and larger land planning scales.

Watershed-Based Storm Water Management

A more recent trend in storm water management is watershed-based planning. This approach is viewed as more cost-effective and environmentally beneficial in terms of controlling runoff and protecting water quality. Controlling storm water runoff at the watershed or subwatershed level through land planning policy, management, and design provides opportunities for nonstructural and preventive solutions as well as more cost-effective structural methods. The more traditional approach to storm water management on a site-by-site basis has primarily resulted in relatively expensive, maintenance-intensive structural solutions.

Although the objectives of site-scale management systems have been well intended, they have not always adequately addressed downstream flooding or water quality issues such as non-point-source pollution. Detention basins, constructed on a site-by-site basis, can actually result in increased stream flooding because of possible simultaneous timing of peak discharges from many basins. In addition, the increased maintenance requirements and associated costs of individual site management systems are rarely considered in the design and implementation stages. As a result, many of these systems are not properly maintained, further reducing their effectiveness.

The development and implementation of a watershed-based management plan require a clearly defined planning process. The first step in this process is to characterize the watershed in terms of flooding, water quality, surface cover, and land use. The second step is to identify, assess, and prioritize problems. The third step is to establish management objectives for the watershed and to identify the nonstructural objectives, such as land acquisition, impervious cover restrictions, and public education, and the structural ones, such as regional detention measures, to achieve objectives. The final step is to implement a long-term monitoring and enforcement program.

Watershed-based zoning is a land planning tool that has evolved from watershed-based management strategies. This technique establishes the intensity of development within a watershed based to some degree on an allowable percentage of impervious cover in relation to specific water quality and stream protection goals.

Site Planning and Water Quality

Specific strategies to protect water resources may be implemented at the site development scale. In some cases, the implementation of these strategies may require regulatory changes, such as subdivision codes, parking requirements, design standards, or other control mechanisms, since existing regulations may actually exacerbate storm water problems.

By its very nature, development is accompanied by increased impervious land cover in the form of buildings and pavements. As pervious surfaces are converted to impervious surfaces, there is less opportunity for storm water infiltration. The consequences of this conversion include increased rate, volume, velocity, and decreased time of concentration of storm water runoff. Research has shown that degradation of water quality in streams takes place when the impervious cover within the drainage area approaches approximately 20%. Above this level stream bank erosion, increased pollution, loss of wildlife habitat, and decreased biodiversity may occur. In addition, pervious surfaces, such as lawns, located directly adjacent to impervious surfaces, such as sidewalks and streets, can also degrade stream quality. Fertilizers, insecticides, and organic matter can be displaced or drift more easily to the impervious surfaces, from which they can be easily flushed into the storm drainage system.

Reducing Imperviousness

As previously stated, impervious surfaces are created by buildings and pavements primarily for roads, walks, and parking lots. The extent of building coverage, referred to as the *building footprint,* is normally regulated by zoning ordinances and is, therefore, a relatively fixed amount for a particular land use. Total site coverage, including all impervious surfaces, is regulated to a much lesser degree, and thus the elements associated with pavements, particularly streets and parking lots, provide the greatest opportunity for reducing impervious cover.

Parking Lots

There are several strategies that can be used to reduce the size and, therefore, the extent of pavement needed for parking lots. One strategy is to use realistic parking demand ratios for a particular land use or development project. Although these ratios are usually stipulated in zoning ordinances, the assumptions used to establish these values may be questioned. In terms of environmental quality, the luxury of basing these ratios on worst-case, highest-demand scenarios no longer exists. To further exacerbate the problem developers often view these ratios as minimums and build additional parking spaces. Lower parking requirements can be achieved by using more realistic demand ratios or by developing a more precise user profile for the project. For some land uses, it may be possible to achieve a 20 to 30% reduction in the number of required parking spaces.

A second strategy is to reduce the dimensions of parking spaces and aisle widths to reflect more accurately the size of today's automobiles. Historically, parking stalls were 10 ft (3.0 m) wide by 20 ft (6.0 m) long. Today many automobiles can be easily accommodated in a 9-ft (2.7-m) by 18-ft (5.5-m) stall, resulting in a reduction in paving by almost 20%. Dimensions as small as 8 ft (2.4 m) by 16 ft (4.9 m) can be achieved for compact cars. The width of the access aisle can also be reduced from 24 ft (7.3 m) to as little as 20 ft (6.0 m). User profiles and turnover rates must be considered in selecting appropriate dimensions.

Management strategies can also be used to reduce the projected parking demand. These strategies include shared parking arrangements, improved mass transit systems, and employee incentives for mass transit use.

Street Width

The geometry of road design is primarily established by the American Association of State Highway and Transportation Officials (AASHTO) and the Institute of Traffic Engineers (ITE) based upon such factors as volume (number of vehicle trips per day), safety, and ease of traffic flow. Standards established by these organizations have been adopted by many communities in establishing street width. Since streets can make up as much as 70% of the impervious surface of a proposed subdivision, careful consideration must be given to the appropriate design width of the proposed streets. Reducing street width from 30 ft (9.1 m) to 26 ft (7.9 m) will result in a 13% reduction of impervious pavement. Any change from established standards requires approval from appropriate governing agencies.

Cluster Development

Cluster development, an established site-planning concept, is used primarily to concentrate residential development while preserving a certain (specified) percentage of the site in open space. This planning tool can be used effectively in managing storm runoff and protecting water quality. Properly executed cluster development can reduce impervious cover through shortened road systems, reduce storm water runoff and requisite infrastructure, increase opportunities for the type and location of storm water management measures, and preserve buffers for stream corridors and environmentally sensitive areas.

PRINCIPLES AND TECHNIQUES

Measures that have been developed to control, store, and/or treat storm water runoff from developed areas for the purpose of reducing flooding or removing pollutants while maintaining or enhancing environmental quality are referred to as *best management practices* (BMPs). The goal of a BMP is to control non-point-source pollution while providing effective storm water management. A BMP for a specific site should be designed to control runoff, maximize pollutant removal, and integrate with the natural and built landscapes while considering maintenance requirements, costs, and responsibilities. Through proper planning and good design, storm water management facilities can serve multiple uses, provide community and aesthetic amenities, create safe environments, and reduce development costs.

BMP selection criteria include storm water management objectives, water quality objectives, and appropriateness to specific site conditions, including climate, soils, topography, proposed and existing land uses, and surface cover. Integration of specific management devices into the existing landscape and proposed development poses a challenge for site planners and landscape architects. The design of a BMP has several components. The nontechnical aspects include aesthetics, site suitability and appropriateness, safety, cost, maintenance, and multiple uses. These aspects will most likely establish the physical framework for the overall drainage concept. The technical aspects include understanding the existing hydrologic characteristics and engineering for the proposed system, which will establish size, storage capacity, discharge, and infiltration rates. Control measures may be used singly or in combination, depending on the size and character of the existing site and the nature of the proposed development.

BMPs commonly used include, but are not limited to, wet ponds, detention facilities, infiltration facilities, and water quality basins, as well as biofilters, green roofs, cisterns, rain gardens, and constructed wetlands, or a combination of these practices. Typical design characteristics and capabilities for each of these are briefly described.

Wet Ponds

Retention (or *wet*) *ponds* are basins that contain a permanent pool of water. This control measure,

through careful planning and design, can serve multiple purposes including storm water management, pollutant removal, habitat improvement, and aesthetic enhancement (Figure 9.3). Potential benefits derived from wet ponds may include increased property values, recreational opportunities, and the creation of wildlife habitat. The configuration and edge treatment of retention ponds

(a)

(b)

Figure 9.3. Examples of retention basins used as site amenities. (a) This pond is an attractive feature at the entrance to a residential development. Jets help to aerate the water to reduce algae growth. (b) The stone edging provides a more refined appearance for this pond used to enhance the setting of a corporate campus.

may be designed to appear refined, naturalized, or wild. Possible disadvantages include safety problems, algae bloom, offensive odors, mosquitoes, or the need for maintenance and sediment removal.

The following features, summarized in Figure 9.4, should be considered when designing a wet pond.

1. Maximize flow length between inlet and outlet. This extends the flow path before the water exits, thus increasing the time for sediment and pollutant settlement. A suggested minimum length-to-width ratio is 3:1. If this ratio cannot be achieved, baffles can be used to break up flow and lengthen the flow path between inlet and outlet.

2. The pond should expand gradually in the direction of flow. Water entering the pond spreads out and uniformly displaces the existing water, thus preventing the creation of "dead zones." Generally, an irregular shoreline is preferred when a more natural appearance is desired.

3. Pool depth should be between 4 and 8 ft (1.2–2.4 m). Depths of less than 4 ft can result in elevated water temperatures and resuspension of sediment due to surface disturbance. A level safety bench at least 10 ft (3.0 m) wide by 1 ft (0.3 m) deep should be provided around the perimeter of the pond to reduce potential safety problems. Where groundwater quality is a concern, the pond should be lined and the basin depth should be above the seasonal high water table to prevent mixing of groundwater and runoff. Obviously, under these circumstances, wet ponds cannot be used to recharge groundwater.

4. The use of a complex and organic geometry for the shape of and the topography within the pond can improve both the feature's treatment of storm water and its habitat value. Rigid rectilinear geometries can lead to zones in the composition that do not perform a treatment function.

Figure 9.4e illustrates a wet pond that has been poorly integrated into the site design. The pond is an unattractive intrusion inappropriately placed in the front yards of the housing units and fails to demonstrate any site or environmental sensitivity. It is essentially a pit edged with steep gabion walls and completely enclosed by a chain link fence. By contrast, Figure 9.4f makes the wet pond a welcoming community attraction.

Detention Facilities

Detention facilities, or *dry basins,* are used as a means of controlling peak discharge rates through the temporary storage of storm runoff. Outflow rates are set at or below predevelopment rates, and flow is metered out of the basin until no water remains. Detention basins may work effectively in reducing downstream flooding and stream bank erosion, depending on the quantity of storm water detained and release rates, but they may not be very effective in enhancing storm water quality. Detention ponds that extend temporary storage time, referred to as *dual-purpose detention basins,* allow for more effective removal of particulate pollutants and provide a technique for improving water quality.

On-site detention can be accomplished in a variety of ways. Surface techniques use ponds, basins, and paved areas, while subsurface techniques use dry wells, porous fill, oversized drainage structures, and cisterns or tanks. Subsurface techniques may be costly, but they reduce land consumption and may be appropriate on very tight sites where space for surface techniques is not available.

The design characteristics of detention basins are similar to those of retention facilities in many ways; however, additional features illustrated in

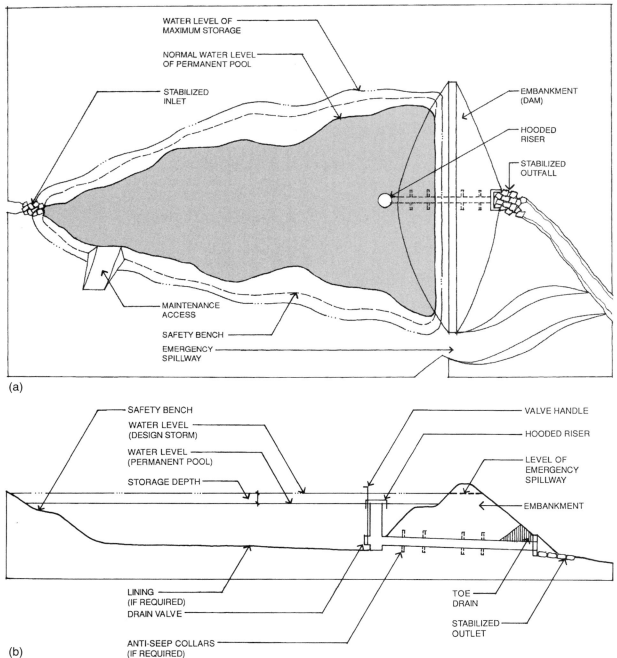

(a)

WATER LEVEL OF
MAXIMUM STORAGE

NORMAL WATER LEVEL
OF PERMANENT POOL

STABILIZED
INLET

EMBANKMENT
(DAM)

HOODED
RISER

STABILIZED
OUTFALL

MAINTENANCE
ACCESS

SAFETY BENCH

EMERGENCY
SPILLWAY

(b)

SAFETY BENCH

WATER LEVEL
(DESIGN STORM)

WATER LEVEL
(PERMANENT POOL)

STORAGE DEPTH

VALVE HANDLE

HOODED RISER

LEVEL OF
EMERGENCY
SPILLWAY

EMBANKMENT

LINING
(IF REQUIRED)

DRAIN VALVE

ANTI-SEEP COLLARS
(IF REQUIRED)

TOE
DRAIN

STABILIZED
OUTLET

(c)

(d)

(e)

(f)

Figure 9.4. Retention basin (wet pond). (a) Plan. (b) Section. (c) Pipe inlet with headwall and apron stabilized with riprap to minimize erosion. (d) Swale directs runoff to this retention basin. Gabions are used to stabilize the inlet point of the swale. (e) A poorly designed retention basin. (f) A well-designed retention basin, acting as a feature for the houses overlooking it and walking paths connecting the surrounding community to it. (See Figure 9.4f in the Color Plates.)

Figure 9.5 are required to increase potential use, enhance appearance, and improve maintainability. Detention basins can be designed to fit into a variety of locations, including lawns, playfields, open spaces, swales, parking lots, and court sport areas. Where multiple use is desired, provisions must be made to prevent standing water and minimize saturated soil conditions. These include the use of a low-flow channel, positive drainage toward the channel and outlet, subsurface drainage for playfields, and a separate sediment basin upstream from the primary basin, easily accessible for maintenance purposes. A vegetated detention basin is illustrated in Figure 9.5f. Vegetation slows flow through

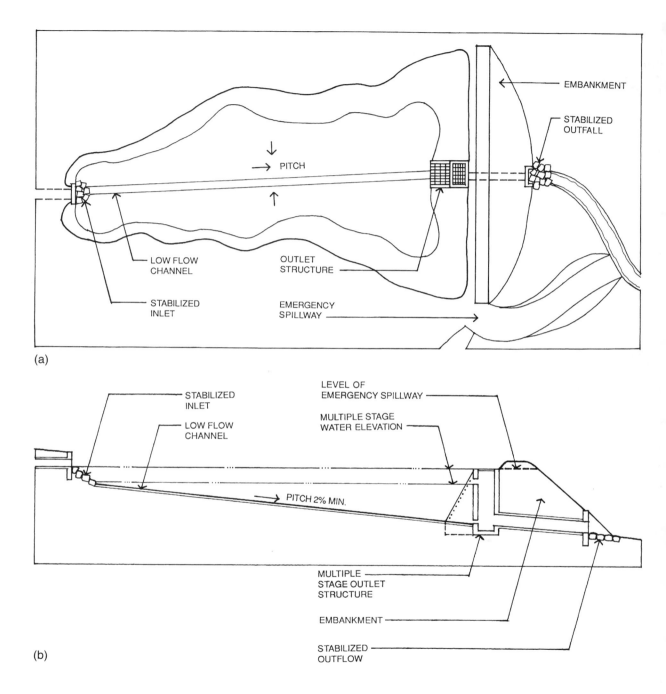

(a)

EMBANKMENT

STABILIZED
OUTFALL

PITCH

LOW FLOW
CHANNEL

OUTLET
STRUCTURE

STABILIZED
INLET

EMERGENCY
SPILLWAY

(b)

STABILIZED
INLET

LOW FLOW
CHANNEL

LEVEL OF
EMERGENCY SPILLWAY

MULTIPLE STAGE
WATER ELEVATION

PITCH 2% MIN.

MULTIPLE
STAGE OUTLET
STRUCTURE

EMBANKMENT

STABILIZED
OUTFLOW

(c)

(d)

(e)

(f)

Figure 9.5. Detention basin (dry pond). (a) Plan. (b) Section. (c) Large detention basin for a residential development. (d) Detailed view of the inlet pipe and headwall pictured in part c. Note the low-flow channel and the use of riprap for soil stabilization. (e) Multiple-stage outlet structure and concrete lined emergency spillway for the detention basin also shown in part c. (f) A well-designed vegetated detention basin. A low-flow channel with a mowed edge is provided for maintenance.

the basin, enhances infiltration, and removes water through plant uptake and transpiration.

1. The length-to-width ratio is not as critical for a detention basin as for a wet pond, but an elongated form is still preferred. Flow length between inlet and outlet should be maximized, and short-circuiting of flow should be prevented.

2. The side slopes of the basin should not be steeper than 3:1 (H:V). Less steep side slopes are preferred, although more area will be required for the basin. The floor of the basin should have a 2% minimum slope toward the outlet to ensure positive drainage. An access way at least 10 ft (3.0 m) wide with a slope of

5:1 or less should be provided for maintenance equipment.

3. A low-flow channel should be provided to reduce drying time and improve usability.

Parking lot detention areas may be an inexpensive way to control runoff, reduce storm sewer pipe sizes, and reduce erosion. Collecting runoff in a parking lot may cause inconvenience to traffic and pedestrians, but if the collection area is properly located, such conflicts can be minimized. Again, on small sites with little area available for detention or retention basins, parking lot detention may be an appropriate alternative.

Safety

Measures should be taken to reduce safety hazards that may be created by retention and detention ponds located in populated areas. Safety issues are related to access, large volumes of flowing water, constrictions created by pipes and culverts, and the intermittent nature of storm water storage. Safety measures may include installing fencing, avoiding steep side slopes or sudden drops, minimizing constriction points, and covering outlets with properly designed grates. As a minimum, the construction of detention and retention basins must meet all applicable federal, state, and local regulations, including state dam safety regulations where appropriate.

Infiltration Facilities

Infiltration techniques are highly beneficial in that they can significantly reduce or eliminate surface runoff while at the same time replenishing groundwater, which supplies wetlands, streams, and wells. Other benefits of infiltration include reduced downstream peak flows, reduced soil settlement caused by depletion of groundwater, preservation of existing vegetation, and lower development costs based on a reduced size of the storm sewer system. Preserving infiltration after development can be one of the most effective mechanisms in preventing adverse impacts to the surface water system. In terms of water quality, infiltration devices filter runoff through the soil layer, where a number of physical, chemical, and biological removal processes occur. However, infiltration practices should not be used to remove sediment or other particulates, since sedimentation will eventually clog the infiltration device and render it useless. Sediment should be removed by the use of filter strips or sediment traps before it enters an infiltration device.

There are practical limitations to the use of infiltration facilities. These include soil permeability rates, potential reduction in permeability rates over time, and the potential for groundwater contamination. Conditions that must be examined to determine the appropriateness of infiltration facilities include depth to groundwater, seasonal variation in groundwater levels, slope and direction of groundwater flow, soil permeability, vegetative cover, and quality of storm water runoff.

Infiltration facilities may be classified as either surface systems, such as basins; subsurface systems, such as trenches; or porous pavement systems.

Infiltration Basins

An infiltration basin is a surface impoundment created by damming or excavating. The purpose of the basin is to store runoff for a selected design storm or specific volume temporarily so that the water will enter the soil over a given time period. These basins, in terms of performance and appearance, are very similar to detention basins, and, in fact, basins are often designed to combine infiltration and detention functions (Figure 9.6). In addition to the limitations mentioned above, infiltration basins may require large areas, are not adaptable to

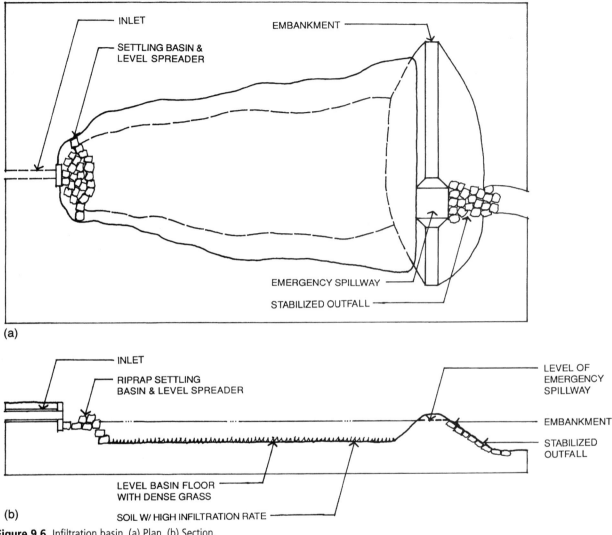

Figure 9.6. Infiltration basin. (a) Plan. (b) Section.

multiple uses, and have high rates of failure due to improper maintenance and installation. In recent years, infiltration basins that have been designed as a depression in the landscape, as opposed to requiring an embankment for containment, have become more commonly known by the name *rain gardens* (see below).

Rain Gardens

A rain garden is a more informal and organic-appearing infiltration basin. Rather than relying on a basin requiring embankment structures, as above, rain gardens are meant to be installed in areas that already show good soil drainage, though the soil can be manipulated to improve its drainage characteristics. Ideally, they are located in already low-lying areas and away from building foundations and septic systems that receive full to partial sun to maximize evaporation and minimize the potential for damage to other site elements. They will also be planted with vegetation that can tolerate occasional inundation. It is important that rain gardens are located close to the source of runoff. On larger sites, this will require multiple rain gardens located throughout a site as opposed to a singular large basin. (See Figure 9.7 in the Color Plates.)

Infiltration Trenches

An infiltration trench is an excavation backfilled with coarse aggregate stone. The voids between the aggregate material provide the volume for temporary storage of storm runoff. Runoff stored in the trench gradually infiltrates the surrounding soil. The surface of the trench may be covered with grass having a surface inlet, or with porous material, such as sand, gravel, or stone. Infiltration trenches are appropriate for relatively small drainage areas. They are flexible systems that can easily be fit into underutilized or marginal areas of a site, and where soil and groundwater conditions allow, they can be easily adapted to retrofitting an existing developed site. An observation well, such as a perforated polyvinyl chloride (PVC) pipe placed vertically in the trench, should be installed to monitor any change in infiltration rate on a periodic basis (Figure 9.8).

Porous Pavement

Usually pavement creates an impervious surface that generates high rates and quantities of runoff.

Figure 9.7. This rain garden is a simple depression with a drain at the lower left for overflow.

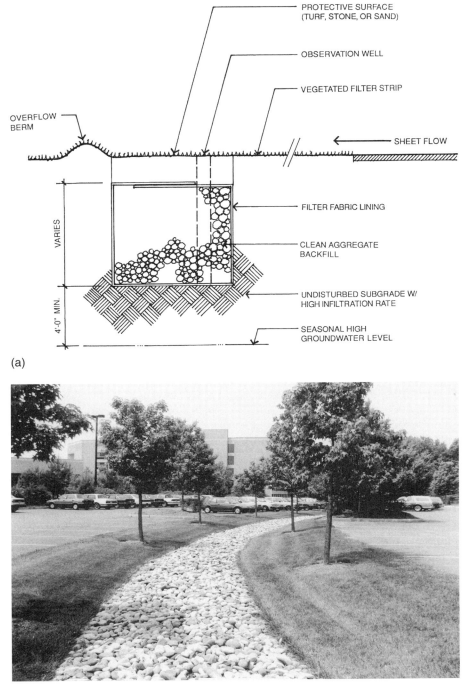

PROTECTIVE SURFACE
(TURF, STONE, OR SAND)

OBSERVATION WELL

VEGETATED FILTER STRIP

OVERFLOW
BERM

SHEET FLOW

VARIES

4'-0" MIN.

FILTER FABRIC LINING

CLEAN AGGREGATE
BACKFILL

UNDISTURBED SUBGRADE W/
HIGH INFILTRATION RATE

SEASONAL HIGH
GROUNDWATER LEVEL

(a)

(b)

Figure 9.8. Infiltration trench. (a) Section. (b) Sheet flow from parking is directed to a stone-lined swale. Stone reduces runoff velocity, which enhances the potential for increased infiltration.

173

The objective of porous pavements is to increase perviousness while still providing a stable, protective surface. There are several types of porous pavement including porous asphalt, open-gridded modular pavement, reinforced sand and gravel paving, and pervious concrete.

Both porous asphalt and pervious concrete use an open-graded aggregate mix that increases the interconnected pore or void space and allows water to percolate through the pavement (Figure 9.9). Open-graded aggregate mixes have only a small amount of small-sized aggregate particles. This allows air voids to occur between the larger aggregate particles. Open-gridded modular pavement is typically constructed of a structural concrete framework with regularly spaced void areas that are filled with pervious material, such as sod, sand, or gravel. This idea is altered to allow for greater surface area coverage of the pervious infill material by reinforcing it with plastic rings. Porous pavements are appropriate for such uses as low-volume roads, driveways, parking lots, bikeways, and emergency lanes.

Porous pavements should be used only where the subgrade soil conditions provide the proper permeability, depth to groundwater does not pose a problem, or contamination will not occur from degraded storm water quality. It should be noted that, in addition to being used in infiltration situations, porous pavements can be combined with subsurface storage facilities on densely developed sites.

The advantages and disadvantages of porous pavements are numerous. Advantages include generally higher recharge rates than natural conditions due to less vegetative uptake, control of both the rate and volume of runoff, reduced potential for swale and channel erosion, preservation of existing vegetation by maintaining proper soil moisture levels, reduced surface puddling, enhanced pollutant removal, and reduced construction costs through decreased infrastructure, such as curbs, drains, and pipes.

A major concern is limited experience with these systems by engineers and contractors. A high level of workmanship is required in preparing the subgrade, placing the base course, and installing the paving material if the system is to perform at the desired level. Another serious drawback is the potential for clogging if the pavement is improperly maintained or installed. Other disadvantages include the potential for groundwater contamination, weakening of the subgrade in saturated conditions, and the development of anaerobic conditions in areas where there are frequent storms. Also, in cold climates, sand and deicing salts cannot be used on porous pavements.

Water Quality Basins

Water quality amelioration is often included in the design of retention and detention basins. In retention (wet) basins, additional volume is provided for the settling out of sediments. Detention (dry) basins may have a small orifice at the bottom of the outlet structure so that runoff from frequent storms, which tends to flush contaminants into the pond, is retained for a prolonged period. The extended detention period resulting from the small orifice allows the contaminants to settle out and the pond to drain gradually.

Landscape Practices

In and of themselves, landscape practices do not provide complete storm water management or water quality enhancement. However, several planting and vegetative measures are an integral part of many BMPs; these measures include vegetated swales, filter strips, basin landscaping, and urban forestry.

Vegetated swales provide an alternative to curbs and gutters and are a common technique for controlling storm water runoff, particularly in

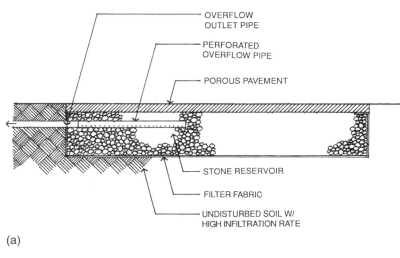

Figure 9.9. Porous pavement. (a) Typical section. (See Figures 9.9b–d in the Color Plates.) (b) Pervious concrete pavement used as a sidewalk in a new residential community. (c) Open-gridded modular pavement infilled with sod. (d) Reinforced gravel paving.

(a)

Labels in diagram:
OVERFLOW OUTLET PIPE
PERFORATED OVERFLOW PIPE
POROUS PAVEMENT
STONE RESERVOIR
FILTER FABRIC
UNDISTURBED SOIL W/ HIGH INFILTRATION RATE

(b)

(c)

(d)

175

residential areas. Benefits derived from the use of swales include increased surface friction, resulting in decreased flow velocities and, consequently, increased times of concentration. The runoff-reducing performance of swales can be improved when combined with other measures, such as check dams and infiltration trenches. Swales have limited capacity and are subject to erosion if improperly designed or maintained.

Filter strips are devices that are typically placed adjacent to impervious surfaces to intercept overland sheet flow. Filter strips can lower runoff velocities, increase the time of concentration, improve infiltration, and contribute to groundwater recharge. They can be designed to fit into the overall site plan as screening, buffers, and spatial delineators. These strips must be properly designed to prevent concentration of runoff, which would eliminate their effectiveness. Grass filter strips should be used to trap sediment to protect the performance of infiltration trenches.

Bioretention is a technique whereby parking lot islands, planting strips, and swales are used to collect and filter storm runoff. Through the use of grass filters, shallow ponding, infiltration, and plant uptake, this technique takes advantage of an underutilized portion of the landscape for water quality enhancement. In terms of land consumption, it normally does not require space in addition to that which is devoted to, or required for, parking lot landscaping. Rain gardens have become a critical part of bioretention practices.

Planting design is an essential component of all storm water basins. The design of retention, detention, and infiltration basins must include appropriate planting measures to ensure optimal performance. Benefits derived from properly designed planting schemes include slope stabilization, pollutant removal, aesthetic enhancement, and the creation of wildlife habitat. Plant selection should respond to specific microclimatic and site

conditions. In particular, it is important to recognize that there may be several different vegetative zones based on depth of water and different soil moisture conditions.

Urban forestry involves the preservation of existing trees and the planting of new trees during the development process. Benefits include the significant interception of precipitation by tree canopies and the increased water storage and infiltration capacity of the ground layer. The amount of runoff generated by areas landscaped with trees, shrubs, and groundcovers may be as much as 30 to 50% less than that generated by lawn areas.

Constructed Treatment Wetlands

Constructed treatment wetlands, sometimes referred to as *artificial* or *created wetlands,* may be designed for a variety of functions including the treatment of point and non-point pollution and/or the control of storm water runoff. Wetlands are dynamic, highly complex ecosystems, and the process for re-creating or duplicating natural systems

Figure 9.10. A constructed treatment wetland. Part of the Pennswood Village case study presented later in this chapter.

is still evolving. As is the case with most BMPs, these artificial systems require an interdisciplinary design approach, which includes the participation of wetland and plant ecologists, hydrologists, soil scientists, geotechnical and civil engineers, and landscape architects.

The physical, chemical, and biological processes that occur in wetlands must be understood to plan, design, and maintain a viable and appropriate constructed wetland ecosystem. Perhaps the most important physical characteristic is the *water budget.* A water budget is the balance of water in the system including inflows (precipitation, runoff, and base flows such as streams), storage (both surface and substrate), and outflows (evaporation, transpiration, percolation, and base and excess flows).

Sediment deposited from inflow water can alter the character of a wetland in terms of storage capacity and the plants and animals supported by the system. To alleviate this potential problem, it is recommended that a sediment basin be located upstream from the constructed wetland. The basin allows for pretreatment of the water before it enters the wetland, as well as offering an area that is more easily accessible for maintenance and sediment removal.

The hydrologic design process for constructed wetlands is similar to that for detention and retention basins in that inflow volumes, storage volumes, outflow rates, and outlet sizing must be determined based on a particular design storm. The planting design should be consistent with the wetland objectives and be appropriate to the site's hydrology, soils, and anticipated variations in water depth. It must be realized that constructed wetlands require a period of time to establish, stabilize, and grow, and that diligent construction supervision, frequent maintenance, and water level monitoring are essential for a successful project.

Constructed wetlands can perform multiple functions, including groundwater recharge, control of storm runoff, enhancement of water quality, and promotion of biodiversity. In some instances, the water quality of constructed wetlands may be better than that of naturally occurring systems because of flow routing patterns, longer detention of inflows, and less short-circuiting of water traveling through the system.

Rainwater Harvesting

Rainwater harvesting, or the collection and storage of rainwater on a site, is becoming a frequently included component of storm water management systems in new construction. Its function is twofold. First, it serves to reduce the load on the site storm water management system until it is full. Second, this water, once treated in the system, is then available for irrigation or consumption. (See Figure 9.11 in the Color Plates.)

A rainwater harvesting system can include as many as six functional components, depending on the end use or desired quality of the water. Every system must include (1) a catchment area, (2) a conveyance system connecting to the storage element, and (3) the storage element or cistern. The other systems that may be included in this system are (4) a roof-wash system, (5) a delivery system, and (6) water treatment systems.

The catchment area is often a roof, but any paved impervious surface can potentially be used as a catchment, though additional filtration will likely be required to deal with the greater contamination of these surfaces by oil and other debris. The composition of the catchment surface plays an important role in determining the water quality. Roofing made of organic materials, including wood or clay, can allow algae and mold to grow readily on their surface and thus are not recommended for use in projects where the goal is potable water. The roofing material may also leach chemicals or minerals. This makes asphaltic and zinc-coated metal

Figure 9.11. Sculptural rainwater harvesting installation. The downspout from the building is considered part of the conveyance system. The corrugated steel is the cistern, and one of the sculptural half-pipes acts as an overflow for times when the cistern is full. The striped rod projecting from the center of the cistern is attached to a float insider that shows the amount of water in the cistern.

roofing less desirable for capture for potable water use. Lead solder should also be avoided in connections on the roof and in any other component of the system. The best options for all types of water use are stainless steel or galvanized steel with a baked-on enamel, lead-free finish.

The conveyance system typically includes gutters, downspouts, and piping. These components can be constructed from a variety of materials, including aluminum, PVC, galvanized steel, stainless steel, or copper. A roof-wash system may be included in the conveyance system that removes the first 10 to 20 gal (38 to 76 L) of water from the system in a separate pipe. This gets rid of the built-up particulate debris on the roof.

The storage component requires early design consideration as both the most costly and the most limiting element in the system. The size of the cistern determines how much water will be on hand for use. The size of this element can range from individual rain barrels to large structures holding thousands of gallons of water. The cistern can also be fabricated out of a wide variety of materials including metal, concrete, mortared stone masonry, fiberglass, polyethylene, and wood. The container must be sealed from UV radiation to prohibit algae growth. It is also typically designed with both an overflow at the desired maximum water level and a drain at the base, should the cistern need to be drained.

The type of treatment systems employed in the rainwater harvesting system depends on the end use of the water. Where the water will be used solely for irrigation, a roof-wash system combined with leaf screens installed at downspout inlets may be adequate. A gravel filter can be substituted for the roof-wash system. This type of filtration entails the addition of a small tank filled with porous, nonlimestone rock before the water enters the cistern. Water enters at the base of the tank and particulate matter is physically filtered as water rises to the top of the tank, where it can be drained into the cistern. If a higher level of water quality is desirable, there is a range of filtration options including more refined physical filters, ozonation, and UV sterilization.

The delivery system takes water from the cistern to the location where it will be used. If the cistern is located at a higher elevation than the one at which the water will be used for irrigation, gravity will be enough to move the water. If this relationship does not exist, a pump will be required to deliver water for use.

Local codes should always be checked to ensure that systems are being designed to work within them or with the understanding that a variance will be sought. Be aware that some municipalities will require a greater degree of treatment in the case of systems to be used for irrigation. Other municipalities may require permits for harvesting the water, because they consider the runoff as part of their local water budget.

Green Roof Systems

Green roofs are engineered systems of roofing designed to support plant life on top of building structures while protecting the underlying structure. There are three types of green roof systems.

Extensive green roofs are comprised of 2 to 6 in. (5 to 15 cm) of lightweight mineral growing medium planted with drought-tolerant species, usually sedums, and subsisting solely on rainwater. They are lightweight, typically weighing between 15 and 30 lb/ft^2 (73 and 146 kg/m^2). (See Figure 9.12 in the Color Plates.)

Figure 9.12. Extensive green roof. Sedum plugs have been planted in an even spacing. The unplanted area is covered with a net straw blanket to keep the lightweight soil in place until the sedum grow to cover the entire roof area. *(Photo: Mathews Nielsen)*

Figure 9.13. Intensive green roof. To allow for the greater soil depth of an intensive roof, soil is often placed in a raised planter or mounded to provide depth. This example shows both in a single composition.

Intensive green roofs have deeper, more organics-rich soil and are planted with a wide range of plants, even trees. The weight of this type of green roof can vary widely and is limited by the structural load that the roof is designed to support. In determining the load an intensive roof will apply, the weight of each material being used in the construction must be taken into account, including the planting medium and the plants themselves. Irrigation will also be required as part of this installation. (See Figure 9.13 in the Color Plates.)

The last type of green roof is a modular system. Whereas the first two systems are installed to be integrated with the roof, this system contains all of its components within a tray that behaves similarly to a potted plant. The tray system is most often used for extensive-type roof plantings, but it can also be designed with greater depth to accommodate intensive-type plantings as well.

There are nine basic components that may be used in a green roof system. Working from the surface of the roof structure upward, they include:

1. *Waterproofing Membrane*. Protects the roof deck from infiltration by water.

2. *Root Barrier*. A secondary membrane that protects the waterproofing membrane and roof deck from incursion by invasive plant roots (Figure 9.14). This element is required only if all or part of the waterproofing membrane contains organic materials that attract root growth.

3. *Protection Board*. An optional component that protects these elements below from damage during the construction process. It is typically a rigid board meant to withstand accidental tool impacts.

Figure 9.14. Root barrier turned up at edge of planted area. *(Photo: Mathews Nielsen)*

Figure 9.15. Drainage and retention layer, with filter fabric attached. *(Photo: Mathews Nielsen)*

Figure 9.16. Sedum plugs. *(Photo: Mathews Nielsen)*

4. *Insulation.* Often required by code to prevent winter heat loss from the building. It can also be used to build up topography or to minimize soil depth. Rigid chlorofluorocarbon (CFC)-free extruded polystyrene is most commonly used as the insulation component.

5. *Drainage and Retention Layer.* Provides aeration to the growing medium while ensuring that it does not become over-saturated (Figure 9.15). These layers are usually constructed from lightweight, strong sheets of plastic in a variety of shapes, all dimpled with peaks and valleys. The valleys in the material or a secondary absorbent mat retain water for times of drought.

6. *Filter Fabric.* Used to separate the drainage layer from growing medium.

7. *Growing Medium.* Different from soil used for growing plants in the ground, the soil typically is composed of a lightweight mineral base and a small amount of organic matter. It must not contain any silt, which will clog the filter fabric. (See Figure 7.7 for an image of lightweight growing medium.)

8. *Plantings.* Can be hydroseeded, hand seeded, rolled out as mats, or planted as plugs or containers. Mats or containers give the most immediate visual impact but also cost the most. Plugs are typically the most successful and cost-effective solution if the plants are not required to look lush and full immediately, but can spread and mature over time (Figure 9.16).

Figure 9.17. Mulching straw blanket. *(Photo: Mathews Nielsen)*

9. *Mulch.* May be included in green roof installations as typical bark mulch. Where high wind
is a concern, the mulch may take the form of a
mulching straw blanket or stone aggregate. The
latter needs to be large enough not to blow off
the roof as well.

The process of designing a green roof requires a
great degree of coordination between the landscape
architect, the architects and engineers on a design
team, and the client. The following set of questions
provide a good summary of the questions that the
team should be aware of and work to answer early
in the design process so that a successful and ele-
gant design can be created.

1. Will there be public access? This will affect the
way planted areas and walking surfaces will be
separated. It will also affect the number of egress-
es required and the design at the roof parapet.

2. Will the roof be visible from the building being
designed or from the surrounding buildings?

3. What is the extent of the green roof surface?
Are there any local codes that limit the area?
Conversely, are there any project goals that
would warrant maximizing the extent of the
green roof? Goals might include obtaining
a green building certification or meeting local
storm water runoff loading requirements.

4. Is there a specific design load that the green
roof area needs to fall within? If there is, this
may determine which of the above options is
viable, unless the design is at a point where
there is still some flexibility.

5. If the design loads have not yet been set, what
kind of plant palette is the team hoping to
use? A design consisting of low-lying patterns
in sedum would imply an extensive roof with
4–6 in. (10 to 15 cm) of soil. A design with a
broader range of vegetation including perenni-
als, grasses, and even shrubs and small trees
would imply an intensive roof system and will
require a minimum of 12 in. of soil, depending
on the type of plant material.

6. Are roof penetrations a factor? Locate all roof
penetrations, with special attention to any that
might be blowing exhaust or vented air directly
on the vegetation. Plants will have difficulty
surviving the stress of continuous exhaust flow,
and the design should reflect this situation.

7. Will the roof be installed on level or sloping surfaces? If the roof is sloping, what is the maximum slope presently being considered? Design
details will be necessary to keep soil from sliding on slopes greater than 3:1.

8. Have wind studies been conducted on the
building design? If so, they need to be reviewed
to evaluate whether a green roof will survive
and what measures may need to be taken to
keep the lightweight growing medium from being blown away.

Though green roof systems are included here
as a potential component of larger storm water
management systems, they have more to add as a

design element than the absorption of rainwater and the slowing of runoff in storm events. The following functions or benefits can be obtained during a careful and considered design process:

1. *Habitat.* Green roofs have great potential to add habitat back to the urban realm.

2. *Open Space.* Similarly, there is great potential for adding open space to the urban environment with green roofs.

3. *Heat Island Effect.* By reflecting solar radiation and ambient cooling through evapotranspiration, green roofs play an active role in mitigating the buildup of heat that is typical in urban environments. As such, a green roof can play a part in obtaining a heat island effect point for the roof.

4. *Storm Water Management.* The green roof can be used as part of a storm water management system, minimizing and slowing down the release of water into the storm sewer.

5. *Energy Performance.* Green roofs provide passive solar cooling on roofs they sit on while providing lower ambient air temperatures at air intakes located adjacent to the roof surface. Both of these benefits may play a part in optimizing energy performance in the building below the green roof.

CASE STUDIES

Pennswood Village[1]

Project Overview

Pennswood Village, located in Bucks County, Pennsylvania, is an excellent example of sustainable design within a civic-minded framework. Pennswood Village, an existing 82-ac (33.2-ha)

[1] Landscape Architect: Wells Appel
Civil Engineer: Pickering, Corts & Summerson
Hydrology and Ecology: Princeton Hydro
Wetland Delineation: Mellon Biological Services

Quaker-directed retirement community, wished to expand the amenities available to its residents, increase the number of housing units, and provide a wider range of housing choices. To accomplish these objectives, the Pennswood Village Association hired the landscape architectural firm of Wells Appel to determine a suitable number of new housing units and develop a new master plan for the community. In the process of developing the plan, two off-site issues were identified. These issues, storm water management and traffic safety, subsequently strongly influenced the land planning concept.

Land Planning Approach

Of the 82 ac (33.2 ha), approximately 50 ac (20.2 ha) were originally developed and about 20 ac (8.1 ha) were leased for farming. Arrival to the community was via a straight entry drive adjacent to the farm field. Although this entrance was somewhat pastoral, it was not particularly interesting. Reexamining the farm field created an opportunity to address the problems of storm water management and traffic safety.

The approach to the new master plan was to maintain a condensed housing core and enhance the sense of arrival while solving a number of functional problems. In addition to management of the storm water and traffic, other issues included access to two adjacent schools, preservation of a historic barn, and accommodating recreation facilities for the Friends School. The proposed plan is illustrated in Figure 9.18. Civic involvement was evidenced by the Village entering into a private–public partnership with Middletown Township to solve the traffic safety and off-site storm water problems.

Storm Water Management Concept

The idea for Pennswood's storm water system was conceived by Wells Appel as a logical expression

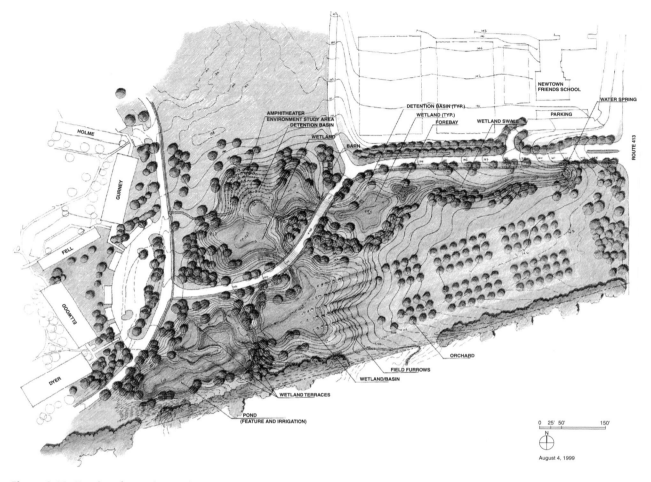

Figure 9.18. Site plan of entry drive and storm water management area. Plan: Wells Appel.

of the community's values in regard to ecology, stewardship, and education. The concept not only addressed the technical challenges, but was envisioned to create a much-needed "sense of entrance" to the community. To achieve this vision, Wells Appel assembled a team of plant ecologists, wildlife biologists, environmental planners, and civil engineers. Although the township's storm water management requirements could have been met by constructing a typical and less costly dry detention basin, Pennswood Village residents preferred a much more naturalistic approach.

By dividing a watershed into a series of small, linked subwatersheds, it is possible to apply and successfully utilize BMPs to create a system that would otherwise be incapable of managing large volumes of runoff. A fundamental feature of the Pennswood Village design is the use of a number of

BMPs, linked in a specific series of passive operations, to manage the quality and quantity of runoff from the site and outlying watersheds.

In Pennswood Village, a riparian buffer type of bioretention system is utilized. The underlying concept associated with this design is the creation of off-line bioretention areas into which runoff can be diverted and treated over a prolonged period of time (18 to 36 hours). This system, which mimics a natural riparian stream corridor, promotes infiltration of runoff, attenuates peak flows, and filters particulate pollutants while creating diverse habitats for a wide variety of organisms.

Consistent with the goal of creating an attractive, naturalized storm water management system, considerable care was taken in the planting design and selection of plant materials. As a reflection of the community's land stewardship philosophy, native plant materials were used to provide habitat for wildlife and create a sense of place (Figure 9.19). In addition, the use of indigenous plants minimized problems with the acclimatization of plant material, maintenance of plantings, and

Figure 9.19. Native plantings add to the natural character of the site. Paths with mowed edges meander through the site to encourage strolling, walking, and biking by the residents.

the ability of the plants to withstand climatic and moisture fluctuations.

Storm Water Management Design

As noted, the functional design of the storm water management system mimics that of a natural riparian stream corridor channel. The system consists of an integrated series of BMPs, each sized and located to address a specific storm water management issue. The alignment and grading of the swales, basins, and wetlands, combined with the careful selection of native grasses, shrubs, and trees, diminishes the velocity of the runoff, biofilters and settles pollutants, and creates opportunities for groundwater recharge. There are four major components to the system: a sedimentation basin, an infiltration basin, a vegetated swale, and a treatment wetland.

Sediment Basin

At the uppermost part of the system is a sediment basin, where runoff is directed by several pipes from the contributing watershed and adjacent highway (Figure 9.20). The sedimentation basin is stone-lined to slow the storm surge, settle out gross particulate material, and contain most of the debris conveyed along with the runoff. A flow dissipater constructed of locally quarried stone reduces the velocity of the concentrated runoff as it enters the basin. A weir regulates the volume of the collected runoff and the length of time it is detained in the sedimentation basin. The basin is easily accessed for routine maintenance and the periodic removal of accumulated sediments.

Infiltration Basin

Runoff discharged from the sedimentation basin is directed into a vegetated swale (Figure 9.21), from which it is conveyed to an infiltration basin.

(a)

Figure 9.21. Vegetated swale leading from the sediment basin to the infiltration basin. *(Photo: Wells Appel)*

(b)

Figure 9.20. Sediment basin. (a) Sediment basin under construction. Pipes convey storm water runoff collected off-site. (b) Completed sediment basin with stone veneer headwall and stone-lined basin to dissipate the energy of the water flowing from the pipes. *(Photos: Wells Appel)*

The predominant soils in this section of the site are highly permeable, with the depth to the seasonal high water table and the depth to bedrock in excess of 6 ft (1.8 m). This combination of good soil permeability and lack of a constraining horizon is conducive to the infiltration of runoff and the recharge of the shallow aquifer. The infiltration basin (Figure 9.22) is sized to manage the first flush runoff volume of a storm event.

Figure 9.22. Vegetated swale and infiltration basin.

Figure 9.23. Meandering swale passes under the entry drive.

Vegetated Swale

When the flow exceeds the infiltration capacity of the basin, it is discharged over a broad crested weir into a long, meandering vegetated swale (Figure 9.23). On either side of this swale is a broad, flat meadow, graded and designed to function in a manner similar to a riparian corridor or stream floodplain. That is, it consists of a series of shallow, stepped terraces that create ever-broader channels, each of which accommodates and detains the runoff from increasingly large storm events. As a result of the different water levels, soil moisture content, and microclimates created by the terraces, the meadow supports a variety of vegetation including grasses, shrubs, or trees, depending on their different flood and drought tolerances.

Constructed Treatment Wetland

The terminus of the system is a constructed treatment wetland (CTW) (see Figure 9.10) and a small wet pond (Figure 9.24). Outflow from the wet pond is controlled by an outlet structure designed to safely pass the volume of a 100-year storm. Initially, during the early part of a storm, runoff

that exceeds the capacity of the infiltration basin flows, via the vegetated swale, into the wet pond. The outlet control structure on the pond causes the runoff to flood back into the CTW. As water is detained in the CTW and wet pond, it backs up farther, eventually overflowing into the broad meadow and the created riparian corridor. The CTW functions as a shallow wetland where pollutant removal is achieved as a result of settling, filtering, and biouptake.

Entry Drive Alignment

The area in which the new storm water management system has been created is analogous to the "front lawn" of Pennswood Village, with the residences set back more than 1,200 ft (366 m) from the adjacent road frontage. Although the treatment of this space is nontraditional in character, it establishes the setting for the sense of arrival and approach to the community.

The entry drive is oriented to heighten the experience of moving through this naturalized but highly manipulated landscape. The two stone

Figure 9.24. A pond area is the terminus of the storm water management system. However, the upstream components of the system have functioned so well that very little water actually reaches or is stored in the pond.

bridges that pass over the meandering swale emphasize the storm water management function of this part of the Pennswood site. The use of reverse curves slows traffic and provides a series of changing views of the landscape.

Conclusion

Pennswood Village is an excellent example of what might be called *second-glance* design. The sculpted landforms, planting design, and storm water function create a very subtle, understated landscape. Without the prior knowledge that this is a completely constructed environment, the immediate perception is that this is a place that has always existed. In addition to providing an attractive recreational and educational environment for Pennswood Village and the community at large, it is a highly functional storm water management system that exceeds the township's requirements.

Street Edge Alternatives[2]

The city of Seattle, Washington, has had a diminishing number of salmon swimming in its urban streams. In an effort to improve the vitality of the salmon population, the city undertook stream restoration projects through its Urban Creeks Legacy Program. However, these restorations would not be effective if steps had not been taken to address the quality and quantity of water running into the streams from the surrounding urban environment. Because impervious surfaces increase the volume and rate of storm water flow and transport nonpoint pollution, Seattle's streets, which make up 25% of the city's total land surface, are a great target for innovative design. The city has begun using the term *natural drainage systems* to describe an

---

[2] Seattle Public Utilities is responsible for the landscape architectural and engineering design.

inventive category of capital improvement projects that offer alternatives to the typical curb and gutter street development. This case study discusses one design already completed under the city's Natural Drainage System Program.

Natural Drainage Systems

The Natural Drainage System Program has a combined goal of improving both the natural environment through storm water management and the visual and social environments of the communities within which its projects take place. More specifically, the objectives of the drainage system include infiltration and slowing of storm water flow, filtering and bioremediation of pollutants by soils and plants, reduced impervious surface, and an increased amount and diversity of vegetation and related pedestrian amenities. Within the system there are a number of design alternatives that can be used to meet the objectives: retaining existing trees on site, enlarging tree pits, creating a meandered infiltration and conveyance trench within the planting strip, inclusion of a linear bioretention system either at grade or subsurface, using porous pavement where feasible, combining rock and vegetation systems where water velocities may be too high, and using interconnected vegetated swales. This last system is the focus of this case study.

SEA Street

The natural drainage system (NDS) uses interconnected vegetated swales as an alternative to the traditional curb and gutter drainage design, while integrating pedestrian environment enhancements and traffic-calming measures. Such a system consists of a narrow curvilinear street with adjacent drainage swales connected by culverts under redesigned on-street parking (Figure 9.25). Sidewalks and a wide assortment of plantings, including new trees, complete the design, which has come to be called a *Street Edge Alternative* design, or SEA street.

Site Selection

Site selection was very important in determining project feasibility. To provide the greatest positive environmental impact, the project is located within the watershed of a salmon-bearing stream. It is also located in one of the more recently incorporated parts of the city, because such areas typically do not have sidewalks, curbs, or gutters that need to be demolished. The area selected in the northwest corner of Seattle is within the Pipers Creek Watershed, adjacent to Carkeek Park. The storm water of the entire neighborhood presently drains into Pipers Creek through a combined system of both natural and asphalt-lined ditches and culverts. The street segment for the SEA demonstration project is a nonarterial through street, is not located near any critical slope areas, and does not have a grade steeper than 4%.

Project Goals

The objective of the project is to reduce the overall runoff rate of surface drainage to the creek while meeting the goals of conveying the 25-year, 24-hour design storm and detaining up to the 2-year storm event to predevelopment conditions. Water quality treatment is inherent in the design, providing treatment for a 6-month, 24-hour design storm event. This is accomplished in the design by both limiting the amount of impervious area and using a flow control structure that causes storm water to back up into swales for detention during storm events. These flow structures also allow high-flow events to bypass the structure so that flooding does not occur within the roadway or on adjacent properties beyond the boundaries of the swales. The soils and vegetation within the swales, as shown in Figure 9.26, also provide some measure of water quality treatment through physical filtration of the water.

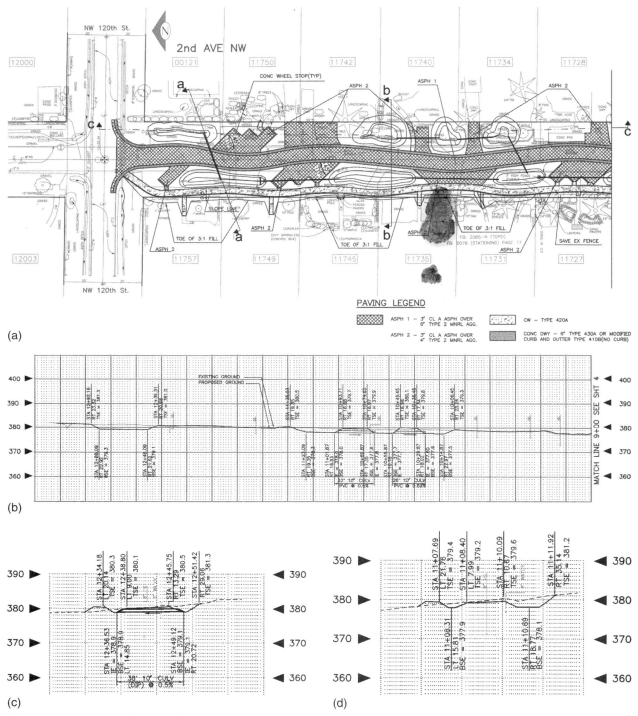

Figure 9.25. Construction drawings of the SEA. Street project. (a) Plan (plan: Seattle Public Utilities). (b) Profile C. (c) Section A. (d) Section B.

190

Figure 9.26. View into the vegetated swale. Notice the culvert opening connecting this swale cell with one across the street.

Two years of flow monitoring, conducted by the University of Washington, showed 98% of all flows fully attenuated for the 2.3 ac (0.9 ha) of the contributing area. The largest storm event during that time period was approximately a 1½-year event.

Residents who have property facing the street also have a role to play. They maintain the city's infrastructure in the form of "street gardens" in front of their homes. Having had an active role during the planning and design of the project, the residents, with a small amount of garden maintenance within the street right-of-way, continue to contribute to their community. This retrofit of a residential street has united the community visually, environmentally, and socially while achieving the project's goals in protecting the creek. This combination of benefits could not be achieved by the construction of a traditional underground pipe system.

This is just the beginning for the NDS program. The program is expanding with a project involving more than 15 blocks, comprising a 32-ac (13-ha) drainage basin, incorporating combinations of SEA streets and other natural drainage systems within the Pipers Creek Watershed. Seattle Public Utilities has also partnered with the Seattle Housing Authority to integrate a natural drainage system into the High Point Neighborhood Redevelopment, the next case study.

High Point Neighborhood Redevelopment[3]

The High Point Neighborhood located within the West Seattle neighborhood of Seattle, Washington, represents an innovative vision for how a community can be redesigned to minimize the impacts of storm water runoff and maximize housing density. The neighborhood prior to this redevelopment contained 716 housing units on a 120-ac (48.6-ha) site. The storm water from the neighborhood was directed from the streets, via underground piping, to a local salmon-bearing creek. The new design, once completed, will have 1,600 units that will be knitted together with an NDS across the 36 blocks of this neighborhood. The NDS in this neighborhood is a larger-scale version of that discussed in the previous case study. It is more complex, with more types of systems involved, including grass-lined

---

[3] Owner/developer: Seattle Housing Authority
Architect: Mithun
Civil Engineering and right-of-way Landscape Architect: SvR Design
Landscape Architect: Nakano Associates

(a)

(b)

(c)

(d)

(e)

Figure 9.27. The High Point NDS. (a) A grassed swale with cuts in the adjacent curb to collect street run-off. (b) A vegetated swale replacing a typical street-edge planter strip. (c) A gravel-lined swale running through the back yards of the community, with pervious concrete in the foreground. (d) Stepped infiltration basins along a more steeply sloping road in the neighborhood. (e) The detention pond is aerated by pumping water uphill to feed the constructed stream at the center of the image.

(a)   (b)

Figure 9.28. Tree preservation. (a) In the midst of the new development. (b) Protected while the second phase is being constructed.

and vegetated swales, porous pavement tiered infiltration basins, and a detention pond (Figure 9.27; see the Color Plates).

To ground the neighborhood, an arborist was hired to survey the existing trees and identify mature, healthy trees that should be saved during the design and construction process. During the first phase of construction, over 100 trees were saved and provide the neighborhood with a mature character lacking in many new developments (Figure 9.28).

SUMMARY

This chapter has introduced basic storm water management principles and the range of BMPs utilized in the management of storm water management. A discussion of erosion and sediment control is presented in Chapter 10. Chapters 11, 12, and 13 discuss methods for calculating storm water runoff volumes, peak discharge rates, flood storage capacity, and system design.

Soil Erosion and Sediment Control

INTRODUCTION

The erosion and sedimentation process involves the detachment, transportation, and deposition of soil particles by the action of water, ice, wind, and gravity. Rainfall impact, flowing water, freezing and thawing, and wind dislodge soil particles, and the movement of water and wind transports the particles and deposits them in a new location. The discussion that follows is limited to erosion caused by the force of falling and flowing water.

Erosion and sedimentation are critical issues in storm water management, especially during construction, when exposed sites are particularly vulnerable. The rate of erosion at construction sites has been estimated to be 5 times that of agricultural land, 10 times that of pastureland, and 250 times that of forestland (Figure 10.1). By volume, sediment is the largest non-point water pollutant. Examples of problems created by excessive erosion include the filling of lakes, ponds, and wetlands; decreased channel capacity in streams and rivers; degraded animal and plant habitats; and increased potable water treatment costs.

REGULATORY REQUIREMENTS

Many states and local jurisdictions have regulations that require the submission of erosion and sediment control plans before granting site plan approval or issuing a building permit. With the passage of the federal Clean Water Act, all states are now responsible for implementing a storm water permitting program that regulates the discharge of runoff from most construction sites. In most cases, it is the responsibility of the site planner to develop an erosion and sediment control plan that complies with all regulatory requirements.

(a)   (b)

Figure 10.1. Examples of severe erosion on a construction site. (a) Concentrated runoff across bare soil results in gully erosion. (b) Sediment deposited on paved surfaces, where it can be easily washed into storm sewers or picked up and transported by car or truck tires.

SOIL EROSION FACTORS

As shown in Figure 10.2, there are four primary factors that determine the potential for erosion: soil type, vegetative cover, topography, and climate. Each of these factors is briefly discussed here.

Soil

The erodibility of a soil is determined by particle size and gradation, soil structure, permeability, and organic content. Soils with a high content of silt and fine sand have a high erodibility potential, whereas soils with increased clay and organic content have a lower potential. Although clay does not erode easily, once in suspension it does not settle out easily. Well-drained, well-sorted gravels and gravel-sand mixtures are highly permeable and easily infiltrated and therefore have the lowest erosion potential. Organic content enhances the permeability and water absorption characteristics of a soil, thus decreasing erodibility. There are a number of models for estimating erosion rates and evaluating various erosion and sedimentation management practices. The Universal Soil Loss Equation (USLE) and the Revised Universal Soil Loss Equation (RUSLE) are perhaps the most

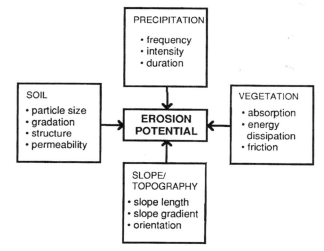

Figure 10.2. Factors affecting erosion potential.

widely known of these. A discussion of the USLE can be found in Barfield et al. (1981).

Vegetative Cover

Vegetation prevents soil erosion in a variety of ways. First, it shields soil from raindrop impact. This serves to dissipate energy that would otherwise dislodge soil particles. Second, it slows runoff velocity through increased surface friction. Finally, plant root systems hold soil in place while increasing its water absorption capacity. The goal of most site development projects should be to retain as much existing vegetation as possible, particularly in vulnerable areas such as steep slopes, stream banks, drainageways, and areas with poor soils.

Topography

The length and steepness of slopes influence the amount and rate of storm water runoff. As the extent and gradient of slope increase, the amount, rate, and velocity of runoff increase, thereby increasing the potential for erosion. To reduce erosion caused by topographic conditions, use the following guidelines: Avoid developing steep slopes, limit the length and gradient of proposed slopes, and protect disturbed slopes as quickly as possible. Slope orientation may influence the ability to reestablish a protective vegetative cover.

Climate

The frequency, intensity, and duration of rainstorms will directly influence the amount of runoff generated on a particular site. Where possible, site construction should be scheduled during months in which low precipitation and low runoff are anticipated, although in some regions of the country this may be very difficult to predict or achieve. Scheduling construction to coincide with optimum seeding periods for a particular region can also promote the establishment of a cover crop for soil stabilization.

EROSION AND SEDIMENTATION PROCESSES

Runoff, whether dispersed or concentrated, can cause significant erosion. Soil detachment that begins with raindrop impact on the ground surface continues as sheet erosion while runoff remains dispersed. As runoff concentrates, small channels or rills form. Rill erosion increases as the rate and volume of runoff increase. When rills progress beyond the size that can be easily removed through smoothing or seasonal weathering cycles, the concentrated flow channels are termed *gullies*. As the rate and volume of runoff continue to increase, significant amounts of soil can be detached and transported as gully erosion. Flowing water transports detached particles, either by carrying them in suspension or by *pushing* them along the bed of the channel. As flow velocity increases, so does the particle size that can be transported. When flow velocity decreases, the larger particles can no longer be held or moved and are deposited as sediment. Sedimentation occurs where channel grades flatten or where water is pooled or slowed by barriers.

EROSION AND SEDIMENT CONTROL PRINCIPLES

Clearing and grading operations associated with site development create water quality problems with regard to soil erosion and sedimentation. Appropriately planned erosion and sediment control, using vegetative and nonvegetative measures, can significantly reduce soil loss if properly installed and maintained from the initial phases to the completion of a construction project. The goal of any plan should be to reduce the detachment and transport of soil.

The guiding principles to achieve this goal include minimizing disturbance, controlling runoff, collecting sediment, and monitoring construction. These practices may also be effective in reducing runoff and non-point pollution and should be employed on any construction site to minimize soil erosion and sediment problems. Through proper planning, many of the control measures can be incorporated into the permanent storm water management system.

Minimizing Disturbance

The area of disturbance and the duration of exposure should be minimized. Minimal disturbance can be achieved by applying five basic principles: Work with existing topography, restrict the area of disturbance, develop compactly, manage site construction, and preserve existing vegetation. The following is a brief discussion of each of these principles.

1. The proposed development should be fit to the existing topography. To the extent possible, the predevelopment drainage pattern and hydrologic conditions (including peak discharge, runoff volume, infiltration capacity, groundwater recharge, and water quality) should be preserved. Construction in or disturbance of natural drainageways should be avoided. Buildings should be designed to step with the topography, and roads should be located so that they do not disrupt the natural drainage patterns. Uses such as playfields and parking lots, which are generally designed as large planes, should be located in relatively flat areas.

2. Disturbance should be restricted to those areas that are necessary for development. These areas normally include buildings, parking areas, accessways, and utilities. Innovative and sensitive site planning techniques (in concert with construction management) are key to the successful implementation of this principle. For example, the alignment of roadways and utilities can be tailored to preserve existing vegetation. Moreover, innovative utility trenching techniques can be used to narrow the width of the disturbance area from 25 ft (7.6 m) to 10–15 ft (3.0–4.5 m), thus reducing adjacent

soil compaction and loss of existing vegetation. Minimizing the number of utility trenches can be achieved by coordinating and placing multiple utility lines in the same trench.

3. Clustering development is the third principle. By clustering structures and other components of a development on one portion of the site, a design can create opportunities to preserve sensitive areas and leave large portions of the site undisturbed.

4. Proper construction management is the fourth principle. Construction equipment, materials, and staging should be limited to only those areas that are necessary to disturb during the construction process. Sound construction management also includes sequencing and phasing of construction operations, to limit the amount of the site exposed, and using effective vegetative and other soil stabilization methods. This can also include locating the staging of potential pollutant sources away from steep slopes, water bodies, and other critical areas of the site.

5. As much of the existing vegetation as possible, particularly woodlands, should be preserved. Woodlands usually generate low runoff volumes, have low rates of soil erosion, and have high filtering capacity in terms of water quality. Concerted efforts should be made to preserve vegetation in environmentally sensitive areas such as stream buffers, steep slopes, floodplains, and wetlands.

Controlling Runoff

Storm water runoff from upslope areas should be prevented from crossing disturbed or exposed soils. Diversion measures can be effectively utilized to redirect runoff. Where diversion is not possible, vegetative buffer strips should be used to reduce runoff velocities.

Storm water runoff generated on-site must be carefully controlled. Low gradients, short slopes, and the preservation of existing vegetation, coupled with stabilization techniques such as sodding, seeding, or mulching, will help to reduce runoff velocities. In addition, runoff must be directed and routed to sediment control devices (such as traps, interceptors, and silt fences) if these measures are to be effective. Where long stretches of steep slopes do exist, they should be altered at regular intervals when possible to intercept runoff and divert the runoff longitudinally along the face of the slope.

Collecting Sediment

Where erosion is unavoidable, which is the case on virtually all construction sites, the resulting sediment should be collected on-site. Sediment traps and basins, inlet protection, silt fences, and similar devices should be employed to prevent the off-site transport of eroded soil. Stabilized construction site access points should be located to reduce the tracking of soil from construction equipment tires onto adjacent streets or other paved surfaces.

Monitoring Construction

A routine maintenance schedule is essential during construction if control measures are to function at optimum levels. Situations such as silt fence or hay bale blowouts and sediment traps that have become filled must be immediately tended to. Poor monitoring and maintenance are often the cause of the failure of these measures.

DEVELOPMENT OF AN EROSION AND SEDIMENT CONTROL PLAN

Preparing a site plan that effectively incorporates soil erosion and sediment control measures requires the designer to have a good understanding of the erosion potential of the area to be developed. Early in the planning process, critical or sensitive areas should be identified. These may include highly erodible soils, steeply sloped topography, stream corridors, and wetlands. Avoid disturbance of these areas by siting structures or improvements in less critical locations.

Conceptually, there are two basic strategies for the development of an erosion and sediment control plan. One strategy focuses primarily on erosion control; here the planner's goal is to keep the soil in place. The erosion potential of the entire site is evaluated along with runoff patterns. A plan is developed that incorporates management practices and measures that will minimize erosion of the disturbed area. The second strategy seeks to minimize the off-site transport of sediment. Because there is greater emphasis on designing measures to capture sediments generated from disturbed areas, fewer erosion control measures may be incorporated in the plan.

Either strategy can be employed to reduce non-point-source pollution associated with sediment transport from construction sites. However, the most effective plans often incorporate both erosion control and sediment control features.

RUNOFF CONSIDERATIONS

Control of erosion during land development is largely achieved by controlling or managing runoff. To develop an effective plan to control runoff, a site designer should (1) review the existing runoff patterns on the undeveloped site, (2) determine what the runoff patterns will be once development is completed, and (3) determine how to manage runoff as the site changes from the existing to the developed condition. Runoff from undisturbed uplands should be diverted from newly graded areas until they are stabilized. Runoff from disturbed areas should be captured and treated to reduce off-site sediment transport.

CONSTRUCTION SEQUENCING

Planning when and how site development takes place is an important part of the erosion and sediment control design process. In drier climates, land disturbance can be scheduled to avoid rainy seasons when there is greater potential for erosion from storm water runoff. In humid regions or in colder climates with short construction seasons, this is not a practical consideration. However, in all regions, construction activities can and should be staged or sequenced to reduce the extent and duration of soil disturbance. For example, a large housing development can be broken down into smaller phases, each one to be completed before the next is begun. Timing the installation of erosion and sediment control measures is also an important consideration. Installation of a sediment control fence parallel to a stream, for example, should be completed before clearing the adjacent upland area. A comprehensive soil erosion and sediment control plan will include a sequence of construction that outlines the timing and order of construction operations.

EROSION CONTROL MEASURES

Erosion control measures can be classified according to how protection is provided; they include both runoff control practices and soil stabilization practices (Figure 10.3). These measures may be either temporary or permanent. Temporary measures are in place only during construction as the site is transformed from the predeveloped to the developed condition. Permanent measures

CONTROL MEASURE	SOIL STABILIZATION	RUNOFF CONTROL	SEDIMENT CONTROL
	VEGETATIVE SOIL COVER	DIVERSIONS	SEDIMENT BASINS
		WATERWAYS	
	NON-VEGETATIVE SOIL COVER	OUTLET STABILIZATION	SEDIMENT FILTERS & BARRIERS
	DIVERSIONS		
		SLOPE PROTECTION	MUD & DUST CONTROL

Figure 10.3. Erosion control measures.

become part of the landscape to provide long-term erosion control. The methods, or particular control devices, used may be either vegetative or nonvegetative (structural). The various practices can be used alone or in combination. Biotechnical measures may incorporate both structural and vegetative elements, typically using woody vegetation.

Runoff Control Practices

Runoff control measures are intended to intercept or control storm water runoff before it can concentrate or before it has reached sufficient volume or velocity to cause damage. Specific measures include diversions, waterway stabilization, slope protection structures, grade control structures, and outlet protection.

> *Diversions* are channels that intercept and redirect the flow of surface runoff. They are typically sited above disturbed locations to divert clean water or within disturbed areas to break up sheet flow concentrations before gullies can form. Runoff is directed to suitable outlets such as existing well-vegetated areas for low discharges or to stable channels for larger flows.

> *Waterways* are natural or constructed channels that provide for the safe disposal of excess water. They may be stabilized vegetatively or with an erosion-resistant lining such as

riprap, modular concrete paving units, or other suitable material. Biotechnical techniques may also be used.

Slope protection structures convey concentrated runoff down steep slopes. The structures typically consist of pipes or chutes. Because of the high velocities, chutes are usually lined with riprap or concrete.

Grade control structures consist of chutes, weirs, or pipe drop spillways installed to prevent the advance of gullies or to reduce the grade in a natural or artificial channel. The slope of a steep channel may be reduced, and thus flow velocity reduced, by a series of low drop structures.

Outlet protection is provided at the end of a pipe or paved channel to allow for energy dissipation and to create a stable transition to a receiving channel. Aprons, roughened surfaces, or shallow pools lined with riprap or precast concrete modular units are commonly used.

Soil Stabilization Practices

Stabilization measures protect the soil surface against particle detachment caused by raindrop impact and from sheet or rill erosion associated with dispersed flow. Generally, concentrated flow must be diverted and managed by other means. Vegetative measures that provide soil stabilization include maintaining and protecting as much of the existing vegetation as possible; retaining existing topsoil for reuse; establishing new vegetative cover, such as seeding on disturbed areas as quickly as possible; and selecting plants and a planting design scheme that are appropriate for the site and will promote long-term stability. Nonvegetative stabilization measures employ materials such as organic and inorganic mulches, gravel, crushed stone, and

geotextiles (meshes, nets, and mats). Synthetic or organic binders or adhesives may be applied to the soil surface to enhance resistance to erosion by sheet flow or wind.

Biotechnical Measures

Soil bioengineering is the use of live, woody, and herbaceous plants to stabilize or protect stream banks, shorelines, drainageways, and upland slopes. It combines biological and ecological concepts with engineering principles to prevent or minimize slope failure and erosion. Vegetation may be used alone or in combination with structural elements, such as rock, wood, concrete, or geotextiles. Techniques include the use of live woody plant cuttings to provide soil reinforcement, as well as conventional plantings of grasses, forbs, and shrubs to prevent surface erosion.

Stems or branch parts of living plants can be used as the initial and primary materials for reinforcing and stabilizing soil. As roots and foliage develop, the vegetation becomes a major structural component of the bioengineering system. Techniques include planting, burying, staking, or driving vegetation into the ground. Live staking and the use of live fascines and brushlayers are examples of such techniques.

Live Staking. An appropriate technique for the repair of small earth slumps that are frequently wet, live staking involves the insertion and tamping of live, rootable cuttings into the ground. As the stakes root, they create a stabilizing mat that reinforces the soil. Excess soil moisture is extracted through water uptake and transpiration.

Live Fascines. Live fascines are long bundles of branch cuttings bound together into sausage-like structures (Figure 10.4) with the branches and bud ends oriented in the same direction. These bundles are capable of propagation. The use of live facines is an effective technique for stabilizing slopes by reducing erosion and face sliding. The

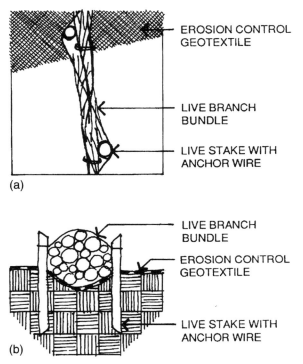

(a)

— EROSION CONTROL GEOTEXTILE

— LIVE BRANCH BUNDLE

— LIVE STAKE WITH ANCHOR WIRE

— LIVE BRANCH BUNDLE

— EROSION CONTROL GEOTEXTILE

— LIVE STAKE WITH ANCHOR WIRE

(b)

Figure 10.4. Typical live fascine detail. (a) Plan. (b) Section.

fascines are placed in shallow trenches parallel to contours for dry slopes, and at an angle to the contours for wet slopes, and are anchored with live and dead stakes.

Brushlayering. Brushlayering is somewhat similar to the live fascine system, except that the brushlayers are oriented primarily perpendicular to the slope. This orientation is more effective in terms of earth reinforcement and mass stability. Brushlayering consists of placing live branch cuttings, usually in a crisscross fashion, on small benches excavated into the slope and then covering them with soil (Figure 10.5).

Branch Packing. Branch packing installations are constructed and function similar to brushlayering, except with the addition of vertical live staking to improve initial structural stability. This installation is used specifically for repairing small localized slumps or holes (Figure 10.6).

Live Cribwall. Live cribwalls are box-like structures fabricated with untreated timbers and filled with layers of live branch cuttings and soil or other appropriate backfill material. This type of structure is employed in place of low walls at the bottom of cut-or

Figure 10.5. Typical section of brushlayering.

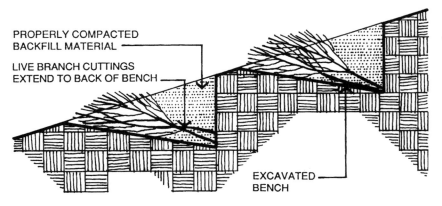

PROPERLY COMPACTED BACKFILL MATERIAL

LIVE BRANCH CUTTINGS EXTEND TO BACK OF BENCH

EXCAVATED BENCH

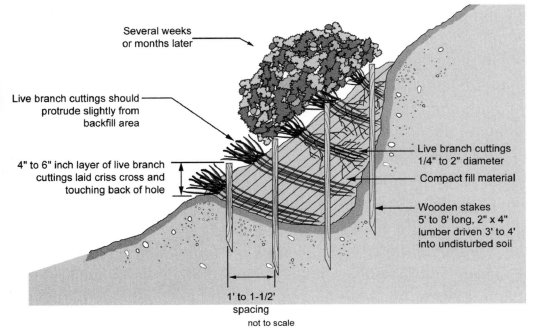

Several weeks
or months later

Live branch cuttings should
protrude slightly from
backfill area

4" to 6" inch layer of live branch
cuttings laid criss cross and
touching back of hole

Live branch cuttings
1/4" to 2" diameter

Compact fill material

Wooden stakes
5' to 8' long, 2" x 4"
lumber driven 3' to 4'
into undisturbed soil

1' to 1-1/2'
spacing

not to scale

Figure 10.6. Typical section of branch packing. *(Source: USDA, Soil Bioengineering: An Alternative to Roadside Management (2002))*

fill-slopes to stabilize the toe of the slope and reduce its overall steepness, providing immediate protection from erosion and sliding. The branch cutting should be installed to extend into the slope. Rooting and establishment of the vegetation will take over the structural functions of the timbers over time (Figure 10.7). This technique can also be used with rock gabions and rock walls.

Fiber Rolls. Fiber rolls are prefabricated tubes consisting of biodegradable materials such as rice straw, wheat straw, coconut fiber, and wood excelsior bound together by netting. The tubes are typically 8 to 12 in. (200 to 300 mm) in diameter. They are used at the toe, top, and face of a slope to intercept and slow runoff, remove sediment, and release runoff as sheet flow. Fiber rolls should be trenched and staked to operate effectively

(Figure 10.8). Rolls may also be used to control erosion along streams, ponds, and lakes. The rolls can be planted with vegetation that will take over the role of the fiber roll as it degrades.

Log Terraces. These are similar in use to fiber rolls, but are both more rigid and longer-lasting. This technique is best deployed in focused areas where erosion is already a problem. There are three typical patterns for constructing the terraces: staggered, ladder, and building block (Figure 10.9). The staggered pattern utilizes logs that cross at least 50% of the erosion area. The ladder pattern should be utilized only where it is possible to use logs that can cross the entire problem area. The building block pattern is similar to the one that occurs on slopes that are eroding.

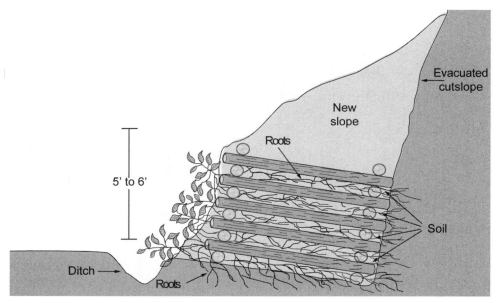

Figure 10.7. Typical section of a live cribwall. *(Source: USDA, Soil Bioengineering: An Alternative to Roadside Management. (2002))*

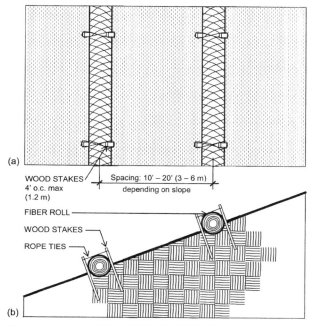

Figure 10.8. Typical fiber roll detail. (a) Plan. (b) Section.

Conventional planting techniques may be supplemented with structural or organic erosion control products, particularly for drainageways, where tensile and shear stresses of soils are limiting factors, and for shorelines, where wave and water action causes erosion. Degradable and non-degradable geosynthetic products can be used to stabilize the soil and protect the vegetation until plantings develop.

Careful consideration must be given to the use of soil bioengineering and the selection of appropriate bioengineering solutions. In some instances, conventional vegetative treatments may be sufficient, but in others, more standard structural engineering methods may be necessary. Regardless of the type of solution, it is important that the treatment be designed to fit the specific site condition, rather than the condition being altered to fit the design based on standardized detailing.

Soil bioengineering is a constantly evolving field, with much knowledge gained through

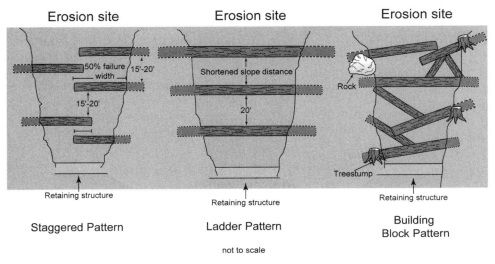

Figure 10.9. Plan view of typical log terrace patterns. *(Source: USDA, Soil Bioengineering: An Alternative to Roadside Management (2000))*

experience and experimentation. Effective, sustainable solutions require an interdisciplinary approach involving soil and geotechnical engineers, plant ecologists, hydrologists, and landscape architects.

Maintenance of Erosion Control Measures

Both temporary and permanent erosion control measures require maintenance in order to function effectively. Vegetative systems must be closely monitored during the first growing season to ensure good establishment. Periodic trimming or mowing, along with supplemental nutrient applications, may be necessary for long-term vigor. Structural measures should be inspected periodically, especially after significant runoff events. Weaknesses or minor failures in structural linings should be repaired promptly. Runoff control systems that handle concentrated flows can experience rapid failure if left untreated. The design team should develop maintenance plans for the construction period and, if

applicable, for the postconstruction period when permanent measures are installed.

SEDIMENT CONTROL MEASURES

Sediment control measures capture sediment on-site before it can be transported downstream or into an existing storm drainage system. Methods of on-site management include the use of sediment basins, silt barriers or fences, vegetative filter strips, and storm drain inlet protection. Sediment barriers and filter strips are most effective where sediments are to be removed from sheet or shallow flows. Concentrated flows should be treated with a sediment basin. As runoff is slowed or contained within a basin, suspended sediments will settle and be deposited. Coarse sediments will settle rapidly, whereas finer sediments require a longer period of time. Filtering through vegetation or other mediums also removes sediments by particle contact. Stone tracking pads at construction egress points are other devices that remove sediments by contact

Figure 10.10. Several erosion control measures have been implemented on this construction site. A silt barrier fence has been installed to collect sediment. An outlet structure in the fence directs runoff toward an existing culvert. Riprap has been used to stabilize the outlet point, and hay bales have been placed across the swale to trap sediment from the outflow before the runoff enters the culvert.

of a tire with the stone surface. Sediment control systems are usually temporary measures that are removed upon final stabilization of disturbed areas at the completion of construction (Figure 10.10).

Maintenance of Sediment Control Measures

Maintenance activities, including periodic removal of trapped sediment, must be performed for sediment control systems to remain effective. As sediment accumulates in a basin, the volume of runoff detained and the settlement time are reduced, which, in turn, reduce the effectiveness of such systems. Generally, it is recommended that sediment be removed when the design storage volume is reduced by half. Silt barriers and filters must also be maintained against clogging and excessive sediment buildup. Maintenance plans should define the appropriate sediment removal periods, address proper disposal methods, and outline procedures for the final removal of the sediment control device.

CASE STUDIES

Loantaka Brook Preserve[1]

Introduction

Loantaka Brook Preserve is an excellent example of how designing with site protection in mind can turn what would normally become a scar in the landscape into a place whose design maintains the integrity of the forest in which it was constructed.

When it becomes necessary to expand a utility company's infrastructure, parks and natural areas are vulnerable to infringement by the construction of new utility lines. In Morristown, New Jersey, a new natural gas pipeline was mandated to be routed through the Loantaka Brook Reservation, a Morris County park, in order to avoid a residential neighborhood that already contained two gas lines. Andropogon Associates, Ltd., was hired by the Park Commission to devise a set of

---

[1] Landscape Architect: Andropogon Associates, Ltd.

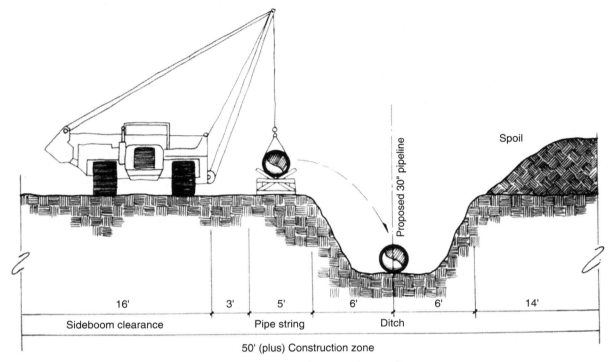

Figure 10.11. Section of a typical pipeline construction technique. *(Image: Andropogon)*

design strategies in cooperation with Algonquin Gas Transmission Company to ensure that the pipeline installation would have no adverse long-term effects on the park.

Nature of the Problem

There are multiple problems with the typical design and construction of utility corridors. They stem from the design process itself and affect the details of implementation. These corridors are designed by pipeline engineers who determine their route and size, with the main focus on successfully navigating the hurdles of the regulatory process and not on fitting the design successfully within its local environmental context.

Many of the decisions that are made in an effort to meet industry regulations are in direct opposition to respect for the environment in which they are constructed. The standard pipeline installation creates a 75-ft to 150-ft (22.8–45.7-m) swath of disturbance (Figure 10.11). The amount of vegetation lost within a forest is significant. This break in the canopy creates a set of edges within the forest that truncates the typical patterns of movement, places the trees adjacent to the opening under stress, and weakens the trees' ability to resist disease and infestation. The use of extremely heavy equipment within the corridor also causes serious soil compaction, limiting the ability of the vegetation to reestablish after construction is completed. After completion, the only vegetative cover mandated within the disturbed pipeline corridor is non-native turf grasses for soil stabilization, which are inappropriate to a shaded forest environment.

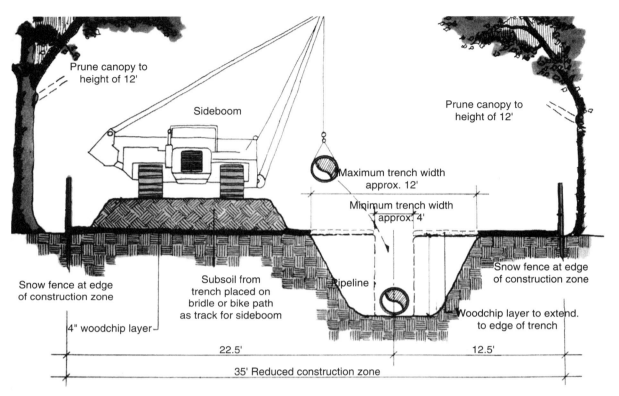

Figure 10.12. Section of a reorganized pipeline construction technique to minimize disturbance. *(Photos: Andropogon)*

Controlling Disturbance and the Grading Process

In an effort to combat these problems, the design team collaborated with the contractors and park officials and came up with three critical design changes. First, the pipeline's route was realigned to follow a gravel horse trail and an asphalt bike path. By utilizing this existing seam of disturbance, the area of forest to be cleared and the area of soil disturbed were minimized. Second, disturbance to adjacent habitat was minimized. The area to be disturbed was fenced off along the entire route before any construction took place. Within the construction zone, all large canopy trees were felled by

qualified arborists and lowered with ropes. Those canopy trees directly adjacent to the construction site were pruned to a height of 18 ft (5.5 m) to allow the necessary clearance for the sideboom used to lay the pipes in place. Wherever possible, tree stumps were left in situ and cut flush with the ground to leave soil undisturbed. Third, the construction zone was also reduced by creatively organizing the construction process (Figure 10.12). The upper layers of forest soil, located where the trench was to be excavated, were harvested in blocks or mats to be returned when the construction was completed. This was accomplished by welding large steel plates to the bucket of the excavating

(a)　　　　　　　　　　　　　　　　　　　(b)

Figure 10.13. View along the trail corridor. (a) Before construction. (b) After construction. *(Photos: Andropogon)*

equipment. The plates were slipped under the top-soil layer, thus removing the soil and herbaceous plants relatively intact. The heavy machinery used to lay the pipe worked on top of spoil material dug out of the trench, which also helped prevent soil compaction. This technique significantly reduced the width of the area to be disturbed. Normally, the excavated material would be placed on one side of the trench while the heavy equipment worked on the other. The pipe itself was welded in the trench instead of alongside it, although OSHA standards would prohibit such measures today without continual shoring of the ditch. Once the backfilling was completed, the forest mats were replaced and mulched with composted leaf litter. This combination of practices not only reduced the construction corridor down to 35 ft (10.7 m), but also provided for quick reestablishment of vegetation within the disturbed area. Just 1 year later, the forest floor showed dense regrowth of ferns, wildflowers, and resprouting of shrubs and trees (Figure 10.13).

SUMMARY

This chapter has introduced the basic principles and measures used in erosion and sedimentation control. Readers are encouraged to investigate the principles and measures that are appropriate to their particular regions and to go beyond the basics in understanding the relationship of storm water management, and construction management and practices, to the management of soil erosion and sedimentation.

CHAPTER 11

Determining Rates and Volumes of Storm Runoff: The Rational and Modified Rational Methods

INTRODUCTION

To design and size storm water management devices, such as grassed swales, drainage pipes, and detention storage ponds, it is first necessary to estimate the rates and volumes of runoff that must be handled. The science of hydrology, which deals with precipitation and runoff, includes a number of models that help predict the runoff to be used as input to the design procedures. Many of these are based on precipitation, since for most development sites long-term rainfall records are available. Unlike the deductions of a science, such as hydraulics, which deals with the flow of water in pipes and channels, over weirs, through orifices, and so forth, and in which model studies can be performed in a laboratory, the projections of hydrology cannot be replicated. Every storm or flood event is unique: the durations and intensities of precipitation vary. In addition, the growth stage of vegetation, the activity of soil organisms influencing infiltration rates, and the soil and air temperatures are not likely to be identical for several events. Nevertheless, experience has shown that the forecasts of storm runoff for various probabilities of occurrence are useful for planning and designing storm water management systems and structures. It must be kept in mind, however, that since only estimates are involved, it would be improper to calculate runoff rates and volumes to too great a degree of precision; that is, final results should be appropriately rounded.

RATIONAL METHOD

A frequently used formula for computing the peak rate of runoff from small drainage areas (i.e., less than about 200 ac or 80 ha) is the *Rational method.* The equation is:

$$q = CiA \qquad \textbf{(11.1)}$$

where

q = peak runoff rate, in cubic feet per second (ft^3/s or cfs)

C = dimensionless coefficient (between 0 and 1)

i = rainfall intensity, inches per hour (iph) for the design storm frequency and for the time of concentration of the drainage area

A = area of drainage area, acres (ac)

The equation is based on the theory that the peak rate of runoff from a small area is equal to the intensity of rainfall multiplied by a coefficient that depends on the characteristics of the drainage area, including land use, soils, and slope, and by the size of the drainage area. The extent of the

drainage area is determined by connecting the high points and ridge lines on a topographic map or grading plan until a closed system is developed (Figure 11.1). Drainage areas may vary in size from several hundred square feet (40 to 50 m²) for an area drain, or several square miles (square kilometers) for a stream, up to thousands of square miles (square kilometers) for a large river, in which case it is called a *watershed.* It must also be realized that drainage area boundaries are independent of property lines. It is important to include all parts of a drainage area, even if they are beyond the property line.

The Rational method makes the simplifying assumptions that the rainfall intensity is uniform for the duration of the storm, which must equal at least the time of concentration, and that the precipitation falls on the entire drainage area during that time. These assumptions obviously cannot be applied to large areas.

One acre-inch (ac-in.) per hour of water may be converted to cubic feet per second as follows:

$$1\,\text{acre} \times \frac{1\,\text{in.}}{\text{hr}} \times \frac{43{,}560\,\text{ft}^2}{\text{acre}} \times \frac{1}{12\,\text{in./ft.}} \times \frac{1}{3{,}600\,\text{sec/hr}}$$
$$= 1.0008\,\text{ft}^3/\text{s}$$

The rate computed by the Rational method is therefore dimensionally incorrect by 0.8%. This is generally ignored since, as previously stated, the field of hydrology is not an exact science.

For the metric system, Equation 11.1 ($q = CiA$) must be modified so that it can be used with the following measurement units:

q = peak runoff rate, cubic meters per second (m^3/s)

C = dimensionless coefficient (between 0 and 1)

i = rainfall intensity, mm/h, for the design storm frequency and for the time of concentration of the drainage area

A = drainage area, hectares (ha)

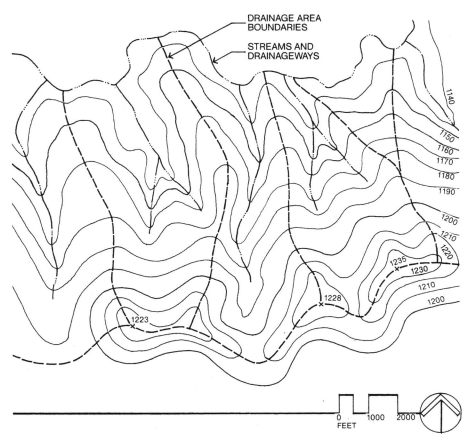

Figure 11.1. Drainage areas. Boundaries for drainage areas are determined by locating ridge lines and high points.

The adjustment factor is derived as follows:

$$q\,(\mathrm{m^3/s}) = C \times \frac{1\ \mathrm{mm}}{\mathrm{hr}} \times \frac{1\ \mathrm{m}}{1,000\ \mathrm{m}}$$

$$\times \frac{1\ \mathrm{hr}}{3,600\ \mathrm{sec}} \times A\,(\mathrm{ha}) \times \frac{10,000\ \mathrm{m^2}}{1\ \mathrm{ha}}$$

$$q\,(\mathrm{m^3/s}) = \frac{C \times i\,(\mathrm{mm/ha}) \times A\,(\mathrm{ha})}{360} \qquad \textbf{(11.2)}$$

When determining area, it is important to remember to convert square meters to hectares for this calculation.

The *runoff coefficient*, C, is a value between 0 and 1. Zero represents a completely pervious surface from which there is no runoff, while 1 represents a completely impervious and wetted surface from which there is total runoff. Table 11.1 contains suggested C values for a variety of surface conditions. For pervious areas, the C value would increase as the soil becomes saturated. Most drainage areas consist of a variety of surfaces with different C values. Runoff volumes may be computed for each surface separately, or an average C value can be computed for the entire drainage area if the locations of the various land uses are mixed throughout the area.

Rainfall intensity, i, is the rate of rainfall in inches per hour (iph) or mm per hour (mm/h)

Table 11.1 Recommended Runoff Coefficients (*C*)

Urban Areas[a]	
Downtown Business	0.70–0.95
Neighborhood Business	0.50–0.70
Single-Family Residential	0.30–0.50
Detached Multiunit Residential	0.40–0.60
Attached Multiunit Residential	0.60–0.75
Suburban Residential	0.25–0.40
Apartment	0.50–0.70
Light Industry	0.50–0.80
Heavy Industry	0.60–0.90
Parks, Cemeteries	0.10–0.25
Playgrounds	0.20–0.35
Railroad Yards	0.20–0.35
Unimproved	0.10–0.30
Urban Surfaces	
Roofs	0.80–0.95
Asphalt and Concrete Pavements	0.75–0.95
Gravel	0.35–0.70

	SOIL TEXTURE		
Rural and Suburban Areas[b]	**Sandy Loam**	**Clay and Silt Loam**	**Clay**
Woodland			
Flat (0–5% slope)	0.10	0.30	0.40
Rolling (5–10% slope)	0.25	0.35	0.50
Hilly (10–30% slope)	0.30	0.50	0.60
Pasture and Lawns			
Flat	0.10	0.30	0.40
Rolling	0.16	0.36	0.55
Hilly	0.22	0.42	0.60
Cultivated or No Plant Cover			
Flat	0.30	0.50	0.60
Rolling	0.40	0.60	0.70
Hilly	0.52	0.72	0.82

[a]From American Iron and Steel Institute (1980).
[b]From Schwab et al. (1971).

for the design storm frequency and for the time of concentration of the drainage area. The *storm frequency* is the number of years during which the design storm, or a storm exceeding it, statistically may be expected to occur once. It must be pointed out that the frequency is based on long-term probabilities and that, for example, a 10-year frequency storm could conceivably occur several times during a period of less than 10 years. This might be compared to throwing a die for which the overall probability of coming up 6 is one out of six throws but that could come up 6 several times in succession. The *design storm* is a storm with a frequency and duration for which the management system is designed. The selection of a design storm is based on economics, environmental context, and the ultimate consequences should the system overflow or it may be prescribed by applicable regulations. Rainfall intensities for various durations may be obtained from National Weather Service publications and charts similar to the one in Figure 11.2.

The *time of concentration* (T_c) is the time required for water to flow from the hydraulically most remote part of the drainage area to the section under consideration. It is important to realize that this is not necessarily the longest distance, since overland and channel flow time is dependent on slope, surface, and channel characteristics. Assuming a theoretical storm of uniform intensity falling uniformly over the entire drainage area with a duration equal to or exceeding the time of concentration, the maximum runoff is reached at the time of concentration. At this time, all parts of the drainage area are contributing simultaneously to the runoff at the section under consideration. Convenient charts that are used to estimate time of concentration are illustrated in Figure 11.3 for overland flow time, which is demonstrated in Example 11.2, and in Figure 11.4 for channel flow time, which is applied in Example 11.4. The USDA Natural Resources Conservation Service (formerly the Soil

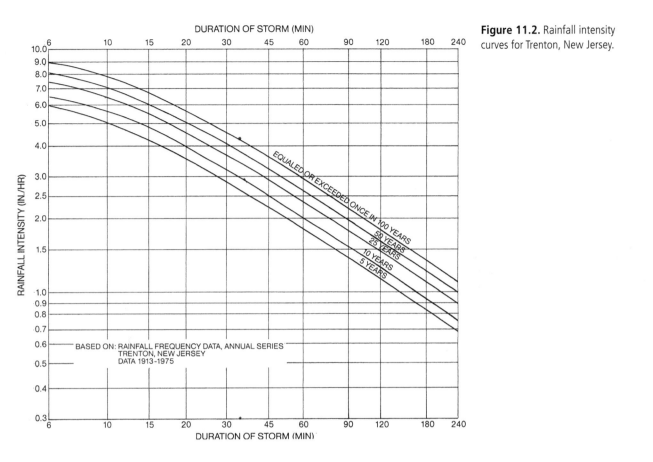

Figure 11.2. Rainfall intensity curves for Trenton, New Jersey.

Conservation Service) methodology for calculating the time of concentration, discussed in the next chapter, may also be used as a basis for determining design storm intensity using the Rational method.

▉ EXAMPLE 11.1

The drainage area for a grassed waterway is an 8.2-ac (3.3 ha) site for a small industrial plant. As shown in Figure 11.5, several different surfaces are dispersed throughout the site. These surfaces include 4.4 ac (1.8 ha) of relatively flat lawn with a silt loam soil, 2.8 ac (1.1 ha) of pavement, and 1.0 ac (0.4 ha) of roof surface. To simplify this

example, the rainfall intensity is assumed to be 2 iph. Calculate the peak rate of runoff for this drainage area.

SOLUTION 1

$A = 4.4$ ac lawn, 2.8 ac pavement, 1.0 ac roof

$i = 2$ iph

From Table 11.1:

$$C_{\text{flat lawn}} = 0.30$$
$$C_{\text{pavement}} = 0.85$$
$$C_{\text{roof}} = 0.95$$

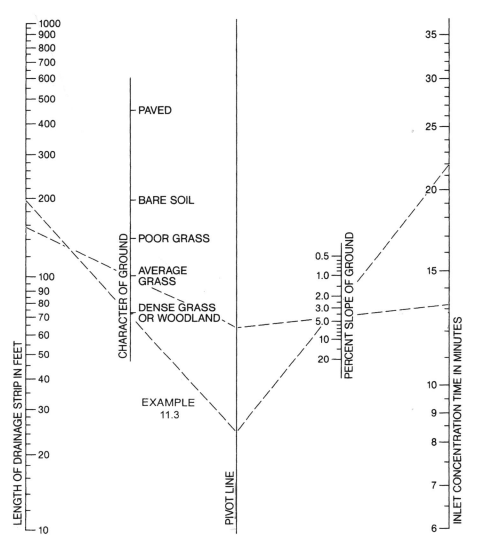

Figure 11.3. Nomograph for overland flow time.

Using the equation $q = CiA$, substitute the known values.

$$q_{lawn} = 0.30 \times 2.0 \times 4.4 = 2.64 \approx 2.6 \text{ ft}^3/\text{s}$$

$$q_{pavt.} = 0.85 \times 2.0 \times 2.8 = 4.76 \approx 4.8 \text{ ft}^3/\text{s}$$

$$q_{roof} = 0.95 \times 2.0 \times 1.0 = 1.9 \text{ ft}^3/\text{s}$$

$$q_{total} = 2.6 + 4.8 + 1.9 = 9.3 \text{ ft}^3/\text{s}$$

SOLUTION 2

$$A_{total} = 4.4 + 2.8 + 1.0 = 8.2 \text{ ac}$$

$$i = 2 \text{ iph}$$

$$C_{ave.} = \frac{(4.4 \times 0.30) + (2.8 \times 0.85) + (1.0 \times 0.95)}{8.2}$$

$$= 0.567 \approx 0.57$$

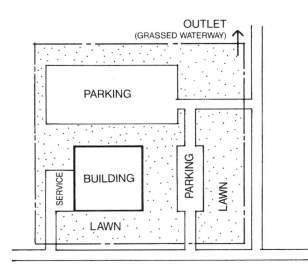

Figure 11.5. Schematic site plan for Example 11.1.

Note that the total q value is the same whether it is computed separately or using an average C value. However, for this example, the average C value provides a more descriptive representation of the actual runoff conditions for the drainage area. ■

■ **EXAMPLE 11.2**

Determine the peak runoff rate for a drainage area consisting of 1.78 ha of lawn with a runoff coefficient (C) of 0.30, 1.13 ha of pavement with $C = 0.85$, and 0.40 ha of roof surface with $C = 0.95$. Use a rainfall intensity of 50.8 mm/h. (Note that this example is a metric conversion of Example 11.1.)

SOLUTION

$A_{total} = 1.78 + 1.13 + 0.40 = 3.31$ ha

$i = 50.8$ mm/h

$C_{ave.} = \dfrac{(1.78 \times 0.30) + (1.13 \times 0.85) + (0.40 \times 0.95)}{3.31}$

$\qquad = 1.8745/3.31 = 0.566 \approx 0.57$

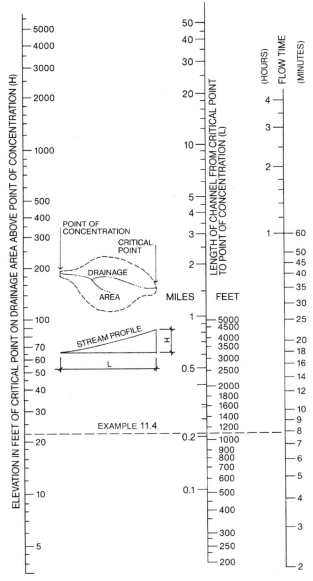

Figure 11.4. Nomograph for channel flow time.

Again substitute the known values into the equation $q = CiA$.

$q_{total} = 0.57 \times 2.0 \times 8.2 = 9.3$ ft^3/s

Substituting the known values into the equation $q = CiA/360$.

$$q_\text{total} = \frac{0.57 \times 50.8 \times 3.31}{360}$$

$$= 0.266 \text{ m}^3/\text{s}$$

The following is a check against Example 11.1:

$$0.266 \text{ m}^3/\text{s} \times 35.315 \text{ ft}^3/\text{m}^3 = 9.4 \text{ ft}^3/\text{s}$$

Example 11.1 resulted in 9.3 ft³/s. However, when the factor 1.008 (previously derived) is applied, this becomes $9.3 \times 1.008 = 9.37 \approx 9.4$ ft³/s. ■

■ EXAMPLE 11.3

The 1.5-ac drainage area in New Jersey, illustrated in Figure 11.6, consists of 0.14 ac of pavement, 0.20 ac of woodland, and 1.16 ac of lawn. The soil

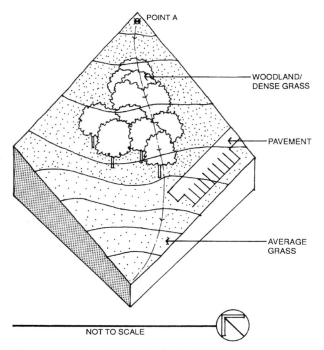

Figure 11.6. Schematic site plan for Example 11.3.

is a silt loam, and the slopes range up to 5%. Calculate the peak rate of runoff leaving the site at the southwest corner. A 10-year design storm is to be used.

SOLUTION

The first step in this problem is to determine the time of concentration in order to establish the rainfall intensity value, i. Additional information is required to compute the overland flow time. From visual inspection, it is determined that point A is the hydraulically most remote point on the site. The *distance* that water must travel to reach the outlet point from point A, the *slope* of its path of travel, and the *surface character* of the path must also be determined. This is summarized in the following table:

Length	Character	Slope	Time of Concentration
200 ft	Woodland/dense grass	2%	22 minutes
160 ft	Average grass	4%	13 minutes
			35 minutes

The time of concentration is determined from the chart in Figure 11.3. First, the travel distance is located along the length line; then the surface character is located on the ground line. A straight line is drawn through these two points until it intersects with the pivot line. Next, the slope of the path is located on the percent slope line, and a straight line is drawn from the point on the pivot line through the point on the slope line until it intersects with the inlet concentration time. This point of intersection represents the time of concentration in minutes. No additional time needs to be computed, since there is no channel flow involved in this example.

The intensity of the design storm can then be obtained from the chart in Figure 11.2. Locate the 35-minute storm duration along the horizontal axis of the chart and extend a vertical line until it intersects with the 10-year frequency curve. From the point on the curve, extend a horizontal line to the left until it intersects with the vertical axis. The value obtained, about 2.8 iph, is the rainfall intensity for the storm duration.

Note that the scales are logarithmic. The chart in Figure 11.2 applies to New Jersey. The appropriate charts or similar information for other states may be obtained from the state department of conservation, water resources agency, or other similar agency, or from the National Weather Service. A sampling of rainfall intensity curves for other regions of the United States is illustrated in Figure 11.7.

The next step is to select an appropriate runoff coefficient from Table 11.1 for the various surfaces.

$$C_{pavement} = 0.90$$
$$C_{woodland} = 0.30$$
$$C_{lawn} = 0.30$$

The last step is to substitute all the known values into the equation $q = CiA$.

$$q_{total} = (0.90 \times 2.8 \times 0.14) + (0.30 \times 2.8 \times 0.20)$$
$$+ (0.30 \times 2.8 \times 1.16)$$
$$= 2.8 \times (0.90 \times 0.14 + 0.30 \times 0.20$$
$$+ 0.30 \times 1.16)$$
$$= 2.8 \times 0.53 = 1.484 \approx 1.5 \text{ ft}^3/\text{s} \blacksquare$$

The following example demonstrates the determination of the time of concentration when overland flow and stream flow are involved.

■ EXAMPLE 11.4

Figure 11.8 shows a 95-ac drainage area that is completely wooded, with a stream flowing through the center. The soil survey report indicates a silt loam. The topographic map shows that the average

drainage area slope is 6%, while the stream slope is 2%. A road culvert is to be installed at the outlet from this drainage area and must be designed for a 50-year storm frequency. What is the peak rate of runoff for which the culvert must be designed?

SOLUTION

An examination of the topographic map shows that A is the hydraulically most remote point. From A to B, the water flows overland for 970 ft along a 4% slope. (The *average* drainage area slope is 6%.) From B to C there is 1,100 ft of stream flow with a 2% slope. Using Figure 11.3 as before, the overland flow is determined as 35 minutes. To obtain the stream flow time, Figure 11.4 must be used. To calculate H, which is the elevation of the critical point above the point of concentration, that is, the evation of point B above point C, distance B–C is multiplied by the slope:

$$H = 1,100 \times 0.02 = 22 \text{ ft}$$

A straight line is drawn from 22 ft on the H scale on the left through 1,100 ft on the L scale to the T scale on the right, which yields about 8 minutes. (Note the rapidity of the stream flow compared to overland flow.) Then the total time of concentration is overland flow time + stream flow time, or 35 + 8 = 43 minutes. The intensity for a 50-year 43-minute storm is about 3.3 iph from Figure 11.2. The C value for woodland on silt loam with an average slope of 6% is 0.35 from Table 11.1. The design peak rate of runoff is thus

$$q = CiA$$
$$= 0.35 \times 3.3 \times 95$$
$$\approx 110 \text{ ft}^3/\text{s}$$

Therefore, the culvert must be sized to accommodate 110 ft³/s.

As demonstrated by the following examples, common sense should be applied when determining the time of concentration, particularly with

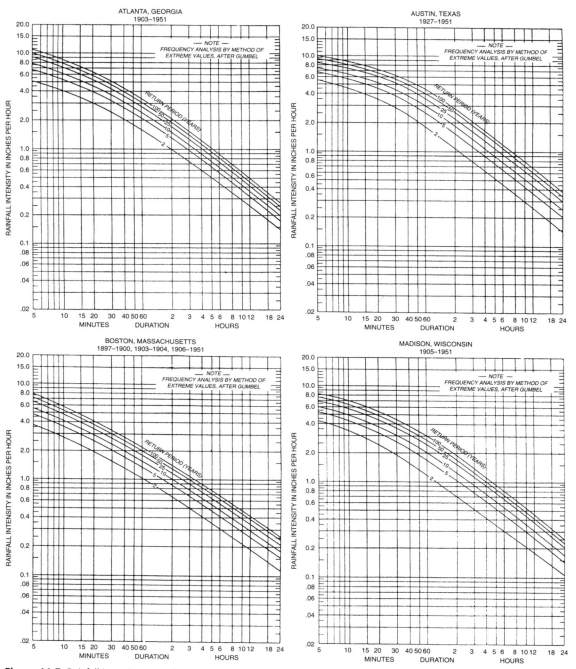

Figure 11.7. Rainfall intensity curves for various U.S. cities.

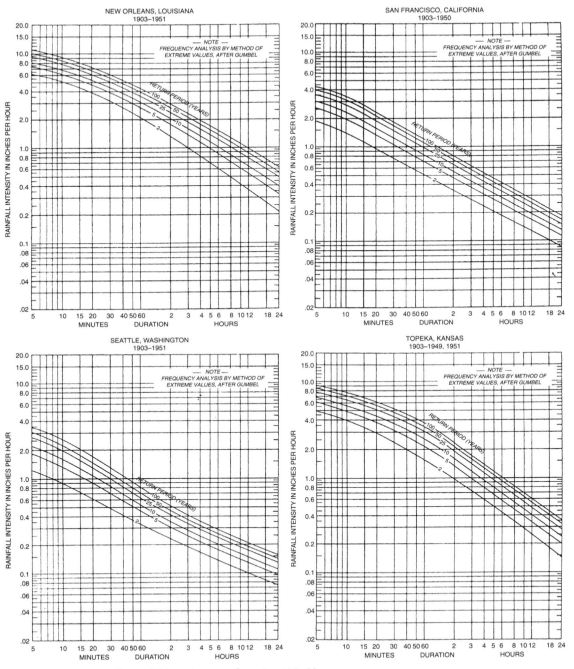

Figure 11.7. (continued). Rainfall intensity curves for various U.S. cities.

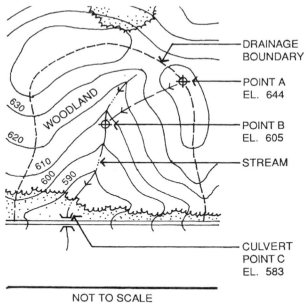

DRAINAGE BOUNDARY

POINT A EL. 644

POINT B EL. 605

STREAM

CULVERT POINT C EL. 583

NOT TO SCALE

Figure 11.8. Schematic site plan for Example 11.4.

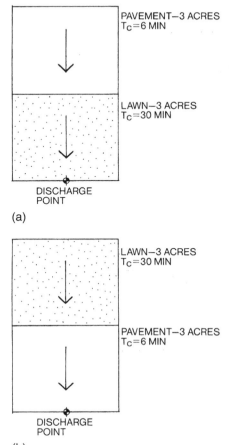

PAVEMENT—3 ACRES $T_C=6$ MIN

LAWN—3 ACRES $T_C=30$ MIN

DISCHARGE POINT

(a)

LAWN—3 ACRES $T_C=30$ MIN

PAVEMENT—3 ACRES $T_C=6$ MIN

DISCHARGE POINT

(b)

Figure 11.9. Schematic plans. (a) Example 11.5A. (b) Example 11.5B.

regard to the location of different surface types (C values) on a site.

■ EXAMPLE 11.5A

Figure 11.9a schematically illustrates a drainage area that consists of 3 ac of pavement ($C= 0.80$) and 3 ac of lawn ($C= 0.30$). In contrast to Example 11.1, where the different surfaces were mixed throughout the site, these two surfaces are concentrated and segregated. Determine the peak rate of runoff at the point of discharge from the site for a 10-year storm frequency. Assume a 6-minute travel time over the pavement and a 30-minute travel time over the lawn. The runoff from the pavement flows over the lawn area to the discharge point.

SOLUTION

Since it takes the hydraulically most remote drop of water 6 minutes to flow over the pavement and

an additional 30 minutes to flow over the lawn before reaching the discharge point, the total time of concentration is 36 minutes (6 + 30). Entering the chart in Figure 11.2 with a storm duration of 36 minutes, a rainfall intensity of approximately 2.8 iph is determined from the 10-year storm frequency curve. From the Rational formula, the peak rate of runoff is calculated as follows:

$$q = CiA$$
$$q_{lawn} = 0.30 \times 2.8 \times 3.0 = 2.52 \approx 2.5 \text{ ft}^3/\text{s}$$

$q_{\text{pavt}} = 0.80 \times 2.8 \times 3.0 = 6.72 \approx 6.7 \text{ ft}^3/\text{s}$

$q_{\text{total}} = 2.5 + 6.7 = 9.2 \text{ ft}^3/\text{s}$ ◼

◼ EXAMPLE 11.5B

All the conditions in this example, including travel times, are the same as in Example 11.5A except that the relationship of pavement to lawn has been reversed. Now the runoff from the lawn flows over the pavement to the discharge point, as illustrated in Figure 11.9b. Again, calculate the peak rate of runoff from the site using a 10-year storm frequency.

SOLUTION

In the previous example, the lawn attenuated the velocity of flow from the pavement, since it was located between the paved area and the point of discharge. However, in this example, the flow from the pavement is not attenuated, and its runoff concentrates at the discharge point in 6 minutes. Therefore, the storm duration for determining the rainfall intensity is 6 minutes for the pavement. Again, referring to Figure 11.2, the rainfall intensity is 6.6 iph on the 10-year storm frequency curve. Thus, the peak rate of runoff from the pavement is

$q_{\text{pavt.}} = 0.80 \times 6.6 \times 3.0 = 15.84 \approx 15.8 \text{ ft}^3/\text{s}$

The runoff rate from the pavement alone is considerably greater than the runoff rate for the entire drainage area in Example 11.5A.

This example demonstrates that great care must be taken to arrive at a realistic estimate of runoff rates. Average C values should not be used unless the various land uses are distributed uniformly throughout a drainage area. For example, if a 40-ac housing development with streets, gutters, and storm sewers were to be constructed in a 200-ac wooded drainage area, the runoff from the dissimilar land uses should be determined separately and

then added. The next section will include procedures for accomplishing this. ◼

MODIFIED RATIONAL METHOD

The Rational method uses runoff coefficients (C) that are constant for all frequencies and all storms and yields only peak runoff rates, using rainfall intensities for a specific storm frequency and duration. Normally, the times of concentration on which these intensities are based are relatively short. It has been recognized that for the less frequent storm events, such as those that may occur with frequencies of 25 to 100 years, the short times of concentration do not adequately represent the total duration of rainfall with its resulting runoff. The durations of storm events used for the Rational method, equal to the time of concentration, are usually parts of larger storm systems with periods of rainfall preceding and extending beyond the time of concentration. Much of the soil's ability to absorb storm runoff has been exhausted by "antecedent precipitation."

The Modified Rational method (MRM) recommends that an *antecedent precipitation factor* (C_A) be included in the Rational formula, so that it becomes:

$$q = CC_A iA \qquad (11.3)$$

Recommended values for C_A are listed in Table 11.2. The product of $C \times C_A$ must never exceed 1, since otherwise the computed runoff rate would be greater than the intensity of the design storm, which is incongruous. The American Public Works Association suggests that the use of the MRM for the determination of required storage volumes be limited to small drainage areas, such as those less than 20 ac (8.1 ha).

While peak runoff rates are sufficient for sizing structures, such as culverts, waterways, and

Table 11.2 Recommended Antecedent Precipitation Factors

Frequency	C_A
2 to 10	1.0
25	1.1
50	1.2
100	1.25

Source: From American Public Works Association (1981).

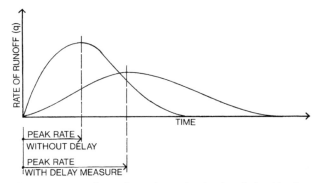

Figure 11.10. Hydrographs. Hydrographs plot the relationship of runoff rate to time. When land development takes place and delay measures such as retention and detention basins are not used, the peak occurs earlier and at a higher rate than if delay measures are used, as qualitatively illustrated in the graph.

pipes, the design of storage ponds and reservoirs requires the determination of inflow and outflow volumes, obtained from hydrographs. A *hydrograph* is a plot of flow rate (q) versus time (T) (Figure 11.10) or the tabular representation of such plots. Hydrographs are labeled by the duration (DUR) of the *rainfall events* producing them, not by the duration of the *runoff*. Thus, a 30-minute storm produces a 30-minute hydrograph, regardless of the duration of the runoff.

Some situations also require the determination of flow rates at any time during the runoff process, which can be obtained from hydrographs. The MRM also permits the determination of runoff for storm durations shorter or longer than the time of concentration.

Three types of simplified hydrographs can be developed by the MRM. For all three types the intensity used to calculate the maximum runoff rate (q_{max}) is that for the duration and frequency of the storm event.

Type A Hydrograph

The duration of the storm event is equal to the time of concentration, as shown in Figure 11.11.

$$q_p = CC_AiA \qquad (11.4)$$

The peak rate of runoff (q_p) is reached at the time of concentration (T_c). The time of recession

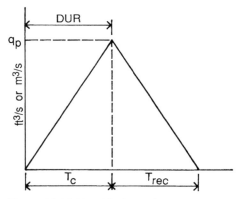

Figure 11.11. Type A hydrograph.

(T_{rec}) equals the time of concentration. This hydrograph represents the maximum potential runoff rate from the drainage area for the specified frequency.

Type B Hydrograph

As illustrated in Figure 11.12, the duration of the storm is greater than the time of concentration.

$$q_{max} = CC_AiA$$

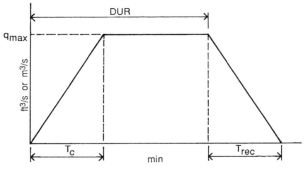

Figure 11.12. Type B hydrograph.

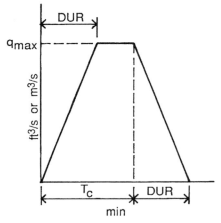

Figure 11.13. Type C hydrograph.

The maximum flow rate (q_{max}) is reached at the time of concentration but is smaller than that of the type A hydrograph, since the intensity for the longer duration is less. The runoff rate remains constant to the end of the storm duration. The time of recession equals the time of concentration.

Type C Hydrograph

The duration of the storm, as depicted in Figure 11.13, is less than the time of concentration.

$$q_{max} = CC_A iA(DUR/T_c) \qquad (11.6)$$

The maximum runoff rate (q_{max}) is reached at the end of the storm duration. It remains constant to the end of the time of concentration. The time of recession equals the duration of the storm. The intensity of the storm is greater than that used for the type A hydrograph. However, since the drainage area has not reached its time of concentration and maximum potential runoff rate, the reduction factor (DUR/T_c) is included in the equation.

■ EXAMPLE 11.6

Develop 10-, 25-, and 50-minute hydrographs for a 15-ac drainage area, having a C-value of 0.3 and a time of concentration of 25 minutes. A 100-year frequency is desired.

SOLUTION (10-MINUTE HYDROGRAPH)

Since the storm duration is less than the time of concentration, this is a type C hydrograph and the equation used is:

$$q_{max} = CC_A iA(DUR/T_c)$$
$$A = 1.25 \text{ (from Table 11.2)}$$
$$i = 7.9 \text{ iph (approx.) (from Figure 11.2)}$$
$$q_{max} = 0.3 \times 1.25 \times 7.9 \times 15 \times 10/25$$
$$q_{max} \approx 17.8 \text{ ft}^3/\text{s}$$

Note that although the duration of the storm event is only 10 minutes, the duration of runoff is 35 minutes. ($T_c + DUR$) (Figure 11.14).

SOLUTION (25-MINUTE HYDROGRAPH)

Since the duration of the storm event equals the time of concentration, this is a type A hydrograph (Figure 11.15). The equation used is:

$$q_p = CC_A iA$$
$$A = 1.25 \text{ (from Table 11.2)}$$
$$i = 5.1 \text{ iph (approx.) (from Figure 11.2)}$$
$$q_p = 0.3 \times 1.25 \times 5.1 \times 15$$
$$q_p \approx 28.7 \text{ ft}^3/\text{s}$$

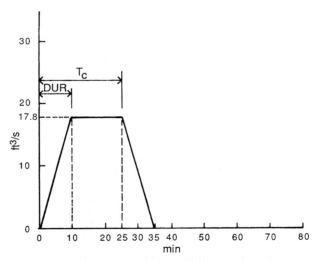

Figure 11.14. The 10-minute hydrograph for Example 11.6.

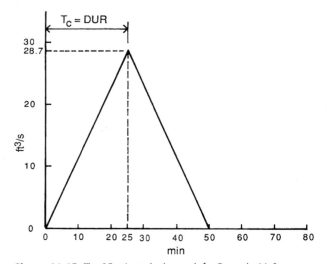

Figure 11.15. The 25-minute hydrograph for Example 11.6.

SOLUTION (50-MINUTE HYDROGRAPH)

Since the duration of the storm event is greater than the time of concentration, this is a type B hydrograph (Figure 11.16).

$$q_{max} = CC_A iA$$
$$A = 1.25 \text{ (from Table 11.2)}$$
$$i = 3.4 \text{ iph (approx.) (from Figure 11.2)}$$
$$q_{max} = 0.3 \times 1.25 \times 3.4 \times 15$$
$$q_{max} \approx 19.1 \text{ ft}^3/\text{s}$$

Figure 11.17a illustrates the computer input for the 50-minute hydrograph for Example 11.6. The computer program is designed to ask a series of questions to obtain the appropriate data to perform the calculations. Storm duration and frequency are inputs, whereas rainfall intensity is determined by the computer based upon digitized rainfall intensity curves. This accounts for the slight variation (19.0 ft³/s vs. 19.1 ft³/s) in the calculated flow rates (Figure 11.17b). ■

Hydrologic theory permits the combination of runoff hydrographs emanating from several subareas and then joining in one flow path. The next example will demonstrate this procedure.

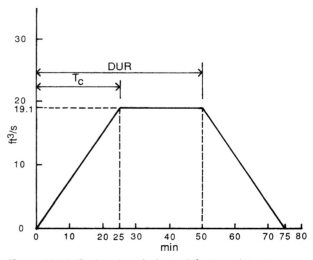

Figure 11.16. The 50-minute hydrograph for Example 11.6.

■ EXAMPLE 11.7

In Example 11.5B, the peak rate of runoff was calculated for the pavement only. By means of separate hydrographs, determine the total runoff from the lawn and pavement.

```
DO YOU WISH TO USE ANTECEDENT PRECIPITATION FACTORS   (Y/N)? Y

RUNOFF COEFFICIENT AND ACREAGE FOR SUBAREA No.1   (C1,A1) ? 0.3,15
RUNOFF COEFFICIENT AND ACREAGE FOR SUBAREA No.2   (C2,A2) ? 0,0
RUNOFF COEFFICIENT AND ACREAGE FOR SUBAREA No.3   (C3,A3) ? 0,0

TIME OF CONCENTRATION IN MINUTES? 25

RETURN PERIOD IN YEARS (FREQUENCY) OF THE DESIGN STORM:
(2,5,10,25,50, OR 100)? 100

STORM DURATION IN MINUTES (FOR TRIANGULAR HYDROGRAPHS DURATION = Tc;
MINIMUM DURATION IS 6 MINUTES, MAXIMUM IS 240 MINUTES.)? 50

TIME INTERVAL (MINUTES) FOR WHICH HYDROGRAPH ORDINATES ARE TO BE COMPUTED.(MUST
BE DIVISIBLE INTO Tc AND INTO DURATION OF STORM)? 25
```
(a)

```
THE RUNOFF COEFFICIENTS FOR AREAS 1 TO 3 ARE    :  0.30  0.00  0.00
THE ACREAGES FOR AREAS 1 TO 3 ARE               : 15.00  0.00  0.00
AVE. C * A.P.F. USED =   0.375        INTENSITY      =  3.38  IPH
ANTEC. PREC. FACT.   =   1.25         TOTAL AREA     = 15.00  ACRES
TIME OF CONCENTR.    = 25.0  MIN.     STORM DURATION = 50.0   MIN.
PEAK FLOW RATE       = 19.0  CFS      FREQUENCY      = 100    YEARS

                TIME, MIN.   FLOW RATE, CFS
                ---------    -----------
                   0.0           0.0
                  25.0          19.0
                  50.0          19.0
                  75.0           0.0
```
(b)

Figure 11.17. (a) Computer input for the 50-minute hydrograph. (b) Computer output for the 50-minute hydrograph. *(Software: MODRAT1© Kurt Nathan)*

SOLUTION

The runoff hydrograph from the pavement is type A, since the storm duration equals the time of concentration of 6 minutes. Listing the runoff by 6-minute intervals, the hydrograph can be represented as follows:

Time, min	Flow Rate, ft³/s
0	0.0
6	15.8
12	0.0

See computations in the solution to Example 11.5B.

The hydrograph for a 6-minute duration and a 36-minute time of concentration for the lawn area is type C, since the duration is shorter than the time of concentration.

$$q_{max} = CC_AiA(DUR/T_c)$$
$$A = 1.0 \text{ (for a 10-year frequency)}$$
$$i = 6.6 \text{ iph}$$
$$q_{max} = 0.3 \times 1.0 \times 6.6 \times 3 \times (6/36)$$
$$= 0.99 \approx 1.0 \text{ ft}^3/s$$

The hydrograph for the lawn is tabulated as follows:

Time, min	Flow Rate, ft³/s
0	0.0
6	1.0
12	1.0
18	1.0
24	1.0
30	1.0
36	1.0
42	0.0

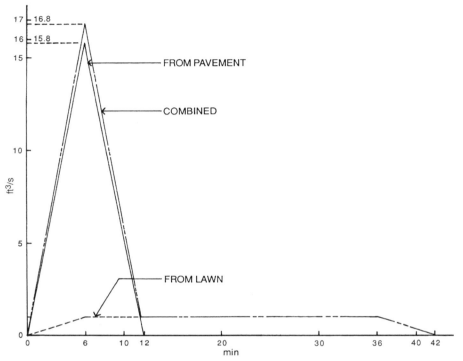

Figure 11.18. Combined hydrograph for Example 11.7.

The two hydrographs may be combined as follows:

Time, min	Flow Rate from Pavement, ft³/s	Flow Rate from Lawn, ft³/s	Total Runoff, ft³/s
0	0.0	0.0	0.0
6	15.8	1.0	16.8
12	0.0	1.0	1.0
18	0.0	1.0	1.0
24	0.0	1.0	1.0
30	0.0	1.0	1.0
36	0.0	1.0	1.0
42	0.0	0.0	0.0

Although the runoff from the lawn is ignored in Example 11.5B, the combined hydrograph shows that the lawn area is contributing 1 ft³/s at the 6-minute T_c for the pavement. Therefore, the peak runoff rate is 16.8 ft³/s, not 15.8, as previously computed (Figure 11.18). Including the lawn in this example does not change the outcome significantly; however, considerable differences may result for larger drainage areas. ■

VOLUMES OF RUNOFF, STORAGE, AND RELEASE

The area under a hydrograph represents the volume of runoff (*Vol*). If the *q*-values on the y-axis are in ft³/s and the *T*-values on the *x*-axis are converted into seconds, the volume can be computed as

$$Vol = ft^3/sec \times sec = ft^3 \qquad (11.7)$$

Since the MRM specifies for each type of hydrograph that the time of recession must equal the time of rise,[1] the volumes for type A and B hydrographs are the products of the *duration* in seconds times the maximum flow rate in ft³/s. For type C hydrographs, the volume is the product of the *time of concentration* in seconds multiplied by the maximum flow rate in ft³. This may be seen conceptually by the diagrams in Figure 11.19.

■ EXAMPLE 11.8

Compute the runoff volumes for the 25- and 50-minute storm durations for the drainage area of Example 11.6.

SOLUTION (25-MINUTE DURATION)
The first step is to convert the duration from minutes to seconds (25 min × 60 sec/min = 1,500 sec). The peak runoff rate for the 25-minute storm is 28.7 ft³/s from the solution for the 25-minute hydrograph. The volume (*Vol*) for the 25-minute storm is computed as follows:

$$Vol = 28.7 \text{ ft}^3/\text{s} \times 1,500 \text{ sec} = 43,050 \text{ ft}^3$$

SOLUTION (50-MINUTE DURATION)
The duration in seconds is 50 min × 60 sec/min = 3,000 sec. The maximum runoff rate for the 50-minute storm is 19.1 ft³/s from the solution for the 50-minute hydrograph. The volume (*Vol*) for the 50-minute storm is computed as follows:

$$Vol = 19.1 \text{ ft}^3/\text{s} \times 3,000 \text{ sec} = 57,300 \text{ ft}^3 \text{ ■}$$

---

[1] This is obviously an oversimplification and there are other systems, such as the NRCS Triangular Unit Hydrograph method, using different proportions. However, for the formulas used here, these configurations, as recommended by the American Public Works Association, must be used.

This shows that short, intense storms (with corresponding high *i*-values and peak runoff rates) do not produce the greatest runoff volumes.

REQUIRED STORAGE FOR DETENTION OR RETENTION PONDS BY THE MODIFIED RATIONAL METHOD

The most important use of the MRM is in the determination of required storage volumes for detention or retention ponds. The procedure is to subtract the volume of outflow from the basin from the inflow volume to the basin for the same duration. The difference is the required storage.

Usually, the initial duration used is the time of concentration. However, as shown in Example 11.8, short, intense storm events do not necessarily yield the greatest volumes. Therefore, the duration is then increased from the time of concentration by equal time intervals until the maximum required storage is reached. The rate of outflow is generally prescribed by governmental regulations. Most often the maximum postdevelopment outflow for specified frequencies cannot exceed the predevelopment rate for the same frequencies.

■ EXAMPLE 11.9

Determine the required storm water storage if the 15-ac drainage area of Example 11.6 is developed so that the average *C* value is increased to 0.75 and the time of concentration is reduced to 15 minutes. The local ordinance states that the postdevelopment 100-year outflow from the area cannot exceed the 28.7 ft³/s predevelopment rate previously computed for the 25-minute T_c.

SOLUTION
Starting with the time of concentration of 15 minutes, *i* for a 100-year frequency, and a 15-minute

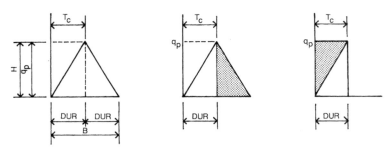

(a) *Type A hydrograph*
By geometry, the area of a triangle is $A = 1/2\ B \times H$
For hydrographs: if
A = Volume
$B = 2 \times$ Duration
$H = q_p$
then $Vol = 1/2 \times (2 \times DUR) \times q_p = DUR \times q_p$

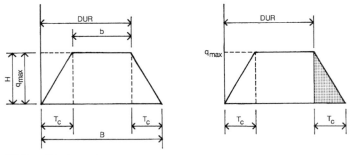
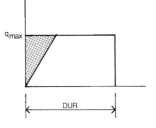

(b) *Type B hydrograph*
By geometry, the area of a trapezoid is $A = [(B + b)/2] \times H$
For hydrographs: if
A = Volume
B = Duration + T_c
b = Duration − T_c
$H = q_{max}$
then $Vol = [(DUR + T_c + DUR − T_c)/2] \times q_{max} = [(2 \times DUR)/2] \times q_{max} = DUR \times q_{max}$

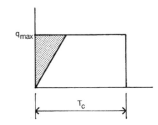

(c) *Type C hydrograph*
Geometry similar to that of type B hydrograph. If
A = Volume
$B = T_c + DUR$
$b = T_c − DUR$
$H = q_{max}$
then $Vol = [(T_c + DUR + T_c − DUR)/2] \times q_{max} = [(2 \times T_c)/2] \times q_{max} = T_c \times q_{max}$

Figure 11.19. Volume diagrams.

Table 11.3 Required Storage at 5-Minute Intervals for Example 11.9

Storm Freq., yr	Duration, min	Intensity, iph [a]	C_A[b]	Maximum Inflow, ft³/s[c]	Maximum Outflow, ft³/s[d]	Inflow Volume, ft³[e]	Outflow Storage, ft³[f]	Required Storage, ft³[g]
100	15	6.8	1.25	95.6	28.7	86,040	25,830	60,210
100	20	5.7	1.25	80.2	28.7	96,240	34,440	61,800
100	25	5.1	1.25	71.7	28.7	107,550	43,050	64,500
100	30	4.6	1.25	64.7	28.7	116,460	51,660	*64,800
100	35	4.2	1.25	59.1	28.7	124,110	60,270	63,840

[a] From Figure 11.2.
[b] From Table 11.2.
[c] From $q = CC_AiA$ for postdevelopment conditions.
[d] Allowable outflow rate from predevelopment conditions.
[e] From duration in sec × inflow rate (ft³/s).
[f] From duration in sec × outflow rate (ft³/s).
[g] Inflow volume − outflow volume.
*Maximum, or critical, storage volume.

duration is 6.8 iph from Figure 11.2. CA is 1.25 from Table 11.2. Using the type A hydrograph, the equation is

$$q_p = CC_AiA$$
$$q_p = 0.75 \times 1.25 \times 6.8 \times 15$$
$$q_p = 95.6 \text{ ft}^3/\text{s inflow rate to pond}$$
$$Vol_i = 95.6 \text{ ft}^3/\text{s} \times 15\text{min} \times 60 \text{ sec/min}$$
$$= 86,040 \text{ ft}^3 \text{ inflow volume}$$
$$Vol_o = 28.7 \text{ ft}^3/\text{s} \times 15 \text{ min} \times 60 \text{ sec/min}$$
$$= 25,830 \text{ ft}^3 \text{ outflow volume}$$

The storage volume required for a 100-year 15-minute storm event is

$$Vol_{stor} = 86.040 \text{ ft}^3 \text{ inflow} - 25,830 \text{ ft}^3 \text{ outflow}$$
$$= 60,210 \text{ ft}^3$$

Using a 5-minute time increment, the required storage for a 20-minute storm is determined next. The intensity, i, for a 100-year frequency and a 20-minute duration is 5.7 iph from figure 11.2.

$$q_{max} = CC_AiA$$
$$q_{max} = 0.75 \times 1.25 \times 5.7 \times 15$$
$$q_{max} = 80.2 \text{ ft}^3/\text{s inflow rate to pond}$$
$$Vol_i = 80.2 \text{ ft}^3/\text{s} \times 20 \text{ min} \times 60 \text{ sec/min}$$
$$= 96,240 \text{ ft}^3 \text{ inflow vol.}$$
$$Vol_o = 28.7 \text{ ft}^3/\text{s} \times 20 \text{ min} \times 60 \text{ sec/min}$$
$$= 34,440 \text{ ft}^3 \text{ outflow vol.}$$

The storage volume required for a 100-year 20-minute storm event is

$$Vol_{stor} = 96,240 \text{ ft}^3 \text{ inflow} - 34,440 \text{ ft}^3 \text{ outflow}$$
$$= 61,800 \text{ ft}^3$$

The procedure is continued with 5-minute intervals. The results are presented in Table 11.3.

In this case, the maximum or "critical" storage requirement for a 100-year event results from a storm duration of 30 minutes. The outlet structure for the pond should discharge 28.7 ft³/s when the pond contains 64,800 ft³. It must be emphasized

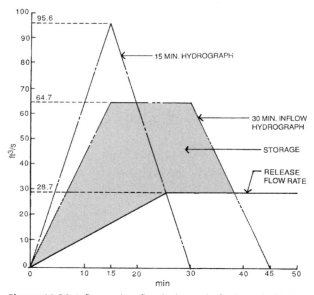

Figure 11.20. Inflow and outflow hydrographs for Example 11.9.

that the procedure yields a volume that is only an estimate, possibly sufficient for a small pond in a situation where failure would not cause serious damage and liability. Where these conditions are not met, the results produce a starting point for design, and the actual required volume must be determined by a detailed analysis of the proposed outlet structure and the actual pond dimensions, which is called *reservoir routing*. A discussion of this topic can be found in engineering hydrology textbooks. Storm water management regulations may require the routing of the runoff from additional storm frequencies.

The inflow and outflow hydrographs for this example are illustrated in Figure 11.20. The maximum release flow does not take place immediately. The MRM specifies that it occurs at the point where the release rate intersects with the

(a)
```
DO YOU WISH TO USE ANTECEDENT PRECIPITATION FACTORS  (Y/N)? Y

RUNOFF COEFFICIENT AND ACREAGE FOR SUBAREA No.1  (C1,A1) ? .75,15
RUNOFF COEFFICIENT AND ACREAGE FOR SUBAREA No.2  (C2,A2) ?
RUNOFF COEFFICIENT AND ACREAGE FOR SUBAREA No.3  (C3,A3) ?

TIME OF CONCENTRATION IN MINUTES? 15

RETURN PERIOD IN YEARS (FREQUENCY) OF THE DESIGN STORM:
(2,5,10,25,50, OR 100)? 100

DESIRED RELEASE RATE FROM DETENTION STORAGE IN CFS? 28.7

STORM DURATION IN MINUTES (FOR TRIANGULAR HYDROGRAPHS DURATION = Tc;
MINIMUM DURATION IS 6 MINUTES, MAXIMUM IS 240 MINUTES.)? 15

TIME INTERVAL (MINUTES) FOR WHICH HYDROGRAPH ORDINATES ARE TO BE COMPUTED.(MUST
BE DIVISIBLE INTO Tc AND INTO DURATION OF STORM)?

POSTDEVELOPMENT

AREA =  15.00 ACRES      C-COEFF.=  0.750      TC =  15.0 MIN.
```

(b)

FREQ. YRS.	DUR. MIN.	INT. IN./HR	A.P.F.	PEAK INFL. CFS	PEAK OUTFL. CFS	REQ.STOR. CUFT
100	15	6.91	1.25	97.2	28.7	61644
100	20	5.70	1.25	80.1	28.7	61714
100	25	5.11	1.25	71.9	28.7	64841
100	30	4.64	1.25	65.2	28.7	65781
100	35	4.24	1.25	59.7	28.7	65090

Figure 11.21. (a) Computer input for Example 11.9. (b) Computer output for Example 11.9. *(software: MODRAT2© Kurt Nathan)*

recession portion of a hydrograph having a duration equal to the time of concentration (type A hydrograph), that is, 15 minutes for this example.

Figure 11.21a is the input to solve Example 11.9 by computer. As in Example 11.6, the program provides a series of prompts (or questions) to solicit the appropriate data. Once again, duration and frequency are inputs and intensity is calculated from digitized intensity curves. In examining the output (Figure 11.21b), the "critical" storm duration of 30 minutes is consistent with the previous calculation. However, the required storage volumes are slightly different, reflecting the variation in the intensity values. ■

■ EXAMPLE 11.10

Converting the units in Example 11.9 to metric units, determine the volume of inflow to the storage pond for a storm duration of 15 minutes and a 100-year frequency.

SOLUTION

$$q_p = \frac{CC_A iA}{360}$$

$$q_p = \frac{0.75 \times 1.25 \times 172.72 \times 6.0705}{360}$$

$$q_p = 2.73046 \ \text{m}^3/\text{s inflow rate to pond}$$

$$Vol_i = 2.73046 \ \text{m}^3/\text{s} \times 15 \ \text{min} \times 60 \ \text{s/min}$$

$$= 2,457.4 \ \text{m}^3 \ \text{inflow volume} \approx 2,457 \ \text{m}^3$$

A comparison with the volume in Example 11.9 can be made as follows:

$$2,457 \ \text{m}^3 \times 35.315 \ \text{ft}^3/\text{m}^3 = 86,768.9 \ \text{ft}^3 \approx 86,769 \ \text{ft}^3$$

The result from Example 11.9 was 86,040 ft³. If the adjustment factor of 1.008 is applied, the result becomes 86,728 ft³ (1.008 × 86,040 ft³ = 86,728 ft³), which is very close to the metric calculation. Since, as previously stated, hydrology is not an exact science, these differences are not significant. Note that when doing calculations, it is preferable not to round intermediate computations. Only the final result should be rounded. ■

SUMMARY

This chapter has described the Rational method for determining storm water surface runoff rates. It has introduced the concept of time of concentration for a drainage area and explained the Modified Rational method (MRM) of developing simplified hydrographs and determining volumes of runoff and required storm water storage. The following chapter will deal with the Natural Resources Conservation Service (NRCS) methodology.

CHAPTER 12

Natural Resources Conservation Service Methods of Estimating Runoff Rates, Volumes, and Required Detention Storage

INTRODUCTION

The USDA NRCS, formerly known as the Soil Conservation Service (SCS), has developed a methodology for determining runoff rates and volumes. Many other government agencies and private consultants have adopted the NRCS hydrologic procedures. These are based on runoff, in inches, resulting from rainfall, in inches, for a specific drainage area and land use and for a specified storm duration.

Normally, this duration is far greater than the time of concentration, in contrast to that of the Rational method, and therefore the rainfall intensity is not constant for the design storm event. However, the assumption that rain falls equally on the entire drainage area still applies.

The inches of precipitation are transformed into inches of runoff by means of a runoff curve number (*CN*), based on soils, land use, impervious areas, interception by vegetation and structures, and temporary surface storage. Figure 12.1 illustrates the relationship between *CN* and direct runoff. Hydrographs are developed by means of unit hydrograph theory and the modified attenuation-kinematic

routing method. A discussion of these two procedures is beyond the scope of this book; this chapter will be limited to the use of the 1986 edition of SCS Technical Release 55, *Urban Hydrology for Small Watersheds* (TR55). Since the original publication was produced by the NRCS under its former name, TR55 will continue to be referred to as an SCS document in this text.

The 1986 edition of TR55 contains methods for estimating runoff rates and volumes that can be performed through the use of charts and simplified hand or calculator computations, which for that reason are presented in this chapter. These procedures are still valid, although the current TR55

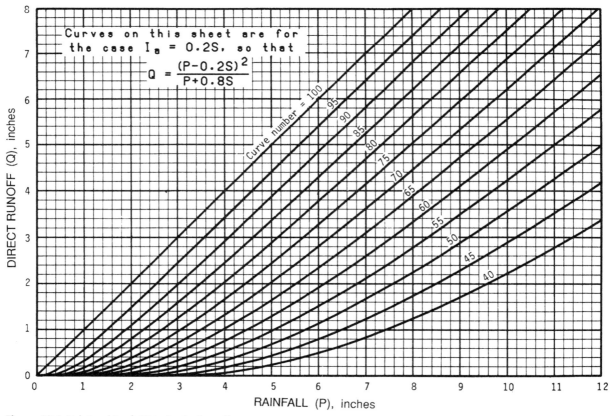

Figure 12.1. Relationship of *CN* to depth of runoff.

software has been enhanced to include more complex hydrologic computational methods. The l986 edition is a simplified condensation of SCS hydrologic procedures, suitable for drainage areas with times of concentration (T_c) of up to 2 hours for the Tabular Hydrograph method and up to 10 hours for the Graphical Peak Discharge method. The publication contains numerous tables and graphs, of which only samples are included in this book. For application to actual projects, the reader is urged to obtain the source document. Also, since NRCS has not converted the TR55 methodology to the metric system, it is not appropriate to apply metric conversions to this chapter.

RAINFALL

Four regional rainfall patterns are used by the SCS. Their approximate geographical boundaries are shown in Figure 12.2. The cumulative proportions of total rainfall depth for all frequencies over a 24-hour period are illustrated in Figure 12.3 for all four distributions. An "intermediate storm" pattern has been used; that is, there is a period of high intensity (a large amount of rainfall in a relatively short period), preceded and followed by more gradual accumulation. For Type II and Type III storms, approximately one-half of the 24-hour precipitation occurs in 1 hour at about the midpoint.

Although SCS hydrology can be applied to storm events of various lengths, a 24-hour duration *must* be used for all applications involving TR55. Twenty-four-hour rainfall depths for frequencies from 2 to 100 years for the eastern and central United States can be interpolated from Figures 12.4 to 12.7. Values for areas not included in the maps can be obtained from NRCS State Conservation Engineers for those areas.

PROCEDURES OF TR55

Figure 12.8 is a flowchart for determining appropriate procedures to be used for various purposes. For example, to estimate peak flow from an area

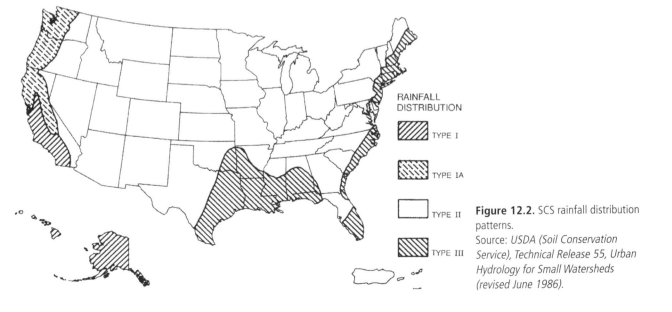

Figure 12.2. SCS rainfall distribution patterns.
Source: *USDA (Soil Conservation Service), Technical Release 55, Urban Hydrology for Small Watersheds (revised June 1986).*

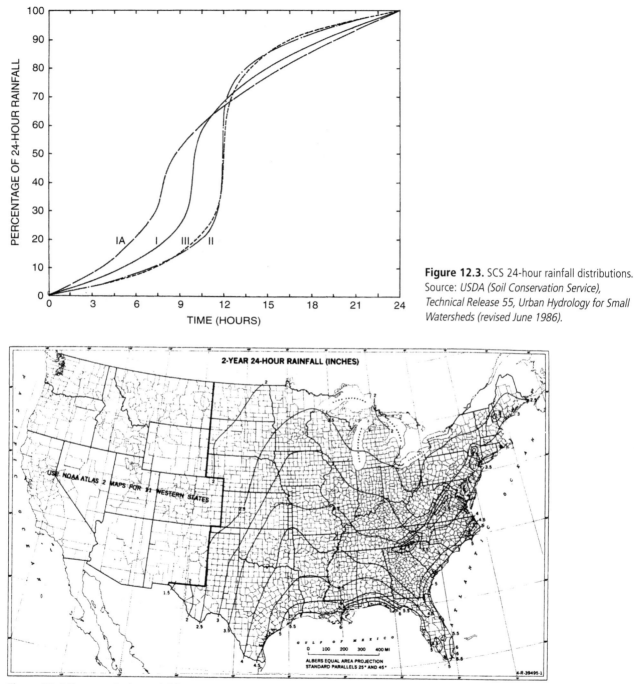

Figure 12.3. SCS 24-hour rainfall distributions. Source: *USDA (Soil Conservation Service), Technical Release 55, Urban Hydrology for Small Watersheds (revised June 1986).*

Figure 12.4. Two-year, 24-hour rainfall.
Source: *USDA (Soil Conservation Service), Technical Release 55, Urban Hydrology for Small Watersheds (revised June 1986).*

238

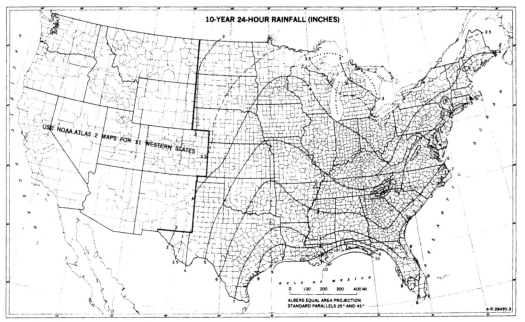

Figure 12.5. Ten-year, 24-hour rainfall.
Source: *USDA (Soil Conservation Service), Technical Release 55, Urban Hydrology for Small Watersheds, (revised June 1986).*

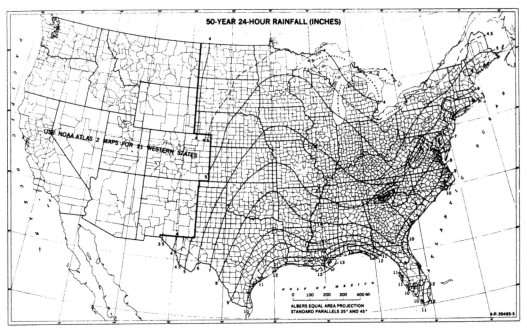

Figure 12.6. Fifty-year, 24-hour rainfall.
Source: *USDA (Soil Conservation Service), Technical Release 55, Urban Hydrology for Small Watersheds (revised June 1986).*

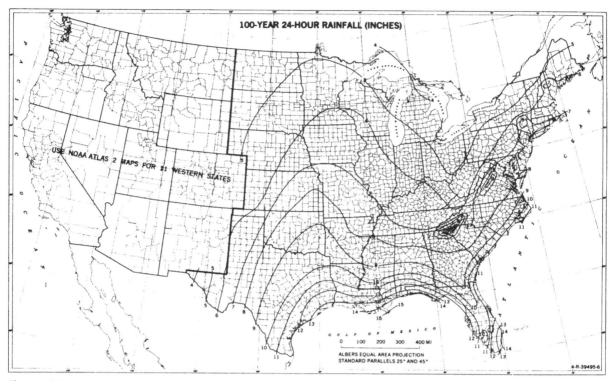

Figure 12.7. One-hundred-year, 24-hour rainfall.
Source: *USDA (Soil Conservation Service), Technical Release 55, Urban Hydrology for Small Watersheds (revised June 1986).*

with homogeneous topographic, soil, and land use conditions, the Graphical Discharge method could be used. However, if there are several subareas in a watershed, each with different characteristics, the Tabular Hydrograph method would have to be used to arrive at the total runoff rate. TR55 deals with surface flow over land and in open channels only. In drainage areas having storm sewers, flow paths and times for large events should be carefully investigated. Most of the runoff will probably be overland flow. The actual flow in the pipes must be determined separately.

Travel Time and Time of Concentration

Travel time (T_t) is the time required for runoff to flow from one point in a drainage area to another,

while *time of concentration* (T_c), is the sum of the consecutive travel times through a watershed. (Previously, this was defined as the time required for water to flow from the hydraulically most remote point in a drainage area to the point of interest, usually the outlet.) With the flow distance and velocity of flow known, travel time can be calculated by dividing the flow length by the velocity:

$$T_t = L/V \qquad (12.1)$$

where

T_t = travel time, seconds (sec)
L = flow length, feet (ft)
V = flow velocity, ft/sec (fps)

(Divide T_t by 3,600 sec/hr to convert to hours of travel time.)

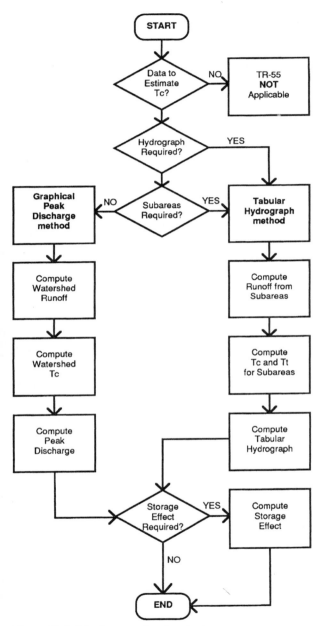

Figure 12.8. Selection procedure flowchart.
Source: *USDA (Soil Conservation Service), Technical Release 55, Urban Hydrology for Small Watersheds (revised June 1986).*

The SCS separates flow into three distinct processes: sheet flow, shallow concentrated flow, and open channel flow. *Sheet flow* is flow over plane, sloped surfaces and normally takes place at the upper end of a flow path. Its maximum permitted length is 100 ft; however, it may be less, and its actual length is best determined by field inspection and observation. Manning's kinematic solution is used to determine travel time for sheet flow:

$$T_t = \frac{0.007 \, (nL)^{0.8}}{(P_2)^{0.5} S^{0.4}} \qquad (12.2)$$

where

T_t = travel time, hours

n = Manning's roughness coefficient for sheet flow (Table 12.1), not to be confused with Manning's n for open channel flow

Table 12.1 Roughness Coefficients *(n)* for Sheet Flow

Surface Description	n[a]
Smooth surfaces (concrete, asphalt, gravel, or bare soil)	0.011
Fallow (no residue)	0.05
Cultivated soils:	
Residue cover ≤20%	0.06
Residue cover >20%	0.17
Grass:	
Short grass prairie	0.15
Dense grasses[b]	0.24
Bermuda grass	0.41
Range (natural)	0.13
Woods[c]	
Light underbrush	0.40
Dense underbrush	0.80

[a]The *n* values are a composite of information compiled by Engman (1986).

[b]Includes species such as weeping love grass, bluegrass, buffalo grass, blue grama grass, and native grass mixtures.

[c]When selecting *n*, consider cover to a height of about 0.1 ft. This is the only part of the plant cover that will obstruct sheet flow.

L = flow length, feet
P_2 = 2-year 24-hour rainfall, inches
S = slope of flow path, ft/ft

If surface flow continues beyond sheet flow, it becomes *shallow concentrated flow*. Velocities for this type of flow may be estimated by the use of Figure 12.9 for paved or unpaved flow paths by entering with the slope in ft/ft from the left until the appropriate line for type of flow is intersected. Projecting a vertical line down from the point of intersection, the velocity in fps may be read. Travel time can then be computed by means of Equation 12.1.

Finally, runoff may enter an *open channel*. The average flow velocity for open channels can be calculated by Manning's equation for open channels:

$$V = \frac{1.486}{n} R^{2/3} S^{1/2} \qquad (12.3)$$

where
V = flow velocity, ft/s
n = Manning's roughness coefficient for open channels (Table 12.2)
R = hydraulic radius, ft (see Figure 12.10)
   = cross-sectional area of flow, ft²/ wetted perimeter, ft
S = channel slope, ft/ft

■ EXAMPLE 12.1

Calculate the time of concentration for the following conditions:

100 ft of sheet flow through woods with light underbrush at a 1% slope

770 ft of shallow concentrated flow through woods at a 4% slope

1,100 ft of open channel flow at a 2% slope

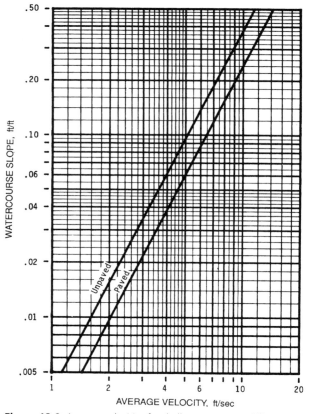

Figure 12.9. Average velocities for shallow concentrated flow. Source: *USDA (Soil Conservation Service), Technical Release 55, Urban Hydrology for Small Watersheds (revised June 1986).*

Table 12.2 Roughness Coefficients *(n)* for Pipes and Channels

Pipe Material	n
Concrete	0.012–0.015
Cast iron	0.013
Corrugated metal	0.024
Plastic (smooth)	0.012
Vitrified clay	0.010–0.015
Channel surface	
Asphalt	0.013–0.016
Concrete	0.012–0.018
Riprap	0.020–0.040
Vegetated	0.030–0.080

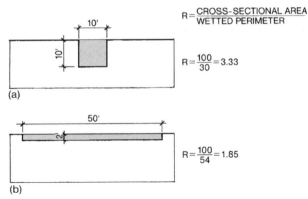

$$R = \frac{\text{CROSS-SECTIONAL AREA}}{\text{WETTED PERIMETER}}$$

$$R = \frac{100}{30} = 3.33$$

(a)

$$R = \frac{100}{54} = 1.85$$

(b)

Figure 12.10. Hydraulic radius. For the same given cross-sectional area, R varies inversely with the wetted perimeter. Although the cross-sectional area in (b) is the same as in (a), the surface area exposed per unit length of channel is much greater, resulting in greater friction between the channel and the water. Consistent with the increased friction, the R value is less than in (a) and the velocity of flow is reduced.

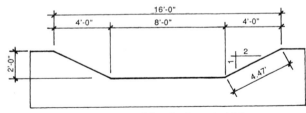

Figure 12.11. Cross section of flow for Example 12.1.

The cross section of flow of the channel approximates a trapezoid with a top width of 16 ft, bottom width of 8 ft, and a depth of 2 ft (Figure 12.11). The roughness coefficient has been estimated as 0.10. The 2-year 24-hour rainfall in the area of the project is 3.3 in.

SOLUTION

Sheet flow:

$$T_{t1} = \frac{0.007(nL)^{0.8}}{P^{0.5}S^{0.4}} = \frac{0.007(0.4 \times 100)^{0.8}}{3.3^{0.5}0.01^{0.4}} \approx 0.47 \text{ hr}$$

Shallow concentrated flow:

$$V = 3.2 \text{ ft/s (from Figure 12.9)}$$
$$T_{t2} = 770 \text{ ft/3.2 ft/s} = 240.6 \text{ sec}$$
$$= 240.6 \text{ sec/3,600 sec/hr} \approx 0.07 \text{ hr}$$

Channel flow:

$$R = A/WP$$
$$A = \frac{B + b}{2} \times h = \frac{16 + 8}{2} \times 2 = 24 \text{ ft}^2$$
$$WP = 2 \times \text{length of sloped slide} + \text{base } (b)$$
$$= 2 \times (4^2 + 2^2)^{0.5} + 8$$
$$= 2 \times 4.47 + 8 = 16.94 \text{ ft}$$
$$R = 24 \text{ ft}^2/16.94 \text{ ft} \approx 1.42 \text{ ft}$$
$$V = \frac{1.486}{n} R^{2/3} S^{1/2}$$
$$= \frac{1.486}{0.10} \times 1.42^{2/3} \times 0.02^{1/2} \approx 2.65 \text{ ft/s}$$
$$T_{t3} = 1,100 \text{ ft/2.65 ft/s} \approx 415.1 \text{ sec}$$
$$= 415.1 \text{ sec/3,600 sec/hr} \approx 0.12 \text{ hr}$$
$$T_c = T_{t1} + T_{t2} + T_{t3}$$
$$= 0.47 + 0.07 + 0.12 = 0.66 \text{ hr}$$

Computer software is available for TR55 hydrologic procedures. A sample of input and output to calculate the time of concentration for Example 12.1 is presented in Figure 12.12. ■

Computing Runoff

The basic runoff equation used by the SCS is

$$Q = \frac{(P - I_a)^2}{(P - I_a) + S} \qquad (12.4)$$

where

Q = runoff, in.
P = rainfall, in.
S = potential maximum retention after start of runoff, in.
I_a = initial abstraction, in.

The initial abstraction—that is, all losses before runoff begins—includes infiltration, evaporation,

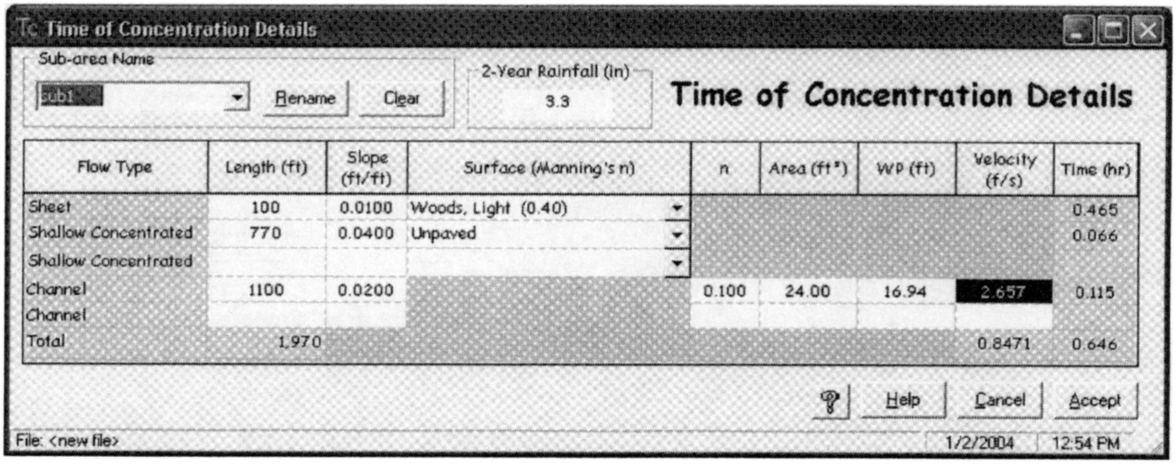

Figure 12.12. Computer input and output for calculating time of concentration for Example 12.1. *(Software: WinTR55)*

interception by vegetation, and water retained in surface depressions. Generally, initial abstraction is estimated as 0.2S. When this is substituted into the runoff equation, it becomes

$$Q = \frac{(P - 0.2S)^2}{(P + 0.8S)} \qquad (12.5)$$

S is defined as 1000/CN − 10, where CN is a runoff curve number, which theoretically varies from 0 to 100 and is somewhat analogous to the runoff coefficient C in the Rational formula. Tables 12.3 and 12.4 list runoff CNs for different urban and natural land uses. TR55 has additional listings for various farming practices and rangelands. When using these numbers, the proportion of impervious areas for the urban land uses and lot sizes on a project site should agree with those listed. Also, the numbers have been developed with the assumption that urban impervious areas are directly connected to a drainage system. If these assumptions do not apply, TR55 includes methods of adjusting the CNs for other conditions.

Hydrologic Soil Groups

The *Hydrologic Soil Group (HSG)* classification indicates how much of the precipitation is likely to enter the soil (infiltrate) and how much will run off. *HSG A* includes sandy soils with high infiltration rates and relatively little runoff, while *HSG D* soils, such as clay loams, and silty clays, have very low infiltration and high runoff potential. *HSG B* and *HSG C* soils have intermediate characteristics.

Soil survey maps indicate the various soils existing on a project site; *HSG* classifications for all soils are listed in Appendix A of TR55, or may be obtained directly from soil survey reports. Normally, the project boundaries and drainage areas are drawn on the applicable soil map to the appropriate scale and the areas of the various soil types, with their *HSG* classification, contained within the drainage areas are measured. As with runoff coefficients for the Rational and Modified Rational methods, a weighted average *CN* may be calculated, where various soil types are intermingled on a site (Figure 12.13).

Table 12.3 Runoff Curve Numbers for Urban Areas[a]

COVER DESCRIPTION		CURVE NUMBERS FOR *HSG* HYDROLOGIC SOIL GROUP			
Cover Type and Hydrologic Condition	Average Percent Impervious Area[b]	A	B	C	D
Fully developed urban areas (vegetation established)					
Open space (lawns, parks, golf courses, cemeteries, etc.):[c]					
Poor condition (grass cover < 50%)		68	79	86	89
Fair condition (grass cover 50% to 75%)		49	69	79	84
Good condition (grass cover > 75%)		39	61	74	80
Impervious areas:					
Paved parking lots, roofs, driveways, etc. (excluding right-of-way)		98	98	98	98
Streets and roads:					
Paved; curbs and storm sewers (excluding right-of-way)		98	98	98	98
Paved; open ditches (including right-of-way)		83	89	92	93
Gravel (including right-of-way)		76	85	89	91
Dirt (including right-of-way)		72	82	87	89
Western desert urban areas:					
Natural desert landscaping (pervious areas only)[d]		63	77	85	88
Artificial desert landscaping (impervious weed barrier, desert shrub with 1- to 2-inch sand or gravel mulch and basin borders)		96	96	96	96
Urban districts:					
Commercial and business	85	89	92	94	95
Industrial	72	81	88	91	93
Residential districts by average lot size:					
1/8 acre or less (town houses)	65	77	85	90	92
1/4 acre	38	61	75	83	87
1/3 acre	30	57	72	81	86
1/2 acre	25	54	70	80	85
1 acre	20	51	68	79	84
2 acres	12	46	65	77	82
Developing urban areas:					
Newly graded areas (pervious areas only, no vegetation)[e]		77	86	91	94
Idle lands (*CN*s are determined using cover types similar to those in Table 12.2)					

[a] Average runoff condition, and $I_a = 0.2S$.

[b] The average percent impervious area shown was used to develop the composite *CN*s. Other assumptions are as follows: Impervious areas are directly connected to the drainage system, impervious areas have a *CN* of 98, and pervious areas are considered equivalent to open space in good hydrologic condition.

[c] *CN*s shown are equivalent to those of pasture. Composite *CN*s may be computed for other combinations of open space cover type.

[d] Composite *CN*s for natural desert landscaping should be computed based on the impervious area percentage (*CN* = 98) and the pervious area *CN*. The pervious area *CN*s are assumed equivalent to desert shrub in poor hydrologic condition.

[e] Composite *CN*s to use for the design of temporary measures during grading and construction should be computed based on the degree of development (impervious area percentage) and the *CN*s for the newly graded pervious areas.

Table 12.4 Runoff Curve Numbers for Other Agricultural Lands[a]

Cover type	Hydrologic Condition	CURVE NUMBERS FOR HSG			
		A	B	C	D
Pasture, grassland, or range—continuous forage for grazing[b]	Poor	68	79	86	89
	Fair	49	69	79	84
	Good	39	61	74	80
Meadow—continuous grass, protected from grazing and generally mowed for hay.	—	30	58	71	78
Brush—brush-weed-grass mixture with brush the major element[c]	Poor	48	67	77	83
	Fair	35	56	70	77
	Good	30[d]	48	65	73
Woods—grass combination (orchard or tree farm)[e]	Poor	57	73	82	86
	Fair	43	65	76	82
	Good	32	58	72	79
Woods[f]	Poor	45	66	77	83
	Fair	36	60	73	79
	Good	30[d]	55	70	77
Farmsteads—buildings, lanes, driveways, and surrounding lots	—	59	74	82	86

[a] Average runoff condition, and $I_a = 0.2S$.

[b] *Poor:* <50% ground cover or heavily grazed with no mulch.
Fair: 50 to 75% ground cover and not heavily grazed.
Good: >75% ground cover and lightly or only occasionally grazed.

[c] *Poor:* <50% ground cover.
Fair: 50 to 75% ground cover.
Good: >75% ground cover.

[d] Actual curve number is less than 30; use $CN = 30$ for runoff computations.

[e] *CNs* shown were computed for areas with 50% woods and 50% grass (pasture) cover. Other combinations of conditions may be computed from the *CNs* for woods and pasture.

[f] *Poor:* Forest litter, small trees, and brush are destroyed by heavy grazing or regular burning.
Fair: Woods are grazed but not burned, and some forest litter covers the soil.
Good: Woods are protected from grazing, and litter and brush adequately cover the soil.

Hydrologic Condition

The term *hydrologic condition* applies to the vegetative cover, residue, and surface roughness of a particular area. Good plant cover and soil surfaces that are not smooth will generally reduce potential runoff and would cause a soil to be considered in good hydrologic condition.

Graphical Peak Discharge Method

The equation used for the graphical peak discharge method is

$$q_p = q_u \times A_m \times Q \times F_p \qquad (12.6)$$

where

q_p = peak discharge, ft³/s

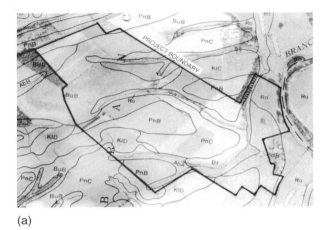

(a)

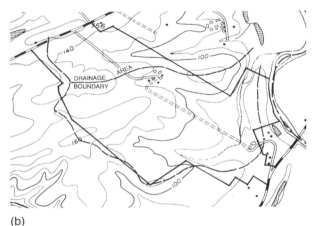

(b)

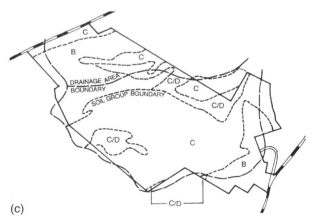

(c)

Figure 12.13. Plotting *HSGs* for a project site. (a) Soils map with project boundary indicated. (b) Topographic map with drainage area boundaries indicated. (c) Boundaries of *HSGs* shown with drainage and project boundaries.

Table 12.5 Pond and Swamp Adjustment Factor (F_p)

Percentage of Pond and Swamp Areas	F_p
0	1.00
0.2	0.97
1.0	0.87
3.0	0.75
5.0	0.72

q_u = unit peak discharge, ft³/s/sq mi/in. of runoff (csm/in.)

A_m = drainage area, sq mi

Q = runoff, in.

F_p = pond and swamp adjustment factor (Table 12.5) (Do not include ponds or swamps that are in the *c* flow path.)

This method can be used for a homogeneous drainage area that can be characterized by a single *CN* if only a peak discharge value is needed.

■ EXAMPLE 12.2

Determine the 50-year 24-hour peak flow rate for a 95-ac wooded drainage area in central New Jersey. The soil on the site is classified as Bucks silt loam in fair hydrologic condition. The time of concentration has been computed as 0.66 hour (Example 12.1). There are no ponds or swamps.

SOLUTION

Appendix A in TR55 lists Bucks silt loam as *HSG* B. The *CN* for *HSG* B woods in fair condition is 60 from Table 12.4.

A_m = 95 ac/640 ac/sq. mi. = 0.148 sq. mi.

P = 6.5 in. (50-year 24-hour precipitation in central New Jersey from Figure 12.6)

$S = (1{,}000/CN) - 10 = (1{,}000/60) - 10 = 6.67\,\text{in.}$

$I_a = 0.2S = 0.2 \times 6.67\,\text{in.} = 1.33\,\text{in.}$

$Q = \dfrac{(P - 0.2S)^2}{P + 0.8S} = \dfrac{(6.5 - 1.33)^2}{6.5 + (0.8 \times 6.67)} = 2.26\,\text{in.}$

$I_a/P = 1.33/6.5 = 0.20$

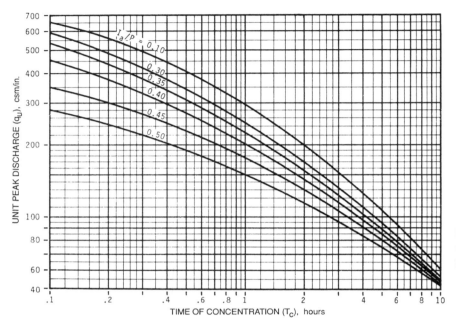

Figure 12.14. Unit peak discharge (q_u) for SCS Type III rainfall distribution. Source: *USDA (Soil Conservation Service), Technical Release 55, Urban Hydrology for Small Watersheds (revised June 1986).*

Using Figure 12.14 for Type III rainfall, 0.66-hr T_c, and $I_a/P = 0.20$, q_u is estimated as 330 csm. Finally:

$$q_p = q_u \times A_m \times Q \times F_p$$
$$= 330 \times 0.148 \times 2.26 \times 1.0 = 110.38 \approx 110 \text{ft}^3/\text{s}$$

Note that approximate Q values may also be obtained directly from Figure 12.1. ∎

Tabular Hydrograph Method

When a hydrograph is required or when a drainage area consists of several distinct subareas having different land uses, topography, or soils, the use of the Tabular Hydrograph method is required, as shown in Figure 12.8. The acreage of the various subareas should not differ by a factor of 5 or more. The equation used for the flow rate at any time during runoff is

$$q = q_t \times A_m \times Q \qquad (12.7)$$

where

q = hydrograph coordinate at hydrograph time t, ft³/s

q_t = tabular hydrograph unit discharge from the tables provided in TR55, csm/in. of runoff

A_m = subarea, sq mi

Q = runoff, in.

∎ EXAMPLE 12.3

Develop a combined 10-year 24-hour hydrograph for the grassed and paved areas of Example 11.6. Properties of the areas are as follows:

Area A: Lawn, fair condition, *HSG B*

$CN = 69$ (from table 12.3)

$T_c = 0.5$ hr

$T_t = 0.1$ hr (over pavement)

Area B: Paved

$CN = 98$ (for all $HSGs$)

$T_c = 0.1$ hr

$T_t = 0.0$ hr

The 10-year 24-hour precipitation (central New Jersey) is 5.2 in., from Figure 12.5. A Type III storm distribution is to be used.

SOLUTION
Area A

$S = (1{,}000/69) - 10 = 4.49$ in.

$I_a = 0.2 \times 4.49 = 0.898 \approx 0.9$ in.

$I_a/P = 0.9/5.2 = 0.17$

$$Q = \frac{(5.2 - 0.9)^2}{5.2 + (0.8 \times 4.49)} = 2.10 \text{ in.}$$

$= 3/640 = 0.0047$ sq mi

Area B

$S = (1{,}000/98) - 10 = 0.20$ in.

$I_a = 0.2 \times 0.2 = 0.04$ in.

$I_a/P = 0.04/5.2 = 0.0077$

$$Q = \frac{(5.2 - 0.04)^2}{5.2 + (0.8 \times 0.2)} = 4.967 \approx 5.0 \text{ in.}$$

$A_m = 0.0047$ sq mi ■

Hydrograph for Area A

Area A has a T_c of 0.5 hr and a T_t of 0.1 hr. The I_a/P values for which hydrographs are listed in TR55 are 0.10, 0.30, and 0.50. The computed I_a/P value can either be rounded to the nearest one of these three values, or the runoff ordinates can be linearly interpolated. For this example, the computed I_a/P of 0.17 will be rounded down to 0.10.

Table 12.6a   Area A Hydrograph for Example 12.3

hr[a]	11.0	11.3	11.6	11.9	12.0	12.1	12.2	12.3	12.4	12.5	12.6	12.7	12.8	13.0	13.2	13.4	13.6	13.8	14.0
csm/in.[b]	19.0	24.0	30.0	43.0	50.0	64.0	86.0	125.0	186.0	273.0	355.0	392.0	390.0	296.0	194.0	129.0	94.0	75.0	65.0
cfs[c]	0.2	0.2	0.3	0.4	0.5	0.6	0.9	1.2	1.8	2.7	3.5	3.9	3.9	2.9	1.9	1.3	0.9	0.7	0.6
hr	14.3	14.6	15.0	15.5	16.0	16.5	17.0	17.5	18.0	19.0	20.0	22.0	26.0						
csm/in.	56.0	49.0	43.0	38.0	33.0	28.0	24.0	21.0	19.0	15.0	14.0	11.0	0.0						
cfs	0.6	0.5	0.4	0.4	0.3	0.3	0.2	0.2	0.2	0.1	0.1	0.1	0.0						

[a] Hydrograph time.
[b] Unit discharge, q_t, from Table 12.9b for $T_c = 0.5$ hr, $T_t = 0.1$ hr, and $I_a/P = 0.10$.
[c] From $q = q_t \times A_m \times Q$.

Table 12.6b   Area B Hydrograph for Example 12.3

hr[a]	11.0	11.3	11.6	11.9	12.0	12.1	12.2	12.3	12.4	12.5	12.6	12.7	12.8	13.0	13.2	13.4	13.6	13.8	14.0
csm/in.[b]	29.0	38.0	57.0	172.0	241.0	425.0	662.0	531.0	345.0	265.0	191.0	130.0	101.0	83.0	68.0	62.0	58.0	54.0	50.0
cfs[c]	0.7	0.9	1.3	4.0	5.7	10.0	15.6	12.5	8.1	6.2	4.5	3.1	2.4	2.0	1.6	1.5	1.4	1.3	1.2
hr	14.3	14.6	15.0	15.5	16.0	16.5	17.0	17.5	18.0	19.0	20.0	22.0	26.0						
csm/in.	44.0	41.0	37.0	32.0	27.0	23.0	21.0	19.0	16.0	14.0	13.0	11.0	0.0						
cfs	1.0	1.0	0.9	0.8	0.6	0.5	0.5	0.4	0.4	0.3	0.3	0.3	0.0						

[a] Hydrograph time.
[b] Unit discharge, q_t, from Table 12.9b for $T_c = 0.1$ hr, $T_t = 0.0$ hr, and $I_a/P = 0.10$.
[c] From $q = q_t \times A_m \times Q$.

Table 12.6c   Combined Hydrograph for Example 12.3

hr	11.0	11.3	11.6	11.9	12.0	2.1	12.2	12.3	12.4	12.5	12.6	12.7	12.8	13.0	13.2	13.4	13.6	13.8	14.0
A cfs	0.2	0.2	0.3	0.4	0.5	0.6	0.9	1.2	1.8	2.7	3.5	3.9	3.9	2.9	1.9	1.3	0.9	0.7	0.6
B cfs	0.7	0.9	1.3	4.0	5.7	10.0	15.6	12.5	8.1	6.2	4.5	3.1	2.4	2.0	1.6	1.5	1.4	1.3	1.2
Total cfs	0.9	1.1	1.6	4.4	6.2	10.6	16.5	13.7	9.9	8.9	8.0	7.0	6.3	4.9	3.5	2.8	2.3	2.0	1.8

hr	14.3	14.6	15.0	15.5	16.0	16.5	17.0	17.5	18.0	19.0	20.0	22.0	26.0
A cfs	0.6	0.5	0.4	0.4	0.3	0.3	0.2	0.2	0.2	0.1	0.1	0.1	0.0
B cfs	1.0	1.0	0.9	0.8	0.6	0.5	0.5	0.4	0.4	0.3	0.3	0.3	0.0
Total cfs	1.6	1.5	1.3	1.2	0.9	0.8	0.7	0.6	0.6	0.4	0.4	0.4	0.0

Line 1 in Table 12.6a lists the hydrograph time, line 2 the unit discharge, q_t, in csm/in. at that time, and line 3 the discharge, q, at that time in ft³/s. Lines 1 and 2 have been obtained from Table 12.7b for $T_c = 0.5$ hr and $T_t = 0.1$ hr. Line 3 was computed by multiplying the csm/in. values by A_m, the area in sq mi, and by Q, the runoff in inches. A_m had previously been determined as 0.0047 and Q as 2.10. These values can be combined as a multiplication factor of 0.0099. All ft³/s values have been rounded to the nearest 0.1 ft³/s.

Hydrograph for Area B

Similarly, using Table 12.7a with $T_c = 0.1$ hr, $T_t = 0.0$ hr, $I_a/P = 0.10$, $A_m = 0.0047$ sq mi, and $Q = 5.0$ in. (multiplication factor of 0.0235), ft³/s values are computed as shown in Table 12.6b.

The two hydrographs can now be combined by adding, as shown in Table 12.6c. The combined 10-year 24-hour hydrograph yields a q_p of 16.5 ft³/s at 12.2 hours (Table 12.6c). The timing of the peak flow reflects the 24-hour rainfall distribution for a Type III storm and a short time of concentration.

VOLUME FOR DETENTION STORAGE

Figure 12.15 provides a method of estimating required detention storage volume when the postdevelopment peak runoff rate from a site into a basin and the limiting peak outflow rate from the basin are known. As with the previously described Modified Rational method, the detention volume obtained by this procedure should normally not be used for a final design, but it can aid in the selection of the pond location and as a starting point for a detailed design. An accurate stage–volume relationship for a basin and the details of the outlet structure must be known to perform the reservoir routing for the final design. A discussion of that procedure can be found in many engineering hydrology textbooks.

To use Figure 12.15, the TR55 graphical peak discharge method or the tabular hydrograph method *must* be used. If the pond is to be located at the outlet of a subarea, travel times downstream of the subarea should not be included in the determination of the peak flow rate from the subarea.

■ EXAMPLE 12.4

The 95-ac wooded area of Example 12.2 is to be developed into 1-ac residential lots. Determine the approximate pond storage required to maintain the 110 ft³/s predevelopment outflow rate for a 50-year 24-hour storm event (previously computed). The postdevelopment 50-year 24-hour peak runoff rate has been determined as 183 ft³/s.

Table 12.7a Tabular Hydrograph Unit Discharges (csm/in.) for Type III Rainfall Distribution ($T_c = 0.1$ hr)

HYDROGRAPH TIME (HOURS)

$I_A/P = 0.10$ $T_C = 0.1$ HR $I_A/P = 0.10$

TRVL TIME (HR)	11.0	11.3	11.6	11.9	12.0	12.1	12.2	12.3	12.4	12.5	12.6	12.7	12.8	13.0	13.2	13.4	13.6	13.8	14.0	14.3	14.6	15.0	15.5	16.0	16.5	17.0	17.5	18.0	19.0	20.0	22.0	26.0
0.0	29	38	57	172	241	425	662	531	345	265	191	130	101	83	68	62	58	54	50	44	41	37	32	27	23	21	19	16	14	13	11	0
.10	26	32	47	98	147	210	353	559	540	410	313	231	164	101	80	67	61	57	53	47	43	39	34	28	24	22	19	17	14	13	11	0
.20	25	31	44	86	127	182	296	471	517	446	357	273	200	117	86	70	63	58	54	48	44	39	34	29	24	22	20	17	14	13	11	0
.30	22	28	37	57	76	110	158	250	398	477	457	390	312	178	111	83	69	62	57	51	45	41	36	31	25	23	20	18	15	13	11	0
.40	21	27	35	53	68	96	137	213	336	430	448	410	345	210	128	90	72	64	58	52	46	41	36	31	26	23	20	18	15	13	11	0
.50	19	24	30	43	49	62	85	120	182	284	382	426	415	305	188	120	86	71	63	55	49	43	38	33	27	24	21	19	15	14	11	0
.75	17	22	27	37	41	49	62	84	120	181	258	327	375	353	264	177	120	88	72	59	52	45	39	34	29	25	22	20	15	14	11	0
1.0	13	17	22	27	30	33	37	43	52	66	91	131	190	315	358	307	220	149	104	72	60	50	43	37	32	27	23	21	16	14	12	0
1.5	9	11	14	18	19	21	23	25	27	29	33	37	44	70	134	229	304	318	269	172	106	68	52	44	38	33	28	24	19	15	12	2
2.0	6	8	10	13	14	15	16	17	19	20	22	24	26	32	45	73	130	207	271	292	216	121	68	51	43	37	32	27	21	16	13	6
2.5	3	4	6	8	9	10	10	11	12	13	14	16	17	20	23	29	38	57	97	189	271	244	136	75	53	44	38	33	24	19	14	9
3.0	1	2	4	5	6	6	7	8	8	9	10	11	12	14	16	19	23	28	38	74	146	256	226	131	74	53	44	37	27	21	14	10

$I_A/P = 0.30$ $T_C = 0.1$ HR $I_A/P = 0.30$

TRVL TIME (HR)	11.0	11.3	11.6	11.9	12.0	12.1	12.2	12.3	12.4	12.5	12.6	12.7	12.8	13.0	13.2	13.4	13.6	13.8	14.0	14.3	14.6	15.0	15.5	16.0	16.5	17.0	17.5	18.0	19.0	20.0	22.0	26.0
0.0	0	0	0	48	106	296	597	496	368	300	221	155	125	106	89	83	79	74	69	62	59	54	47	40	35	32	28	25	22	20	17	0
.10	0	0	0	35	82	225	473	488	408	336	260	190	147	113	94	85	80	75	70	63	59	54	48	40	35	32	29	25	22	20	17	0
.20	0	0	0	7	26	64	171	372	449	422	365	295	225	142	109	92	84	79	74	66	61	56	50	43	36	33	30	26	22	20	17	0
.30	0	0	0	5	19	49	130	291	397	414	381	323	258	161	118	96	86	80	75	68	62	57	50	43	37	33	30	27	22	20	17	0
.40	0	0	0	0	3	14	37	99	227	340	389	384	343	229	152	113	94	85	79	71	65	59	52	46	38	34	31	28	23	21	17	0
.50	0	0	0	0	2	10	28	75	177	286	355	374	354	256	170	123	99	87	80	73	66	60	53	46	39	35	31	28	23	21	18	0
.75	0	0	0	0	0	1	4	13	35	86	161	238	296	325	266	194	141	110	93	80	71	63	56	50	43	37	33	30	24	21	18	0
1.0	0	0	0	0	0	0	0	2	6	19	48	99	165	282	311	264	197	144	112	88	77	67	59	52	45	39	34	31	24	22	18	0
1.5	0	0	0	0	0	0	0	0	0	0	1	4	29	99	197	265	277	236	162	113	84	69	60	53	46	39	35	28	23	19	2	
2.0	0	0	0	0	0	0	0	0	0	0	0	0	1	8	35	94	172	233	253	196	124	83	68	59	52	45	39	31	25	20	8	
2.5	0	0	0	0	0	0	0	0	0	0	0	0	0	0	2	11	37	88	184	235	201	122	83	67	59	52	45	34	27	21	13	
3.0	0	0	0	0	0	0	0	0	0	0	0	0	0	0	0	1	7	38	110	222	202	131	88	69	60	52	39	31	22	15		

$I_A/P = 0.50$ $T_C = 0.1$ HR $I_A/P = 0.50$

TRVL TIME (HR)	11.0	11.3	11.6	11.9	12.0	12.1	12.2	12.3	12.4	12.5	12.6	12.7	12.8	13.0	13.2	13.4	13.6	13.8	14.0	14.3	14.6	15.0	15.5	16.0	16.5	17.0	17.5	18.0	19.0	20.0	22.0	26.0
0.0	0	0	0	0	0	107	226	282	258	209	155	130	123	107	97	95	91	87	82	78	74	69	61	52	47	43	39	35	32	29	25	0
.10	0	0	0	0	0	71	174	246	254	224	178	146	130	112	100	96	92	88	83	78	75	70	62	53	48	44	40	35	32	29	25	0
.20	0	0	0	0	0	0	48	132	208	239	229	195	162	127	109	99	95	91	87	80	77	72	65	56	49	45	41	36	32	30	25	0
.30	0	0	0	0	0	0	32	99	172	216	225	205	176	136	113	101	96	92	88	81	77	72	65	57	50	45	41	37	32	30	26	0
.40	0	0	0	0	0	0	0	21	73	139	191	213	208	164	131	111	100	95	91	85	79	74	68	60	51	47	43	38	33	30	26	0
.50	0	0	0	0	0	0	0	14	53	110	164	197	204	174	139	116	103	97	92	86	80	75	68	60	52	47	43	39	33	30	26	0
.75	0	0	0	0	0	0	0	5	22	54	96	137	166	180	159	134	115	103	96	89	83	77	70	63	54	48	44	40	33	31	26	0
1.0	0	0	0	0	0	0	0	0	0	2	10	29	60	132	175	169	146	124	109	97	89	81	74	67	59	52	47	43	34	31	27	0
1.5	0	0	0	0	0	0	0	0	0	0	0	0	2	17	58	112	150	159	148	122	104	91	81	74	67	59	51	46	38	32	28	1
2.0	0	0	0	0	0	0	0	0	0	0	0	0	0	0	4	20	54	98	133	149	133	108	90	80	73	66	58	51	42	34	29	7
2.5	0	0	0	0	0	0	0	0	0	0	0	0	0	0	0	2	12	35	87	131	141	111	92	81	74	66	59	46	38	30	18	
3.0	0	0	0	0	0	0	0	0	0	0	0	0	0	0	0	0	1	4	22	63	120	136	110	91	81	73	66	51	42	31	22	

RAINFALL TYPE = III $T_C = 0.1$ HR

Table 12.7b Tabular Hydrograph Unit Discharges (csm/in.) for Type III Rainfall Distribution (T_c = 0.1 hr)

HYDROGRAPH TIME (HOURS)

I_A/P = 0.10 — T_C = 0.5 HR — **I_A/P = 0.10**

TRVL TIME (HR)	11.0	11.3	11.6	11.9	12.0	12.1	12.2	12.3	12.4	12.5	12.6	12.7	12.8	13.0	13.2	13.4	13.6	13.8	14.0	14.3	14.6	15.0	15.5	16.0	16.5	17.0	17.5	18.0	19.0	20.0	22.0	26.0
0.0	21	27	35	54	70	97	144	217	316	397	411	388	330	214	139	99	78	67	60	52	47	42	36	31	26	23	21	18	15	13	11	0
.10	19	24	30	43	50	64	86	125	186	273	355	392	390	296	194	129	94	75	65	56	49	43	38	33	28	24	21	19	15	14	11	0
.20	18	23	29	40	47	58	77	109	161	235	315	367	382	318	218	145	103	80	68	57	50	44	39	33	28	24	22	19	15	14	11	0
.30	16	21	26	34	38	44	53	69	95	139	203	278	337	367	289	199	135	98	77	62	54	46	40	35	30	25	22	20	16	14	11	0
.40	16	20	25	33	36	41	49	62	84	121	176	244	306	358	306	220	151	107	83	64	55	47	41	35	30	25	23	20	16	14	12	0
.50	14	18	22	28	31	35	39	46	57	75	106	152	213	323	346	282	202	140	102	73	59	50	42	37	32	27	23	21	16	14	12	0
.75	12	16	20	25	28	30	34	38	45	56	75	104	145	246	319	308	252	187	135	89	67	53	44	39	33	28	24	22	17	14	12	0
1.0	10	12	16	20	22	23	25	28	31	34	39	47	60	110	197	280	309	279	220	138	90	63	49	42	37	31	26	23	18	15	12	0
1.5	6	8	10	13	14	15	17	18	19	21	23	25	27	34	49	82	143	218	283	271	203	116	68	51	43	37	32	27	21	16	13	4
2.0	3	5	7	9	10	11	12	13	14	15	16	17	19	22	27	34	50	82	135	226	265	211	114	67	50	42	37	31	23	18	13	8
2.5	2	3	4	6	7	7	8	9	10	10	11	12	13	16	18	22	26	34	50	102	182	249	197	111	67	50	42	36	26	20	14	9
3.0	1	1	2	3	4	4	5	5	6	6	7	8	8	10	12	14	16	19	23	34	63	144	238	201	121	72	52	43	31	23	15	10

I_A/P = 0.30 — T_C = 0.5 HR — **I_A/P = 0.30**

TRVL TIME (HR)	11.0	11.3	11.6	11.9	12.0	12.1	12.2	12.3	12.4	12.5	12.6	12.7	12.8	13.0	13.2	13.4	13.6	13.8	14.0	14.3	14.6	15.0	15.5	16.0	16.5	17.0	17.5	18.0	19.0	20.0	22.0	26.0
0.0	0	0	0	1	4	15	40	101	198	295	345	345	325	232	161	122	100	88	80	72	65	59	53	46	39	34	31	28	23	21	18	0
.10	0	0	0	1	3	11	30	77	158	249	313	335	329	253	178	132	106	91	82	73	66	60	53	47	40	35	31	28	23	21	18	0
.20	0	0	0	0	2	8	23	59	125	208	278	316	324	271	196	144	112	95	85	75	67	61	54	47	40	35	32	28	23	21	18	0
.30	0	0	0	0	0	2	6	17	45	98	171	242	291	313	249	182	136	108	92	80	71	63	56	49	42	36	33	29	24	21	18	0
.40	0	0	0	0	0	1	4	13	34	77	140	208	264	304	263	198	148	115	97	81	72	64	57	50	43	37	33	30	24	21	18	0
.50	0	0	0	0	0	0	1	3	10	26	60	113	177	276	295	244	185	140	111	88	77	67	59	52	45	39	34	31	24	22	18	0
.75	0	0	0	0	0	0	0	1	4	12	29	60	104	204	271	263	222	174	136	101	83	70	61	54	47	40	35	32	25	22	18	0
1.0	0	0	0	0	0	0	0	0	0	1	2	6	16	67	155	235	263	242	198	138	102	80	66	58	51	44	38	34	27	23	19	1
1.5	0	0	0	0	0	0	0	0	0	0	0	0	0	4	22	67	138	205	241	221	167	110	79	66	58	51	44	38	30	24	20	5
2.0	0	0	0	0	0	0	0	0	0	0	0	0	0	0	0	3	13	42	93	182	225	191	119	83	67	58	51	44	34	27	21	12
2.5	0	0	0	0	0	0	0	0	0	0	0	0	0	0	0	0	1	4	15	62	139	213	180	117	82	67	58	51	38	30	22	15
3.0	0	0	0	0	0	0	0	0	0	0	0	0	0	0	0	0	0	0	1	10	41	127	203	171	114	81	66	57	43	33	23	16

I_A/P = 0.50 — T_C = 0.5 HR — **I_A/P = 0.50**

TRVL TIME (HR)	11.0	11.3	11.6	11.9	12.0	12.1	12.2	12.3	12.4	12.5	12.6	12.7	12.8	13.0	13.2	13.4	13.6	13.8	14.0	14.3	14.6	15.0	15.5	16.0	16.5	17.0	17.5	18.0	19.0	20.0	22.0	26.0
0.0	0	0	0	0	0	0	3	24	68	124	174	190	190	162	133	114	103	97	92	85	80	75	68	60	52	47	43	39	33	30	26	0
.10	0	0	0	0	0	0	2	17	51	100	149	177	186	169	140	119	106	99	93	86	81	75	69	61	52	47	43	39	33	30	26	0
.20	0	0	0	0	0	0	1	12	38	79	126	160	181	173	147	124	109	101	95	88	81	76	69	62	53	48	44	39	33	30	26	0
.30	0	0	0	0	0	0	0	1	8	28	62	105	141	176	165	141	120	107	99	91	84	78	71	64	56	49	45	41	33	31	26	0
.40	0	0	0	0	0	0	0	1	6	20	48	86	123	172	172	146	125	111	101	92	85	79	72	65	56	50	45	41	34	31	26	0
.50	0	0	0	0	0	0	0	0	4	15	37	70	105	157	167	151	130	114	104	94	87	79	73	66	57	50	46	42	34	31	27	0
.75	0	0	0	0	0	0	0	0	0	1	6	17	37	91	139	157	150	134	119	103	93	84	76	69	62	54	48	44	35	32	27	0
1.0	0	0	0	0	0	0	0	0	0	0	1	3	9	40	91	135	153	149	135	113	99	88	79	72	65	57	50	45	37	32	27	1
1.5	0	0	0	0	0	0	0	0	0	0	0	0	0	0	5	24	59	101	132	144	130	107	90	80	73	65	57	51	41	34	29	6
2.0	0	0	0	0	0	0	0	0	0	0	0	0	0	0	0	1	7	25	55	106	138	130	105	89	79	72	65	57	45	37	30	15
2.5	0	0	0	0	0	0	0	0	0	0	0	0	0	0	0	0	0	2	9	36	81	133	133	104	88	79	71	64	50	41	31	21
3.0	0	0	0	0	0	0	0	0	0	0	0	0	0	0	0	0	0	0	0	5	24	74	128	122	103	88	78	70	55	45	32	23

RAINFALL TYPE = III T_C = 0.5 HR

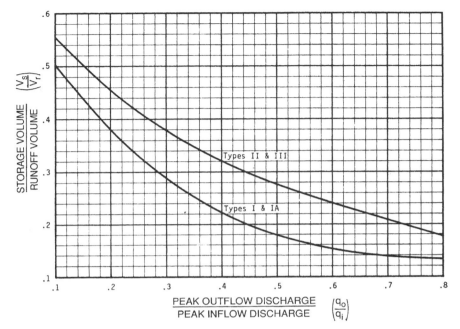

STORAGE VOLUME / RUNOFF VOLUME $\left(\dfrac{V_s}{V_r}\right)$

PEAK OUTFLOW DISCHARGE / PEAK INFLOW DISCHARGE $\left(\dfrac{q_o}{q_i}\right)$

Types II & III

Types I & IA

Figure 12.15. Approximate detention basin routing.
Source: *USDA (Soil Conservation Service), Technical Release 55, Urban Hydrology for Small Watersheds (revised June 1986).*

SOLUTION

The ratio of peak outflow rate/peak inflow rate equals 110 ft³/s/183 ft³/s = 0.60. Drawing a vertical line upward on Figure 12.15 from 0.60 on the *x*-axis to the Type III curve (New Jersey) and then a horizontal line to the left, a storage volume/runoff volume (V_s/V_r) ratio of about 0.24 is obtained.

$P = 6.5$ in. for a 50-year 24-hour storm event (central New Jersey)

$CN = 68$ for 1-ac lots on *HSG B* soil (Table 12.3)

$Q = 3.1$ from Figure 12.1

The volume of runoff (V_r) is computed as follows:

V_r=3.1 in. × 95 ac=294.5 ac-in.

=294.5 ac-in./12 in./ft=24.54 ac-ft

The required storage volume (V_s) can then be determined using the V_s/V_r ratio obtained from Figure 12.15.

$V_s/V_r = 0.24$

$V_s = V_r \times 0.24 = 24.54$ ac-ft³ × 0.24

$= 5.89 \approx 5.9$ ac-ft

If, for planning purposes, an average depth of 4 ft is assumed for the storage facility, then an area of approximately 1.47 ac (5.9 ac-ft/4 ft) would be required for the pond. ■

SUMMARY

The NRCS TR55 methodologies for calculating time of concentration and travel time, computing peak runoff rates, developing hydrographs, and estimating required detention storage have been presented in this chapter. Although examples of the various procedures have been shown, numerous graphs and tables from the source document are not included in this book and the reader is urged to obtain the original publication if the procedures are to be applied on an actual project.

CHAPTER 13

Designing and Sizing Storm Water Management Systems

MANAGEMENT SYSTEMS

The purpose of managing runoff is to ameliorate safety and health hazards, including flooding and property damage, stagnation, earth slides, and reduced soil-bearing capacity; to increase the usability of areas through the elimination of unwanted water; to provide better growing conditions for plants by increasing soil aeration and reducing soil saturation; and to prevent erosion by reducing the rate of flow and volume of runoff. There are a variety of management techniques that may be used to control storm water runoff. The context, that is, the purpose and environmental conditions, will influence the selection of appropriate techniques.

The selection of an appropriate drainage system is based on a variety of factors. The scale and intensity of development, the amount and location of paved and unpaved surfaces, and the proposed uses, ecological impacts, and aesthetic concerns must be addressed in making a choice. Physical factors, such as soil erodibility, extent and steepness of slopes, and expected rainfall intensities, must also be considered. In addition, the availability and suitability of a potential drainage outlet and the character of existing local systems may help determine the type of system proposed. Building and environmental codes or other regulatory requirements, such as maximum rate and volume of runoff, water quality, and method of connection to an existing system, must be met. The ultimate objective in designing most storm drainage systems is not to exceed the rate of flow that existed prior to the development of a site for all storm frequencies.

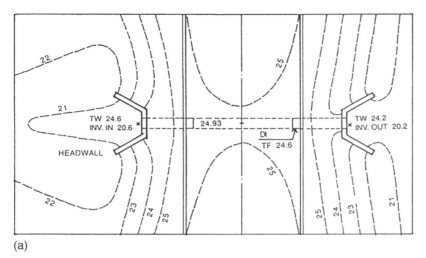

(a)

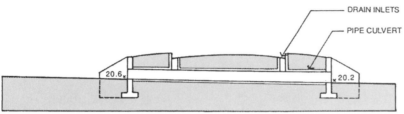

(b)

(c)

Figure 13.1. Culvert. (a) Plan. (b) Section. (c) Runoff from swale is directed into a culvert beneath an entrance drive.

Components of Storm Water Management Systems

Some components of storm water management systems have already been presented in Chapter 9. Other components common to management systems, as well as a review of those previously discussed, are presented here.

Swale

This is a constructed or natural drainage channel used to direct surface flow. Constructed swales have parabolic, trapezoidal, or triangular cross sections. See Chapter 5 for a more complete discussion (Figure 13.1).

Culvert

This is any structure, not classified as a bridge, that allows a water course to flow beneath a road, walk, or highway (Figure 13.1). A *pipe culvert* has a circular, elliptical, or arch cross section, and a *box culvert* has a rectangular cross section.

Catch Basin

This is a structure, typically concrete block or precast concrete rings, 2.5 to 4 ft (800 to 1200 mm) in diameter, that is used to collect and divert surface runoff to an underground conduction system (Figure 13.2). A general rule of thumb is that one catch basin may be used for each 10,000 ft² (930 m²) of paved surface. At the base of the catch basin is a sump or sediment bowl to trap and collect debris. Catch basins may also be rectangular.

Drain Inlet

This structure allows surface runoff to enter directly into a drain pipe. It does not contain a sump (Figure 13.3).

Area Drain

A prefabricated structure, similar to a floor drain, that collects runoff from paved areas (Figure 13.4). Usually one is used for each 1,000 to 2,000 ft² (90–180 m²) of pavement.

Trench Drain

This is a linear inlet structure used to collect sheet flow runoff in paved areas (Figure 13.5).

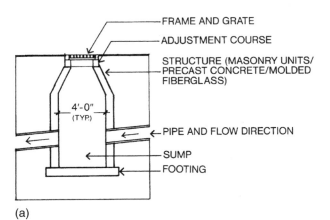

FRAME AND GRATE
ADJUSTMENT COURSE
STRUCTURE (MASONRY UNITS/PRECAST CONCRETE/MOLDED FIBERGLASS)
4'-0" (TYP.)
PIPE AND FLOW DIRECTION
SUMP
FOOTING

(a)

(b)

Figure 13.2. Catch basin. (a) Section. (b) Catch basin with curb inlet under construction.

FRAME AND GRATE

ADJUSTMENT COURSE

STRUCTURE

VARIES

SLOPE TO PIPE OUTLET

FOOTING

(a)

(b)

Figure 13.3. Drain inlet. (a) Section. (b) Grate and frame for drain inlet.

GRATE

CAST FRAME

SEDIMENT BUCKET

OUTLET

(a)

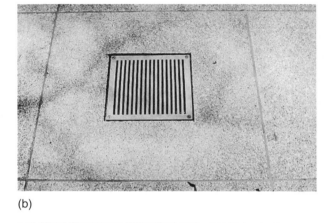

(b)

(c)

(d)

Figure 13.4. Area drain. (a) Section. (b) Area drain grates. Notice how the placement of the grates is coordinated with the paving pattern. (c) Grate size and location not coordinated with paving pattern. (d) Excessive warping of pavement to direct runoff to area drains.

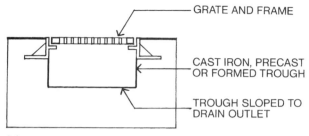

GRATE AND FRAME

CAST IRON, PRECAST
OR FORMED TROUGH

TROUGH SLOPED TO
DRAIN OUTLET

(a)

(b)

Figure 13.5. Trench drain. (a) Section. (b) Trench drain under construction. A prepared base course (see Chapter 7) and a grade stake are also illustrated.

Manhole

This is a structure, often 4 ft (1,200 mm) in diameter, made of concrete block, precast concrete, or fiberglass-reinforced plastic rings, that allows a person to enter a space below ground. For storm drainage purposes, manholes are used where there is a change in the size, slope, or direction of underground pipes. It is more cost-effective if catch basins and manholes are combined. Manholes may be rectangular as well.

Green Roof

This is a combination of waterproofing, roofing protection, drainage mat growing medium, and vegetation installed on top of a structure. For storm

drainage purposes, green roofs can be designed to absorb varying amounts of storm runoff volume as well as slowing the release of the remaining flow that passes through the system. The system can also be designed to provide some storm water quality treatment. Design of green roofs to meet specific criteria for storm water quality and quantity varies from region to region and as of the writing of the fifth edition of this book has not yet been standardized (see Chapter 9).

Cistern or Other Runoff Storage Measure

This is a structure connected to drains from roof structures or other impervious surfaces. Once captured in this structure, the storm water may be released slowly after the storm events' peak has passed or it may be used for irrigation of plantings. In the latter case, the amount of treatment before the water is suitable for use is dependent both on the type of surface the water has been captured from and on local code requirements (see Chapter 9).

Detention and Retention Basin

This is an impoundment area constructed to collect storm runoff from a management system for the purpose of reducing peak flow and controlling the rate of flow. A *retention basin* has a permanent pool, whereas a *detention basin* is normally dry (see Chapter 9).

Sediment Basin

This is an impoundment area or structure that slows the velocity of runoff in order to allow sediment particles to settle out. Retention basins also function as sediment basins, although the reverse is not necessarily true. Retention, detention, and sediment basins require periodic cleaning to remove sediment.

Infiltration Basin or Rain Garden

This is an open-surface storage area with no outlet except an emergency spillway (see Chapter 9).

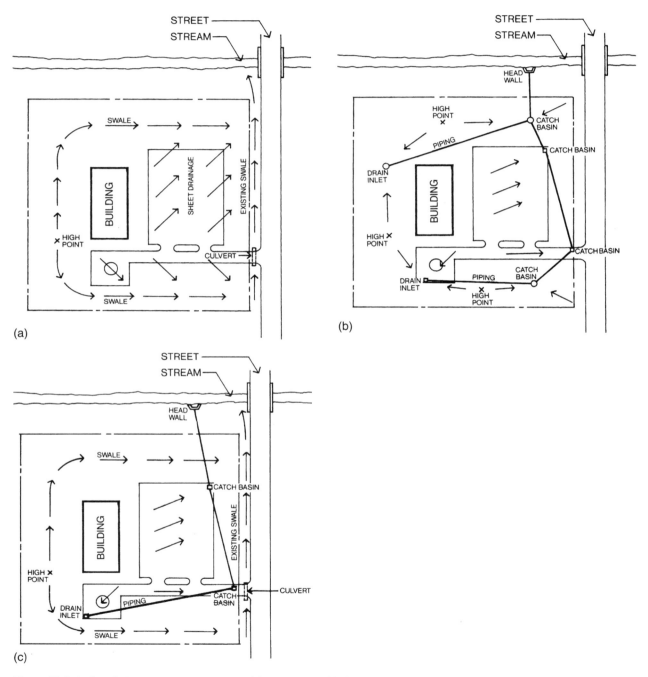

Figure 13.6. Surface drainage management systems. (a) Open system. (b) Closed system. (c) Combination system.

Open Drainage System

In an open drainage system (Figure 13.6a), all surface runoff from paved and unpaved areas is collected and conveyed on the ground, primarily by swales. The system is discharged or directed to an on- or off-site drainageway, stream, or other natural water course, an existing street or municipal storm drainage system, or an on-site retention or sediment pond. The components of a system may include swales, gutters, channels, culverts, and detention, retention, sediment, or infiltration basins. In designing the system, consideration must be given to the volume and velocity of runoff to prevent swale erosion, and to the means of controlling discharge at the outlet in order to collect sediment. If necessary, flow energy must also be dissipated to prevent erosion.

Closed Drainage System

For a closed drainage system, surface runoff from paved and unpaved areas is collected at surface inlets and conveyed by underground pipes to an outlet either on or off the site (Figure 13.6b). The advantage of this system is that the runoff may be intercepted before the volume and velocity increase to the point of causing erosion. Disadvantages include increased cost and complexity of the system, potential for erosion at the discharge point due to the greater concentration of runoff, reduced filtering of sediment because of increased velocity of the storm water in the pipes, and reduced opportunity for storm water to infiltrate the soil. Structures commonly associated with closed systems are catch basins, drain inlets, area drains, trench drains, manholes, and piping. There are various piping materials, including reinforced concrete, vitrified clay, corrugated metal, and plastic.

Combination System

In many cases, the system is a combination of open and closed drainage (Figure 13.6c). Typically, the open system is used in unpaved areas with the intent of providing more opportunity for the storm water to infiltrate the pervious surface, whereas the closed system is used in paved areas. The advantages of this system are reduced construction costs, as compared with a totally closed system, lower potential for soil erosion because of reduced volumes of surface runoff, and lower potential for erosion problems at the outfall because of lower volumes in the pipes.

DESIGN AND LAYOUT OF DRAINAGE SYSTEMS

Surface Drainage

The three basic functions of any storm drainage system are to *collect, conduct,* and *dispose* of storm runoff. In order to proceed with the design of a system, each of these functions must be appropriately analyzed as follows.

Collection

To determine where runoff originates, it is necessary to analyze the existing and proposed drainage patterns. To begin with, it is important to analyze off-site patterns, since very few sites exist as isolated entities. The extent of the surrounding drainage area, its effect on the site, and the effect of the proposed site development must be evaluated. The character of the drainage area, including soils, slopes, and surface cover, has to be determined.

The character of the existing and proposed on-site patterns must also be investigated. This includes the location of high points, low points, ridges, valleys, swales, points of concentration, and streams. Also, by analyzing the on-site patterns, the critical areas where runoff should be collected or intercepted may be determined. Drainage structures, such as catch basins, drain inlets, and area drains, and interception measures, such as diversions and trench drains, must be located at these critical points. By understanding the nature, direction, and extent of these patterns, it is possible to estimate the rate of runoff expected from the individual drainage areas. The analysis of where runoff originates also provides an opportunity to reexamine the grading scheme to determine whether it is functioning properly with regard to storm drainage. Remember that to ensure positive drainage, all surfaces must slope; also remember that, in most cases, it is illegal to increase or concentrate flow across adjacent property.

Disposal

The question of where the water is going must be answered before the question of how it is going to get there, because the outlet will have a direct influence on the method of conduction. It must first be determined whether the runoff will be disposed of on- or off-site and whether the connection is to a natural system (such as a stream, river, or lake) or an engineered system (such as a drainage channel, storm sewer, or detention/retention basin). However, as discussed in Chapter 9, traditional methods of off-site disposal must be seriously reconsidered. Storm water management goals must be to reduce excess runoff from development and to capture as much as possible of the excess on-site.

Failure to consider the suitability of the outlet and the nature of the connection has, in some cases, resulted in systems that do not function properly, in addition to wasted money or even litigation brought about by damages caused by concentrated water flowing from drainage pipes or channels onto adjacent properties. Finally, the connection and means of disposal must comply with all building codes, zoning ordinances, and environmental regulations.

Conduction

Storm runoff may be conducted in an open, closed, or combination system. Some factors that could influence the type, layout, components, and extensiveness of a system have been previously mentioned. These include surface cover and soil type; environmental and ecological consequences; type of land use (e.g., residential development, park, or urban plaza); and visual appearance. This last point is particularly important to landscape architects and site planners. In addition, rainfall characteristics, such as frequency, duration, and intensity of storms, have to be considered. In most cases, it is not difficult to develop a storm drainage management system that functions properly hydraulically. However, to develop a system that is integrated with the overall design concept and does not become visually distracting or environmentally damaging requires a certain amount of care, finesse, and understanding of basic engineering and ecological principles. Based upon current philosophies, runoff should be conducted at low velocities through open systems to the extent possible, and the enhancement of water quality should be integrated into the collection and conduction system.

A general rule of thumb is to make the management system as inconspicuous and unobtrusive as possible. This does not mean that costly measures should be taken to disguise or hide a system or that, in some designs, it is not appropriate to use the management system as an element that is significant to the design concept. It does mean that generally, for open systems, swales should be broad, with gentle, rounded cross sections, rather than narrow and ditch-like, and retention/detention basins should be integrated into the overall site design rather than located as an afterthought. For closed systems, structures should be placed logically and inlet openings not unnecessarily oversized. Where drainage inlets are placed in pavement, the location should be coordinated with the paving pattern, and the sloping of the pavement to direct runoff should be minimized to reduce a warped appearance of the surface (Figure 13.4).

Regardless of whether an open, closed, or combination system is used, the typical conduction pattern will appear tree-like. This pattern results from a hierarchical collection of runoff from a series of small drainage areas that, in most instances, will terminate at one disposal point. It must also be realized that generally the conduction component (swales or pipes) must increase in size as it progresses toward the outlet point, since the volume of runoff continues to increase.

In laying out piping patterns for closed systems, it is important to avoid buildings, subsurface structures such as other utilities, retaining walls, and trees. For most small-scale site development projects, pipes are designed as straight lines, because this reduces the potential for clogging and makes the system easier to clean. It is possible, however, to lay out piping using curved alignments, particularly for large pipes [36-in. (900-mm) diameter or larger]. Since pipes are placed underground, they are independent of the surface slope. However, avoid running pipe contrary to the surface slope, since this increases the amount of trench excavation required. Finally, storm water flows through pipes by gravity; therefore, all pipes must *slope*.

APPLICATIONS

Designing and Sizing Grassed Swales (Waterways)

Grassed swales are common components of open drainage systems. Generally, grassed swales should not carry continuous flows or even be continuously wet. Where this might occur, alternative methods should be used. These include the use of lined waterways or subsurface drains that leave the swale to carry flow only during and after storms, or vegetated swales that are designed to slow runoff and induce infiltration. When designing the layout of a management system, it may be possible to retain an existing natural drainageway or it may be necessary to construct new waterways. Constructed waterways generally have a smooth, shallow, and relatively wide cross section that is called *parabolic,* since it represents part of a parabolic curve. Although the discussion here will be limited to parabolic waterways, there are several other cross-sectional shapes that apply. The dimensions of the cross section are specified by the width, *W,* and the depth, *D,* as illustrated in Figure 13.7. Usually swales are seeded with the same seed mixtures that would be used for lawns in that particular location or with native grasses if a naturalized effect is desired. Newly constructed vegetated waterways should be protected from the erosive effect of flowing water until a good stand of grass has been established.

Grassed waterways are constructed to a design slope that is staked out and controlled during construction by profile leveling. It is preferable to design swales so that the velocity of the water flowing in them will not be decreased, since a reduction in flow velocity will result in siltation. Velocity could be reduced by a change in slope from steep to flat, by enlarging the cross section without also increasing the slope, or by an increase in the frictional resistance of the surface caused by tall vegetation being placed down slope from a stand of short vegetation. However, there are situations where a decrease in velocity, which filters out sediment, is desired. Yet, it must be realized that sedimentation changes the character and capacity of a swale, thus increasing the level of maintenance. Generally, grassed waterways are maintained the same way as any turf area. Two points of critical concern, though, are the prompt repair of any erosion damage and the removal of accumulated sediment.

The required dimensions for grassed swales may be determined analytically or by a variety of published nomographs or other design aids. To determine the required dimensions of a swale, the rate of runoff to be handled must be known. This may be computed using the Rational formula or by

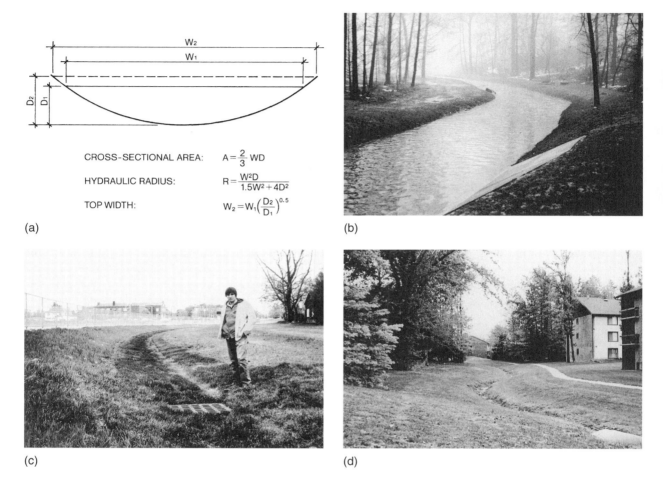

CROSS-SECTIONAL AREA: $A = \frac{2}{3} WD$

HYDRAULIC RADIUS: $R = \frac{W^2 D}{1.5W^2 + 4D^2}$

TOP WIDTH: $W_2 = W_1 \left(\frac{D_2}{D_1}\right)^{0.5}$

(a)

(b)

(c)

(d)

Figure 13.7. Parabolic swales. (a) Elements of parabolic swales. (b) A parabolic swale flowing full. *(Photo: Robert Moore)* (c) A diversion swale with a drain inlet. (d) A swale that is not functioning properly. A broader cross section or longer stand of grass could be used to slow the velocity of flow and reduce the potential for erosion.

SCS hydrology, as previously discussed. Stable (i.e., nonerodible) channels are usually designed to conform to either the maximum permissible velocity concept or the maximum permissible shear stress concept. The discussion in this book is confined to the former.[1] With the runoff rate known, the next step is to determine the slope for the proposed swale and the design velocity of flow. The slope is generally determined by the proposed grading plan,

the elevation of the outlet point, and the existing topography. The permissible maximum design velocity depends on the type and condition of the vegetation, the erodibility of the soil, and the slope

---

[1]Readers interested in swale design by shear stress are referred to *Stability Design of Grass-lined Open Channels*, Agriculture Handbook No. 667, USDA-NRCS, 2007 or *Design of Roadside Channels with Flexible Linings,* Federal Highway Administration, 1988.

of the swale. Recommended velocities for various conditions may be found in Table 13.1. In situations where excessive velocities cannot be avoided (such as steep slopes and channel width limitations), structural linings, such as riprap, gabions, or concrete, should be used. A discussion of the design of such linings may be found in engineering hydrology textbooks.

Table 13.1 Permissible Velocities for Vegetated Swales and Channels

		Permissible Velocity[a]	
Cover	Slope Range[b] %	Erosion-Resistant Soils[c] m/s/(ft/s)	Easily Eroded Soils[d] m/s/(ft/s)
Bermudagrass	<5 5–10 Over 10	2.43 (8) 2.13 (7) 1.82 (6)	1.82 (6) 1.22 (4) 0.91 (3)
Bahiagrass Buffalograss Kentucky bluegrass Smooth brome Blue grama Tall fescue	<5 5–10 over 10	2.13 (7) 1.82 (6) 1.52 (5)	1.52 (5) 1.22 (4) 0.91 (3)
Grass mixture Reed canarygrass	<5[b] 5–10		1.22 (4) 0.91 (3)
Sericea lespedeza Weeping lovegrass Yellow bluestem Redtop Alfalfa Red fescue	<5[e]	1.06 (3.5)	0.75 (2.5)
Common lespedeza[f] Sudangrass[f]	<5[g]	1.06 (3.5)	0.76 (2.5)

[a]Use velocities exceeding 1.52 m/s (5 ft/s) only where good covers and proper maintenance can be obtained.
[b]Do not use on slopes steeper than 10% except for vegetated side slopes in combination with a stone, concrete, or highly resistant vegetative center section.
[c]Cohesive (clayey) fine-grained soils and coarse-grained soils with cohesive fines with a plasticity index of 10 to 40 (CL, CH, SC, and CG).
[d]Soils that do not meet requirements for erosion-resistant soils.
[e]Do not use on slopes steeper than 5% except for vegetated side slopes in combination with a stone, concrete, or highly resistant vegetative center section.
[f]Annuals—use on mild slope or as temporary protection until permanent covers are established.
[g]Use on slopes steeper than 5% is not recommended.

Since the friction, or resistance to flow, of the vegetation varies with its length (which is short right after mowing and relatively long just before mowing), the range of heights must be determined. Also, as the flow depth increases, long vegetation will bend over and offer less resistance than it would with only a shallow depth. For this reason, various resistance, or retardance, factors have been experimentally determined and are listed in Table 13.2.

If the length of vegetation changes, the final design should always be checked for channel stability with maximum velocity (short vegetation) and capacity with minimum velocity (long vegetation). As a minimum, swales should be designed to carry the peak flow for a 10-year storm frequency.

Swale Design by Hydraulics

There are two formulas, Manning's equation for open channels (Equation 12.3) and the continuity equation, which are used in determining the dimensions of open channels, including swales. The *continuity equation* relates the cross-sectional area to the design flow, and the average flow velocity and is defined as

$$q = AV \qquad (13.1)$$

where
q = flow in ft³/s (m³/s)
A = cross-sectional area of flow in ft² (m²)
V = velocity of flow in ft/s (m/s)

If the hydraulic radius and the required cross-sectional area are known, the design dimensions can be determined.

■ EXAMPLE 13.1

A grassed waterway with a slope of 4% must carry 50 ft³/s of runoff. The soil is easily eroded. Design a vegetated drainage swale with a parabolic cross section. The vegetative cover will be a good stand of bluegrass sod, mowed to be kept at a 2-in. height.

Table 13.2 Retardance Factors for Grassed Swales

Retardance	Cover	Condition
A	Weeping lovegrass	Excellent stand, tall (average 30 in.)
	Reed canarygrass or yellow bluestem ischaemum	Excellent stand, tall (average 36 in.)
B	Smooth bromegrass	Good stand, mowed (average 12 to 15 in.)
	Bermudagrass	Good stand, tall (average 12 in.)
	Native grass mixture (little bluestem, blue grama, and other long and short midwest grasses)	Good stand, unmowed
	Tall fescue	Good stand, unmowed (average 18 in.)
	Sericea lespedeza	Good stand, not woody, tall (average 19 in.)
	Grass-legume mixture—Timothy, smooth bromegrass, or orchardgrass	Good stand, uncut (average 20 in.)
	Reed canarygrass	Good stand, uncut (average 12 to 15 in.)
	Tall fescue, with birdsfoot trefoil or ladino clover	Good stand, uncut (average 18 in.)
	Blue grama	Good stand, uncut (average 13 in.)
C	Bahiagrass	Good stand, uncut (6 to 8 in.)
	Bermudagrass	Good stand, mowed (average 6 in.)
	Redtop	Good stand, headed (15 to 20 in.)
	Grass-legume mixture—summer (orchardgrass, redtop, Italian ryegrass, and common lespedeza)	Good stand, uncut (6 to 8 in.)
	Centipedegrass	Very dense cover (average 6 in.)
	Kentucky bluegrass	Good stand, headed (6 to 12 in.)
D	Bermudagrass	Good stand, cut to 2.5-in. height
	Red fescue	Good stand, headed (12 to 18 in.)
	Buffalograss	Good stand, uncut (3 to 6 in.)
	Grass-legume mixture—fall, spring (orchardgrass, redtop, Italian ryegrass, and common lespedeza)	Good stand, uncut (4 to 5 in.)
	Sericea lespedeza or Kentucky bluegrass	Good stand, cut to 2-in. height; very good stand before cutting
E	Bermudagrass	Good stand, cut to 1.5-in. height
	Bermudagrass	Burned stubble

SOLUTION

From Table 13.1, the permissible velocity for the given conditions is determined as 5 ft/s, while the roughness coefficient (Table 12.2) is taken as 0.04. The known values are substituted into Manning's equation:

$$V = \frac{1.486}{n} R^{2/3} S^{1/2}$$

$$S = \frac{1.486}{0.04} R^{0.67} 0.04^{0.50}$$

$$R^{0.67} = \frac{5 \times 0.04}{1.486 \times 0.04^{0.50}}$$

$$R^{0.67} \approx 0.67$$

$$R \approx 0.67^{1/0.67}$$

$$R \approx 0.67^{1.5}$$

$$R \approx 0.55 \text{ ft}$$

The minimum cross-sectional area is determined by substituting the runoff volume, 50 ft³/s, and the permissible velocity, 5 ft/s, into the continuity equation:

$$q = AV$$

$$50 = A \times 5$$

$$A = \frac{50}{5} = 10 \text{ ft}^2$$

At this point, the required cross section for the drainageway is obtained by successive approximations. For small parabolic swales an initial trial depth may be taken as 1.5R, which in this case is 1.5 × 0.55 or 0.825 ft. As indicated in Figure 13.7, the *area* of a parabolic cross section is:

$$A = 2/3 \, WD \qquad \textbf{(13.2)}$$

where

A = cross-sectional area in ft^2 (m^2)

D = depth at the center in ft (m)

W = top width in ft (m)

Substituting into the equation, a trial width of 18.18 ft is obtained as follows:

$$10 \text{ ft}^2 = 2/3 \, W \times 0.825 \text{ ft}$$

$$W = \frac{10 \times 3}{0.825 \times 2} = 18.18 \text{ ft}$$

The *hydraulic radius* of a parabolic channel is expressed as

$$R = \frac{W^2 D}{1.5 \, W^2 + 4D^2} \qquad \textbf{(13.3)}$$

where

R = hydraulic radius, ft (m)

W = top width, ft (m)

D = depth at the center, ft (m)

For this problem a trial hydraulic radius is obtained by substituting $D = 0.825$ and $W = 18.18$ into the equation.

$$R = \frac{18.18^2 \times 0.825}{(1.5 \times 18.18^2) + (4 \times 0.825^2)}$$

$$R = 0.547 \text{ ft (or approximately 0.55 ft)}$$

Since this agrees with the hydraulic radius for a velocity of 5 ft/s, the design dimensions of $W = 18.18$ ft and $D = 0.825$ ft are satisfactory. In any approximation, the final area should be close to but *not less* than the calculated area (in this case, 10 ft^2), and the final hydraulic radius should be close to but *not greater* than the calculated hydraulic radius (0.55 ft in this problem). Thus, the final design dimensions for this example are

```
         DESIGN FOR STABILITY

         REQUIRED CAPACITY IN CFS?  50

         DESIRED VELOCITY IN FPS?  5

         SLOPE IN PERCENT?  4

         RETARDANCE CLASS?  D

(a)      FREEBOARD (IF ANY) IN FT?  O

         RETARDANCE CLASS        = D

         CONSTRUCTED WIDTH       = 18.1 FT

         WIDTH AT WATER SURFACE  = 18.1 FT

         CONSTRUCTED DEPTH       = 0.83 FT

         FLOW DEPTH              = 0.83 FT

         CAPACITY                = 50.0 CFS

         MANNING'S n             = 0.0403

         HYDRAULIC RADIUS        = 0.55 FT

         VELOCITY                = 5.0 FPS

         SLOPE                   = 4.0 PERCENT

         FREEBOARD               = 0.0 FT

         CRITICAL VELOCITY       = 4.2 FPS

(b)      90 PERCENT OF CRIT. VEL. = 3.8 FPS
```

Figure 13.8. (a) Computer input for Example 13.1. (b) Computer output for Example 13.1. *(Software: GRASCHAN © Kurt Nathan)*

$W = 18.18$ ft (or 18 ft) and $D = 0.83$ ft (or 10 in). If the first trial dimensions do not accomplish this, new dimensions must be assumed and tested. Computer input and output for the design of the grassed waterway in Example 13.1 are shown in Figure 13.8. Retardance class (an input) and critical velocity (an output) are discussed in subsequent sections of this chapter.

The constant of 1.486 is eliminated when metric units are used with Manning's equation. Thus, the equation can be rewritten as follows:

$$V = \frac{R^{2/3}S^{1/2}}{n} \qquad (13.4)$$

where

$V =$ flow velocity, m/s

$n =$ Manning's roughness coefficient for open channels (Table 12.2)

$R =$ hydraulic radius, m [A/WP, m²/m (see Figure 12.10)]

$S =$ gradient, % (m/m) ∎

∎ EXAMPLE 13.2

Calculate the flow velocity of the channel for Example 12.1 (Figure 12.11) when flowing full with $S = 0.02$ and $n = 0.10$. The dimensions of the channel are converted from feet to meters as follows:

$$16 \text{ ft}/3.281 \text{ ft/m} = 4.877 \text{ m}$$

$$8 \text{ ft} = 2.438 \text{ m}$$

$$4.47 \text{ ft} = 1.362 \text{ m}$$

$$2 \text{ ft} = 0.610 \text{ m}$$

SOLUTION

$$A = \frac{B+b}{2} \times h = \frac{4.877 + 2.438}{2} \times 0.610$$
$$= 2.231 \text{ m}^2$$

$$WP = 2 \times \text{length of sloped side} + \text{base } (b)$$
$$= 2 \times 1.362 + 2.438 = 5.162 \text{ m}$$

$$R = A/WP = 2.231 \text{ m}^2/5.162 \text{ m } 0.4322 \text{ m}$$

$$V = \frac{R^{2/3}S^{1/2}}{n} = \frac{0.4322^{2/3} \times 0.02^{1/2}}{0.10} = 0.81 \text{ m/s}$$

The velocity can be checked against the velocity determined in Example 12.1 as follows:

$$0.81 \text{ m/s} \times 3.281 \text{ ft/m} \approx 2.66 \text{ ft/s}$$

Using the continuity equation (Equation 13.1), determine the flow rate with this velocity.

$$q = AV$$
$$= 2.231 \text{ m}^2 \times 0.81 \text{ m/s} = 1.807$$
$$q \approx 1.81 \text{ m}^3/\text{s} \ ∎$$

Swale Design with Charts

Since the hydraulic design of swales is somewhat involved and since the n value of vegetation is variable, charts for the solution of Manning's equation (Equations 12.3 and 13.4) have been developed. These charts aid in finding the required hydraulic radii for various vegetative retardance classes and maximum permissible velocities and are shown in Figure 13.9. An example will illustrate their use.

∎ EXAMPLE 13.3

Storm water runoff from part of a townhouse development is to be conducted through a vegetated waterway (swale). The area in which this swale is located will be mowed twice during the growing season so that the height of the vegetation, which will be a good stand of Kentucky bluegrass, will vary between 2 and 10 in. The soil survey report shows the existing soil to be easily eroded. The site plan indicates that the swale will have a 5% gradient, and it is to be designed to carry 36 ft³/s.

SOLUTION

The maximum permissible velocity for this swale with Kentucky bluegrass on a 5% gradient and on an easily eroded soil is determined to be 4 ft/s from Table 13.1. In Table 13.2, the vegetative retardance factor for the cut condition is specified as D and for uncut condition as C. To design for stability, Figure 13.9d (Retardance D) is used. Entering horizontally from the left with 4 ft/s velocity until the 5% slope line is intersected, a vertical line is extended upward from the point of intersection and the required hydraulic radius is determined as 0.43 ft.

As in the previous example, the minimum required cross-sectional area is determined from $q = AV$:

$$36 = A \times 4$$

$$A = 36/4 = 9 \text{ ft}^2$$

The trial depth is again $1.5 \times R$ or 1.5×0.43, which is 0.65 ft. From $A = 2/3WD$, $9 = 2/3W \times 0.65$. Solving for W:

$$W = \frac{9 \times 3/2}{0.65} = 20.8 \text{ ft}$$

The dimensions $W = 20.8$ ft and $D = 0.65$ ft are satisfactory for stability with the vegetation in the mowed condition.

When the grass is long, retardance factor C is indicated. Since the velocity will be reduced below the allowable 4 ft/s because of the greater retardance, the cross-sectional area will have to be increased so that the swale will still be able to handle 36 ft³/s. This is done by deepening and widening the swale, retaining the same parabolic shape. A trial-and-error procedure must be employed. Assume a flow depth of 0.75 ft. Then the hydraulic radius from $D = 1.5R$ is $D/1.5 = R = 0.5$ ft. Entering Figure 13.9c (Retardance C) vertically with $R = 0.5$ until the 5% slope line is intersected

and then extending a horizontal line to the left, a velocity of 3.4 ft/s is obtained.

From the simplified equation of a parabola ($y = fx^2$ or $D = fW^2$), the width is proportional to the square root of the depth, and thus the new top width is computed as $W2 = W1(D2/D1)^{0.5} = 20.8 \times (0.75/0.65)^{0.5} = 22.3$ ft. The new area is $2/3WD = 2/3 \times 22.3 \times 0.75 = 13.15$ ft². From $q = AV$, the swale under these conditions will handle $13.15 \times 3.4 = 37.9$ ft³/s, which is a little more than required and is satisfactory.

It must be pointed out that state or local review agencies may have regulations specifying permissible velocities and retardance classifications for various types of vegetation different from those listed in Tables 13.1 and 13.2. Applicable regulatory agencies should be consulted to determine specific requirements for a particular project. ■

Critical Velocity

To enhance the stability of vegetated waterways by avoiding possible turbulence, some regulatory agencies suggest that design flow velocities be no greater than 90% of the *critical velocity*. Critical velocity (which occurs at the critical depth) is attained when the specific energy of the flowing water is at the minimum. For a given rate (ft³/s or m³/s), flows at less than the critical depth (with higher velocities) are called *supercritical* and those at depths greater than critical (with lower velocities) are called *subcritical* (Figure 13.10). For a full discussion of the critical flow phenomenon, the reader is referred to textbooks on fluid mechanics or hydraulics. (Of course, flow velocities should never exceed the allowable velocities stipulated in Table 13.1).

For parabolic waterways, the critical velocity is a function of the flow depth and can be computed from the equation

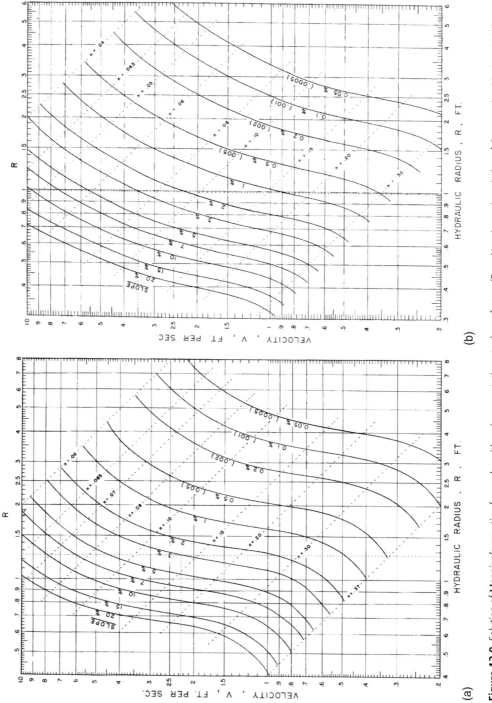

(a)

(b)

Figure 13.9. Solution of Manning's equation for swales with various vegetative retardance factors (From New Jersey Association of Conservation Districts, 1987). (a) Retardance A. (b) Retardance B.

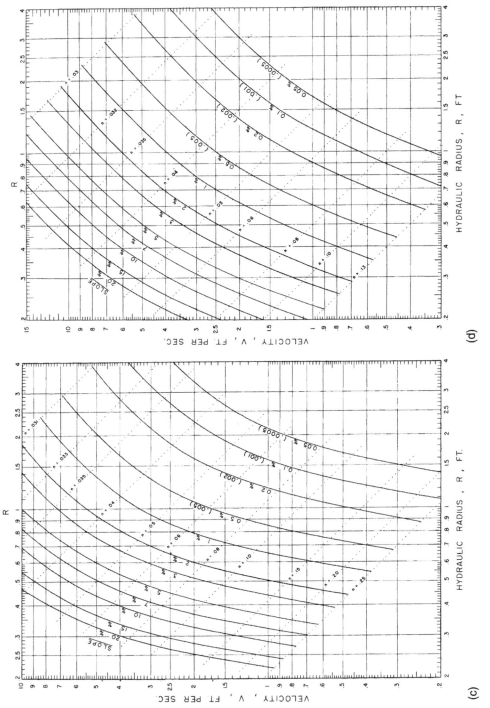

Figure 13.9 (continued). Solution of Manning's equation for swales with various vegetative retardance factors (From New Jersey Association of Conservation Districts, 1987). (c) Retardance C. (d) Retardance D.

(c)

(d)

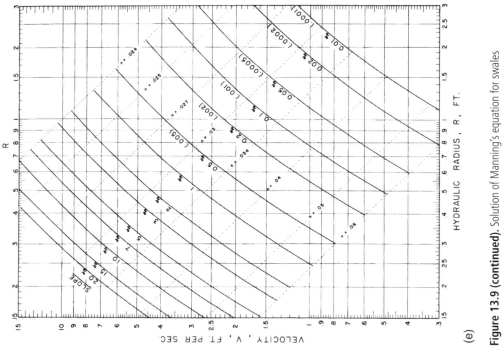

Figure 13.9 (continued). Solution of Manning's equation for swales with various vegetative retardance factors (From New Jersey Association of Conservation Districts, 1987). (e) Retardance E.

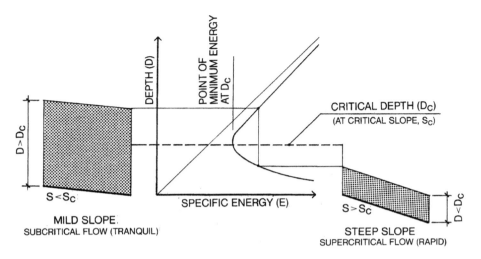

Figure 13.10. Critical flow depth. Critical flow depth, D_c, occurs at the point of minimum energy of the specific energy curve. Above the minimum energy point there, are two depths at which flow can occur with the same specific energy for the same q. One depth is greater than D_c and results in subcritical or tranquil flow, while the other is less than D_c and results in supercritical or rapid flow.

$$V_c = 4.63D^{0.5}$$

where

V_c = critical velocity, in ft/s

D = flow of depth of parabolic channel, in ft

Table 13.3 lists values of critical velocities and hydraulic radii for parabolic waterways of various depths. The following examples will illustrate how to design for subcritical flow velocity.

■ EXAMPLE 13.4A

A grassed waterway with a slope of 4% must carry 50 ft³/s of runoff. The soil is easily eroded. The vegetative cover will be a good stand of bluegrass sod, which will be kept mowed to a 2-in. height. Design a vegetated drainageway with a parabolic cross section. The regulatory agency limits the design flow velocity to a maximum of 90% of the critical

velocity. (Note that, except for the critical velocity requirement, this is the same as Example 13.1.)

SOLUTION

For a good stand of vegetation 2-in. high, the retardance factor for allowable velocity is determined as D from Table 13.2. The swale design must agree with both Table 13.3 and Figure 13.9d. From the solution for Example 13.1, it is known that the velocity corresponding to a 0.825-ft depth is 5 ft/s. According to Table 13.3, this is too great to meet the critical velocity requirement. Therefore, a trial depth of 0.7 ft with 0.90 V_c of 3.49 ft/s and R of 0.47 ft is selected. Entering Figure 13.9d vertically with $R = 0.47$ until the "4% slope line" (between 3 and 5%) is intersected, a horizontal line is extended from the point of intersection to the left and a velocity of about 3.7 ft/s is obtained. This is more than the 3.49 ft/s indicated in Table 13.3 as 0.90 V_c for a depth of 0.7, and D and R must be reduced.

Table 13.3 Critical Velocities and Hydraulic Radii for Parabolic Waterways.

Critical Depth (ft)	Critical[a] Velocity (fps)	90% of Crit. Velocity (fps)	Approx. Hydraulic Radius[b] (ft)
0.5	3.27	2.95	0.33
0.6	3.59	3.23	0.40
0.7	3.87	3.49	0.47
0.8	4.14	3.73	0.53
0.9	4.39	3.95	0.60
1.0	4.63	4.17	0.67
1.1	4.86	4.37	0.73
1.2	5.07	4.56	0.80
1.3	5.28	4.75	0.87
1.4	5.48	4.93	0.93
1.5	5.67	5.10	1.00
1.6	5.86	5.27	1.07
1.7	6.04	5.43	1.13
1.8	6.21	5.59	1.20
1.9	6.38	5.74	1.27
2.0	6.55	5.89	1.33
2.1	6.71	6.04	1.40
2.2	6.87	6.18	1.47
2.3	7.02	6.32	1.53
2.4	7.17	6.46	1.60
2.5	7.32	6.59	1.67

[a]Computed from $V_c = 4.63D^{0.5}$.
[b]Computed from $R = D/1.5$.

A depth of 0.6 with a corresponding R of 0.40 is tried next, resulting in a velocity of about 2.8 ft/s from Figure 13.9d. This is less than the 3.23 ft/s indicated as 0.90 V_c and would meet the velocity restriction. However, by deepening the channel somewhat, the width, which would be required to carry the design flow rate with a depth of 0.6 ft, can be reduced.

For a depth of 0.65, $R = 0.65/1.5 = 0.43$, $V_c = 4.63 \times D^{0.5} = 4.63 \times 0.65^{0.5} = 3.73$, and 0.90 $V_c = 3.36$. (These values could also have been determined from Table 13.3 by interpolation.) From Figure 13.9d, $V = 3.30$ for $R = 0.43$ at 4% slope. This is less than 90% of the critical velocity. The n value from the same figure is 0.051. From

$$q = AV$$
$$50 = A \times 3.30 \text{ ft}^2$$
$$A = \frac{50}{3.30} = 15.2 \text{ ft}^2$$

From

$$A = 2/3WD$$
$$15.2 = 2/3W \times 0.65$$
$$W = \frac{15.2 \times 3}{0.65 \times 2} = 35.1 \text{ ft}$$

The design dimensions are:

$$D = 0.65 \text{ ft}$$
$$W = 35.1$$

Note that in this case the width necessary to reduce the velocity to subcritical is almost twice that of the previous design for allowable velocity (Example 13.1).

As a check, R, V, and Q should be computed from the design dimensions.

$$R = \frac{W^2D}{1.5W^2 + 4D^2} = \frac{35.1^2 \times 0.65}{1.5 \times 35.1^2 + 4 \times 0.65^2} = 0.43$$

$$V = \frac{1.486}{n}R^{0.67}S^{0.5} = \frac{1.486}{0.051} \times 0.43^{0.67} \times 0.04^{0.5} = 3.31$$

$$q = AV = 15.2 \times 3.31 = 50.3 \text{ ft}^3/\text{s}$$

Thus, all requirements have been met.

If conditions permit, other methods could be used to reduce flow velocities, such as increasing the retardance factor by letting the vegetation grow to a greater height and/or reducing the gradient. This will be demonstrated in the next example. ■

■ EXAMPLE 13.4B

It has been decided that the swale of Example 13.4A requires too great an area, and it will therefore be relocated on the site plan. To decrease the width and cross-sectional area, the flow velocity will be increased to near the permissible velocity of 5 ft/s while still remaining 90% of the critical velocity or less. The vegetation is to remain retardance D. What will be the dimensions and the required slope for this swale?

SOLUTION

Table 13.3 indicates that a parabolic swale with a depth of 1.4 ft has a hydraulic radius of about 0.93 ft with 90% of the critical velocity of 4.93 ft/s. The intersection of $R = 0.93$ and $V = 4.93$ on Figure 13.9d indicates a slope of 1.67% and an n value of 0.036 (by interpolation).

$$q = AV$$

$$50 = A \times 4.93$$

$$A = \frac{50}{4.93} = 10.14 \approx 10.1 \text{ ft}^2$$

$$A = 2/3 \, WD$$

$$10.1 = 2/3 \, W \times 1.4$$

$$W = \frac{10.1 \times 3}{1.4 \times 2} = 10.82 \approx 10.8 \text{ ft}$$

Thus, the trial design dimensions are

$$D = 1.4 \text{ ft}$$

$$W = 10.8 \text{ ft}$$

and the trial design slope is 1.67%.

When these values are checked by the method previously shown, the resulting velocity slightly exceeds 4.93 ft/s, which is 90% of the critical velocity. Recalculating with $D = 1.34$ ft (90% $V_c = 4.8$ ft/s) and checking again leads to values that are within acceptable limits, and the final design measurements are

$$D = 1.34 \text{ ft}$$

$$W = 11.9 \text{ ft}$$

$$S = 1.6\%$$

Where it is appropriate, increasing the retardance of the vegetation may be more practical than reducing the slope by relocating the swale.

Some designers increase the depth from 0.3 to 0.5 ft (0.1 to 0.15 m) after the hydraulic design procedure. This will also result in widening of the channel. The increased depth is called *freeboard*. ■

Designing and Sizing Pipe Systems

It is often more practical to dispose of or direct excess surface water by means of subsurface piping or closed systems rather than by open drainage channels. As previously mentioned, in designing any drainage system, the first step is to determine the availability of an adequate outlet. The next step for a closed system is to determine surface slopes and configuration and the location of collection points where the inlet structures will be placed for the piping system. Generally, it is best to locate these structures away from trees, main walks, and buildings, since occasional clogging may cause flooding. The collection points are then connected on the drawing, usually by straight lines that represent the subsurface pipes. The network should be designed with the minimum adequate amount of pipe for economy. Where two or more pipes join, or where pipes join at different elevations, structures such as manholes, junction boxes, or catch basins should be used. A 3-ft (900-mm) minimum depth for pipes is recommended to protect pipes from being crushed by traffic and, in northern climates, to reduce potential frost problems.

Most often using the Rational method, the peak rate of runoff (q_p) is calculated for the drainage area collected by each pipe, keeping in mind that the volume is cumulative proceeding downgrade as additional inlets are connected to the system. By selecting a slope for the pipe, a pipe size for the calculated runoff can be determined using Manning's equation (Equations 12.3 and 13.4) and the continuity equation (Equation 13.1). This process is illustrated in the following example.

■ EXAMPLE 13.5

Calculate the pipe size required to carry 10 ft³/s at a 10% slope. Use vitrified clay pipe with an *n* value of 0.015.

SOLUTION

The cross-sectional area of a circular pipe flowing full is r^2, the area of a circle. The wetted perimeter of a circular pipe flowing full is equal to the circumference, or $2\pi r$. Thus, the hydraulic radius is

$$R = \frac{\pi r^2}{2r\pi} = \frac{r}{2}$$

where

R = hydraulic radius, in ft (m)

r = inside radius of pipe section, in ft (m)

As stated before, Manning's equation (in U.S. Customary units) is

$$V = \frac{1.486}{n} R^{0.67} S^{0.05}$$

and the continuity equation is $q = AV$. These two equations can be combined as follows:

$$q = A \frac{1.486}{n} R^{0.67} S^{0.50}$$

By substituting the known values for the problem, the equation becomes

$$10 = \pi r^2 \frac{1.486}{0.015} (r/2)^{0.67} (0.1)^{0.50}$$

$$r^2 \times r^{0.67} = \frac{10 \times 0.015 \times 2^{0.67}}{\pi \times 1.486 \times 0.1^{0.50}}$$

$$r^2 \times r^{0.67} = 0.16$$

$$r^{2.67} = 0.16$$

$$r = 0.16^{1/2.67} = 0.50 \text{ ft}$$

Therefore, a pipe with a 0.50-ft radius, or a 1.0-ft diameter, is an adequate size for this problem.

In most cases, several pipes are interconnected to create a closed drainage system. A procedure for sizing pipes for such a system is demonstrated in Examples 13.5 and 13.6. In Example 13.6, a method for determining runoff rates from various drainage areas, which contribute to a piping system, is discussed. ■

■ EXAMPLE 13.6

Figure 13.11 schematically illustrates two drainage areas and a proposed drainage system consisting of two catch basins and required piping. The characteristics of the drainage areas are:

Drainage Area X: A = 1.2 ac

$$C = 0.3$$

$$T_c = 45 \text{ min}$$

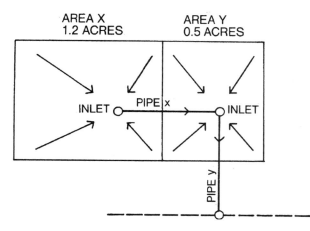

Figure 13.11. Schematic plan for Example 13.6.

Drainage Area Y: $A = 0.5$ ac

$$C = 0.7$$

$$T_c = 20 \text{ min}$$

Determine the peak rate of runoff that must be handled by pipes x and y for a 10-year storm frequency.

SOLUTION

The first step is to determine the rainfall intensity from Figure 11.2 for each of the drainage areas. This is 2.5 iph for area X and 4.0 iph for area Y. Using the Rational formula, the rate of runoff for each drainage area can be calculated.

$$q_x = 0.3 \times 2.5 \times 1.2$$

$$q_x = 0.9 \text{ ft}^3/\text{s}$$

$$q_y = 0.7 \times 4.0 \times 0.5$$

$$q_y = 1.4 \text{ ft}^3/\text{s}$$

Pipe x must handle only the runoff from drainage area X; therefore, it can be sized for 0.9 ft^3/s. However, pipe y must handle the runoff from area Y plus the water flowing in pipe x. As determined above, the peak rate of flow for area Y is 1.4 ft^3/s. This rate is reached in 20 minutes, but at that time pipe x is still not flowing full, since area X does not peak until 45 minutes after the beginning of the design storm. If q_x and q_y were simply added, the pipe may be oversized. Using the definition of time of concentration as the time for water to flow from the hydraulically most remote point of the drainage area to the point of interest, this would be 45 minutes (T_c for area X) plus the time of flow in the pipe from area X to area Y [for distances less than 150 ft (45.0 m) this time is usually negligible]. The rate of runoff for the longer time of concentration is

$$q_y = 0.7 \times 2.5 \times 0.5$$

$$= 0.88 \text{ ft}^3/\text{s} \approx 0.9 \text{ ft}^3/\text{s}$$

Therefore, the rate of flow that pipe y must handle is 0.9 + 0.9, approximately 1.8 ft^3/s. This is above the peak rate of 1.4 ft^3/s, which occurs in 20 minutes for area Y but below 2.3 ft^3/s, which would have resulted if the two rates had been added.

A more accurate and sophisticated procedure is to utilize the maximum flow rates obtained from the MRM.

For a storm duration of 20 minutes, the maximum flow rate for area X is

$$q = C \times C_A \times i \times A \times Dur/T_c$$

since 20 minutes is less than the time of concentration of 45 minutes. Therefore,

$$q = 0.3 \times 1.0 \times 4.0 \times 1.2 \times 20/45$$

$$= 0.64 \approx 0.6 \text{ ft}^3/\text{s}$$

The total runoff rate for pipe y is 0.6 + 1.4 = 2.0 ft^3/s. This is more than the 1.8 ft^3/s previously determined and should be used for design.

It is important to analyze each project carefully to make sure that pipes are designed to handle peak flows regardless of the time of concentration upstream. ■

■ EXAMPLE 13.7

In this problem, the site plan (Figure 13.12) for a small office building indicates proposed grades, location of drainage structures, and the piping pattern. For this site plan all parking areas, drives, and streets have 6-in.-high curbs, and all areas not paved are lawn with a silt loam soil texture. The off-site drainage area consists of 2 ac of woodland. The longest overland distance for this runoff, which enters the site at the north corner, is 200 ft, with an average slope of 4% and, again, a silt loam soil texture. Use a 10-year storm frequency for the design of the drainage system, which is located in New Jersey. Runoff from the building roof must be accommodated in the design.

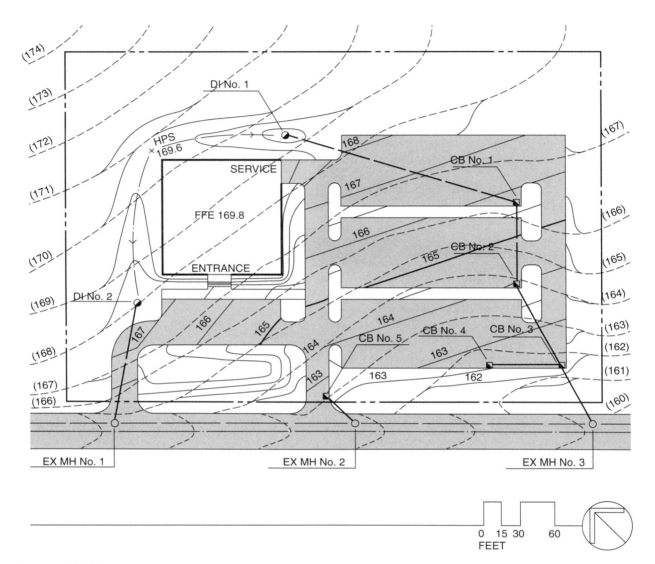

Figure 13.12. Site plan for Example 13.7.

SOLUTION

Step 1. The first step is to develop an orderly procedure for recording and organizing all necessary information for sizing and laying out a closed drainage system. This required information is arranged in tabular form, as illustrated in Table 13.4.

Step 2. The next step is to determine the extent of the drainage areas, the surface characteristics, and the area of each surface type for each drainage structure (Figure 13.3). The selected surface coefficients (C) for each surface type and the respective areas (A) are recorded in the

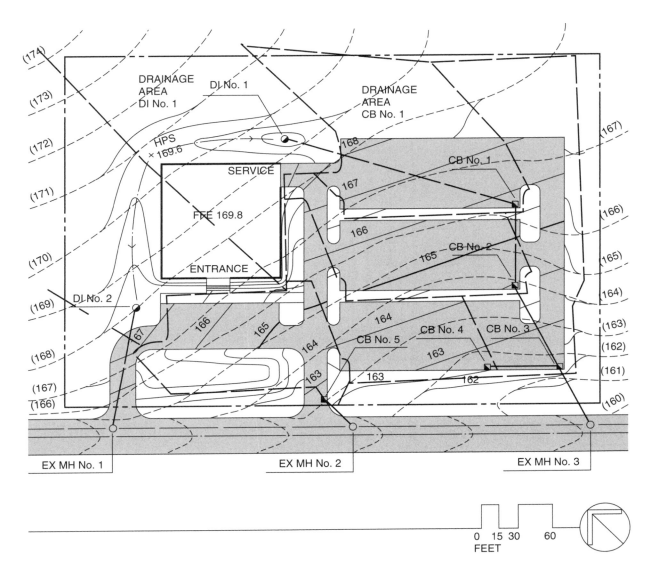

Figure 13.13. Drainage areas for Example 13.7.

table. In this problem, the assumption is that one-half of the off-site drainage area (or 1 ac) is directed toward drain inlet No. 1 and the other half toward drain inlet No. 2. The same assumption is made for the roof runoff.

Step 3. The third step is to determine the overland flow time (time of concentration) for each

of the drainage areas by using the nomograph in Figure 11.3. An adjusted rainfall intensity value (i) can then be obtained from the rainfall intensity curves in Figure 11.2. A 10-year frequency curve for central New Jersey is used. The information from Steps 2 and 3 can be substituted into the Rational formula, $q = CiA$, to

Table 13.4 Data for Example 13.7

Area	to	c	T[a] (min)	i (iph)	A (ac)	q_{sub} (cfs)	q (cfs)	D (in.)	S (ft/ft)	L (ft)	V (fps)	n	INV in	INV out	TF[c]
½ Roof	DI No. 1	0.92	37	2.8	0.12	0.31									
DI No. 1	CB No. 1	0.30		2.8	1.45	1.22	1.53	12	0.0024	210	1.9	0.015		156.79	167.60
CB No. 1	CB No. 2	0.30	37	2.8	0.20	0.17									
		0.90		2.8	0.21	0.53	2.23	12	0.0055	75	2.8	0.015	156.29	156.29	165.70
CB No. 2	CB No. 3	0.90	37	2.8	0.30	0.76	2.99	12	0.0095	80	3.7	0.015	155.88	155.88	163.90
CB No. 4	CB No. 3	0.30	10[b]	5.8	0.04	0.07									
		0.90		5.8	0.25	1.31	1.38	8	0.018	50	3.9	0.015		156.02	162.60
CB No. 3	MH No. 3	0.30	37	2.8	0.07	0.06									
		0.90		2.8	0.28	0.71	5.14	15	0.0095	55	4.3	0.015	155.12	154.87	162.00
CB No. 5	MH No. 2	0.30	10	5.8	0.12	0.21									
		0.90		5.8	0.18	0.94	1.15	8	0.011	30	3.2	0.015		157.06	162.50
½ Roof	DI No. 2	0.92	40	2.7	0.12	0.30									
DI No. 2	MH No. 1	0.30		2.7	1.36	1.10	1.40	8	0.018	105	3.9	0.015		161.16	167.20

[a]Flow times in pipes between drainage structures have not been included, since the distances between structures are relatively short and the resultant flow times are negligible. However, for longer distances the flow time in pipes must be included in the time of concentration. (To determine the travel time in pipes, the length of the pipe is divided by the flow velocity. For example, the travel time in a 500-ft-long pipe with a 2.5-fps flow velocity is 500 ft./2.5 fps = 200 sec. or 3.33 min.)

[b]Since it takes several minutes for rain to wet a surface thoroughly, many municipalities permit the use of minimum times of concentration, such as 10 or 15 minutes. This will reduce the intensity used for the computation of the runoff rate and thus the required pipe size.

[c]Top of frame.

calculate the peak rate of runoff to be carried in each pipe. Remember that these rates are additive moving downgrade. For example, the pipe between catch basin No. 1 and catch basin No. 2 must carry the runoff from the catch basin No. 1 drainage area as well as the runoff from the drainage inlet No. 1 and one-half of the roof runoff.

Step 4. At this point, the pipes may be sized. However, rather than using equations to calculate the required sizes, the nomograph in Figure 13.14 is used. There are five components to the nomograph: discharge in ft³/s, diameter of pipe in inches, roughness coefficient, velocity in ft/s, and slope. The figure is actually two nomographs. The first directly relates discharge, diameter of the pipe, and

velocity. Knowing any two values will allow the determination of the third. The other nomograph relates slope and roughness coefficient to diameter of pipe and discharge. Two values on the same side of the pivot line must be known (or selected) in order to determine the other two values. The use of the nomograph is demonstrated by sizing the pipe from drain inlet No. 1 to catch basin No. 1.

Two issues related to pipe sizing must be discussed before proceeding. The first is the pipe size. To reduce clogging and maintenance problems, a 12-in. (300-mm)-diameter pipe is recommended as a minimum size for landscape applications. This minimum does not apply to roof drain and area drain conditions. Also, there are standard pipe sizes for the different pipe materials, and manufacturers'

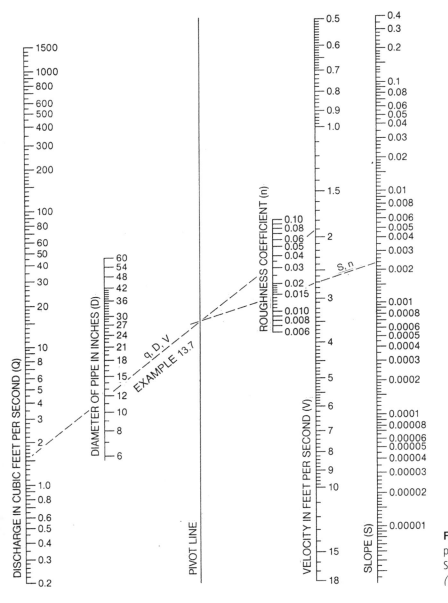

Figure 13.14. Nomograph for circular pipes flowing full (Manning's equation). Source: *American Iron and Steel Institute (1980).*

catalogs should be consulted. The second issue is velocity. A recommended range for the velocity of water in pipes is 2.5 to 10 ft/s (0.75 to 3.0 m/s). A minimum of 2.5 ft/s (0.75 m/s) is used to ensure self-cleaning, while a maximum of 10 ft/s (3.0 m/s)

is suggested to reduce potential scouring and pipe wear, which may occur above this velocity. Also from the nomograph, it can be seen that there is an inverse relationship between pipe size and slope and velocity.

For drainage inlet No. 1 to catch basin No. 1, the discharge flowing in the pipe is 1.53 ft³/s. Experience shows that this is a comparatively low rate flow; therefore, the use of a minimum pipe size is anticipated. In applying the nomograph, the discharge (q) is known and a 12-in.-diameter pipe size is selected. The procedure for determining the remaining values is as follows:

1. Locate 1.53 ft³/s on the discharge line.
2. Locate 12 in. on the diameter of pipe line.
3. Draw a straight line through the two points, crossing the pivot line, until it intersects with the velocity line.
4. Read the value of the velocity line at the point of intersection. In this case, the velocity is 1.9 ft/s, somewhat below the recommended minimum. However, rather than reduce the pipe to an 8-in. diameter (the next lower standard size for reinforced concrete pipe), the 12-in. diameter is maintained.
5. Next, return to the intersection point of the line drawn in Step 3 with the pivot line.
6. Locate 0.015 on the roughness coefficient line. This is the selected n value for the piping material (reinforced concrete pipe) used in this problem (see Table 12.2).
7. Draw a straight line from the point on the pivot line through 0.015 on the roughness coefficient line until it intersects with the slope line.
8. Read the value on the slope line at the point of intersection, which is 0.0024.
9. Record all appropriate values in Table 13.4.

The same procedure is applied to the remaining pipes. All data for the problem are recorded in Table 13.4.

Two additional points with regard to the design of pipe systems must be made here. The first is that pipe size should *never* decrease proceeding downgrade. The diameter of the outlet pipe from a drainage structure should be equal to or larger than the diameter of the inlet pipe. Note that the pipe size at catch basin No. 4 can be less, since it is a branch line. The second design point is that, to prevent silting and clogging, it is preferable *not* to decrease pipe flow velocity proceeding downgrade. This is one reason that the 8-in.-diameter pipe was not used at drainage inlet No. 1. The velocity for an 8-in. pipe would have been greater than 4 ft/s, which would have been greater than the subsequent velocities. However, 8-in.-diameter reinforced concrete pipe is used for catch basins Nos. 4 and 5. The smaller diameter was necessary in order to ensure a reasonable velocity due to the very low flow rate.

Step 5. The last step is to determine the invert elevations for the pipes and draw a profile of the system. *Invert elevation* is the elevation of the bottom of the pipe *opening* in a drainage structure, as illustrated in Figure 13.15. The invert elevation of the outlet pipe must be equal to or lower than the invert elevation of the inlet pipe. One technique used to ensure this relationship is to match top of pipe elevations.

Inlet elevations are determined by proceeding backward from the point at which the proposed

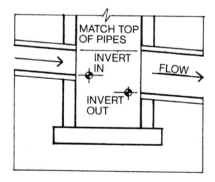

Figure 13.15. Invert elevation. The invert elevation for a drainage structure is the lowest point of the internal cross section of the entering and exiting pipes. The invert of the entering pipe is referred to as the invert *in*, while for the exiting pipe it is referred to as the invert *out*. The invert in must not be lower than the invert out. This relationship can be assured by matching the top of pipe elevations.

system connects to the existing system. The difference in elevation between the existing invert elevations and the proposed invert elevation is calculated by multiplying the pipe slope by the pipe length. To calculate the outlet invert for catch basin No. 3 (CB No. 3), work back from the existing invert elevation of manhole No. 3 (MH No. 3), which is 154.35.

$$\text{MH No. 3 inv. elev.} = 154.35 \text{ ft}$$

$$\text{Pipe Slope} = 0.0095 \text{ ft/ft}$$

$$\text{Pipe Length} = 55.0 \text{ ft}$$

$$0.0095 \times 55.0 = 0.52 \text{ ft}$$

$$154.35 + 0.52 = 154.87 \text{ ft outlet invert}$$
$$\text{elevation at CB No. 3}$$

Once this invert elevation is determined, the remaining elevations may be calculated using the same technique.

After all of the invert elevations have been calculated, a profile may be constructed for the entire system (Figure 13.16). A *profile* is a longitudinal

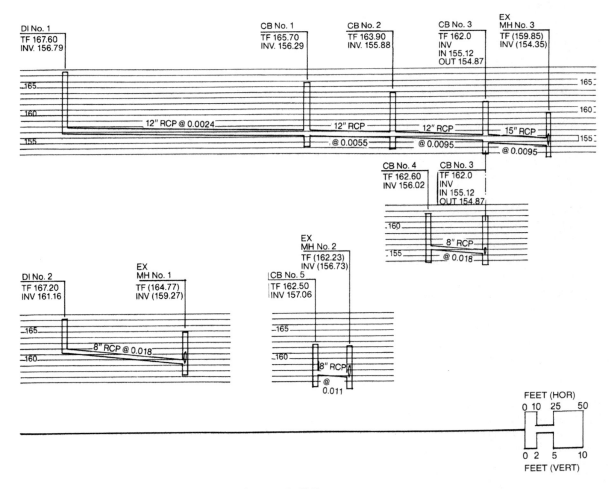

Figure 13.16. Profiles of a storm drainage system for Example 13.7.

section usually taken along the centerline of a linear project, such as storm drainage piping or a road. A profile is a good checking device to evaluate whether pipes slope properly and if invert relationships are correct. It also provides an opportunity to analyze whether pipes are placed too deep, thus requiring excessive trenching, or too shallow, thus resulting in insufficient cover and protection for the pipe. If either situation exists, the system must be reevaluated and redesigned. ■

SUBSURFACE DRAINAGE

The purpose of subsurface drainage is to maintain the water table at a level that provides desirable plant growth conditions and increases the usability of areas for recreational or other purposes. Subsurface drains remove only excess water, not water that plants can use. Water available to plants is held in the soil by capillary, or surface tension, forces, while excess water flows by gravity into the drains. Subsurface drainage is accomplished by means of clay tile or perforated or porous pipe laid in a continuous line at a specified depth and grade (Figures 13.17 and 13.18). Free water enters the drains through the joints, perforations, or porous walls of the pipe and flows out by gravity. Although subsurface drainage is somewhat similar to a closed system, it must be emphasized that water

percolates through the soil and is then removed by drains placed below the ground surface.

The major components of a subsurface drainage system are mains, submains, laterals, and drainage outlets. The laterals collect the free water from the soil and carry it to the submains and mains. These, in turn, conduct the water to the drainage outlet. The installation procedure for perforated pipe is to place the perforations at the bottom of the pipe to minimize the amount of soil particles entering the pipe. For clay tile a small gap is left between pipe segments. Tar paper is placed over the top of the gaps, or permeable filter strips are wrapped around the pipe to minimize the entrance

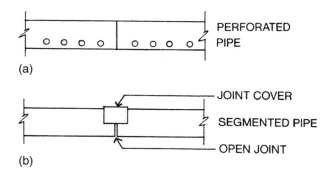

Figure 13.17. Pipe installation for subsurface drainage. (a) Perforated pipe with perforations placed toward the bottom of the pipe. (b) For segmented pipe, such as clay tile, a gap is left between pipe segments. A cover or filter is placed over the open joint to prevent sediment from entering the pipe.

Figure 13.18. French drain with subsurface drainage. A french drain is a trench filled with porous material that is used to collect and conduct surface runoff. French drains may also be used in conjunction with subsurface drainage as illustrated.

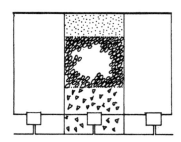
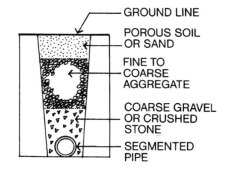

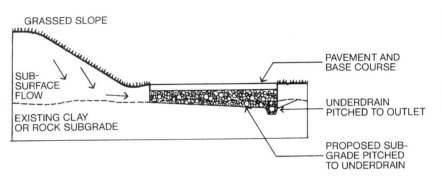

GRASSED SLOPE

SUB-SURFACE FLOW

EXISTING CLAY OR ROCK SUBGRADE

PAVEMENT AND BASE COURSE

UNDERDRAIN PITCHED TO OUTLET

PROPOSED SUB-GRADE PITCHED TO UNDERDRAIN

Figure 13.19. Underdrainage. The section illustrates a condition in which a buildup of water could occur beneath a pavement, thus causing damage by pressure or frost action. To reduce these problems, the new subgrade is sloped to an underdrain that carries off the excess water.

of silt particles into the pipe. Finally, under certain conditions, surface inlets may be used in conjunction with a subsurface drainage system.

Underdrainage is a specific type of subsurface drainage used to maintain proper structural conditions. Examples include footing and foundation drains and lateral drains placed behind retaining walls (see Chapter 5). Pavements placed over clay soils or rock or at the bottom of steep slopes may need underdrains to reduce the possibility of perched water and hydrostatic pressure (Figure 13.19).

Designing and Sizing Subsurface Systems

Subsurface systems may be laid out either to collect water from poorly drained, wet areas or to drain complete areas. The piping pattern for the former condition is typically random, whereas gridiron or herringbone arrangements are typical for the latter (Figure 13.20). *Cutoff* drains are pipes placed across a slope to intercept water that would otherwise be forced to the surface by an outcropping of an impermeable layer such as a tight subsoil (Figure 13.21).

The pipe size required to drain a certain acreage depends on the pipe gradient, since an increase in gradient will result in a greater velocity of flow and will permit the pipe to drain a larger area. Pipes are placed at constant gradients, or variable gradients with the gradient increasing toward the

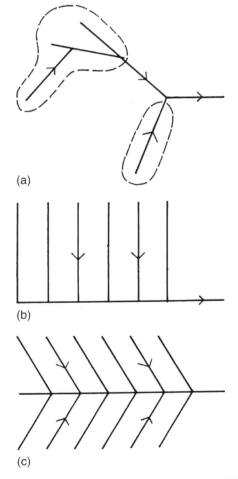

(a)

(b)

(c)

Figure 13.20. Piping patterns for subsurface drainage. (a) Random system. (b) Gridiron system. (c) Herringbone system.

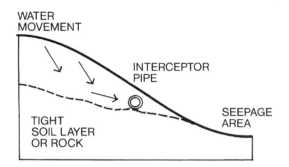

Figure 13.21. Cutoff drain.

outlet. The gradients should never decrease, since the velocity of flow would decrease and silt would be deposited in the pipe. Typically, pipe gradients for lawn areas vary from a minimum of 0.1% to a

maximum of 1.0%. Tables 13.5 and 13.6 show the relationship between pipe size, gradient, and maximum acreage drained for smooth clay or concrete drainage lines and corrugated plastic tubing. These tables were computed by Manning's equation and the continuity equation with n values of 0.011 for the clay and concrete pipe and 0.016 for the corrugated plastic tubing. A drainage coefficient (DC) of $3/8$ in. (or 0.0312 ft) was used. *Drainage coefficient* is defined as the depth of water removed over the drainage area in 24 hours. In humid areas of the United States, a DC of $3/8$ in. is normally used for mineral soils. For organic soils, the acreages of the tables should be reduced by one-half. This may also be done for mineral soils if more rapid drainage is desired.

Table 13.5 Maximum Acreage[a] Drained by Various Pipe Sizes: Clay or Concrete Pipe (n = 0.011, DC = $3/8$ in./24 hr)

Pipe Size (in.)	Slope(%)									
	0.1	0.2	0.3	0.4	0.5	0.6	0.7	0.8	0.9	1.0
4	4.51	6.38	7.82	9.03	10.1	11.1	11.9	12.8	13.5	14.3
5	8.19	11.6	14.2	16.4	18.3	20	21.7	23.2	24.6	25.9
6	13.3	18.8	23.1	26.6	29.8	32.6	35.2	37.6	39.9	42.1
8	28.7	40.5	49.6	57.3	64.1	70.2	75.8	81.1	86	90.6
10	52	73.5	90	104	116	127	138	147	156	164
12	84.5	120	146	169	189	207	224	239	254	267

[a]Reduce these acreages by one-half for a ¾-in. DC.

Table 13.6 Maximum Acreage[a] Drained by Various Pipe Sizes: Corrugated Plastic Tubing (n = 0.016, DC = $3/8$ in./24 hr)

Tubing Size (in.)	Slope (%)									
	0.1	0.2	0.3	0.4	0.5	0.6	0.7	0.8	0.9	1.0
4	3.10	4.39	5.38	6.21	6.94	7.60	8.21	8.78	9.31	9.81
5	5.62	7.96	9.75	11.3	12.6	13.8	14.9	15.9	16.9	17.8
6	9.15	12.9	15.8	18.3	20.5	22.4	24.2	25.9	27.5	28.9
8	19.7	27.9	34.1	39.4	44.1	48.3	52.1	55.7	59.1	62.3
10	35.7	50.5	61.9	71.5	79.9	87.5	94.5	101	107	113
12	58.1	82.2	101	116	130	142	154	164	174	184

[a]Reduce these acreages by one-half for a ¾-in. DC.

Depth and Spacing

The depth at which drainage lines are installed generally depends on the outlet conditions. However, there should be a *minimum* of 2 ft (0.6 m) of cover in mineral soils and 2.5 ft (0.75 m) in organic soils. Drainage lines should always be deep enough to prevent possible frost damage.

The spacing of drainage lines depends on the texture of the soil to be drained. Sandy soils permit more rapid movement of water than heavy clay soils, and, therefore, lines may be spaced farther apart and deeper in sandy soils than in clay soils. If drains are spaced too far apart, however, the central portion between lines will remain poorly drained. Suggestions for depth and spacing of drainage lines are given in Table 13.7.

To design subsurface drainage systems for some soils, such as organic soils and fine sandy loams, a qualified drainage engineer should be consulted, since special precautions must be taken.

Drainage Area

In order to determine the size of pipe, the acreage that each line has to drain must be known. For a gridiron or herringbone system, the area drained by each line may be computed by multiplying the length of the individual lines by the spacing between lines. Where surface inlets are connected to the subsurface system, the total area graded toward the inlets must also be included. The following examples demonstrate the procedure for determining drainage areas and pipe sizes.

Table 13.7 Typical Depths and Spacings of Drainage Lines for Various Soil Textures.

	Spacing (ft)	Depth (ft)
Clay, clay loam	30–70	2.5–3.0
Silt loam	60–100	3.0–4.0
Sandy loam	100–300	3.5–4.5
Organic soils	80–200	3.5–4.5

■ EXAMPLE 13.8

A plan for a gridiron drainage system with proposed pipe gradients indicated is illustrated in Figure 13.22. Determine the pipe sizes for the various parts of the system for a mineral soil and clay pipe. There are no surface inlets.

SOLUTION

The laterals are 300 ft long and are spaced 100 ft apart. This means that each line drains 50 ft on either side. Therefore, the drainage area for each lateral is 300 ft by 100 ft (50 + 50), which equals 30,000 ft^2, or approximately 0.69 ac. Based on Table 13.5, a 4-in. pipe is sufficient for all laterals. The main line at the outlet must accommodate the flow from the five laterals (or approximately 3.44 ac) plus its own drainage area of 500 ft by 50 ft, which equals 25,000 ft^2, or about 0.57 ac, since it provides drainage on one side. The total drainage area of the system is about 4.0 ac (3.44 + 0.57). Table 13.5 shows that a 4-in. pipe is also sufficient for the main

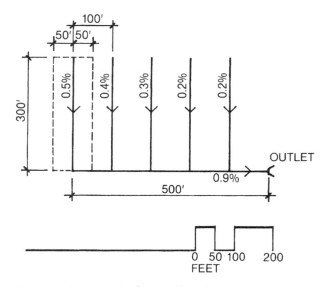

Figure 13.22. Piping plan for Example 13.8.

line. It might be preferable to increase the pipe size to 5 in., particularly if silting is anticipated.

In certain situations, it may be necessary to increase the size of the drainage line, particularly a main line, as it proceeds toward the outlet. This is referred to as a *tapered line*. Thus, it may start as a 5-in. line, increasing to 6 in. and perhaps to 8 in. as greater quantities of flow must be accommodated. This condition is illustrated in the following example. ■

■ EXAMPLE 13.9

Figure 13.23 shows a plan for a herringbone system with the spacing indicated. All laterals have a 0.2% gradient, and the main slopes at 0.3%. Determine the pipe sizes required for a mineral soil, using clay or concrete pipe.

SOLUTION

There are 16 laterals, each of which drains an area 500 ft by 100 ft or 50,000 ft², which is approximately 1.15 ac. Since a 4-in. pipe at a 0.2% grade can drain

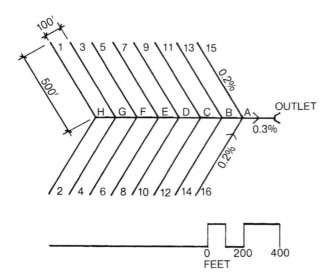

Figure 13.23. Piping plan for Example 13.9.

6.38 ac according to Table 13.5, all laterals may be 4 in. in size.

The main line has a 0.3% grade. From Table 13.5, the maximum acreage that a 4-in. pipe at 0.3% can drain is 7.82 ac. The number of laterals that can be accommodated by a 4-in. main line is determined by dividing the allowable area by the area for each lateral.

$$\frac{7.82 \text{ ac}}{1.15 \text{ ac/lateral}} = 6 \text{ laterals } (6.80)$$

This means that the main line from junction H to junction E can be 4-in. pipe. At junction E two more laterals are added, and the drainage area at this point exceeds 9 ac.

Again, from Table 13.5, a 5-in. pipe at 0.3% can drain an area of 14.2 ac. This means that a 5-in. main line can accommodate 12 laterals.

$$\frac{14.2 \text{ ac}}{1.15 \text{ ac/lateral}} = 12 \text{ laterals } (12.35)$$

From junction E to junction B a 5-in. pipe is used, since at junction B laterals Nos. 13 and 14 are added that increase the drainage area beyond the allowable 14.2 ac. At a gradient of 0.3%, a 6-in. pipe can drain 23.1 ac, which is more than the entire area of the proposed system. Therefore, a 6-in. pipe may be used from junction B to the outlet. Again, to reduce the potential for problems, it would be preferable to use 5-in. pipe for all laterals and 6-in. pipe for the entire main line. Various types of pipe junctions, such as couplings, reducing couplings, tees, reducing tees, end caps, 45° and 90° ells, and Y's, are available to complete drainage systems. ■

■ EXAMPLE 13.10

If the herringbone system of Example 13.9 is to be installed in an area that requires a DC of ¾ in., determine the drain sizes using corrugated plastic tubing.

SOLUTION

As previously determined, each lateral drains about 1.15 ac. However, to use the drainage tables with a ¾-in. DC, all acreages therein have to be reduced by one-half. Therefore, 2.30 ac (2 × 1.15), which when reduced one-half will yield 1.15 ac, must be used to obtain the size for each lateral. Table 13.6 shows that 4-in. tubing is sufficient for all laterals, since it can drain up to 4.39 ac with a ⅜-in. DC and 2.20 ac with a ¾-in. DC.

At a 0.3% slope, Table 13.6 shows the following maximum acreages for various tubing sizes:

Tubing Size, in.	Drainage coefficient	
	⅜ in. max. acreage	¾ in. max. acreage
4	5.38	2.69
5	9.75	4.88
6	15.8	7.90
8	34.1	17.1
10	61.9	31.0

The number of laterals that each pipe size can accommodate is

4 in. 2.69/1.15 = 2.3 or 2

5 in. 4.88/1.15 = 4.2 or 4

6 in. 7.90/1.15 = 6.9 or 6

8 in. 17.1/1.15 = 14.9 or 14

10 in. 31.0/1.15 = 26.95 or 26

Therefore, the minimum tubing sizes for the design of the main are:

Tubing Junction	Size (in.)
H to G	4
G to F	5
F to E	6
E to A	8
A to outlet	10

The system can be simplified by using 6-in. tubing from H to E.

Outlets

Subsurface drainage systems may discharge into open or closed drainage systems, streams, or drainage channels. Where drainage discharges into a stream or channel, a headwall or drop structure should be installed at the outlet to prevent erosion.

Wetlands

With wetland restrictions now in effect, it is suggested that state and federal regulations be consulted before planning to install a subsurface drainage system.

SUMMARY

A number of principles regarding drainage system design have been presented in this chapter. However, it must be realized that storm runoff and hydraulics are highly complex subjects. The intent here is to provide a familiarity with the basic principles so that the reader may be conversant with these subjects. In most cases, the handling of storm water runoff will be a collaborative effort between qualified, technically competent engineers and site designers.

14
Site Layout and Dimensioning

The term *layout* can be interpreted in two ways. As a noun, it is a set of instructions *for* the contractor and/or surveyor presented in the form of a drawing, usually referred to as the *layout plan, dimensioning and materials plan,* or *staking plan*, that locates the site elements to be constructed. As a verb (i.e., to *lay out*), it is the actual on-site process of staking out the location of these elements *by* the contractor and/or surveyor that can be seen in Figure 14.1. This chapter presents methods and practices associated with developing the layout plan.

The purpose of the layout plan is to establish the *horizontal* position, orientation, and extent of all proposed constructed elements. The *vertical* position is established by the grading plan. The layout plan, together with the grading plan and site details, provides sufficient information for both the site planner and the contractor to calculate the needed quantities of construction materials and estimate the cost of a project.

Figure 14.1. Field staking a project prior to construction of site elements.

As with grading plans, there is no one correct way in which to present information on a layout plan. However, there are basic methods and guidelines that should be followed. Information should be conveyed in a logical, well-organized manner that reinforces geometric relationships and the

291

intent of the design while demonstrating an understanding of construction processes and sequencing. Long-standing standards and practices have been established to facilitate communication and understanding among the practitioners of a variety of disciplines, including landscape architects, architects, engineers, surveyors, and contractors. These graphical and notational conventions are consistent regardless of whether a drawing is CAD-generated or hand-drawn.

The amount of dimensional information provided on a layout plan must be sufficient to allow all proposed constructed elements to be located in an efficient and cost-effective manner. Underdimensioning results in greater interpretation by the contractor and loss of control of the design outcome by the site planner. Overdimensioning can lead to confusion and error, produce drawings that are difficult to read, and imply inflexibility in accommodating field conditions.

HIERARCHY OF DIMENSIONING

Priorities should be established in terms of accuracy and precision for locating site elements. These priorities are based on a number of factors such as legal requirements, methods of construction, dimensional tolerances of construction materials, and design intent. Unnecessary levels of precision should be avoided, because such demands will tend to increase the cost of a project.

There are three categories that denote the degree to which dimensions are critical: fixed dimensions, semifixed dimensions, and flexible dimensions.

Fixed Dimensions

Fixed dimensions locate site elements with a high level of accuracy, usually for legal purposes. Legal examples may include property lines, rights-of-way lines, building locations, building setbacks, and those governed by other code requirements. These elements are normally located by a licensed land surveyor using accurate and appropriate surveying techniques. Fixed dimensions are also used to locate elements or baselines on which semifixed dimensions may depend.

Semifixed Dimensions

Semifixed dimensions are located in reference to fixed dimensions. Points, lines, and planes located by fixed dimensions serve as the bases to which semifixed dimensions are referenced. Site features that would be located in this manner include sidewalks, terraces, parking areas, walls, fences, and other landscape elements.

Semifixed dimensions can also be used to locate other semifixed and floating dimensions. In most circumstances, the majority of site dimensions are semifixed dimensions.

The term *semifixed* should not be interpreted to mean a lower degree of accuracy. For example, the length of a masonry wall based on a specific brick module and bond pattern, or a paving pattern that fits within the column spacing of a loggia, must be computed and accurately dimensioned.

Flexible Dimensions

Flexible dimensions locate site elements that do not require exactness in terms of their form and positioning and suggest greater tolerance with regard to acceptable levels of accuracy. The dimensions may be adjusted based on field conditions as long as there are no legal ramifications as a result of these modifications and the overall intent of the design is not compromised. Because of their flexibility, these dimensions are often referred to as *floating dimensions* and are indicated by +/– signs. Features included in this category include free-form geometries like curvilinear walks and paths and planting bed lines, as well as utility lines and structures. It should be noted that plantings and movable furnishings such as tables and chairs, planters, and trash receptacles are generally *not* dimensioned.

Field dimensions are dimensions that can be determined only after construction has progressed to a point where an actual measurement can be taken. For example, consider the construction of a wood gate in a dry-laid fieldstone wall. The fieldstone wall would be constructed, and then the width of the opening for the gate would be measured. Field dimensions must still meet standards of accuracy, based on the nature and tolerances of the construction materials.

DIMENSIONING GUIDELINES

Accuracy and Tolerances

The ability to measure distances (or any quantity) is limited by such factors as the quality of the measuring device, atmospheric conditions, and the skill of the personnel operating the device. These limitations, combined with the desired level of accuracy, will influence the manner in which values are expressed on a layout plan. It is important to note that not all elements on a site must be located with the same degree of exactness.

With respect to construction, the expressed value of a dimension implies a certain level of precision. This level of precision is normally assumed to be one-half of the smallest unit indicated. For example, a dimension of 84 ft implies a preciseness of ± 6 in. (½ foot), and 84'-3" implies a preciseness of ± ½ in.

The way in which units are presented will also affect implied precision. Although 84'-3" and 84.25' represent the same distance, they represent different levels of implied precision [± ½ in. for the former and ± 0.005 ft (or about ¹⁄₁₆ in.) for the latter]. In the metric system, 36 m implies a precision of ± 0.5 m, and 36.4 m implies a precision of ± 0.05 m (5 cm).

The level of precision should reflect the tolerances that can be achieved in terms of construction materials and workmanship. For example, indicating the location of a dry-laid, rough-cut stone wall with a dimension of 25'-10½" indicates a precision of ± ¼ in. However, this level of precision is unrealistic, since the dimension of the stone material may vary by 1 in. or more.

Referencing and Construction Sequencing

In order to locate points or lines in the landscape, there must be a known reference or *point of beginning*, a specified distance, and a specified direction. It is important that the reference lines and points be fixed locations in the landscape that will not be disturbed during the construction process. Elements located from these fixed points can also serve as references. As indicated previously, features located by fixed dimensions often become references for semifixed dimensions.

In developing layout plans, it is important to understand the sequence in which elements will be constructed. This is particularly true where elements that are located by semifixed dimensions become the references for other semifixed dimensions. If the construction sequence anticipated by the site planner is incorrect, some dimensions could be referenced from points or lines that have not yet been constructed and are therefore nonexistent.

Dimensional Notation

Landscape architecture typically employs architectural convention in denoting dimensions rather than engineering convention. In other words, distances

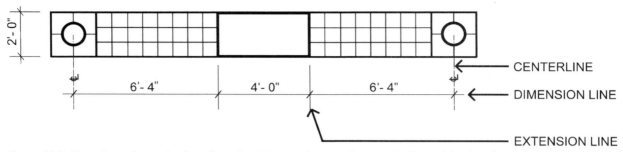

Figure 14.2. Dimension and extension lines. There should be a gap between the extension line and the object being dimensioned. However, centerlines used as extension lines should extend through the object.

are indicated by feet and inches (e.g., 12′-9″) rather than as feet and decimals of a foot (e.g., 12.75′). The basis for this practice is that most construction modules are expressed in feet and inches (e.g., 16″, 2′-0″, 4′-0″), and site contractors normally use measuring devices that are marked off in feet and inches.

For whole-foot dimensions, inches should always be expressed. For example, 12 ft is expressed as 12′-0″, not 12′. On the other hand, for dimensions of less than 1 ft, feet are *not* indicated. For example, 6 in. is expressed as 6″, not 0′-6″.

In the metric system, units for linear measurement are restricted to meters and millimeters. *Centimeters are not used in construction.* Whole numbers always indicate millimeters, and decimalized numbers indicate meters; thus, unit symbol notations are not required after dimensions. For example, dimensions 100, 300, 600, and 1200 are in millimeters and 0.100, 0.300, 0.600, 1.200, and 12.00 are in meters. However, unit notations are indicated in this book to avoid confusion between feet and meters.

Dual units [International System (SI) and U.S. Customary] should not be used on construction drawings. This practice increases dimensioning time and the chance for error and makes drawings confusing and more difficult to read.

For dimensioning purposes, converting from one notational or measurement system to another should generally be avoided. Conversions from decimalized feet to feet and inches, from SI to U.S. Customary, or vice versa, have inherent errors and different levels of implied accuracy.

Graphic Convention and Organization

Dimension and extension lines are used to identify the distance between two points. A *dimension line* ties two extension lines together. *Extension lines* extend at a right angle from the dimension line to the face, edge, or centerline of an object and establish the limits of the dimension line (Figure 14.2). Extension lines should not be used as dimension lines except where they are used as offsets from a baseline, as noted previously.

The intersection of dimension and extension lines should be clearly delineated by an arrow, tick mark, or bullet, as shown in Figure 14.3. A hierarchy of line weights should also be established, with extension lines slightly lighter than dimension lines and dimension lines lighter than site elements. Dimension lines should not be broken, and dimension labels should be placed above the line. Labels should be oriented so that they read from the bottom or righthand side of the sheet.

Dimension lines should be strung together and a clear hierarchy of information established. Overall dimensions should be placed farthest from the object, with successively more detailed dimensioning closer to the object (Figure 14.4). Points of beginning, centerlines, faces of walls, and other dimension alignments should be clearly indicated.

Figure 14.4 also shows an example of potential overdimensioning, where the 4'-0" central dimension could be removed, because it is implied between the overall 16'-8" dimension and the equal 6'-4" dimensions to the sides. Unless there is a specific code issue or design element that requires that area to be 4'-0", this is a place where some design flexibility might be acknowledged by the removal of the 4'-0" dimension.

The organization of information is also important in determining of the clarity and readability of drawings. Crossing dimension lines and extension lines should be avoided, as should the crossing of other labeling, information, and lines on the drawing. Where extension lines must cross, one should be broken and the other should pass through. Where possible, it is preferable to group dimension lines together. This approach consolidates the information and avoids the confusion of a disjointed or scattered appearance.

HORIZONTAL LAYOUT METHODS

A number of horizontal layout methods, or systems, have been developed that are appropriate for laying out site elements. One or more of these methods may be used on the same site. The key to any system is to clearly indicate the point of beginning. On some sites, there may be multiple points of beginning. The following sections present several basic systems that are commonly used in site planning.

Perpendicular Offsets

The *perpendicular offset* system is a common, convenient, easy-to-use method for site layout. It is most appropriate to use this method where a considerable

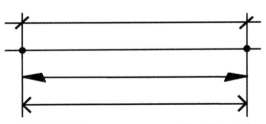

Figure 14.3. Ticks, bullets, or arrows are used to delineate the intersection of dimension and extension lines. When ticks (and sometimes bullets) are used, the dimension line extends beyond the extension line.

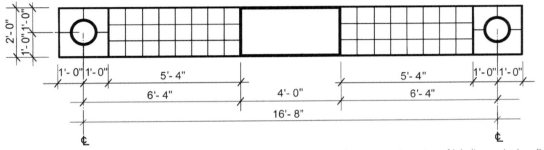

Figure 14.4. A more detailed version of Figure 14.1, this drawing illustrates the proper orientation of labeling, stringing dimensions together, and hierarchy of dimension lines.

proportion of the site elements are located perpendicular or parallel to property lines or proposed buildings. Constructed elements (usually building walls), property lines, and established baselines serve as reference lines from which dimension lines are offset. The locations of faces, edges, and centerlines of proposed elements are established by dimension lines that are perpendicular to the reference lines. Points and corners are located by the implied intersection of extension lines. Laying out elements using a series of dimensions, referred to as a *string* or *chain*, is often associated with this system. A layout plan using the perpendicular offset method is illustrated in Figure 14.5.

In some instances, it may be appropriate to use a rotated baseline. Such cases include situations

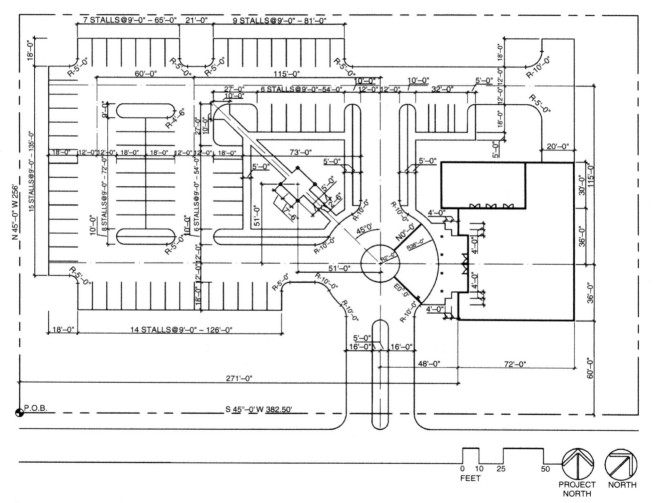

Figure 14.5. Example of a perpendicular offset dimensioning system. The point of beginning (POB) is located at the southerly intersection of the property lines. The location of the building is established by fixed dimensions. The site elements are located by semifixed dimensions that are referenced to the building.

where a proposed element or group of elements is positioned at other than a right angle to a building or property line or where rotating the baseline would reinforce important design relationships (Figure 14.6).

Baseline System

Baseline dimensioning is a variation of the perpendicular offset method. This method is normally used with curvilinear elements that do not require a high degree of accuracy, such as informal walks and paths and edges of planting beds. The location

of the baseline may be arbitrarily established or referenced to a building wall, another constructed element, or a property line. Offsets, usually at fixed intervals, are taken from the baseline to the edge or centerline of the proposed site element. Offsets from baselines are among the few exceptions where extension lines also serve as dimension lines (Figure 14.7).

The accuracy of the shape is limited by the offset interval, because the form must be interpolated between offset points. A short interval may be appropriate for complex forms or where a high level of control is desired, whereas a longer interval

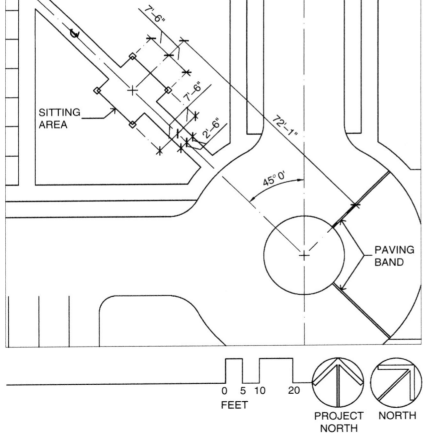

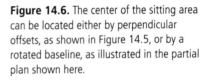

Figure 14.6. The center of the sitting area can be located either by perpendicular offsets, as shown in Figure 14.5, or by a rotated baseline, as illustrated in the partial plan shown here.

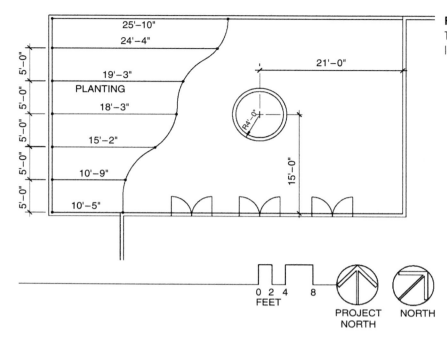

Figure 14.7. Example of a baseline system. The curvilinear edge of the planting area is located by offsets from the courtyard wall.

may be suitable for simple forms or where there is less concern for the final form. Locating offsets at key or critical points can be used in addition, or as an alternative, to regularly spaced offset intervals. Normally, the staking of offsets is approved by the site planner prior to commencing construction.

Coordinate System

A *coordinate system* is essentially a Cartesian system that uses a pair of distances along a horizontal axis (x) and a vertical axis (y), which define the unique geographical position of a point. Distances are indicated as north or south and east or west from a known reference point either defined by an established benchmark or arbitrarily established for the particular project. The known reference point is referred to as the *point of origin* (PO) or *point of beginning* (POB).

The point of origin may be site specific, such as the corner of a property, or in reference to a local,

state, or national system. For example, in the United States, the National Geodetic Survey (NGS) of the National Oceanographic and Atmospheric Administration defines and manages a national coordinate system referred to as the National Spatial Reference System (NSRS). In addition, the NGS has established the State Plane System to provide local reference systems that are tied to a national datum.

For site-specific coordinate systems, the point of origin is usually located in the lower left corner of the site plan (usually southwest, if north is oriented to the top of the sheet) so that the coordinate values remain positive and in the northeast quadrant. With a site-specific system, it may also be necessary to establish a north orientation that does not coincide with geographic north. Both the point of origin and the coordinate orientation should be clearly delineated. In addition, a grid may be placed on the layout plan to serve as a reference and checking device. Methods of coordinate notation are illustrated in Figure 14.8.

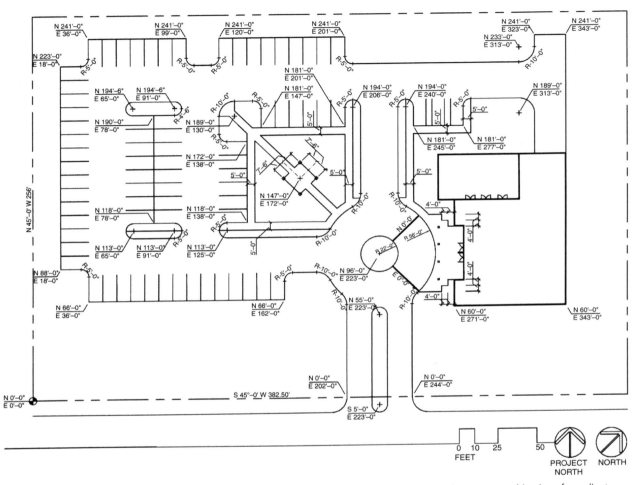

Figure 14.8. Example of a coordinate system. The site plan is the same as in Figure 14.5. This layout plan uses a combination of coordinates, perpendicular offsets, and angles and bearings.

There are two advantages of the coordinate system. The first is the elimination of the clutter of dimension lines, which makes the layout plan easier to read. The second is that, as opposed to a string of dimensions in which errors can become cumulative, coordinates are independent measurements, thus eliminating cumulative error problems.

Latitude and Departure

Where necessary, coordinates may also be calculated by using latitudes and departures. From plane surveying, *latitude* is the north/south orthographic projection of a line and *departure* is the east/west orthographic projection, as shown in Figure 14.9. Given a bearing angle (β) and length of line (L), latitude and departure may be calculated as follows:

$$\text{Lat} = \cos \beta \times L$$

$$\text{Dep} = \sin \beta \times L$$

When providing dimensions on a layout plan, *either* the bearing and length *or* latitude and departure should be given, but not both.

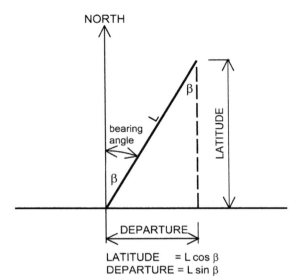

LATITUDE   = L cos β
DEPARTURE = L sin β

Figure 14.9. Latitude and departure.

Angles, Bearings, and Arcs

The layout of complex angular and curvilinear designs may require the use of angles, bearings, and arcs. A *bearing* is the direction of a line specified by a given angle between the line and an established meridian, usually the north/south axis. A bearing is an acute angle and is located within one of four quadrants: NE, SE, SW, or NW. A bearing line can also serve as a reference from which other angles can be measured.

An *arc* is a segment of a circle. It is defined by a center point, a radius, and an internal angle. To spatially locate an arc, its end points and orientation must be defined. Horizontal curve principles can be used to lay out arcs and circular elements. Horizontal curves are discussed in Chapter 15. An example using arcs and radii is illustrated in Figure 14.10.

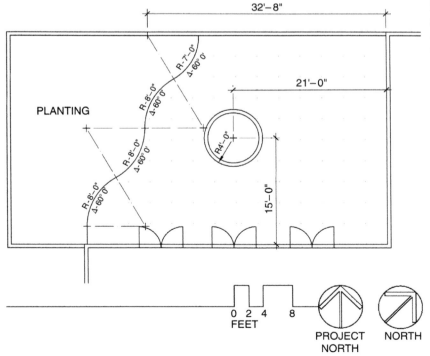

Figure 14.10. Example of an angle and arc system. The curvilinear edge of the planting area illustrated in Figure 14.7 is located using internal angles and radii.

Stationing

Stationing is a technique used to lay out linear and curvilinear elements such as the centerlines of roads, paths, and utilities. This technique requires bearings, tangent lengths, and the computation of distances. A more complete discussion of stationing is presented in Chapter 15.

LAYOUT PLANS

Dimensioning and Computer-Aided Design (CAD)

The same graphic and organizational conventions apply whether drawings are hand-drawn or produced by computer using appropriate CAD software. It is important to configure software applications to conform to these conventions rather than simply rely on the default configurations.

The advantages of CAD systems, particularly as they relate to drawing production, layering of information, and repetitive use of data, are extensive. Spatial coordination and the sharing of information among members of the project team are greatly facilitated.

CAD drawings are generated by data defined by Cartesian coordinates either in two dimensions (x, y) or three dimensions (x, y, z). Points are referenced to a point of origin within a single plane or to one that is established by the intersection of the three reference planes.

Lengths, areas, and volumes can be easily calculated when CAD drawing files are properly constructed. Generally, as mentioned previously with respect to coordinate systems, the point of origin is positioned in the lower left corner of the drawing to ensure that all coordinates are positive and, subsequently, that all area, volume, and dimensional calculations are positive.

Spatial coordination among members of the design team is essential to creating accurate and reliable construction drawings. Without such coordination, there is little control over the drawing production process. Again, consistent with a coordinate system, a grid is commonly established on the site survey that is referenced either to an established benchmark or to a temporary benchmark specifically related to the site.

Generally, dimensions should be derived from the underlying coordinate system using the "associative dimensioning" function of the CAD software. These dimensions should be based on "full-size" model space. Preferably, dimensions should not be added as text, inasmuch as this is a graphic format that has no connection to the coordinate system and such use can lead to spatial coordination problems. An advantage of the associative dimensioning function is that any changes in the position or layout of site elements will be reflected automatically in the dimensioning. Dimensional systems (customary and SI units) and notational and graphic standards should be established by the design team at the start of a project so that the information is presented in a consistent format.

A significant organizational advantage of CAD systems is the ability to structure information in layers. This process easily allows information to be presented in a hierarchical manner. For complex sites, information can be separated based on importance (e.g., fixed dimensions) or the category of elements to be constructed. For example, for a project consisting of a grouping of buildings, roadways, and parking, the building location dimensions may be shown on one drawing, the dimensions for the roadways and parking lot layout on another, and the location of the site structures (walks, stairs, walls, etc.) on a third. An important aspect of this approach is the need to maintain consistent spatial referencing and spatial coordination.

Global Positioning Systems (GPS)

Although this chapter has not addressed specific measurement and surveying methods and techniques, GPS technology warrants discussion because of its potentially broad applicability to land planning, site engineering, and site construction. GPS was originally developed by the U.S. military to provide the capability of locating any point on the earth's surface at any time in any weather condition. With the successful development of this technology, civilian applications, particularly for navigation and surveying purposes, became readily apparent.

GPS is a worldwide radio navigation system that uses a constellation of 24 satellites and ground stations to calculate an accurate position. The degree of accuracy is highly variable, depending on equipment, techniques, line of sight to the sky (difficult in urban situations), integration with other systems, and postprocessing of information. For highly sophisticated systems, an accuracy of less than 1 cm is achievable. The type of application will determine the necessary level of accuracy and the appropriate equipment and methods.

GPS receivers are highly compact devices that can be handheld, offering easy accessibility and great flexibility for field use. In order to calculate location in terms of latitude, longitude, and elevation above sea level, at least four (and preferably six) satellites must be perceptible from the receiver. Satellite perceptibility can be a problem in urban and densely forested locations due to both tall buildings and tree canopy interference with reception.

Applications

In terms of accuracy, GPS can be divided into three basic categories: recreational, mapping, and survey. Recreational GPS is used for orientation and wayfinding for hiking, fishing, boating, and the like. Horizontal accuracy is usually within 50 ft (15 m).

Mapping GPS is appropriate for the collection of field data for land planning and site analysis. GPS provides landscape architects and site planners with the ability to locate natural and cultural features in the field. A significant advantage of this process is that the data collected can be easily interfaced with CAD and Geographic Information System (GIS) software. Attributes may be assigned in the field to describe the feature, and these data can also be integrated with GIS. Typical levels of horizontal accuracy for mapping GPS range from about 20 in. (50 cm) to about 16 ft (5 m).

Surveying GPS is used where a very high degree of accuracy is required, such as in construction layout, including grading, and for legal purposes such as in property surveys and platting. Accuracy to $3/8$ in. (1 cm) is achievable. Surveying GPS should be conducted by appropriately trained and licensed professionals. The integration of GPS, GIS, and CAD should lead to a seamless flow of spatial information for the entire land planning and land development team.

CHAPTER 15

Horizontal Road Alignment

Generally, landscape architects and site designers are involved in the design of low-speed residential and park roads, entry and service drives, and parking areas. Involvement with high-speed roads is limited to corridor or route selection but, for the most part, is not concerned with highway engineering. The purpose of this chapter and the next is to present the basic engineering necessary to lay out roads and drives in the landscape. Visual, experiential, and environmental issues, traffic engineering, and traffic management techniques are not addressed here but may be found in *Residential Streets,* by the American Society of Civil Engineers (1990), and various publications of the American Association of State Highway and Transportation Officials (AASHTO) and the Institute of Traffic Engineers (ITE).

In order to create safe, enjoyable, and easily maneuverable vehicular circulation, roads must be engineered in both the horizontal and vertical planes. The horizontal plane is concerned with the alignment of roads *through* the landscape, referred to as *horizontal alignment.* The vertical plane is concerned with the alignment of roads *over* the landscape, which is accommodated by vertical curves (for further discussion, see Chapter 16). Figure 15.1 shows a complex example of horizontal alignment in the form of a Formula 1 racetrack.

TYPES OF HORIZONTAL CURVES

In the horizontal plane, road alignment consists of two basic geometric components: the straight line, or *tangent,* and the *curve.* The tangent is the most common element of road alignment. It represents the shortest distance between two points, and it is easy to lay out. In flat or featureless terrain or in urban grid situations, its use may be appropriate. However, due to its predictability and limiting

Figure 15.1. The Bahrain International Racing Circuit in Sakhir, Bahrain, showcases a complex example of horizontal alignment when viewed in plan. *(Image: Google Earth™ mapping service and Europa Technologies, Ltd.)*

viewpoint, a straight line in the landscape may become aesthetically and experientially uninteresting. To create interest and respond to natural features, such as topography and vegetation, tangents may change direction. Two basic types of curves are used to accommodate this change in direction.

Circular Curves

As the name implies, circular curves are circular arcs with a constant radius. They are easy to calculate and lay out and may be used in four basic configurations (Figure 15.2).

Simple Curve

This is a curve with a single radius and is the most common configuration for low-speed roads.

Compound Curve

This is a curve consisting of two or more radii in the same direction. For continuity and ease of handling, the difference in the length of the radii should not be greater than 50%.

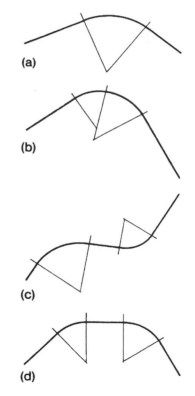

Figure 15.2. Types of horizontal curves. (a) Simple curve with a single radius. (b) Compound curve. (c) Reverse curve. (d) Broken-back curve.

Reverse Curve

This curve consists of two arcs in *opposite* directions. Usually, a tangent is required between the two arcs, the length of which is determined by the design speed of the road.

Broken-Back Curve

This consists of two curves in the *same* direction connected by a tangent. Where the tangent distance is relatively short, these curves may be uncomfortable to maneuver and visually disjointing. Therefore, if possible, this condition should be avoided by using one larger curve.

Spiral Transitional Curves

The normal path through a curve at high speeds is not circular but through a series of curves with a constantly changing radius. This phenomenon is reflected in road alignment design by the use of spiral curves. The major disadvantage of this type of curve is that it is more difficult to calculate and lay out. For the design speeds and scale of roads in which landscape architects are involved, circular curves are sufficient. Therefore, spiral curves are not discussed further here.

CIRCULAR CURVE ELEMENTS

Figure 15.3 illustrates the elements of circular curves that are defined as follows:

Point of Curvature (PC)

This point marks the beginning of the curve at which the road alignment diverges from the tangent line in the direction of stationing.

Point of Tangency (PT)

This point marks the end of the curve at which the road alignment returns to a tangent line in the direction of stationing.

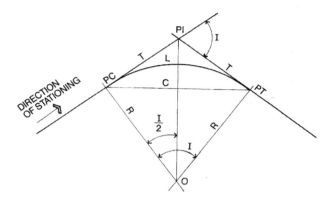

Figure 15.3. Elements of horizontal curves.

Point of Intersection (PI)

This is the point at which the two tangent lines intersect.

Included Angle (I)

This is the central angle of the curve, which is equal to the deflection angle between the tangents.

Tangent Distance (T)

This is the distance from the PI to either the PC or the PT. These distances are *always* equal for simple circular curves.

Radius (R)

This is the radius of the curve.

Length of Curve (L)

This is the length of the arc from PC to PT.

Chord (C)

This is the distance from PC to PT measured along a straight line.

Center of Curve (O)

This is the point about which the included angle I is turned.

CIRCULAR CURVE FORMULAS

Using basic trigonometric and geometric relationships in conjunction with the preceding definitions, the following formulas may be derived for circular curves:

$$T = R\tan\frac{I}{2} \qquad (15.1)$$

$$C = 2R\sin\frac{I}{2} \qquad (15.2)$$

Note that the radius is always perpendicular to the tangent line at PC and PT. The two relationships can be derived from Figure 15.3. The arc length L can be computed as part of the total circumference of a circle by proportion as follows:

$$\frac{L}{2\pi R} = \frac{I}{360°}$$

$$L = \frac{(2\pi R) \times I}{360} \qquad (15.3)$$

where

L = length of curve

I = included angle

$2\pi R$ = circumference of circle

$360°$ = total degrees in circle

■ EXAMPLE 15.1

Two tangent lines intersect at point B, as illustrated in Figure 15.4. The bearing of tangent line AB is N76°30′E, while the bearing of tangent line CB is S15°20′E. A circular curve with a 100-ft radius is to be constructed to connect the two tangent lines. Find the included angle, the tangent distance (the distance from point B to the beginning or end of the curve), the length of the curve (arc), and chord distance.

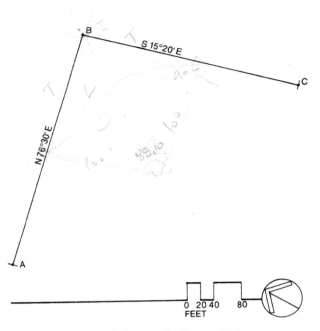

Figure 15.4. Tangent line bearings for Example 15.1.

SOLUTION

Using Figure 15.5, the deflection angle between the tangent lines is determined to be 88°10′. As previously noted, the deflection angle and the included angle are equal; therefore, the included angle for this circular curve is 88°10′.

The formula for calculating the tangent distance is

$$T = R\tan\frac{I}{2}$$

By substituting the known values, the equation becomes

$$T = 100\tan\frac{88°10′}{2}$$

$$= 100\tan 44°5′$$

$$= 100 \times 0.9685$$

$$= 96.85 \text{ ft}$$

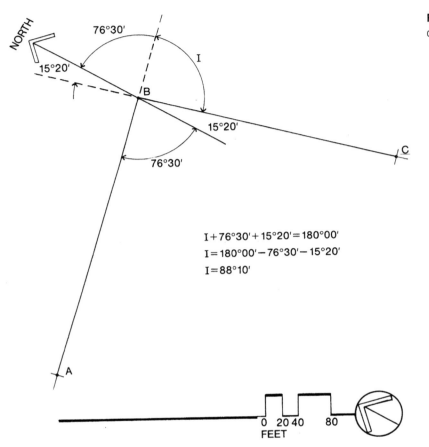

Figure 15.5. Diagram for calculating the deflection and included angles.

$I + 76°30' + 15°20' = 180°00'$

$I = 180°00' - 76°30' - 15°20'$

$I = 88°10'$

The length of the curve is determined by substituting the known radius into the following proportion:

$$L / 2\pi R = I/360°$$

$$L/2\pi 100 = \frac{88°10'}{360°}$$

$$L = \frac{2\pi 100 \times 88.167°}{360°}$$

$$= 153.88 \text{ ft}$$

Note that the minutes (and seconds if applicable) of the included angle are converted to decimals

of degrees before being used in multiplication or division.

Finally the chord length is determined by the following equation:

$$C = 2R \sin \frac{I}{2}$$

$$= 2 \times 100 \sin 44°5'$$

$$= 2 \times 100 \times 0.6957$$

$$= 139.14 \text{ ft } \blacksquare$$

■ EXAMPLE 15.2

For a curve having an included angle of 88°10′ and a radius of 30.0 m, determine the tangent distance, length of curve, and chord distance.

Equation 15.1 is again used to calculate the tangent distance:

$$T = R \tan \frac{I}{2}$$

By substituting the known values, the equation becomes

$$T = 30 \tan \frac{88°10′}{2}$$

$$= 30 \tan 44°05′$$

$$= 30 \times 0.9685$$

$$= 29.055 \text{ m} \approx 29.06 \text{ m}$$

The length of the curve is determined by substituting the known radius and included angle into Equation 15.3:

$$L/2\pi R = I/360°$$

$$L/2\pi 30 = 88°10′/360°$$

$$L = \frac{2\pi 30 \times 88.167°}{360°}$$

$$= 46.16 \text{ m}$$

Finally, the chord length is determined by Equation 15.2:

$$C = 2R \sin \frac{I}{2}$$

$$= 2 \times 30 \sin 44°05′$$

$$= 2 \times 30 \times 0.6957$$

$$= 41.74 \text{ m} ■$$

DEGREE OF CURVE

Some organizations, such as highway departments, simplify their computations for curve layouts and establish minimum curve standards by using the designation *degree of curve*. There are two definitions for degree of curve. The *chord definition* defines it as the angle subtending a 100-ft chord, while the *arc definition* defines it as the angle subtending a 100-ft arc. This discussion will be limited to the latter definition, since it is the one most commonly used today.

From the relationship illustrated in Figure 15.6, the following proportion may be established (the same proportion used to determine length of curve):

$$100/D = 2\pi R/360° \qquad (15.4)$$

where
  D = subtended angle (degree of curve)
  R = radius of curve

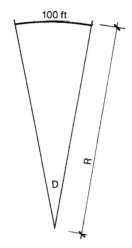

Figure 15.6. Degree of curve.

Thus

$$R = \frac{100 \times 360°}{2\pi D°}$$

$$R = 5{,}729.578/D \approx 5{,}730/D$$

Therefore, the degree of curve D is inversely proportional to the radius. This relationship is illustrated by the following example: A curve with a radius of 2,865 ft would have a degree of curvature of 2°, while a curve with a radius of 286.5 ft would have a degree of curvature of 20°.

■ EXAMPLE 15.3

Determine the radius, tangent distance, length of curve, and chord length for a 10° curve with an included angle of 60°00'.

SOLUTION

The radius is calculated from the following proportion:

$$R = 5729.578/D = 5{,}729.578/10$$

$$= 572.96 \text{ ft}$$

The remaining information is calculated using the formulas applied in Example 15.1.

Tangent Distance

$$T = R \tan \frac{I}{2}$$

$$= 572.96 \tan \frac{60°}{2}$$

$$= 572.96 \tan 30°$$

$$= 572.96 \times 0.57735 = 330.80 \text{ ft}$$

Length of Curve

$$L/2\pi R = I/360°$$

$$L = 2\pi R \times I/360$$

$$= 2\pi(572.96) \times 60/360$$

$$= 600.00 \text{ ft}$$

It should be noted that the following proportion, based on degree of curve, may also be used to calculate the length of arc:

$$L/100 = I/D$$

$$L = 100 \times 60/10$$

$$= 600 \text{ ft}$$

Chord Distance

$$C = 2R \sin \frac{I}{2}$$

$$= 2 \times 572.96 \sin \frac{60°}{2}$$

$$= 2 \times 572.96 \sin 30°$$

$$= 2 \times 572.96 \times 0.5000$$

$$= 572.96 \text{ ft} ■$$

■ EXAMPLE 15.4

Determine the degree of curve for Example 15.1.

SOLUTION

The degree of curve is calculated from the proportion

$$R = 5{,}729.578/D$$

The proportion may be arranged as follows:

$$D = 5{,}729.578/R$$

As given in the problem, R equals 100 ft; therefore,

$$D = 5,729.578/100$$

$$= 57.29578°$$

$$= 57°17'45'', \text{ or approximately } 57°18' \blacksquare$$

STATIONING

Stationing is a measurement convention applied to route surveying for streets, power lines, sanitary and storm sewers, and so on. Stationing is marked out continuously along a route centerline from a starting point designated as station 0 + 00. In addition, critical points, such as high and low points, street intersections, and beginnings and ends of curves, are located by station points.

In the U.S. Customary system, full stations are at 100-ft (1 + 00) intervals and half stations at 50-ft intervals. For the metric system, full and half stations are at 100 m (1 + 00) and 50 m, respectively. In addition, partial stations of 20 or 30 m may be used for construction staking. For highway layout, 1,000-m stationing may be used, which is indicated as 0 + 000, 1 + 000, and so on. The typical manner for noting station points is illustrated in Figure 15.7. As shown in this figure, a separate stationing system is used for each road.

■ EXAMPLE 15.5

This example illustrates the procedure for stationing roads that contain horizontal circular curves. Using Example 15.1, locate the 100-ft stations, the stations for PC and PT, and the station at the end of the road.

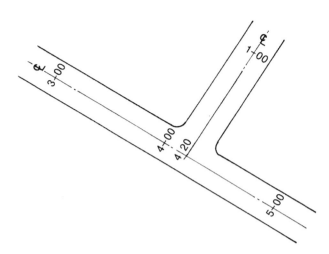

Figure 15.7. Typical centerline stationing.

SOLUTION

Step 1. The first step in the process is to determine the bearings and lengths of the tangent lines. In addition to the bearings that were previously established in Example 15.1, lengths have now been assigned to tangent line AB (372.25 ft) and tangent line BC (326.90 ft). This information is summarized in Figure 15.8. Note that point A is the beginning of the road and point C is the end of the road.

Step 2. The next step is to establish the horizontal curves and calculate all necessary horizontal curve data (R, T, L, and I). As previously calculated, this information is as follows:

$$I = 88°10'$$

$$R = 100.00 \text{ ft}$$

$$T = 96.85 \text{ ft}$$

$$L = 153.88 \text{ ft}$$

Step 3. The third step is to calculate the station points for PC and PT (Figure 15.9). PC is located by subtracting the horizontal curve tangent length T from the total length of tangent line AB.

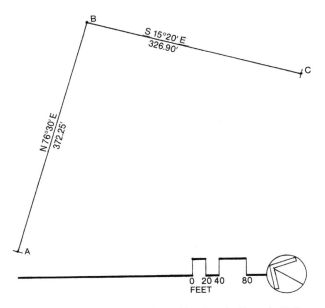

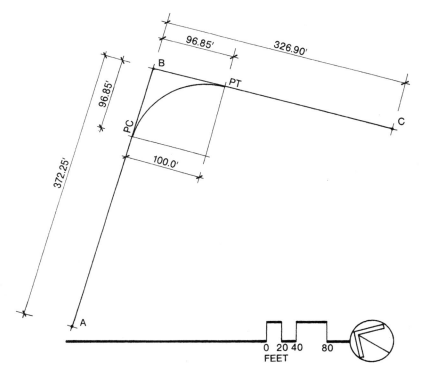

Figure 15.8. Tangent line lengths and bearings for Example 15.5.

372.25 ft

−96.85 ft

275.40 ft = station 2 + 75.40 PC

The station at PT is determined by adding the length of the arc L to the previously determined station of PC.

275.40 ft

+ 153.88 ft

429.28 ft = station 4 + 29.28 PT

Step 4. The last step is to station the tangents and circular curves completely, including 100-ft station intervals and the station at the end of the road (Figure 15.10). The distance along tangent line AB to PC is 275.40 ft; therefore, stations 1 + 00 and 2 + 00 must occur along this length. Since

Figure 15.9. Circular curve tangent distances for Example 15.5.

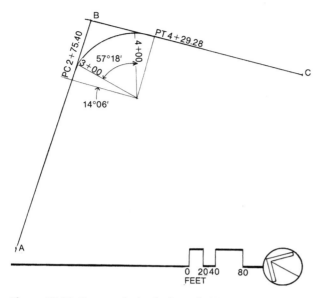

Figure 15.10. Curve stationing for Example 15.5

the station at PT is 4 + 29.28, stations 3 + 00 and 4 + 00 must occur along the arc. These stations can be located by using the following proportion:

$$L/2\pi R = I/360$$

This will determine the angle formed by the known length of the arc. To locate station 3 + 00, the length of arc from PC (station 2 + 75.40) is determined.

$$\begin{array}{r} 3 + 00.00 \\ - \ 2 + 75.40 \\ \hline L = 24.60 \text{ ft} \end{array}$$

The angle subtending this length can now be calculated by substituting L into the proportion.

$$I/360 = 24.60/2\pi 100$$

$$I = [24.60/2\pi 100] \times 360$$

$$= 14.095$$

$$= 14°05'41'' \text{ (or approximately } 14°06')$$

Marking off an angle of 14°06' at the center of the curve from PC will locate station 3 + 00.

To locate station 4 + 00, substitute 100 ft for L, since stations 3 + 00 and 4 + 00 are 100 ft apart.

$$I/360 = 100/2\pi 100$$

$$I = (100/2\pi 100) \times 360$$

$$= 57.30$$

$$= 57°18'$$

Marking off an angle of 57°18' the center of the curve from station 3 + 00 will locate station 4 + 00. Note that, consistent with the degree of curve definition, the included angle for the 100-ft arc agrees with the degree of curve previously calculated in Example 15.4.

Finally, the end-of-road station is calculated by determining the length of the tangent line from PT to point C. This distance can be determined by subtracting the horizontal curve tangent length T from the total length of tangent line BC.

$$\begin{array}{r} 326.90 \\ - \ \ 96.85 \text{ (T)} \\ \hline 230.05 \text{ ft} \end{array}$$

This distance is then added to the station at PT.

$$\begin{array}{r} 429.28 \text{ ft} \\ +230.05 \text{ ft} \\ \hline 659.33 \text{ ft} = \text{station } 6 + 59.33 \text{ (end of road)} \end{array}$$

Thus, the total length of this road is 659.33 ft (Figure 15.11).

For alignments containing more than one horizontal curve, the procedure is the same as outlined above. However, once the stations have been determined for the first curve, the next step is to determine the tangent distance from the PT of the first curve to the PC of the second curve (Figure 15.12). This distance is then added to the station of

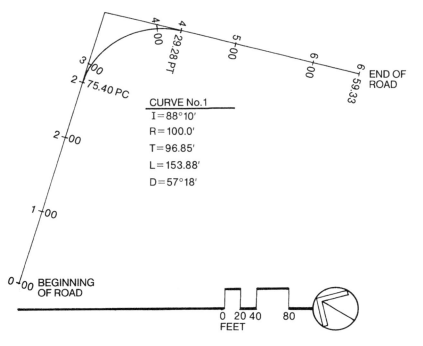

Figure 15.11. Complete alignment stationing and circular curve data for Example 15.5. Circular curve data are normally shown directly on construction plans as indicated.

CURVE No.1
I = 88°10′
R = 100.0′
T = 96.85′
L = 153.88′
D = 57°18′

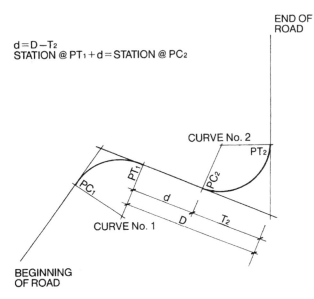

$d = D - T_2$
STATION @ PT₁ + d = STATION @ PC₂

Figure 15.12. Determining stationing for alignments with more than one horizontal curve.

the first PT to determine the station at the second PC. This process is applied to each successive curve.

It must be emphasized that stationing and curve data are usually determined for the *centerline* of a route alignment. ■

HORIZONTAL SIGHT DISTANCE

A visual obstruction close to the inside edge of a horizontal curve restricts the driver's view of the road ahead, as illustrated in Figure 15.13. Preferably, the forward sight distance should not be less than the safe stopping distance for the design speed of the curve, thus providing the driver sufficient time to stop once an object has been spotted in the roadway. If the curve is drawn to scale and the obstruction is properly located, the sight distance can be obtained by scaling. Sight distances may also be determined analytically.

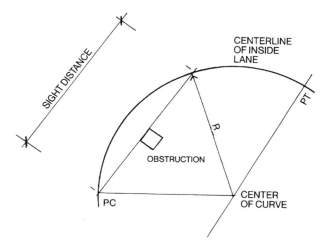

Figure 15.13. Horizontal sight distance.

CONSTRUCTION DRAWING GRAPHICS

For identification purposes, horizontal curves are usually assigned numbers on construction drawing. The information presented on drawings includes the following:

1. Included angle (I)
2. Radius (R)
3. Tangent distance (T)
4. Length of curve (L)
5. Degree of curve (D) (optional)
6. Station points for PC and PT
7. Centerline stationing
8. Bearings for tangent lines
9. Length and bearing of chord (C) (optional)

The presentation of the information may be arranged in a variety of formats. One typical format is illustrated in Figure 15.11. Where the scale or complexity of the drawing makes this format difficult, the curve data may be summarized in separate charts or tables.

HORIZONTAL ALIGNMENT PROCEDURES

To this point, the problems presented in this chapter have been structured, since specific circular curve data have been predetermined. Here, the initial procedures involved in establishing the horizontal alignment of a road or path will be discussed.

Step 1

The first step in the process is to establish *desire lines* on the site plan based on an analysis of natural and cultural conditions as well as the criteria to be used for the road design. Desire lines indicate the optimal path of travel according to the analysis of the site and function of the road and are typically drawn as tangent lines (Figure 15.14). As mentioned at the beginning of the chapter, an in-depth discussion of these considerations may be found in other textbooks. However, a brief list of the items of information usually required is presented here for awareness and reference purposes.

Natural site conditions, including topography, soils, vegetation, drainage patterns, and wildlife habitats, should be inventoried and analyzed. In addition, cultural considerations, including neighborhood context, existing traffic patterns, views both to and from the proposed alignment, safety, and potential air and noise pollution, should be analyzed. In order to establish physical design standards, such as minimum horizontal curve radius (see Table 15.1 for guidelines), maximum slopes, sight and stopping distances, number of traffic lanes, and cross-sectional design, a profile for the type of use that the proposed alignment will receive must be developed. This includes design speed, type of vehicles, estimated traffic volumes, direction of flow, timing of flow both hourly and seasonally, and so on. Cost is an additional consideration for any proposed alignment.

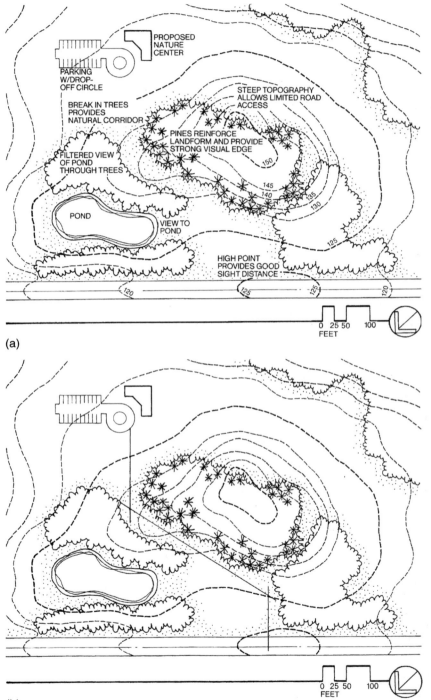

Figure 15.14. Horizontal alignment procedure. (a) Conduct site analysis to determine the best location for the proposed road or drive. (b) Draw in lines along the desired path of travel. These become the tangent lines for the proposed alignment.

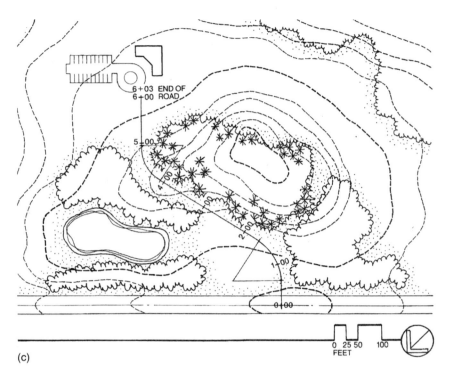

(c)

Figure 15.14. (cont'd) Horizontal alignment procedure. (c) Draw in curves and station the road and drive. Usually, the curves will first be drawn freehand and then circular curves will be designed to approximate the desired curves.

Step 2

Next, transform the desire lines into a preliminary alignment for the road centerline. This is done by establishing tangents and horizontal curves.

Step 3

Once the centerline has been drafted, horizontal curve data can be computed. In order to do the calculations, however, two values of the circular curve equation must be known. Typically, the deflection angle is measured or determined by bearings if possible. Then either the tangent distance or radius is determined by scaling the drawing (or lengths are assigned). *The deflection angle and the tangent length or radius are the only quantities that are predetermined or measured*; all other information must be calculated. It should be noted that computer programs are available that can easily perform steps 2 and 3.

Step 4

The last step is to check the horizontal curve calculations against the design criteria and review the entire alignment with regard to the site analysis. Where problems arise, the alignment should be reworked. Finally, the horizontal alignment should be completely stationed.

It should be noted that the formulas and procedures described in this chapter for circular road curves can also be applied to laying out any other circular site feature, such as paths, walls, and fences.

SUPERELEVATION

When a vehicle travels around a curve, a centrifugal force acts on it. To partially counteract this force, road surfaces are usually banked or tilted inward toward the center of the curve. The banking of horizontal curves is called *superelevation* and is

Table 15.1 Alignment Standards in Relation to Design Speed

a. Miles per hour[a]

Design Speed (mph)	Minimum Radius of Horizontal Curves (ft)	Maximum Percentage of Grade	Minimum Length of Vertical Curve for Each 1% of Algebraic Difference (ft)
20	100	12	10
30	250	10	20
40	450	8	35
50	750	7	70
60	1,100	5	150
70	1,600	4	200

[a] Adapted from Lynch (1971)

b. Kilometers per hour[b]

Design Speed (km/h)	Minimum Radius of Horizontal Curves (m)	Maximum Percentage of Grade	Minimum Length of Vertical Curve for Each 1% of Algebraic Difference (m)
20	25	12	2.75
30	30	12	3
40	50	11	5
50	80	10	6.5
60	120	9	9
70	170	8	15
80	230	7	22
90	290	6	30
100	370	5	45
110	460	4	60

[b] Adapted from Lynch and Hack (1984).

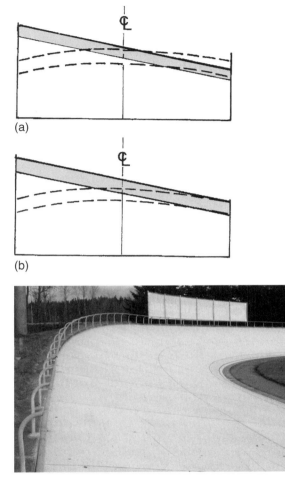

(a)

(b)

(c)

Figure 15.15. Superelevation. (a) Rotated about the centerline. (b) Rotated about the inside edge. (c) An example of superelevation in a bicycle racing velodrome.

generally accomplished by rotating the road surface about its centerline or, in cut situations, preferably about its inside edge (Figure 15.15).

Superelevation does not occur abruptly at the PC or PT; instead, there is a gradual change as the curve is approached along the tangent lines. The length over which this gradual change occurs is referred to as the *runoff distance* (Figure 15.16), which is sometimes computed by adding the rate of crown of the road in in./ft to the rate of superelevation in in./ft and multiplying the sum by 160.

Superelevation can be determined by the formula

$$S = 0.067 \frac{V^2}{R} \qquad \textbf{(15.5)}$$

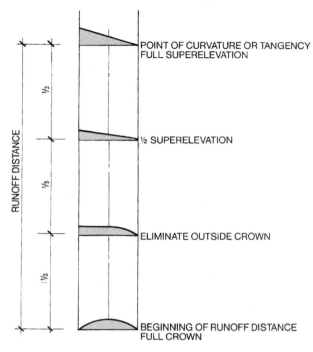

Figure 15.16. Transition to complete superelevation along the runoff distance.

where

S = superelevation in ft/ft of pavement width

V = design speed in mph

R = radius of curve in ft

Where snow and ice are a consideration, S should not exceed 1in./ft or 0.083 ft/ft. If snow and ice are not a problem, a preferred maximum value is 1.5 in./ft or 0.125 ft/ft.

■ EXAMPLE 15.6

Determine the superelevation and runoff distances for a 400-ft radius curve on a road with a 30-mph design speed in a snowy climate. The road has a crown of 0.25 in./ft.

SOLUTION

The superelevation is calculated by substituting into the equation

$$S = 0.067 \frac{V^2}{R}$$

$$= 0.067(30^2/400)$$

$$= 0.15 \text{ ft/ft of width or } 1.8 \text{ in./ft of width}$$

This value exceeds the recommended maximum of 1.0 in./ft; therefore, the proposed superelevation for this curve is 1.0 in./ft or 0.083 ft/ft.

The runoff distance is calculated by adding the crown rate (0.25 in./ft) and the superelevation rate (1 in./ft) and multiplying by the constant (160).

$$(0.25 + 1.0) \times 160 = 200 \text{ ft}$$

This means that the banking of the road begins at a gradual rate 200 ft before the PC and PT. A technique for handling the transition from the total crown cross section to the total superelevation cross section is illustrated in Figure 15.16. The full rate of superelevation occurs at the PC and PT and is maintained through the entire curve. As a safety factor, roads are usually widened on the inside of horizontal curves. ■

CASE STUDY

Morris Arboretum[1]

Originally a private estate, the 175-ac Morris Arboretum, located in Philadelphia, Pennsylvania, lacked the necessary physical infrastructure to fulfill its function as a cultural and university institution. In 1976, under the leadership of Dr. William M. Klein, the Arboretum hired the ecological planning and design firm of Andropogon Associates, Ltd., to develop a master plan. Part of the challenge of the master plan was to tie together the various landscapes and

[1] Landscape Architect: Andropogon Associates.

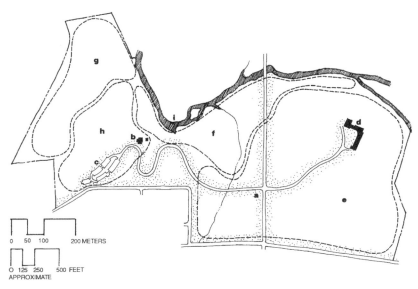

Figure 15.17. Schematic plan of the Morris Arboretum. (a) Northwestern Avenue entrance. (b) Widener Education Center. (c) Parking area. (d) Horticultural Center. (e) Working landscape. (f) Natural landscape. (g) Park landscape. (h) Garden landscape. (i) Wissahickon Creek.

land holdings of which the arboretum is comprised and to develop a meaningful entry and arrival experience to the Arboretum (Figure 15.17).

Entrance Road

The new entrance on Northwestern Avenue (which bisects the Arboretum) is designed to connect the natural, park, and garden landscapes of the former estate on one side of the street with the working landscape of the maintenance, nursery, and research centers on the other. The location and alignment of the road address concerns expressed by adjacent residents (traffic, glare from headlights and night lighting, views to and from the site, and neighborhood character) and respond to physical limitations and opportunities on the site. The alignment consists of a long, sweeping curve across the lower meadow and reverse curves (switchbacks, which are necessary to lessen the road gradient) on the steep hillside leading to the Education Center and parking area.

Two different techniques were used to handle storm runoff from the road. Granite cobble gutters were installed along the steeper portions of the road to collect and conduct runoff to surface inlets so that

Figure 15.18. Long, sweeping curve through the lower meadow. Eliminating curbs or gutters enhances pastoral character of the road.

potential erosion problems are averted. From the surface inlets the water is directed to recharge trenches, where it infiltrates the soil and replenishes the groundwater. By eliminating curbs and gutters on the flatter portions through the lower meadow (Figure 15.18), sheet flow from the road runoff is continued and the problems associated with concentrated runoff are avoided (Figure 15.19).

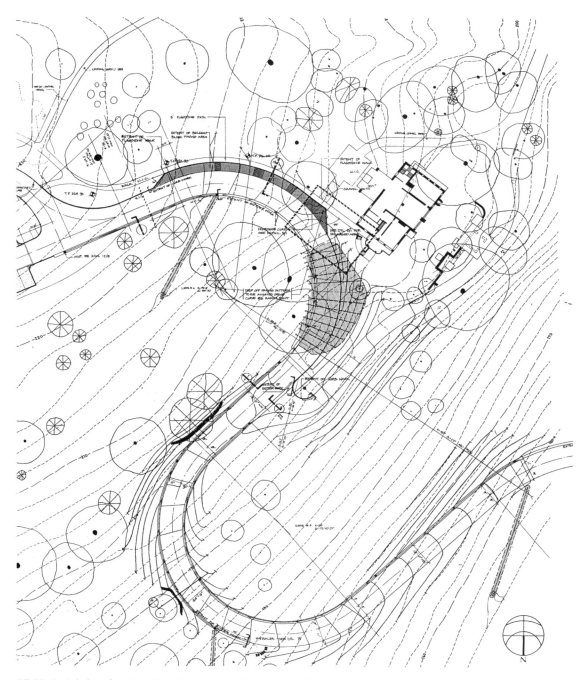

Figure 15.19. Partial plan of road grading. The drawing is the actual grading construction plan for the area pictured in Figure 15.20. Notice the configuration of the contour lines as the road cross section changes from crowned to cross-sloped.

The two techniques also reinforce the landscape character of the arrival sequence. Since curbs are not used, the image of a country road and a pastoral landscape is preserved, while the use of the cobble gutters projects a village-like appearance as the more intensely developed portion of the site is approached (Figure 15.20).

Parking Area

The parking area is placed on top of the hill, facilitating convenient access to the Education Center and the gardens of the former estate and providing views of the lower meadow, creek, and working landscape. The parking area is terraced to fit the topography of the hilltop. The slope separating the two levels of parking helps visually to reduce the apparent scale of the parking area while providing a substantial area for planting.

Management of storm water runoff from the parking area is accomplished by the use of porous asphalt pavement and subsurface stone recharge beds. Porous asphalt pavement is used for the parking bay areas only, while standard asphalt pavement is used for the aisles and entrance road (Figure 15.21). This technique recognizes the reduced strength of porous pavement and minimizes potential problems that may be caused by traffic. Damage to porous paving, if it occurs, appears to result from shear stress caused by the acceleration or braking of vehicles and causes surface scuffing rather than structural cracking. Storm water rapidly percolates through the porous asphalt to the recharge reservoirs beneath the pavement, where water is held in the pore space of the open-graded aggregate and slowly infiltrates the soil. These recharge beds are designed to hold the 100-year storm and are 18 to 24 in. (45 to 61 cm) deep at the Morris Arboretum. A recharge bed, unlike a retention basin, does not function by holding accumulated runoff until it can be released to a storm drain, but rather by leaking water continuously into the subsoil to replenish groundwater. With porous asphalt, the surface is level to allow for even infiltration of storm water. Pipes direct overflow water to recharge trenches and surface outlets.

It must be stressed that the design of porous asphalt pavement systems must be site specific and that such systems are not applicable to every site. Constraints and limitations include soil infiltration rates, depth to water table and bedrock, and traffic type and volume. In particular, porous paving should *not* be installed in areas where the water table is at or near the surface or on limestone substrates, where direct contact with water may dissolve the bedrock.

Particular care must be exercised during the construction of porous asphalt pavements. Fine particulates must be prevented from entering and clogging the pavement and recharge basin, heavy equipment must be prevented from compacting the base of the basin, and the filter fabric must be properly installed.

Figure 15.20. Reverse curve across a steep slope. Cobble gutters are used to collect and conduct runoff to prevent erosion. Note that the curves have been cross-sloped to create a superelevated condition.

(a)

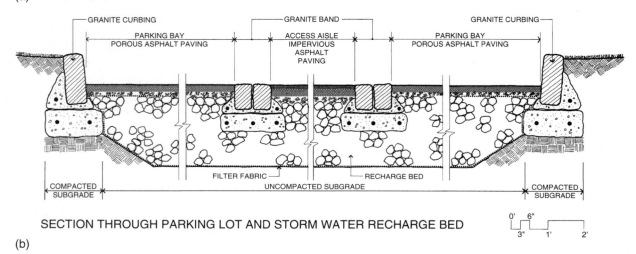

(b)

SECTION THROUGH PARKING LOT AND STORM WATER RECHARGE BED

Figure 15.21. Parking area. (a) The flush cobble strip separates the standard asphalt pavement of the aisle from the porous asphalt pavement of the parking bays. The darker appearance of the porous pavement is caused by the slightly rougher texture of the larger, open-graded aggregate used in the asphalt mix. (b) Section through the parking lot illustrating the stormwater recharge bed and the separation of the impervious pavement of the access aisle from the porous pavement of the parking bays.

The design of the Morris Arboretum's entrance clearly expresses the role of the institution. It takes what would normally be treated as a utilitarian component (e.g., access and parking) and elevates it to one that informs, educates, and contributes to the experience of the place.

Vertical Road Alignment

Vertical curves are used to ease the transition whenever there is a vertical change in direction (slope). Such transitions eliminate awkward bumps along the vehicular path, allow for proper sight distances, and prevent scraping of cars and trucks on the pavement at steep service drives and driveway entrances. A valuable example of the power of this design element can be found in the engineering of highway systems, where vertical curves are used to create complex geometries at the intersection of multiple highways in underpasses and overpasses (Figure 16.1).

Generally, vertical curves are required for low-speed roads and drives when the vertical change exceeds 1%. This vertical change is computed by determining the algebraic difference between the tangent gradients, with tangents in the uphill direction assigned positive values and those in the downhill direction negative values. Thus, the vertical change for a +2.0% gradient intersecting with a −2.0% gradient is 4.0% [+2.0 −(−2.0) = 4.0].

Figure 16.1. Spaghetti Junction in Atlanta, Georgia, is an example of a complex weaving of horizontal and vertical curves.
(Image: Google Earth™ mapping service, and Europa Technologies, Ltd.)

323

There are six possible variations for grade alignment changes. The first is the *peak curve*, in which the entering tangent gradient is positive and the exiting tangent gradient is negative in the direction of stationing. The resultant curve profile is *convex*. The second is the *sag curve*, with the entering gradient negative and the exiting gradient positive. The resultant curve profile is *concave*. The four remaining variations are *intermediate peak* or *sag curves*, in which the change in slope occurs in the same direction, that is, both values either positive or negative, as illustrated in Figure 16.2.

It is important to note that the computation of horizontal and vertical alignments for roads are *separate* procedures; thus, horizontal and vertical curves may partially or completely overlap or may not overlap at all. There are certain relationships between the two curves that affect safety and perception of motion. For example, sharp horizontal curves should be avoided at the apex of peak vertical curves. A more thorough discussion of these relationships should be pursued in other textbooks referenced in the Bibliography. Also, do not become confused by the similarity in terminology between horizontal and vertical curves. Realize that tangent lines for horizontal curves are *direction* lines in the horizontal plane (*through* the landscape), while tangent lines for vertical curves are *slope* lines in the vertical plane (*over* the landscape).

VERTICAL CURVE FORMULA

Generally, parabolas are used for vertical curves, since they lend themselves to simple computation and leveling procedures. For parabolas, the offset distances from the tangent line to the curve vary as the square of the horizontal distances from either end of the curve (see Figure 16.3).

The components of vertical curves are illustrated in Figure 16.3. Note that the illustration depicts a sag curve. There are two types of vertical curves: equal tangent curves and unequal tangent curves. For *equal tangent curves* the horizontal distance from

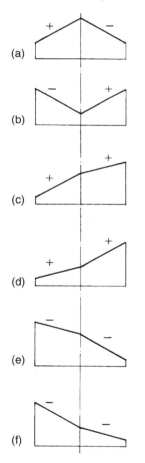

Figure 16.2. Vertical curve tangent variations. (a) Peak curve. (b) Sag curve. (c) Intermediate peak curve. (d) Intermediate sag curve. (e) Intermediate peak curve. (f) Intermediate sag curve.

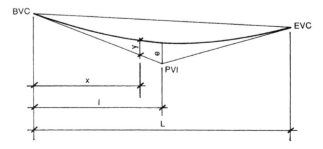

Figure 16.3. Elements of equal tangent vertical curves.

the beginning of curve (BVC) to the point of vertical intersection (PVI) equals the horizontal distance from the PVI to the end of curve (EVC). For *unequal tangent curves,* also called *asymmetrical curves,* the horizontal distance from BVC to PVI does not equal the horizontal distance from PVI to EVC.

EQUAL TANGENT CURVES

Most vertical curves are designed as equal tangent curves. The formulas for computing equal tangent curves are

$$e = \frac{l^2}{200 \times 2 \times l} \times A \qquad (16.1)$$

where

e = tangent offset at PVI, in ft (m)
l = one-half of length of curve, in ft (m)
A = algebraic differences between tangent gradients, in %

and

$$y = e(x/l)^2 \qquad (16.2)$$

where

y = tangent offset distance, in ft (m)
x = horizontal distance from BVC (or EVC) to a point on the curve, in ft (m)
l = one-half the length of curve, in ft (m)
e = tangent offset at PVI, in ft (m)

Points located at the same horizontal distance from the BVC and EVC will have the same tangent offset distance but not necessarily the same curve elevation. This is demonstrated in the following example.

▮ EXAMPLE 16.1

On a preliminary profile of the centerline of a road, a −2.0% grade intersects a +1.5% grade at station 79 + 00.

The elevation at the PVI is 123.50 ft. A vertical curve with L = 800 ft is desired. Calculate

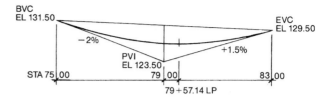

Figure 16.4. Vertical curve for Example 16.1.

the elevations of the curve at all 100-ft stations (Figure 16.4).

SOLUTION

The first step is to calculate the elevations at BVC and EVC and at 100-ft intervals along both tangent lines. Since the curve is symmetrical about the PVI, the station at BVC is 75 + 00 and the station at EVC is 83 + 00. Elevations at these points can now be determined by applying the slope formula.

$(400 \times 0.02) + 123.50 = 131.50$ elevation at BVC

$(400 \times 0.015) + 123.50 = 129.50$ elevation at EVC

The elevations at 100-ft intervals along the tangent lines are easily determined, since, for the entering tangent, a −2.0% gradient results in a 2.0-ft drop in elevation for every 100 ft of distance from the BVC. For the exiting tangent, the change in elevation is 1.5 ft for every 100 ft. The tangent elevations at the 100-ft stations are summarized in Table 16.1.

Next, the tangent offset at PVI must be calculated using Equation 16.1.

$$e = \frac{l^2}{200 \times 2 \times l} \times A$$

$$= \frac{400^2}{200 \times 2 \times 400} \times 3.5 = 3.50 \text{ ft}$$

The elevation of the curve at the PVI station 79 + 00 is 123.50 + 3.50 = 127.0 ft.

With e known, the tangent offsets can be calculated for the desired 100-ft intervals.

Table 16.1 Vertical Curve Data for Example 16.1

Station	Point	TANGENT Elevation	CURVE Elevation	TANGENT Offset	FIRST Difference	SECOND Difference
75 + 00	BVC	131.50	131.50	0.00		
76 + 00		129.50	129.72	0.22	0.22	0.44
77 + 00		127.50	128.38	0.88	0.66	0.43[a]
78 + 00		125.50	127.47	1.97	1.09	0.44
79 + 00	PVI	123.50	127.00	3.50	1.53	
79 + 57.14	LP	124.36	126.93	2.57		
80 + 00		125.00	126.97	1.97		
81 + 00		126.50	127.38	0.88		
82 + 00		128.00	128.22	0.22		
83 + 00	EVC	129.50	129.50	0.00		

[a]Descrepency due to rounding.

Station

$$75 + 00: y_0 = 3.5\,(0/400)^2 = 0.00 \text{ ft}$$
$$76 + 00: y_1 = 3.5\,(100/400)^2 = 0.22 \text{ ft}$$
$$77 + 00: y_2 = 3.5\,(200/400)^2 = 0.88 \text{ ft}$$
$$78 + 00: y_3 = 3.5\,(300/400)^2 = 1.97 \text{ ft}$$
$$79 + 00: y_4 = 3.5\,(400/400)^2 = 3.50 \text{ ft}$$

Station 79 + 00 is the center of the curve.

Since both tangent lines are the same horizontal length from the ends of the curve to the PVI, the tangent offsets are symmetrical about the PVI and do not have to be computed again for the curve from PVI to EVC.

Since this is a sag curve, the tangent offset distances are added to the corresponding tangent elevations to determine the elevations of the curve. The resultant vertical curve is plotted in Figure 16.5. For peak curves, the tangent offset distances would be subtracted from the tangent elevations. The data for the curve are summarized in Table 16.1. Table 16.1 also demonstrates a convenient check for vertical curve computations. The *second*

differences of the tangent offsets at *equal horizontal intervals* are constant. (The discrepancy between 0.44 and 0.43 occurs due to rounding.) ∎

CALCULATING THE LOCATIONS OF HIGH AND LOW POINTS

The locations of low points are needed to position drainage structures, while those of high points may be required to determine sight distances. The location of both high and low points may be necessary to determine critical clearances under structures such as bridges.

The high or low point of a vertical curve coincides with the midpoint of an equal tangent curve only when the gradients of the tangent lines are equal. In all other cases, the high or low point is located on the side of the PVI *opposite* the steepest gradient.

The formula for locating the high or low point of a vertical curve is

$$d = Lg_1/(g_1 - g_2) \qquad \textbf{(16.3)}$$

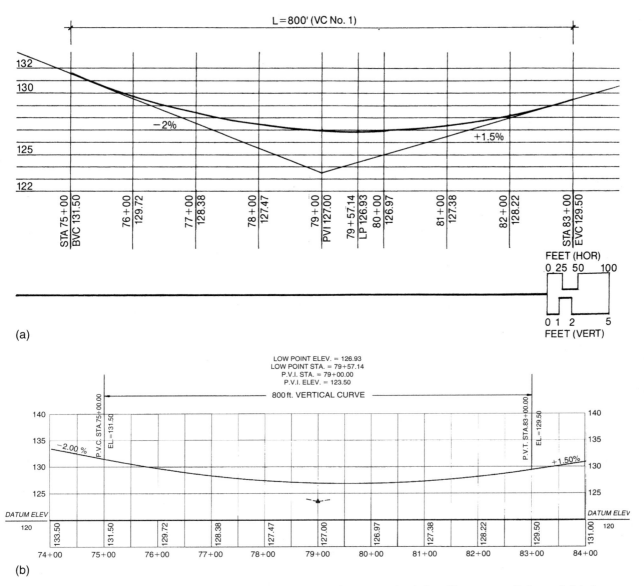

Figure 16.5. (a)Vertical curve profile for Example 16.1. (b)Vertical curve profile computed and plotted by computer. *(Software: Softdesk Civil/Survey Pack Version 7.21)*

where
  d = distance from BVC to HP or LP, in ft (m)
  L = total length of curve, in ft (m)
  g_1 = gradient from BVC to PVI
  g_2 = gradient from PVI to EVC

■ EXAMPLE 16.2

A drain outlet is to be installed at the low point of the curve in the previous example. Find its location and elevation.

SOLUTION

To determine the distance from BVC, substitute the known values into the equation.

$$d = 800 \times (-0.02)/-0.02 - (+0.015)$$
$$= -16.0/-0.035 = 457.14 \text{ ft}$$

Thus, the low point occurs 457.14 ft from the BVC, which is station 79 + 57.14.

Next, compute the tangent elevation at station 79 + 57.14. This location is 57.14 ft past the PVI; therefore, the tangent elevation is $123.50 + (57.14 \times 0.015) = 124.36$ ft. The distance from the EVC is $400.00 - 57.14 = 342.86$ ft, and the tangent offset is determined as

$$y_{lp} = 3.5 \, (342.86/400)^2 = 2.57 \text{ ft}$$

The elevation of the low point on the curve is $124.36 + 2.57 = 126.93$ ft. Note that this elevation is for the centerline of the road. If the drain inlet is located at the edge of the road, an adjustment based on the road cross section would be necessary to determine the top-of-frame elevation. For example, if the crown height of the proposed road is 0.25 ft, the elevation for the drain is $126.93 - 0.25 = 126.68$ ft. ■

■ EXAMPLE 16.3

On a preliminary profile of the centerline of a road, a +2% grade intersects a –3% grade at station 3 + 90.

The elevation at the PVI is 211.8 m. A vertical curve with L = 180.0 m is desired. Calculate the elevations of the curve at all 30.0-m stations and the location and elevation of the high point (Figure 16.6).

SOLUTION

The first step is to calculate the elevations at the BVC and EVC and at 30.0-m intervals along both tangent lines. Since the distances from the BVC to the PVI and from the PVI to the EVC are equal, the station at BVC is 3 + 00 and the station at EVC is 4 + 80. Elevations at these points can now be determined by applying the slope formula.

$$211.8 - (90.0 \times 0.02) = 210.0 \text{ elevation at BVC}$$
$$211.8 - (90.0 \times 0.03) = 209.1 \text{ elevation at EVC}$$

The elevations at 30.0-m intervals along the tangent lines are easily determined, since, for the entering tangent, a +2.0% gradient results in a 0.6 m rise in elevation for every 30.0 m of distance from the BVC. For the exiting tangent, the change in elevation is 0.9 m for every 30.0-m. The tangent elevations at the 30.0-m stations are shown in Table 16.2.

Next, the tangent offset at PVI must be calculated using Equation 16.1.

$$e = \frac{l^2}{200 \times 2 \times l} \times A$$
$$= \frac{90^2}{200 \times 2 \times 90} \times 5 = 1.125 \text{ m}$$

The elevation of the curve at the PVI station 3 + 90 is $211.80 - 1.125 = 210.675$ m.

With e known, the tangent offsets can be calculated for the desired 30.0-m intervals.

Station
  3 + 00: $y_0 = 1.125 \, (0/90)^2 = 0.0$ m
  3 + 30: $y_1 = 1.125 \, (30/90)^2 = 0.125$ m

Table 16.2 Vertical Curve Data for Example 16.3

Station	Point	TANGENT Elevation	CURVE Elevation	TANGENT Offset	FIRST Difference	SECOND Difference
3 + 00	BVC	210.0	210.0	0.0	0.125	
3 + 30		210.6	210.475	0.125	0.375	0.25
3 + 60		211.2	210.7	0.5	0.625	0.25
3 + 72	HP	211.44	210.72	(0.72)		
3 + 90	PVI	211.8	210.675	1.125		
					0.625	
4 + 20		210.9	210.4	0.5		0.25
					0.375	
4 + 50		210	209.875	0.125		0.25
					0.125	
4 + 80	EVC	209.1	209.1	0.0		

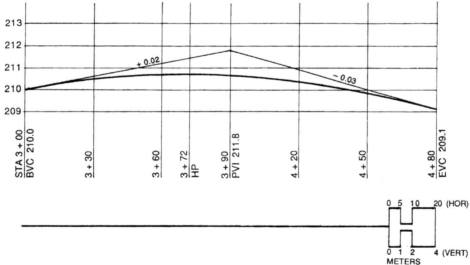

Figure 16.6. Vertical curve profile for Example 16.3.

$3 + 60$: $y_2 = 1.125\ (60/90)^2 = 0.5$ m

$3 + 90$: $y_3 = 1.125\ (90/90)^2 = 1.125$ m

Station $3 + 90$ is the center of the curve.

Since both tangent lines have the same horizontal length from the ends of the curve to the PVI,

the tangent offsets are symmetrical about the PVI and do not have to be computed again for the curve from PVI to EVC.

Since this is a peak curve (as opposed to the sag curve in Example 16.1), the tangent offset distances are subtracted from the corresponding tangent elevations to determine the elevations of the curve. The resultant vertical curve is plotted in Figure 16.6. The data for the curve are summarized in Table 16.2. Again, Table 16.2 demonstrates the principle of *second differences*.

The formula (Equation 16.3) for locating the high point of the curve is:

$$d = Lg_1/(g_1 - g_2)$$

To determine the distance from the BVC to the high point, substitute the known values into the equation.

$$d = 180 \times (+0.02)/(+0.02 - (-0.03))$$
$$= 3.6/0.05 = 72.0 \text{ m}$$

Thus, the high point occurs 72.0 m from the BVC, which is station 3 + 72.

Next, compute the tangent elevation at station 3 + 72. This location is 72.0 m from the BVC; therefore, the tangent elevation is 210.0 (elevation at BVC) + (72.0 × 0.02) = 211.44 m. The tangent offset is determined as

$$y_{hp} = 1.125 \ (72/90)^2 = 0.72 \text{ m}$$

The elevation of the high point on the curve is 211.44 − 0.72 = 210.72 m. Note that this elevation is for the centerline of the road. ■

UNEQUAL TANGENT CURVES

The discussion to this point has dealt with equal tangent vertical curves for which the distance from BVC to PVI equals the distance from PVI to EVC. In some cases, it may be more desirable to make these distances unequal in order to fit topographic conditions better. Although formulas exist to compute unequal tangent curves, a simple approach is to design an unequal tangent curve as a combination of two equal tangent curves using the following procedure (Figure 16.7):

1. Connect the midpoints of the two tangents (points A and B) by line AB.

2. Draw lines from BVC and EVC to point M on line AB. Point M is located at the same station as PVI.

3. Determine the gradient (S) of line AB using the slope formula (Equation 2.2) and calculate the elevation of point M.

4. Design two equal tangent vertical curves, one from BVC to M and the other from M to EVC. Both curves are tangent to line AB at point M, and a smooth vertical curve will result.

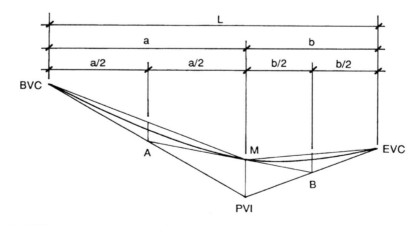

Figure 16.7. Procedure for dividing unequal tangent curves into two equal tangent curves.

■ EXAMPLE 16.4

For the preliminary profile for a road centerline, a +2.0% grade intersects a −3.0% grade at station 35 + 40. The elevation at the PVI is 261.40 ft. The horizontal length of the entering tangent is 200 ft, while the length of the exiting tangent is 300 ft. Design a vertical curve for this situation and calculate the elevations of this curve at all 100-ft stations (Figure 16.8).

SOLUTION

First, connect the midpoints of the two tangents by line AB and draw lines from BVC and EVC to point M. Then determine the elevations at points A and B.

$$\text{EL. } A = 257.40 \text{ (el. at BVC)} + (0.02)(100)$$
$$= 257.40 + 2.0 = 259.40 \text{ ft}$$
$$\text{STA} = (33 + 40) + (1 + 00) = 34 + 40$$

$$\text{EL. } B = 261.40 \text{ (el. at PVI)} - (0.03)(150)$$
$$= 261.40 - 4.5 = 256.90 \text{ ft}$$
$$\text{STA} = (35 + 40) + (1 + 50) = 36 + 90$$

The next step is to determine the gradient, S, of line AB and determine the elevation of point M. The gradient (S) of line AB is equal to DE/L.

$$S = (259.40 - 256.90)/250 = 2.5/250$$
$$= -0.01$$
$$\text{EL. } M = 259.40 \text{ (el. at } A) - (0.01)(100)$$
$$= 258.40 \text{ ft}$$

or

$$\text{EL. } M = 256.90 \text{ (el. at } B) + (0.01)(150)$$
$$= 258.40 \text{ ft}$$

The last step is to design two equal tangent curves, one from BVC to M (Curve 1) and the other from M to EVC (Curve 2).

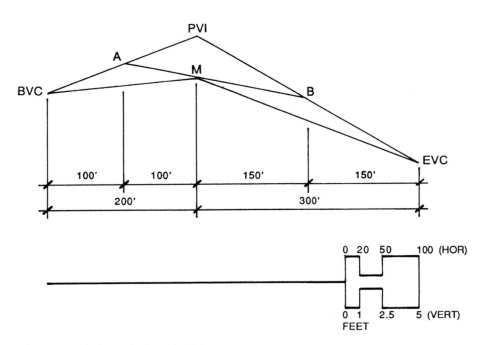

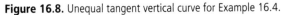

Figure 16.8. Unequal tangent vertical curve for Example 16.4.

Curve 1 Point A is the PVI at station $34 + 40$. The total length of Curve 1 is 200 ft, the entering tangent is $+2\%$, and the exiting tangent is -1% (Figure 16.9). The tangent offset at PVI is calculated using Equation 16.1.

$$e = \frac{l^2}{200 \times 2 \times l} \times A$$

$$= \frac{100^2}{200 \times 2 \times 100} \times 3 = 0.75 \text{ ft}$$

The elevation of the curve at the PVI station $34 + 40$ is $259.40 - 0.75 = 258.65$ ft. The data for Curve 1 are shown as follows:

STA	Point	Tan. El.	Tan. Offset	Curve El.
33 + 40	BVC	257.40	0.00	257.40
34 + 40	A	259.40	0.75	258.65
35 + 40	M (EVC)	258.40	0.00	258.40

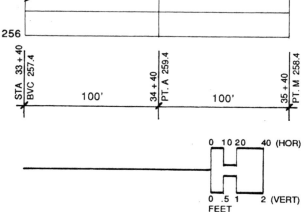

Figure 16.9. Curve 1 for Example 16.4.

Curve 2 Point B is the PVI at station $36 + 90$. The total length of the curve is 300 ft, the entering tangent is -1%, and the exiting tangent is -3% (Figure 16.10). The tangent offset at PVI is calculated using Equation 16.1.

$$e = \frac{l^2}{200 \times 2 \times l} \times A$$

$$= \frac{150^2}{200 \times 2 \times 150} \times 2 = 0.75 \text{ ft}$$

The elevation of the curve at the PVI station $36 + 90$ is $256.90 - 0.75 = 256.15$ ft. The data for Curve 2 are shown as follows:

STA	Point	Tan. El.	Tan. Offset	Curve El.
35 + 40	M (BVC)	258.40	0.00	258.40
36 + 90	B	256.90	0.75	256.15
38 + 40	EVC	252.40	0.00	252.40

The next step is to locate the high point of the entire unequal tangent curve. By inspection, the high point is located in Curve 1, which is consistent with the high or low point located on the side of the PVI *opposite* the steepest gradient for the entire curve.

The formula (Equation 16.3) for locating the high point of the curve is

$$d = Lg_1/(g_1 - g_2)$$

To determine the distance from the BVC to the high point for Curve 1, substitute the known values into the equation.

$$d = 200 \times (+0.02)/(+0.02 - (-0.01))$$

$$= 4/0.03 = 133.333 \text{ ft}$$

Thus, the high point occurs 133.3 ft from the BVC, which is station $34 + 73.3$ [$(33 + 40) + (1 + 33.3)$]. This location is 33.3 ft past the PVI. Therefore, the tangent elevation is 259.40 (El. at PVI)

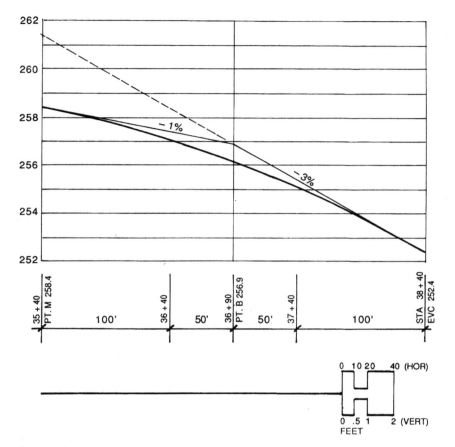

Figure 16.10. Curve 2 for Example 16.4.

$-(33.333 \times 0.01) = 259.067$ ft. The tangent offset is determined as

$$y_{hp} = 0.75 \, (133.33/200)^2 = 0.333 \text{ ft}$$

The elevation of the high point on the curve is $259.067 - 0.333 = 258.734 \approx 258.73$ ft.

The data for the two curves are combined, and the completed curve is illustrated in Figure 16.10.

Additional points along the curve, such as even 100-ft stations, can be determined by computing tangent elevations and offsets (Table 16.3). Note that the 100-ft stations have been computed for the profile. ■

CONSTRUCTION DRAWING GRAPHICS

Unlike horizontal curves, for which all data are presented on the layout plan, vertical curve data are presented on a profile of the road centerline. The presentation format for vertical curves is shown in Figure 16.5 (Example 16.1) and Figure 16.11 (Example 16.4). Information provided on profiles includes:

1. Vertical curve number (for identification purposes)

2. Total length of curve L

Table 16.3   Vertical Curve Data for Example 16.4

Station	Point	Tangent Elevation	Tangent Offset	Curve Elevation
33 + 40	BVC	257.40	0.00	257.40
34 + 00		258.60	0.27	258.33
34 + 73.3	HP	259.067	0.333	258.73
35 + 00		260.60	1.92	258.68
35 + 40	PVI	261.40	3.00	258.40
36 + 00		259.60	1.92	257.68
37 + 00		256.60	0.65	255.95
38 + 00		253.60	0.05	253.55
38 + 40	EVC	252.40	0.00	252.40

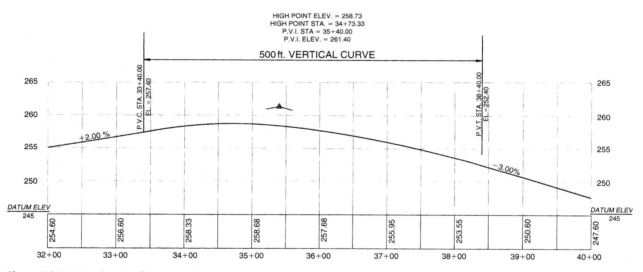

Figure 16.11. Completed profile computed and plotted by computer for Example 16.4. *(Software: Softdesk Civil/Survey Pack Version 7.21)*

3. Stationing at BVC, PVI, EVC, HP or LP, and specified intervals

4. Curve elevations for all stations in No. 3

5. Tangent gradients

Figures 16.5 and 16.11 indicate the profile of only one curve. However, the entire road from station 0 + 00 to the end would normally be profiled.

In addition, the profile of the edge of the road may be indicated by a dashed line on the same drawing.

It should be noted that the *horizontal* alignment must be calculated before the profile can be constructed, since stationing occurs along the centerline of horizontal curves. A profile is then constructed from the beginning to the end of the road and represents the total length along the curved as well as straight portions.

VERTICAL SIGHT DISTANCES

There are two types of sight distance. The first is safe stopping sight distance, or the distance required to react, brake, and stop a vehicle at a given speed. The second is safe passing sight distance. Both of these are a concern on peak curves, since the convex profile shortens the line of sight. For low-speed roads in which landscape architects are involved, passing will most likely be prohibited; therefore, safe stopping distance is of greater concern. Roads requiring safe passing sight distances should be designed by qualified highway engineers.

In determining safe stopping sight distance, generally an eye height of 3.75 ft (1.15 m) and an object height of 0.50 ft (0.15 m) are used. Although formulas may be used to calculate the minimum length of the vertical curve necessary to maintain a safe stopping distance at a given speed, sight distances for vertical curves can be determined to a certain degree by measuring from the height of the eye to the height of the object on the profile, as shown in Figure 16.12. Where the measured distance is less than the safe stopping sight distance, the vertical curve must be redesigned. Again, a highway engineer should be consulted if sight distances are a critical concern.

ROAD ALIGNMENT PROCEDURE

The following outline is a systematic procedure that may be used to ease the task of laying out both horizontal and vertical alignment for roads, drives, walks, and paths.

Step 1

As discussed briefly in Chapter 15, the first step is to develop design criteria and constraints for both horizontal and vertical curves and to conduct a site analysis to determine the best route or corridor location (Figure 15.14a).

Step 2

Once Step 1 has been completed, desire lines can be established *through* the landscape. Desire lines represent movement along the horizontal plane; therefore, it is necessary to design horizontal curves to make this movement or flow as smooth as possible. During this step, horizontal curves should be preliminarily designed, all necessary data calculated, and the centerline of the road or path completely stationed (Figures 15.14b and c).

Step 3

Next, a profile of the *existing* grades along the *proposed* centerline is constructed (Figure 16.13).

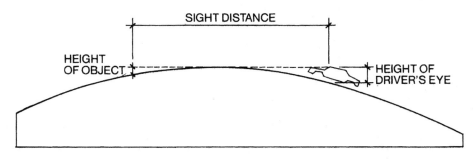

Figure 16.12. Sight distance for peak curves.

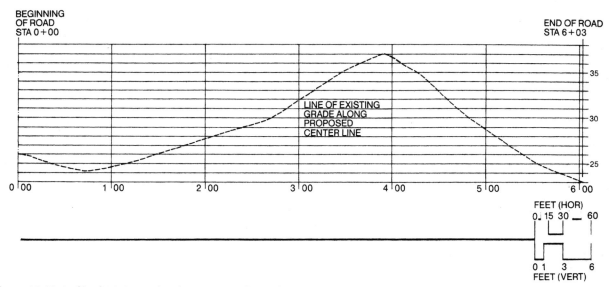

Figure 16.13. Profile of existing grades along a proposed centerline.

Step 4

At this point, the alignment over the landscape can be designed. To begin, the proposed vertical curve tangent lines are placed on the profile of existing grades. The actual placement of these tangent lines is influenced by many factors, including balancing cut and fill, design speed, roughness of topography, and horizontal curve placement. (Figure 16.14).

Step 5

From the profile, station points and elevations for the intersections of the proposed vertical curve tangent lines are established (Figure 16.15). The differences in elevation between intersection points can now be determined. Since the distances between the intersection points can be calculated from the stationing, the slopes of the tangent lines can be computed.

Step 6

The next step is to determine the lengths of the vertical curves required. This depends on such factors as design speed, topography, aesthetics, and sight distances. Vertical curves may be designed as equal tangent curves or unequal tangent curves (Figure 16.16).

Step 7

At this point, the slope of the tangents, lengths of curves, elevations at points of vertical intersection, and the stations for all BVCs, PVIs, and EVCs are known. Therefore, all data necessary to calculate the vertical curves are available, and the profile can be completed.

Step 8

Once the profile has been completed, the *proposed* grades are transferred from the profile to

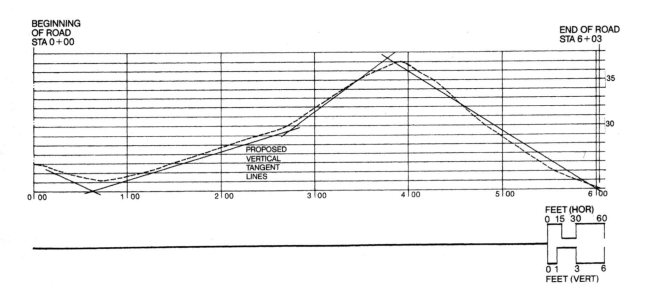

Figure 16.14. Proposed vertical tangent lines.

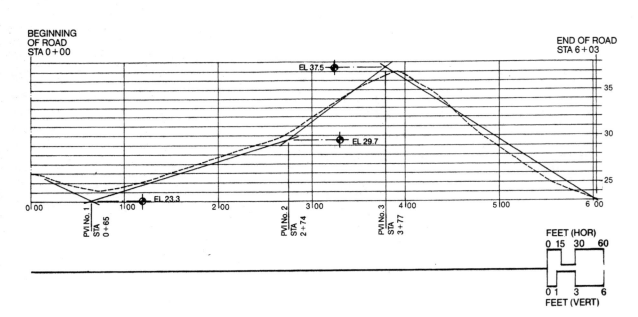

Figure 16.15. Stations and elevations for proposed points of vertical intersection.

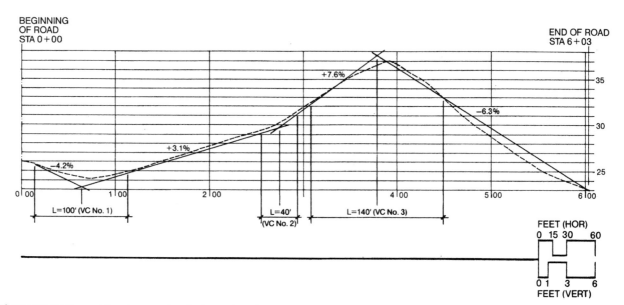

Figure 16.16. Tangent line slopes and vertical curve lengths.

Figure 16.17. Reverse horizontal curve with a sag vertical curve.

Figure 16.18. Reverse horizontal curve with a peak vertical curve. The curving wall reinforces horizontal alignment, while constant wall height emphasizes vertical alignment.

the centerline of the horizontal alignment on the plan. The road (or other linear system such as a walk or path) is graded according to the proposed cross-sectional design, and the proposed contour lines are appropriately connected to the existing contour lines. The proposed grading plan is now analyzed for problem areas, such as steep slopes, excessive cuts or fills, drainage, and removal of vegetation. Where problems arise, either the vertical alignment (profile), horizontal alignment (plan), or both must be restudied and adjusted accordingly. Examples of completed roads with combined horizontal and vertical curves are shown in Figures 16.17 and 16.18.

Appendix I

TABLE OF METRIC EQUIVALENTS

LENGTH

1 in. = 25.4 mm
1 ft = 304.8 mm = 0.3048 m
1 yd = 914.4 mm = 0.9144 m
1 m = 39.37 in. = 3.281 ft
1 km = 1,000 m = 0.621 mi.

AREA

1 ft^2 = 0.0929 m^2
1 m^2 = 10.764 ft^2
1 yd^2 = 0.8361 m^2
1 ac = 43,560 ft^2 = 4047 m^2 = 0.4047 ha
1 ha = 10,000 m^2 = 107,640 ft^2 = 2.471 ac
1 km^2 = 0.386 mi^2

VOLUME

1 ac-ft = 43,560 ft^3 = 1,233.5 m^3
1 yd^3 = 27 ft^3 = 0.7646 m^3
1 ft^3 = 0.0283 m^3
1 m^3 = 35.315 ft^3 = 1.308 yd^3

Appendix II

METRIC DRAWING SCALES

Metric construction drawing scales are directly proportional. U.S. construction drawing scales are not *expressed* as direct proportions (e.g., 1″ = 20′ or ½″ = 1′-10″). Metric construction drawing scales are typically expressed in millimeters (mm). For example, 1:50 means that 1 mm on the drawing represents 50 mm of actual construction.

To determine the *approximate* U.S. construction drawing equivalent scale, divide the metric scale by 12. For example, the U.S. architectural scale of ¼″ = 1′-0″ (1″ = 4′) is approximately equal to the metric scale of 1:50 (50/12 = 4.17). To convert U.S. construction drawing scales to direct proportional scales, multiply the number of units *per inch* by 12. For example, the direct proportional scale for ¼″ = 1′-0″ (1″ = 4′) is 1:48 (4 × 12 = 48); for 1″ = 40′ the direct proportional scale is 1:480 (40 × 12 = 480). Preferred drawing scales and their relationship to U.S. Customary scales are presented in the following table.

Drawing Purpose	Recommended Metric Scales	U.S. Customary Scales
Regional Planning	1:20,000	1″ = 2000′ (1:24,000)
	1:10,000	1″ = 1000′ (1:12,000)
Land Planning	1:5000	1″ = 400′ (1:4800)
	1:2000	1″ = 200′ (1:2400)
	1:1000	1″ = 100′ (1:1200)
	1:500	1″ = 50′ (1:600)
Site Planning	1:500	1″ = 40′ (1:480)
	1:200	1″ = 20′ (1:240)
	1:100	1″ = 10′ (1:120)
Architectural Layout Plans	1:200	1/16″ = 1′-0″ (1:192)
	1:100	1/8″ = 1′-0″ (1:96)
	1:50	1/4″ = 1′-0″ (1:48)
Construction Detailing	1:20	1/2″ = 1′-0″ (1:24)
	1:10	1″ = 1′-0″ (1:12)
	1:5	3″ = 1′-0″ (1:4)

Glossary

Abrasion Wearing away by friction.

Alignment The course along which the centerline of a roadway or channel is located.

Angle of repose The angle that the sloping face of a bank of loose earth or gravel or other material makes with the horizontal.

Antecedent precipitation Rainfall that has recently preceded the storm event being analyzed.

Area drain A structure for collecting runoff from relatively small, paved areas.

Backfill Earth or other material used to replace material removed during construction, such as in pipeline and culvert trenches and behind retaining walls.

Base (Course) A layer of specified or selected material of planned thickness, constructed on the subbase or on the natural subgrade to distribute the load and provide drainage, or on which a wearing surface or a drainage structure is placed.

Bearing capacity (soil) The load-supporting capacity of a soil.

Bench A horizontal or sloping step in a slope.

Bioretention A technique that uses parking lot islands, planting strips, or swales to collect and filter storm water.

Blading Planing or smoothing the ground surface.

Borrow Fill material imported to a site.

Borrow area A source of earth fill materials used in the construction of embankments or other earth fill structures.

Brushlayering Live branch cuttings laid in crisscross fashion on benches between successive lifts of soil.

Caisson Similar to pile; however, rather than driven, holes are drilled into the ground and filled with concrete.

Catch basin A receptacle, with a sediment bowl or sump, for diverting surface water to a subsurface pipe.

Centerline The survey line in the center of a road, ditch, or similar project.

Channel A natural stream, or a ditch or swale constructed to convey water.

Cluster development A land planning technique to concentrate buildings on a portion of a site in order to preserve open space and environmentally sensitive areas.

Compaction The densification of a soil by a mechanical process.

Constructed wetland Artificially created wetland primarily to treat point and non-point sources of water pollution.

Continuity equation A formula expressing the principle of conservation of mass as applied to the flow of water (or other fluids of constant density). It states that the product of cross section of flow and velocity at any point in a channel is a constant.

Contour line An imaginary line, or its representation on a map, following all points at the same elevation above or below a given datum.

Critical depth The depth of flow in an open channel at which critical flow occurs. For a given flow rate, depths greater than critical result in subcritical, or tranquil, flow. Those smaller than critical result in supercritical, or rapid, flow.

Critical flow An unstable flow condition in an open channel that occurs at critical depth.

Critical velocity The velocity at which unstable flow conditions begin to occur.

Crown The rise or difference in elevation between the edge and the centerline of a roadway.

Culvert Any structure, not classified as a bridge, that provides a waterway or other opening under a road.

Cut section (or cut) The part of the ground surface that, when graded, is lower than the original ground.

Datum A horizontal reference plane used as a basis for computing elevations.

Detention basin (dry pond) An impoundment, normally dry, for temporarily storing storm runoff from a drainage area to reduce the peak rate of flow.

Dimension

Field Dimension that must be measured on site, usually after site elements have been constructed.

Fixed Dimension that locates site elements with a high level of accuracy.

Flexible Dimension that has greater tolerance with regard to acceptable levels of accuracy.

Semifixed Dimension located in reference to a fixed dimension.

Discharge (q) Flow rate in a culvert, pipe, or channel.

Diversion A channel, with or without a supporting ridge on the lower side, constructed across a slope to intercept surface runoff.

Drainage Interception and removal of groundwater or surface water by artificial or natural means.

Drainage area The area drained by a channel or subsurface water by artificial or natural means.

Edaphology The study of the soil from the standpoint of higher plants and crop production.

Elevation (a) The altitude relative to a given datum. (b) A scale drawing of the facade of a structure.

Embankment A bank of earth, rock, or other material constructed above the natural ground surface.

Emergency spillway A channel for safely conveying flood discharges exceeding the capacity of the principal spillway of a detention or retention pond.

Erodibility Susceptibility of soil material to detachment and transportation by running water or wind.

Erosion Detachment and movement of soil or rock fragments by water, wind, ice, and gravity.

Excavation (a) The act of taking out materials. (b) The hollow or depression after the materials have been removed.

Fiber rolls Prefabricated tubes consisting of biodegradable materials such as coconut fiber or rice and wheat straw.

Fill section (or fill) The part of the ground surface that, when graded, is higher than the original ground.

Filter strip A vegetated buffer zone for removing sediments and pollutants before runoff reaches ponds, waterways, or other drainage facilities.

Fine grade Preparation of the subgrade preceding placement of surfacing materials.

Foundation The portion of a structure (usually below ground level) that distributes the pressure to the soil or to artificial supports.

Free water Soil water that moves by gravity, in contrast to capillary and hydroscopic water.

French drain A trench filled with coarse aggregate (with or without a pipe) for intercepting and conveying groundwater.

Gabion A compartmented rectangular container made of steel wire mesh and filled with stone. Gabions are used for erosion control and retaining wall purposes.

Geosynthetics Degradable and nondegradable products used for a variety of purposes including soil and slope stabilization, erosion and sediment control, soil reinforcement, and subsurface drainage.

Geotextiles Woven and nonwoven permeable fabrics and grids used for soil-related construction projects.

Grade

Finished grade The completed surfaces of lawns, walks, and roads brought to grades as designed.

Natural grade The undisturbed natural surface of the ground.

Subgrade The grade established in preparation for top surfacing of roads, lawns, etc.

Gradient The degree of inclination of a surface, road, or pipe, usually expressed as a percentage.

Grading Modification of the ground surface by cuts and/or fills. Fine or finish grading is light or thin grading to finish a prepared earth surface.

Grassed waterway A natural or constructed channel, usually broad and shallow, covered with erosion-resistant vegetation, used to conduct surface runoff.

Gravel Aggregate composed of hard, durable stones or pebbles, crushed or uncrushed, often mixed with sand.

Groundwater Free subsurface water, the top of which is the water table.

Gutter An artificially surfaced and generally shallow waterway, usually provided at the sides of a roadway for carrying surface drainage.

Headwall A vertical wall at the end of a culvert to support the pipe and prevent earth from spilling into the channel.

Hydraulic radius The cross-sectional area of flow of a pipe or channel divided by the wetted perimeter.

Hydrograph A graph showing, for a given point on a channel, the discharge, stage, velocity, or other property of water with respect to time.

Hydrologic condition A term describing the vegetative cover, residue, and surface roughness of a soil as they may affect potential runoff.

Hydrologic cycle The concept of a closed system, involving the transformation of water from the vapor phase to the liquid (and solid) phase and back to the vapor phase, and the movement of that water.

Hydrologic Soil Group (HSG) A soil classification system based on infiltration and potential runoff characteristics.

Imperviousness The property of a material through which water will not flow under ordinary hydrostatic pressure.

Infiltration The downward entry of water into the immediate surface of a soil or other material, as contrasted with percolation, which is movement of water through soil layers or material.

Infiltration basin An open-surface storage area with no outlet, except an emergency spillway, that permits runoff to infiltrate the soil.

Initial abstraction (I_a) Losses before runoff begins, including infiltration, evaporation, interception by vegetation, and water retained in surface depressions.

Inlet An arrangement for conveying surface water to an underdrain.

Intercepting ditch An open drain to prevent surface water from flowing down a slope by conducting it around the slope. See also *diversion*.

Interpolation (topographic) The process of determining the location of elevations from the plotted locations of known elevations.

Invert The lowest point of the internal cross section of a pipe or channel.

Layout plan Drawing that dimensionally located site elements to be constructed.

Lift Fill or base course material placed in successive layers. Each layer is properly compacted prior to the placement of the next layer.

Live fascines Bound, elongated, sausage-like bundles of live cut branches that are placed in shallow trenches, partly covered with soil, and staked in place to arrest erosion and soil slippage.

Live stake Cuttings from living branches tamped or inserted into the earth that will eventually root and leaf out.

Low-flow channel A small ditch constructed in flat bottoms of larger ditches or detention basins to facilitate their drainage during periods of low flow.

Manhole A structure, covered with a lid, that allows a person to enter a space below ground level.

Manning's equation A formula for calculating the velocity of flow in a channel as a function of relative roughness, cross-sectional configuration, and gradient.

Maximum potential retention (S) The greatest proportion of precipitation that could possibly be retained by a specific soil and land use combination.

Modified Rational method (MRM) An extension of the Rational method for calculating the rate of runoff from a drainage area. It includes provisions for antecedent precipitation and for developing hydrographs.

Moisture content The percentage, by weight, of water contained in soil or other material, usually based on dry weight.

Monument A boundary stone or other permanent marker locating a property line or corner.

NRCS Natural Resources Conservation Service (formerly Soil Conservation Service), a federal agency in the Department of Agriculture, dealing with erosion and flood control.

Outlet Point of water disposal from a stream, river, lake, tidewater, or artificial drain.

Peak discharge The maximum instantaneous flow rate resulting from a given storm condition at a specific location.

Pedology The study of the soil as a natural body, including its origin, characteristics, classification, and description.

Percolation Movement of soil water toward the water table.

Perron An exterior platform at a building entrance, usually with steps leading up to it.

Pervious The property of a material that permits movement of water through it under ordinary hydrostatic pressure.

pH A measure of alkalinity or acidity, with pH 7 being neutral and pH 6.5 being a desirable degree of soil acidity.

Pile Vertical structural member made of concrete or steel that is driven into the ground by a pile driver until there is significant resistance or bedrock is reached to support the intended load.

Point of beginning (POB) Establishes a reference point that serves as the origin for site dimensioning.

Porous Having many small openings through which liquids may pass.

Porous pavement A pavement constructed from a material that permits percolation of storm water to the subgrade.

Principal spillway A component of retention or detention ponds, generally constructed of permanent materials. It is designed to regulate the normal water level, provide flood protection, and/or reduce the frequency of operation of the emergency spillway.

Rainfall intensity (*i*) The rate at which rain falls, measured in inches per hour (iph) or millimeters per hour (mm/h).

Ramp An inclined plane serving as a way between two different levels.

Rational method A formula for calculating the peak runoff rate from a drainage area based on land use, soils, land slope, rainfall intensity, and drainage area.

Recession, or receding limb (of a hydrograph) The portion of a hydrograph that occurs after the peak when the flow rate decreases.

Retaining wall A wall built to support a bank of earth.

Retention basin (wet pond) A reservoir, containing a permanent pool, for temporarily storing storm runoff and reducing the storm runoff rate from a drainage area.

Right of way The entire strip of land dedicated for highway purposes.

Riprap Stones or other material placed on a slope to prevent erosion by water.

Rising limb (of a hydrograph) The portion of a hydrograph preceding the peak when the flow rate increases.

Rough grade Stage of grading operation in which the desired landform is approximately attained.

Roughness coefficient (*n*) A factor in the Manning formula representing the effect of channel or conduit roughness on energy losses in the flowing water.

Runoff That part of precipitation carried off from the area on which it falls. Also, the rate of surface discharge of the above. (The ratio of runoff to precipitation is a coefficient, expressed as a decimal.)

Runoff curve number (*CN*) A parameter used in NRCS (SCS) hydrological techniques, based on soil characteristics and land use.

SCS Formerly the Soil Conservation Service, now known as the Natural Resources Conservation Service (NRCS), a federal agency in the Department of Agriculture, dealing with erosion and flood control.

Sediment Solid material, both mineral and organic, in suspension, being transported, or having been moved from its original site by air, water, gravity, or ice.

Sediment basin A reservoir formed by the construction of a barrier or dam built at a suitable location to permit the settling out of sediments (e.g., rock, sand, gravel, silt, or other material) before releasing the water.

Shallow concentrated flow Flow in shallow rills.

Shear stress (channel) Force per unit area exerted on the wetted area of a channel, acting in the direction of flow.

Sheet flow Flow over plane, sloped surfaces in a thin layer.

Shoulder The portion of roadway between the edge of the hardened wearing course and the ditch or embankment.

Sight distance The distance between approaching vehicles when first visible to one another on a horizontal or vertical curve.

Slide Movement of soil on a slope resulting in a reduced angle of repose, usually occurring as a result of rainfall, high water, or thaw.

Slope The face of an embankment or a cut section. Any ground whose surface makes an angle with the horizontal plane.

Soil bioengineering Use of live, woody vegetative cuttings to repair slope failures and increase slope stability.

Splash block A masonry block with its top close to the ground surface, which receives roof drainage and prevents erosion below the spout.

Storage (runoff) Runoff that is temporarily impounded to permit control of the runoff rate and/or to improve water quality.

Storm sewer A conduit used for conveyance of rainwater.

Structure Anything constructed that requires a permanent location on the ground or is attached to something having a permanent location on the ground.

Subdrain A pervious backfilled trench containing a pipe with perforations or open joints for the purpose of intercepting groundwater or seepage.

Superelevation The rise of the outer edge of the pavement relative to the inner edge at a curve in the highway, expressed in feet per foot, intended to overcome the tendency of speeding vehicles to overturn when rounding a curve.

Swale A constructed or natural grassed or vegetated waterway.

Tangent A straight road segment connecting two curves.

Terrace An essentially level and defined area, usually raised, either paved or planted, forming part of a garden or building setting.

Time of concentration (T_c) The time for water to flow from the hydraulically most remote point in a drainage area to the point of interest.

Time of recession (T_{rec}) The period of time from the peak of a hydrograph until it reaches the beginning flow rate.

Time of rise (of a hydrograph) (T_{rise}) The period of time from the beginning flow rate until the peak flow rate is reached.

Travel time (T_t) The time for runoff to flow from one point in a drainage area to another.

Trench drain A linear structure that collects runoff from a paved area.

Vegetated structures A retaining wall system in which living plants or cuttings have been integrated into the structure.

Vegetative cuttings Live, cut stems and branches of plants that will root when embedded or inserted in the ground.

Water quality basin A reservoir that has a provision for removing pollutants from storm runoff by retaining the runoff from high-frequency storms (i.e., those with 1- or 2-year frequencies) for prolonged periods (i.e., from 18 to 36 hours).

Watershed Region or area contributing to the supply of a stream or lake. (Also, a drainage basin or catchment area.)

Water table The level below which the ground is saturated.

Waterway A natural course, or a constructed channel, for the flow of water.

Weephole A small hole, as in a retaining wall, to drain water to the outside.

Weir An opening in the crest of a dam or an embankment to discharge excess water; also used for measuring the rate of discharge.

Wetted perimeter The length of the wetted contact between the water and the containing conduit, measured along a plane that is perpendicular to the conduit.

Bibliography

American Association of State Highway and Transportation Officials. 1984. *A Policy on Geometric Design of Highways and Streets*. Washington, DC: American Association of State Highway and Transportation Officials.

American Association of State Highway and Transportation Officials. 2004. NCHRP 25-25(04) *Final Report on Environmental Stewardship Practices, Procedures, and Policies for Highway Construction and Maintenance*. Washington, DC: American Association of State Highway and Transportation Officials.

American Concrete Pipe Association. 1980. *Concrete Pipe Design Manual*. Vienna, VA: American Concrete Pipe Association.

American Iron and Steel Institute. 1980. *Modern Sewer Design*. Washington, DC: American Iron and Steel Institute.

American Public Works Association, 1981. "Practices in Detention of Urban Storm water." *Special Report 43*.

American Society for Testing and Materials (ASTM) D421-85. 1998. *Standard Practice for Dry Preparation of Soil Samples for Particle-Size Analysis and Determination of Soil Constants*. West Conshohocken, PA: ASTM International.

ASTM D422-63. 1998. *Standard Test Method for Particle-Size Analysis of Soils*. West Conshohocken, PA: ASTM International.

ASTM D2487-00. 2000. *Standard Practice for Classification of Soils for Engineering Purposes (Unified Soil Classification System)*. West Conshohocken, PA: ASTM International.

ASTM D4318-00. 2000. *Standard Test Methods for Liquid Limit, Plastic Limit, and Plasticity Index of Soils*. West Conshohocken, PA: ASTM International.

Arnold, C. A., and Gibbons, C. J. 1996. "Impervious Surface Coverage." *Journal of the American Planning Association* 62 (Spring): 243–258.

American Society of Civil Engineers, National Association of Home Builders, and the Urban Land Institute. 1990. *Residential Streets,* 2nd ed. New York: American Society of Civil Engineers; Washington, DC: National Association of Home Builders; and Washington, DC: Urban Land Institute (ULI).

American Society of Landscape Architects. 2007. *Professional Awards: General Design Honor Award— Olympic Sculpture Park*. http://www.asla.org/awards/2007/07winners/267_wmct.html. Washington, DC: American Society of Landscape Architects.

Asphalt Institute. 1984. *Drainage of Asphalt Pavement Structures*. College Park, MD: The Asphalt Institute.

Austin, G. 1995. *Layout Techniques for Landscape Architecture*. Champaign, IL: Stipes Publishing.

Bader, C. D. 1996. "The Changing Directions of Drainage." *Erosion Control* 3 (January/February): 35–41.

Bader, C. D. 1996. "Creating and Restoring Wetlands." *Erosion Control* 3 (May/June): 22–27.

Barfield, B. J., Warner, R. C., and Haan, C. T. 1981. *Applied Hydrology and Sedimentology for Disturbed Areas*. Stillwater: Oklahoma Technical Press.

Brockway, T., and Kinkead, K. 2006. "Rain Gardens: Effective Natural and Cheap." *Daily Journal of Commerce* (August 31). http://www.djc.com/news/co/11181766.html.

Building Officials and Code Administrators, Inc. 1993. *Basic Building Code*, 12th ed. Country Club Hills, IL: Building Officials and Code Administrators, International.

Cabalka, D., and Trotti, J. 1996. "The Grassed-Lined Channel." *Erosion Control* 3 (November/December): 42–50.

Cahill, T. H., Adams, M. C., and Horner, W. R. 1988. *The Use of Porous Paving for Groundwater Recharge in Stormwater Management Systems*. Floodplain/Stormwater Management Symposium. State College: Pennsylvania Department of Environmental Resources.

Cernica, J. N. 1995. *Geotechnical Engineering: Soil Mechanics*. New York: John Wiley & Sons.

Chow, Ven, T. (ed.). 1964. *Handbook of Applied Hydrology*. New York: McGraw-Hill Book Company.

City of Seattle Department of Planning and Design. 2006. *High Point Green Home Case Study*. http://www.seattle. gov/dpd/stellent/groups/pan/@pan/@sustainableblding/ documents/web_informational/dpds_007254.pdf. Seattle, WA: City of Seattle Department of Planning and Design.

Corish, K. A. 1995. *Clearing and Grading Strategies for Urban Watersheds*. Washington, DC: Metropolitan Washington Council of Governments.

Day, G. E., and Crafton, C. S. 1978. *Site and Community Design Guidelines for Stormwater Management*. Blacksburg: College of Agriculture and Urban Studies, Virginia Polytechnic Institute and State University.

De Carlo, G. 1994. "Wachstum im Zeitraffer." *Deutsche Bauzeitung 128* (June): 130–135.

Duncan, C. I., Jr. 1992. *Soils and Foundations for Architects and Engineers*. New York: Van Nostrand Reinhold.

Earthpledge. *Green Roofs: Ecological Design and Construction*. Atglen, PA: Schiffer Publishing, 2005.

Evett, J. B. 1991. *Surveying*, 2nd ed. Englewood Cliffs, NJ: Prentice Hall.

Federal Highway Administration. 1988. *Design of Roadside Channels with Flexible Linings*. http://www.fhwa.dot .gov/engineering/hydraulics/pubs/hec/

Ferguson, B., and Debo, T. N. 1990. *On-site Stormwater Management: Applications for Landscape and Engineering*, 2nd ed. New York: Van Nostrand Reinhold.

Georgia Soil and Water Conservation Commission. 1994. *Guidelines for Streambank Restoration*. Atlanta: Georgia Soil and Water Conservation Commission.

Goldman, S. J., Jackson, K., and Bursztynsky, T. A. 1986. *Erosion and Sediment Control Handbook*. New York: McGraw-Hill Book Company.

Gray, D. H., and Leiser, A. T. 1982. *Biotechnical Slope Protection and Erosion Control*. New York: Van Nostrand Reinhold.

Gray, D. H., and Sotir, R. B. 1996. *Biotechnical and Soil Bioengineering Slope Stabilization*. New York: John Wiley & Sons.

Grzimek, G. 1972. *Spiel und Sport in der Stadtlandschaft: Olympialandschaft Oberwiesenfeld*. Munich: Verlag Georg D. W. Callwey.

Halevy, L. S. 1995. "Landscape Architects and Urban Erosion Control." *Erosion Control 2* (July/August): 52–58.

Hammer, D. A. 1992. *Creating Freshwater Wetlands*. Boca Raton, FL: Lewis Publishers.

Harris, C., and Dines, N. 1988. *Time-Saver Standards for Landscape Architecture*. New York: McGraw-Hill Book Company.

Hughes, A. H. 1990. "Making a Parking Lot into an Exhibit." *The Public Garden* (January).

Institute of Traffic Engineers. 1976. *Transportation and Traffic Engineering Handbook*. Englewood Cliffs, NJ: Prentice-Hall.

Kassler, E. B. 1986. *Modern Gardens and the Landscape*, rev. ed. New York: Museum of Modern Art.

Kavanagh, B. F. 1989. *Surveying with Construction Applications*. Englewood Cliffs, NJ: Prentice Hall.

Leica Geosystems, AG. 1999. *Introduction to GPS, Version 1.0*. Heerbrugg, Switzerland: Leica Geosystems, AG.

Lewis, L. 2000. *Soil Bioengineering—An Alternative to Roadside Management—A Practical Guide*. Technical Report 0077-1801-SDTDC. San Dimas, CA: U.S. Department of Agriculture, Forest Service, San Dimas Technology and Development Center.

Linsley, R. K., Jr., Kohler, M. A., and Paulhus, J. L. H. 1986. *Hydrology for Engineers*. New York: McGraw-Hill Book Company.

Liu, C., and Evett, J. B. 1992. *Soils and Foundations*, 3rd ed. Englewood Cliffs, NJ: Prentice Hall.

Lynch, K. 1971. *Site Planning*, 2nd ed. Cambridge, MA: MIT Press.

Lynch, K., and Hack, G. 1984. *Site Planning*, 3rd ed. Cambridge, MA: MIT Press.

Marble, A. D. 1992. *A Guide to Wetland Functional Design*. Boca Raton, FL: Lewis Publishers.

Moshiri, G. A. 1993. *Constructed Wetlands for Water Quality Improvement*. Boca Raton, FL: Lewis Publishers.

Munson, A. E. 1974. *Construction Design for Landscape Architects*. New York: McGraw-Hill Book Company.

Nathan, K. 1975. *Basic Site Engineering for Landscape Designers*. New York: MSS Information Corp.

New Jersey Association of Conservation Districts. 1987. *Standards for Soil Erosion and Sediment Control in New Jersey*. Trenton: New Jersey Department of Agriculture.

New Jersey Department of Environmental Protection and New Jersey Department of Agriculture. 1994. *Stormwater and Nonpoint Source Pollution Control Best Management Practices Manual*. Trenton, NJ: Department of Environmental Protection.

New Jersey State Soil Conservation Committee. 1997. *Standards for Soil Erosion and Sediment Control in New Jersey, Draft Revisions*. Trenton: New Jersey Department of Agriculture.

Ocean County Soil Conservation District, Schnabel Engineering Associates, Inc. and USDA—Natural Resources Conservation Service. 2001. *Impact of Soil*

Disturbance During Construction on Bulk Density and Infiltration in Ocean County, New Jersey. Forked River, NJ: Ocean County Soil Conservation District.

Osmundson, T. 1999. *Roof Gardens: History, Design and Construction.* New York: W. W. Norton & Company.

Parker, H., and Macguire, J. W. 1954. *Simplified Site Engineering for Architects and Builders.* New York: John Wiley & Sons.

Pira, E. S., and Hubler, M. J. n.d. *Tile Drainage Systems.* Amherst: University of Massachusetts.

Poertner, H. G. (ed.). 1981. *Urban Storm Water Management.* Special Report No. 49. Chicago: American Public Works Association.

Raistrick, A. 1968. *The pennine Dales.* London: Eyre & Spottiswoode Ltd.

Reed, D. P., and Hilderbrand, G. 2003. "Ordering and Terracing in the Leventritt Garden." *Arnoldia,* 62(2): 16–19.

Roberts, J. M. 1983. *The Building Site.* New York: John Wiley & Sons.

Rosenberg, D. 1996. "The Art and Architecture of Erosion Control." *Erosion Control* 3 (July/August): 30–35.

Schoeneberger, P. J., Wysocki, D. A., Benham, E. C., and Broderson, W. D. (eds.). 2002. *Field Book for Describing and Sampling Soils, Version 2.0.* Lincoln, NE: Natural Resources Conservation Service, National Soil Survey Center.

Schroeder, W. L., and S. E. Dickinson. 1996. *Soils in Construction.* Upper Saddle River, NJ: Prentice Hall.

Schueler, T. R. 1987. *Controlling Urban Runoff: A Practical Manual for Planning and Designing Urban BMPs.* Washington, DC: Metropolitan Washington Council of Governments.

Schueler, T. R. 1995. *Site Planning for Urban Stream Protection.* Washington, DC: Metropolitan Washington Council of Governments.

Schwab, G. O., Frevert, R. K., Barnes, K. K., and Edminster, T. W. 1971. *Elementary Soil and Water Engineering.* New York: John Wiley & Sons.

Schwab, G. O., Frevert, R. K., Edminster, T. W., and Barnes, K. K. 1981. *Soil and Water Conservation Engineering.* New York: John Wiley & Sons.

Sears, B. 1988. "Retaining Walls." In *Handbook of Landscape Architecture Construction,* Vol. 2, edited by M. Nelischer. Washington, DC: Landscape Architecture Foundation.

Seattle Art Museum. 2008. "Olympic Sculpture Park." http://www.seattleartmuseum.org/visit/OSP/AboutOSP/.

Seelye, E. E. 1968. *Data Book for Civil Engineers: Design,* 3rd ed. New York: John Wiley & Sons.

Snow, B. 1959. *The Highway and the Landscape.* New Brunswick, NJ: Rutgers University Press.

Soil Quality Institute. 1999. *Soil Quality Test Kit Guide.* USDA, Agricultural Research Service and Natural Resources Conservation Service. Auburn, AL: National Soils Lab.

Souza S. J., Gallagher M., and Appel, S. 2002. *The Pennswood Village Stormwater System: The Design and Construction of a Multifunctional Riparian Corridor for the Management of Stormwater Quality.* Ringoes, NJ: Princeton Hydro.

Stahre, P., and Urbonas, B. 1990. *Stormwater Detention for Drainage, Water Quality, and CSO Management.* Englewood Cliffs, NJ: Prentice Hall.

Steele, F. 1981. *The Sense of Place.* Boston: CBI Publishing.

Stoltz, R. 1985. "Metric Practice." In *Handbook of Landscape Architectural Construction,* Vol. 1, edited by M. Nelischer. Washington, DC: Landscape Architecture Foundation.

Sue, J. 1985. "Landscape Grading Design." In *Handbook of Landscape Architectural Construction,* Vol. 1, edited by M. Nelischer. Washington, DC: Landscape Architecture Foundation.

Thompson, J. W. 1996. "Let That Soak In." *Landscape Architecture* 86 (November): 60–67.

Trimble Navigation Limited. 2003. *GPS Tutorial.* Sunnyvale, CA: Trimble.

Untermann, R. K. 1978. *Principles and Practices of Grading, Drainage and Road Alignment: An Ecologic Approach.* Reston, VA: Reston Publishing Co.

URS Corporation. 2001. *How to Select, Install and Inspect Construction Site Erosion and Sediment Control BMPS for NPDES Storm Water Permit Compliance.* Steamboat Springs, CO: International Erosion Control Association.

US Army. 1997. *Field Manual FM 5-410, Military Soils Engineering.* Washington, DC: Department of the Army.

USDA—Natural Resources Conservation Service (formerly SCS). 1985. "Hydrology." Section 4 in *National Engineering Handbook.* Springfield, VA: National Technical Information Service.

USDA—Natural Resources Conservation Service (formerly SCS). 1986. *Urban Hydrology for Small Watersheds.* Technical Release Number 55. Springfield, VA: National Technical Information Service.

USDA—Natural Resources Conservation Service, 2007. *Stability Design of Grass-lined Open Channels.* Agriculture Handbook No. 667. Springfield, VA: National Technical Information Service.

USDA—Natural Resources Conservation Service (formerly SCS). 1986. "Streambank and Shoreline Protection."

Chapter 16 in *Engineering Field Handbook*. Springfield, VA: National Technical Information Service.

USDA—Natural Resources Conservation Service (formerly SCS). 1989. *Soil Survey of Monmouth County, New Jersey*. Springfield, VA: National Technical Information Service.

USDA—Natural Resources Conservation Service (formerly SCS). 1992. "Wetland Restoration, Enhancement, or Creation." Chapter 13 in *Engineering Field Handbook*. Springfield, VA: National Technical Information Service.

USDA—Natural Resources Conservation Service (formerly SCS). 1992. "Soil Bioengineering for Upland Slope Protection and Erosion Reduction." Chapter 18 in *Engineering Field Handbook*. Springfield, VA: National Technical Information Service.

USDA—Natural Resources Conservation Service. 2002. *Soil Bioengineering: An Alternative to Roadside Management*. San Dimas, CA: San Dimas Technology and Development Center.

USDA—Natural Resources Conservation Service. 2002. *Field Book for Describing and Sampling Soils, Version 2.0*. Lincoln, NE: National Soil Survey Center.

Whipple, W., Grigg, N. S., Grizzard, T., Randall, C. W., Shubinski, R. P., and Tucker, L. S. 1983. *Stormwater Management in Urbanizing Areas*. Englewood Cliffs, NJ: Prentice Hall.

Winterbottom, D. 2000. "Rainwater Harvesting; An Ancient Technology—Cisterns—Is Reconsidered." *Landscape Architecture* 89 (April): 40–46.

Young, D., and Leslie, D. 1974. *Grading Design Approach*. Landscape Architecture Construction Series. Washington, DC: Landscape Architecture Foundation.

Zolomij, R. 1988. "Vehicular Circulation." In *Handbook of Landscape Architectural Construction*, Vol. 2, edited by M. Nelischer. Washington, DC: Landscape Architecture Foundation.

Zolomij, Robert W. n.d. *Construction Drawings Course Manual*.

Index

Accessibility and universal design, 52–54
Americans with Disabilities Act, 54
Americans with Disabilities Act Accessibility Guidelines, 54
Alignment:
 horizontal, 303
 vertical, 323
Anchor Environmental, 58
Andropogon Associates, 206, 318
Angle:
 deflection, 305
 inclusion, 305
Antecedent precipitation factor, 223
Area drain, 257, 258
Arnold Arboretum, 2–4
Artificial wetland, 176
Aspect Consulting, 58
Atterberg limits, 130
Average End Area Method, 141–143

Base, 140
Basin:
 catch, 257
 detention, 165
 infiltration, 170
 retention, 164
 sediment, 259
 water quality, 174
Bayer, Herbert, 5
Beebe Springs Creek Restoration, 19–20
Behnish, Günther, 62
Bench, 56–57
Berm, 15
Best Management Practices, 163
Bioretention, 176
Borrow, 141
Borrow Pit Method, 146–148
Branch packing, 202, 203
Brown & Caldwell Engineering, 7
Brushlayering, 202

Caissons, 124
Catch basin, 257

Central Park, 9–12, 16, 17
Channel flow:
 Mannings's equation for, 242
 time, 214, 217
Charles Anderson Landscape Architecture, 58
Circular curve(s), 304–306
 elements of, 304–305
 formulas, 306
Compaction 136–137, 140
Concentration, time of, 214
Constraints:
 environmental, 23–27
 functional, 27–36
Continuity equation, 265
Contour(s):
 area method, 144–146
 characteristics, 42
 closed, 37
 definition, 37
 degree of accuracy, 40, 41
 interval, 41
 line, 37
 signatures, 44, 85–86, 98–100
Cribwall, live, 202, 204
Critical velocity, 269, 273, 274
Crown:
 height, 91
 parabolic section, 91
 reverse, 91, 92
 road, 91
 tangential section, 91–92
Culvert, 256, 257
Curb(s), 92
 batter-faced, 92
 beveled, 92
 and gutter, 92
 ramp, 50, 51
 rounded, 92
Curvature, point of, 305
Curve(s):
 broken-back, 304, 305
 center of, 305

Curve(s): *(cont'd)*
   chord of, 305
   circular, 304–305
   compound, 304
   degree of, 308–309
   horizontal, 303–305
   length of, 305
   peak, 324
   radius of, 305
   reverse, 304, 305
   sag, 324
   simple, 304
   spiral transition, 305
   vertical, 323–339
Cut, 140
Cut-and-fill volumes:
   adjusting, 148–150
   balancing, 150–155
   by computer, 150
   computation of, 141
Cut-off drain, 285

Datum, 37
Deflection angle, 305, 306
Degree of curve:
   arc definition, 308
   chord definition, 308
Departure, 299
Depression, 44, 45, 48
Design storm, 214
Detention basin:
   Dual-purpose, 165
Digital elevation model, 80
Digital terrain model, 82–83
Dimension line, 294
Dimension(s):
   field, 293
   fixed, 292
   flexible, 292
   floating, 292
semifixed, 292
Dimensional notation, 293–294
Dimensioning and materials plan, 291
Dimensioning systems:
   angles, bearings, and arcs, 300
   baseline, 297–298
   coordinates, 298–299
   perpendicular offsets, 295–297
Dimensioning:
   accuracy and tolerances, 293
   associative, 301
   and computer-aided design, 301
   graphic convention and organization, 294–295

Distance:
   runoff, 317
   tangent, 305
Diversion, 200
Dragonfly Irrigation, 7
Drain:
   area, 257, 258
   cut-off, 285
   French, 284
   inlet, 257, 258
   trench, 257, 259
Drainage area, 212
Drainage system:
   closed, 260, 261
   combination, 260, 261
   design and layout, 260–263
   open, 260, 261
Drainage, subsurface, 284–285
Dry basin, 165
Dry pond, 169

Earthworks Park, 4–7
Elevation, invert, 282
Environmental constraints, of grading:
   drainage, 24
   vegetation, 24
   soils, 24
topography, 23
Erosion and sediment control:
   plan, 199
   principles, 197–199
   regulatory requirements, 195
Erosion and sedimentation processes, 197
Erosion control measures, 200–205
   maintenance, 205
Extension lines, 294

Fiber rolls, 203
Field dimensions, 293
Fill, 136, 140
Filter strip, 176
Finished floor elevation, 115, 140
Finished grade, 139
Fixed dimension, 292
Flexible dimension, 292
Floating dimension, 292
Flow:
   open-channel, 242
   shallow concentrated, 242
   sheet, 241
Footings, 124
Foundation(s), 29, 124
   continuous wall, 29

pole, 29
slab, 29
French drain, 284
Functional constraints, of grading:
    activities and uses, 28
    economics and maintenance, 35
    restrictive conditions, 27

Gasworks Park, 61–64
Geotextiles, 132–133
Global positioning systems, 302
Grade, 76
Grade change devices, 48
Grade, finished, 139
Gradient, 76
Grading:
    athletic facilities, 34
    construction sequence, 133–137
    critical constraints, 36
    of linear elements, 85
    path cross-slope, 86–89
    of planar areas, 98
    positive drainage, 100
    by proportion, 96
    of roads, 91, 95–96
    standards, 35
    terrace, 101
Grading design:
    aesthetics, 2
    architectonic, 2, 3
    geomorphic, 2
    naturalistic, 2, 9
    perception, 12
    sculptural, 2, 4
    spatial considerations, 15
Grading plan:
    construction, 117–121
    graphics, 117
    symbols and abbreviations, 120
Grading process:
    application, 111–117
    for areas, 107
    design development, 109–110
    design implementation, 110
    inventory and analysis, 109
Graphical Peak Discharge Method, 246–248
Green Associates, 3
Green roof systems, 179
    extensive, 179
    intensive, 180
    modular, 180
Grzimek, Günther, 62
Gutter, paved, 92

Haag, Richard, 61
Hart Crowser, 58
High Point Neighborhood Redevelopment, 191–194
Horizontal alignment:
    construction drawing graphics, 314
    procedures, 314–316
    standards, 314
Horizontal curves, 303–305
Horizontal sight distance, 313
Hydraulic radius, 242, 243
Hydrograph, 224
Hydrologic:
    changes, 159
    condition, 246
    cycle, 158
    soil group, 244

Included angle, 305
Infiltration:
    basin, 170
    facilities, 170
    trench, 172, 173
Interpolation, 72
    between contour lines, 75–76
    between spot elevations, 72–75
    graphic, 73–74
Intersection, point of, 305
Invert elevation, 282

Jacob Javits Federal Courthouse Plaza, 2
Jones + Jones, 7
Jordan, Lorna, 7–9

Latitude, 299
Layout plan, 291
Leventritt Garden, 2, 3–4
Lift, 136
Live fascines, 201–202
Live staking, 201
Loantaka Brook Preserve, 206–209
Log terraces, 203, 205

Magnusson Klemencic Associates, 58
Manhole, 259
Mellon Biological Services, 183
Microclimate modification, 21
Mithun, 191
Modified Rational Method, 223–227
Morris Arboretum, 318–322

Nakano Associates, 191
Natural Resources Conservation Service:
    Graphical Peak Discharge Method, 235–253

Natural Resources Conservation Service: *(cont'd)*
  procedures, 237, 240
  rainfall patterns, 238–240
  Tabular Hydrograph Method, 248–250
  TR 55, 236
Nomograph:
  for channel flow time, 217
  for circular pipes flowing full, 281
  for overland flow time, 216

Olmsted, Frederick Law, 9
Olympic Park, 62, 64–70
Olympic Sculpture Park, 58–61
Otto, Frei, 62
Overland flow time, 216

Pavement, porous, 172, 174, 175
Peak curve, 324
Pennswood Village, 183–188
Perception:
  channeling, 16
  concave and convex slopes, 13
  elevation change, 12
  enclosure, 15
  enhancement, 14
  separation, 15
  slope, 12
  spatial considerations, 15
Permissible velocities, 265
Pickering, Corts & Summerson, 183
Piles, 124
Pipe systems, designing and sizing, 275–284
Point of:
  beginning, 293
  curvature, 305
  intersection, 305
  tangency, 305
Porous pavement, 172, 175
Precipitation factor, antecedent, 223
Princeton Hydro, 183
Profile:
  road, 336, 337, 338
  storm drainage, 283

Radius, hydraulic, 243
Rainfall intensity, 212
Rainfall intensity curve(s):
  Atlanta, 220
  Austin, 220
  Boston, 220
  Madison, 220
  New Orleans, 221
  San Francisco, 221

Seattle, 221
Topeka, 221
Trenton, 215
Rain garden, 171–172
Rainwater harvesting, 177
Ramp(s), 50–52
  grading at, 51
  stairs, 52
Rational method, 212–223
Reed Hilderbrand, 3
Retaining wall(s), 54–55, 56
  grading at, 55, 56
  section, 54
Retardance factors, for grassed swales, 266
Retention basin, 164–165, 166–167
Retention pond, 164–165, 166–167
Ridge, 44, 45, 47
Road alignment procedures, 335–339
Roughness coefficients:
  for pipes and channels, 242
  for sheet flow, 241
Runoff coefficient(s), 212, 213
  recommended, 214
Runoff curve number,
  for other agricultural lands, 246
  for urban areas, 245
Runoff:
  distance, 317–318
  storm, 157
  subsurface, 157
  surface, 157
  volume, 227

Saddle, 93, 94
Sag curve, 324
Seattle Housing Authority, 191
Seattle Public Utilities, 188
Section, 41–42
Sediment:
  control measures, 205–206
  maintenance, 206
Sellen Construction, 58
Semifixed dimension, 292
Shallow concentrated flow, 242
Shannon & Wilson, 321
Sheet flow, 241
  Manning's equation for, 241
Sight distance, horizontal, 313
Slope(s), 55
  analysis, 79–82
  calculating, 76
  concave, 13, 45, 46, 48
  convex, 13, 45, 46, 48

direction of, 42, 43
  expressed as degrees, 78–79
  expressed as ratios, 78–79
  formula, 77
  perception, 12
  steepest, 42
  for surface drainage, 99
  uniform, 42, 45
Soil bioengineering, 201–205
Soil characteristics:
  phases, 127
  physical properties, 127–128
Soil classification systems, 128
Soil classification:
  Unified System, 128, 129
  USDA, 128
Soil erosion factors, 196–197
Soil survey, 125–126
Soil volume-weight relationships, 127
Soil(s):
  bearing capacity, 130
  bulk density, 128
  critical conditions, 127
  drainage requirements, 125
  engineering properties, 130
  erodibility, 26
  frost penetration, 131
  gap-graded, 131
  geotechnical investigation, 125
  grain size analysis, 129
  land use feasibility, 125
  lightweight, 132
  liquid limit, 130
  organic and nutrient content, 27
  pH level, 27
  placing and compacting, 136
  plastic limit, 130
  poorly graded, 129
  shear strength, 130–131
  shrinkage and swell, 131
  shrinkage limit, 130
  structural, 131
  unit weight, 128
  well-graded, 131
Specifications, earthwork,
      137–138
Spot elevation, 72, 119
Stair(s), 49–50
  grading at, 50
  section, 49
Stationing, 301, 310–313
Storm frequency, 213
Storm runoff, 157

Storm water management:
  philosophy, 16,
  principles and techniques, 163
  reducing imperviousness, 162
  strategies, 161
  systems, 255–261
  water quality, 162
  watershed-based, 161
Street Edge Alternatives, 188–191
Streets:
  diagonal to contours, 32, 34
  parallel to contours, 32
  perpendicular to contours, 32, 33
Sub-Base, 140
Subgrade, 139–140
  compacted, 140
  undisturbed, 139
Subsurface drainage, 284–289
  area, 286
  and spacing, 287
  drainage coefficient, 286
  piping patterns, 285
  runoff, 157
  system design, 285–289
Summit, 44, 45, 47
Superelevation, 316–318
Surcharge, 124
Surface runoff, 157
SvR Design, 191
Swale(s):
  designing and sizing, 263–269
  to divert runoff, 106–107
  parabolic, 263, 264
  vegetated, 174
  vegetated parabolic, 92
Swale design:
  by charts, 268–269
  by hydraulics, 265–268

Tabular Hydrograph Method, 248–250
Tangency, point of, 305
Tangent, 303
Tangent distance, 305
Terrace(s), 56–57
  in cut, 105–106
  on fill, 101–105
  sections, 57
Thompson, Mary, 3
Time of concentration, 214, 240
Topographic data, 71
Topographic map, 40
Topography, visualizing from contour lines, 98
Topsoil, 140

Travel time, 240
Trench drain, 257, 259

Underdrainage, 285
Universal Design, 52
URS Engineers, 5

Valley, 44, 45, 47
Velocity:
    critical, 269, 273, 274
    permissible, 265
    subcritical, 269
    supercritical, 269
Vertical alignment, 323–339
Vertical curve(s),
    calculating high and low points, 326–330
    construction drawing graphics, 333–335

elements of, 324
equal tangent, 325–330
sight distances, 335
unequal tangent, 330–333
Volume:
    for detention storage, 250–253
    storage for detention and retention ponds, 229–233

Water budget, 177
Watershed, 212
Waterway, 200
Waterworks Gardens, 5, 7–9
Weiss/Manfredi Architects, 58
Wells Appel, 183
Wetlands, constructed, 176
Wet pond, 164
Wildlife habitat enhancement, 17